The Alchemy of Finance

INTRODUCING WILEY INVESTMENT CLASSICS

There are certain books that have redefined the way we see the worlds of finance and investing—books that deserve a place on every investor's shelf. *Wiley Investment Classics* will introduce you to these memorable books, which are just as relevant and vital today as when they were first published. Open a *Wiley Investment Classic* and rediscover the proven strategies, market philosophies, and definitive techniques that continue to stand the test of time.

The Alchemy of Finance

GEORGE SOROS

WILEY

John Wiley & Sons, Inc.

Published by John Wiley & Sons, Inc., Hoboken, New Jersey.
Published simultaneously in Canada.

For general information on our other products and services, or technical support, please contact our
Customer Care Department within the United States at (800) 762-2974, outside the United States at
(317) 572-3993 or fax (317) 572-4002.

Wiley also publishes its books in a variety of electronic formats. Some content that appears in print
may not be available in electronic books.

For more information about Wiley products, visit our web site at www.wiley.com.

ISBN 0-471-44549-5

Printed in the United States of America.

10 9 8 7 6 5 4 3 2 1

TO SUSAN,

without whom this book would have been ready much sooner

Acknowledgments

A number of people have read all or part of the manuscript at various stages of its development. They are too numerous to be listed, but I want to thank them all for their help and criticism. Byron Wien, in particular, has gone beyond the call of duty in reading and commenting on the manuscript at three different stages of development. Special thanks are due to Antonio Foglia, who generated the graphics that illustrate the real-time experiment. Larry Chiarello supplied the figures.

I also want to thank the team that contributed to the performance of Quantum Fund during the experiment: Bill Ehrman, Gary Gladstein, Tom Larkin, Robert Miller, Steven Okin, Joe Orofino, Stephen Plant, Allan Raphael, and Anne Stires.

Many people have read the new Introduction, and I have received many helpful comments. I should like to single out Anders Aslund, Gary Becker, Leon Botstein, Mario Bunge, Charles Calomiris, Flavia Cymbalista, Meghnad Desai, Yehuda Elkana, Jeffrey Frankel, Roman Frydman, John Kay, Allan Meltzer, Bill Newton-Smith, Peter Osnos, Thomas Palley, Edmund Phelps, Adam Posen, Alan Ryan, Robert Skidelsky, and Robert Solow. They bear no responsibility for my views, with which some of them continue to disagree.

Contents

Part Three
THE REAL-TIME EXPERIMENT

Part Four
EVALUATION

Part Five
PRESCRIPTION

Foreword to the New Edition

Some years ago, students in my seminar on international finance wanted exposure to a "real live" speculator. George Soros kindly agreed to spend an evening at Princeton, interacting with an enlarged group, including a number of the economics faculty.

We all got more than we bargained for. George announced at the start that the concept of equilibrium has no relevance to the way financial markets operate. Thinking in those terms would be counterproductive in terms of trading success. Traders make money by following the perceived trend. Markets react to participants' expectations, and those perceptions influence prices, tending to validate themselves in a self-reinforcing process until some unpredictable event jolts expectations.

With the assembled professors listening in intense silence, I valiantly, but without much conviction, tried my best to state the standard case for efficient markets and for the "fundamentals" determining exchange rates. George didn't give much ground. He had on his side the empirical fact of wide fluctuations in market rates that are hard to reconcile with the fundamentals or any understandable concept of efficient markets. In the words of his new Introduction to *The Alchemy of Finance*, "the very idea that financial markets tend toward . . . equilibrium seems to be contradicted by the evidence."

For me, the spirit of that evening was well characterized when one of the younger professors finally summoned the courage to challenge our guest. "Mr. Soros," he said, "you underestimate the work of academic economists in understanding exchange markets. There are interesting and promising developments in chaos theory."

Well, I confess that I am not familiar with chaos theory. I also have difficulty at times in following the subtleties of George Soros's mind as he elaborates his concept of reflexivity. But I understand enough to welcome his effort to restate (and simplify) his thinking in his continuing effort to find a new paradigm for market, and indeed human, behavior.

To my mind, he does decisively puncture the standard textbook model of efficient markets and rational expectations, what he labels "market fundamentalism" that can only lead to "false claims and misleading results."

It's not that market participants are irrational or inefficient in the everyday sense of those words. Nor are expectations unimportant; anyone familiar with asset markets knows that it is expectations that move prices. But Soros goes beyond that observation to emphasize that expectations cannot and will not arrive at a stable equilibrium precisely because the thinking, and therefore the actions, of market participants will affect market behavior: the market will in turn influence the "fundamentals" and shape new expectations in a continuing reflexive process. More broadly, as Soros returns to his first love of philosophy, he sees the reflexive process as an innate part of human existence; "thinking is part of the reality that people have to think about."

George Soros has made his mark as an enormously successful speculator, wise enough to largely withdraw when still way ahead of the game. The bulk of his enormous winnings is now devoted to encouraging transitional and emerging nations to become "open societies," open not only in the sense of freedom of commerce but—more important—tolerant of new ideas and different modes of thinking and behavior.

At the same time, he has written with insight and passion about the strains and instabilities that have accompanied—have in good part been a consequence of—the globilization of financial markets. Over and over again, he makes a point reminiscent of Walter Bagehot's nineteenth-century dictum that money cannot manage itself. In the Soros view, "the belief that financial markets tend toward equilibrium and it is only government interference that prevents them from assuring a best allocation of resources . . . [is] both false and misleading." It is in that critique that his intellectual efforts find application to the policy and practical world of international finance.

George himself has been working to build upon the foundation of acute observation and intellectual analysis a structure of workable and broadly supported reform to better assure the growth and stability of the emerging world. That has been the goal of other books and other writings. No doubt there will be further efforts on his part.

For now, one thing seems to me certain: Soros has from his unique perspective brought a clarity to deep-seated problems of international finance that have been too little recognized in either the world of academia or that of policymakers. Approaches that would ignore the systemic implications of his observations will, in my judgment, fail to develop the full potential of globalized finance for well-developed and underdeveloped economies alike.

The Alchemy of Finance in its original, and even in its "succinct" and "updated" new Introduction, isn't by any means a quick and easy read. But what you read is what you get: an honest struggle by an independent and searching mind to break through an old and stale orthodoxy with new and meaningful insights into financial—and human—behavior. On almost every page, you will suddenly be rewarded by a paragraph, a sentence, or a phrase that will provide fresh insight and challenge your thinking. What remains is what George, or any of us, can do to build new theories and new policy approaches that better reflect the reality he describes.

PAUL A. VOLCKER

Foreword to
the First Edition

Four hundred seventy-three million to one. Those are the odds against George Soros compiling the investment record he did as the manager of the Quantum Fund from 1968 through 1993. His investing record is the most unimpeachable refutation of the random walk hypothesis ever!

As a trader coming of age in the latter half of the frenetic 1970s and the 1980s, *The Alchemy of Finance* was somewhat of a revolutionary book. Remember, this was the period when trend following and indexation were the vogue in investing. It was a time when technical analysis (the study of price movement as a forecasting tool) reached its zenith. Traders of my generation armed themselves with charts and computer-generated graphics that predicted future price direction. We sat day after day in front of screens, mesmerized by blinking lights and ever-changing numbers in a deafening cacophony of information overload. With the possible exception of Elliott Wave Theory, an intellectual framework for understanding the course of social, political, and economic events was noticeably forgotten in favor of just making sure that one was part of the ever-quickening process.

The Alchemy of Finance was a shot out of the dark for me. It let me take a giant step forward by first taking a step backwards, clarifying events that appeared so complex and so overwhelming. During an era when so much money was made in larger than life events, from the Hunt brothers' squeeze of the silver market in 1979 to KKR's takeover of RJR Nabisco in 1989, Mr. Soros's theory of reflexivity is the first modern, nontechnical effort to describe and forecast the dynamic interplay between the participants in the process. That is the brilliance of this book. It describes the dynamics of the path between points of extreme valuation and equilibrium in the marketplace. This is particularly important for the average investor. How many times have we been correctly long near the bottom or short near the top of a major market move? But our staying power with these positions has been weak (as well as our returns) because of a lack of understanding of the path of big price moves. Soros gives us critical insight into that path and thus more confidence in our investments. This constitutes 70% of any successful investing campaign.

When I enter the inevitable losing streak that befalls every investor, I pick up *The Alchemy* and revisit Mr. Soros's campaigns. Studying how he coped with adversity provides an excellent tutorial for breaking the string of negative behaviors that occasionally besets any investor. Winning is infectious. And this book is replete with examples of trading behaviors all would want to emulate. Importantly, Mr. Soros's intellect gives him the confidence and strength of his own convictions to stay with his positions even during trying periods. In that sense, *The Alchemy* joins Edwin Lefèvre's *Reminiscences of a Stock Operator* as a timeless instructional guide of the marketplace. And as such, Soros should beware! In the World War II movie *Patton*, my favorite scene is when U.S. General George S. Patton has just spent weeks studying the writing of his Germany adversary Field Marshall Erwin Rommel and is crushing him in an epic tank battle in Tunisia. Patton, sensing victory as he peers onto the battlefield from his command post, growls, "Rommel, you magnificent bastard. I read your *book!*" Enough said.

The Alchemy is also an excellent economic and political history of recent times. From unknowingly providing a blueprint as to how the savings and loan fiasco in the United States would be resolved six years in advance (page 129) to predicting the stock market crash of 1987 two years in advance (page 186), Soros reveals himself as the great market visionary of our time.

History will probably remember Mr. Soros as the speculator who tilted against the Bank of England in 1992 (and freed the English people from recession). His billion-dollar score is simply too compelling a story for scribes to overlook. Mr. Soros himself would probably like to be remembered as a great economist or even scientist. But I am going to remember him for something even more important, for which he does not receive the credit he deserves. He is someone who genuinely cares about the state of the human condition and tries to better it. His myriad and monumental philanthropical efforts will qualify him as one of history's great benefactors. Even today at age 62, he pursues the activities of his six foundations with the vigor and work ethic of a young turk on the way up the financial ladder, working 18-hour days around the globe on behalf of his causes. He does not just write checks, which any wealthy person can do. He is a hands-on workaholic who materially impacts the quality of the lives of people less fortunate than he. Now this, this is a sign of greatness.

PAUL TUDOR JONES II

New Preface

Much has happened in the past few years to make the theory of reflexivity that is expounded in this book more relevant and more acceptable. Financial markets have been in turmoil. The breaking of the currency peg in Thailand in August 1997 unleashed a financial crisis that spread from one country to another like a wrecking ball. The Russian default in August 1998 put Long Term Capital Management, a hedge fund operating on the efficient market hypothesis, into jeopardy and only the timely intervention of the Federal Reserve Bank of New York prevented a meltdown. Subsequently the spread of the Internet and other innovations in information technology touched off a boom/bust sequence that was eerily reminiscent of the conglomerate boom analyzed in this book. These phenomena could not be reconciled with the theory of rational expectations and the hypothesis of efficient markets. Some academic economists recognized the failure of the prevailing paradigm and started using more realistic approaches. The concept of multiple equilibria begins to recognize reflexivity as a phenomenon, although it fails to deal with it the right way. So the theory of reflexivity should not be as alien to the thinking of academic economists as it was at the time the book was first published.

Yet the theory of reflexivity has made surprisingly few inroads into public discourse. The prevailing view remains that leaving financial markets to their own devices will assure the optimum allocation of resources. Indeed, market fundamentalism has become even more influential than it was 15 years ago.

Undoubtedly, I must accept responsibility for having failed to communicate my ideas effectively. The central thesis, that the bias prevailing in the financial markets can affect the so-called fundamentals that markets are supposed to reflect, does not seem to have registered. I feel obliged to make another try at explaining my view of the world. My own thinking has also evolved in the past 15 years, and I ought to be able to explain myself better.

Accordingly, I have written a comprehensive new Introduction that replaces the original Introduction as well as what was Chapter 1 of the book. I have left the rest of the text entirely untouched. After 15 years in print, there is some merit in exposing it to the test of time. I believe it passes that test quite well.

The new Introduction is rather dense but that cannot be helped because it deals with highly abstract philosophical ideas. My goal is very ambitious: I seek to lay the groundwork for a new paradigm that is applicable not only to financial markets but to all social phenomena.

My comments fall under four main headings. First, I try to make my critique of the prevailing equilibrium theories about financial markets more complete and conclusive and establish the case for a paradigm shift. In this context, I also examine the weaknesses in my original arguments. Then I lay the groundwork for a new paradigm based on the recognition that our understanding never corresponds to reality, and the divergence—which varies from person to person and case to case—is an important but not determining factor in shaping the course of events. The implications of this paradigm reach far beyond the financial markets. Finally, I explore the alchemy—as distinct from science—of finance further. In the book I conducted a real-time experiment that gave a blow-by-blow account of my investment decisions over a period of time, but I did not delve into my own decision-making process; on this occasion I shall make an attempt to reveal "the secret of my success."

GEORGE SOROS

The Alchemy
of Finance

New Introduction*

CRITIQUE OF THE PREVAILING PARADIGM

I started the original introduction by saying that in a very real sense this book represents my life's work. This remains true today. Although my sphere of activities has expanded from the financial to the social and political, I apply the same conceptual framework to those fields as I do to the financial markets. That is why I am so keen to bring the book up to date and to incorporate in it what I have learned in the past 15 years. Understanding reality, and financial markets in particular, is a never-ending process. With the benefit of hindsight, I can see many weaknesses in my previous exposition; rather than correcting them, I shall try to provide a succinct statement of my current thinking on the subject.

First, I must specify what the subject is. The book is about financial markets but my life's work is not confined to that arena. I was interested in philosophy long before I became engaged in financial markets. As I wrote in the original Introduction, "The abstract came first. Ever since I became conscious of my existence I have had a passionate interest in understanding it, and I regarded my own understanding as the central problem that needed to be understood." I developed a theoretical framework based on the concept of reflexivity to explain the relationship between thinking and reality, and I used the financial markets as a laboratory to test my theory. It is in that sense that this book constitutes my life's work. I hope that this summing up will bring it to fruition.

*The New Introduction replaces the Introduction and Chapter 1 from the first edition.

In recent years, my attention has veered in other directions. First I became engaged in the transition from closed to open societies that was made possible by the collapse of the Soviet system. More recently I have become preoccupied with the problems of globalization. It would be inappropriate to discuss these subjects in detail here, especially as I have written about them in other books. However, I feel obliged to restate the conceptual framework with which I have approached both problem areas—the transition to open society and globalization.

The Concept of Reflexivity

The concept of reflexivity is very simple. In situations that have thinking participants, there is a two-way interaction between the participants' thinking and the situation in which they participate. On the one hand, participants seek to understand reality; on the other, they seek to bring about a desired outcome. The two functions work in opposite directions: in the cognitive function reality is the given; in the participating function, the participants' understanding is the constant. The two functions can interfere with each other by rendering what is supposed to be given, contingent. I call the interference between the two functions "reflexivity." I envision reflexivity as a feedback loop between the participants' understanding and the situation in which they participate, and I contend that the concept of reflexivity is crucial to understanding situations that have thinking participants. Reflexivity renders the participants' understanding imperfect and ensures that their actions will have unintended consequences.

The nature of the interference between the cognitive and participating functions is not so simple, and its implications are still not properly understood. The assertion that our understanding of the world in which we live is imperfect is so banal that it hardly needs any elaboration. The way our senses work, the way our language is structured, and many other factors combine to render our understanding imperfect; but the imperfection introduced by reflexivity is more specific and needs further elucidation. The imperfection I am concerned with arises because we are participants. When we act as outside observers we can make statements that do or do not correspond to the facts without altering the facts; when we act as participants, our actions alter the situation we seek to understand. As a consequence, we cannot base our decisions on knowledge. We may know many things, and the more we know the better we are placed to make the right decisions, but knowledge alone is not a sufficient basis for making decisions. We are confronted with a situation that is inherently unknowable in the sense that what needs to be a fact to make knowledge possible is, in fact, contingent on the participants' view of the situation. If the participants' views corresponded to the situation, the situation would not be unknowable and participants could act on the basis of knowledge. But that is not the case. The situation is unknowable because the participants' views do not correspond to the situation. If this seems like circular logic, well, it is. Participants are caught in a situation characterized by a circular feedback I have called reflexivity, and trying to understand it forces them—and us, observers who seek to understand situations that have thinking participants—into circular logic. That is the point that requires further elucidation.

The traditional correspondence theory of truth sees knowledge as being expressed by true statements. The statement X is true if, and only if, the fact described by X actually happens. Facts have to be independent of the statements that refer to them in order to constitute a reliable criterion of truth. But the participants' decisions relate to the future, and the future is contingent on the participants' decisions in the present. Therefore, future facts do not constitute an independent criterion by which the current thinking of the participants could be qualified as knowledge. Even if the outcome happened to correspond to some participants' expectations, that would not qualify those expectations as knowledge because the correspondence may have been brought about by the various participants' decisions. To claim that expectations are based on knowledge is to deny that reflexivity plays any role in shaping the course of events.

Reflexivity and Economic Theory

The assertion that future outcomes are fully reflected in current expectations seems absurd, yet it is very much alive. It is at the basis of the prevailing paradigm in financial economics. Market prices are seen as passive reflections of the underlying fundamentals. The efficient market hypothesis claims that market prices fully reflect all extant information. The closely related rational expectations theory holds that, in the absence of exogenous shocks, financial markets tend toward an equilibrium that accurately reflects the participants' expectations. Together, these theories support the belief that financial markets, left to their own devices, assure the optimum allocation of resources.

This paradigm is in deep trouble; the idea that financial markets tend toward such an equilibrium seems to be contradicted by the evidence. Most economists now recognize that financial markets are capable of producing multiple equilibria. Yet the idea that free, unregulated markets assure the optimum allocation of resources has not been abandoned. Great efforts have gone into reconciling the actual behavior of financial markets with the efficient market hypothesis, adopting ever more elastic definitions of rationality and ever more modest definitions of efficiency. These modifications do not go far enough. It is time for a paradigm shift.

The Alchemy of Finance was meant to be a frontal assault on the prevailing paradigm, but it ran into a stone wall. Professional economists dismissed the theory of reflexivity as the work of an amateur whose financial success has gone to his head. I was accused either of ignoring the latest advances in economic theory or of restating the obvious. No doubt, I have to bear some of the responsibility. I gave my critics a wide opening by freely admitting that I was not familiar with the theories of rational expectations and efficient markets because, as a practitioner, I felt I was better off without them. My exposition also suffered from other limitations that I need not belabor here because readers will be able to judge for themselves. Nevertheless, the theory of reflexivity has gained ground among practitioners, and *The Alchemy of Finance*, with all its shortcomings, has found a place in the reading lists of business schools as distinct from economics departments.

I should like to use this opportunity to drive my critique of the old paradigm home. I may be flogging a dead horse by now, but the exercise is necessary because the prevailing paradigm has become deeply ingrained in people's thinking. Even as the experts have modified their views, public policy in the United States and elsewhere is still guided by the belief that financial markets tend toward an equilibrium that assures the best allocation of resources and it is only government interference that stands in the way. I have called this dogma "market fundamentalism" and it remains very influential.

Let me first dispose of the theory of rational expectations. The theory, as I understand it, asserts that market participants, in pursuing their self-interest, base their decisions on the assumption that the other participants will do the same. This sounds reasonable, but it isn't, because participants act not on the basis of their best interests but on their *perception* of their best interests, and the two are not identical. Their understanding is imperfect and their actions have unintended consequences.

There is a lack of correspondence between expectations and out-comes—between *ex ante* and *ex post*—and it is not rational for people to act on the assumption that there is no divergence between the two.[1]

Rational expectations theory seeks to overcome this difficulty by claiming that the market as a whole always knows more than any individual participant—sufficiently so that markets manage to be always right. People may get things wrong, and misunderstandings may cause random disturbances; but in the ultimate analysis all market participants use the same model of how the world works, and when they do not, they learn from experience so that in the end they converge on the same model. I work with a different model, and the fact that I have been successful using it as a market participant makes nonsense out of rational expectations.

I contend that financial markets are always wrong in the sense that they operate with a prevailing bias, but the bias can actually validate itself by influencing not only market prices but also the so-called fundamentals that market prices are supposed to reflect. That is the point that people steeped in the prevailing paradigm have such difficulty grasping.

The ways in which the prevailing bias can validate itself are discussed in detail in the book, with many concrete examples. Beyond a certain point the self-validating feedback loops become unsustainable. That is how reflexivity gives rise to initially self-fulfilling but eventually self-defeating prophesies and processes. The most spectacular manifestation is in the boom/bust sequences that are characteristic of financial markets. The theory of reflexivity can explain such bubbles, while the efficient market hypothesis cannot. A whole new literature has sprung up to explain away bubbles within the prevailing paradigm. But bubbles are not the only manifestations of reflexivity. There are also many subtler forms described in the book, such as Reagan's Imperial Circle or the mergermania of the 1980s. They cannot be explained without discarding the efficient market hypothesis.

We can see, then, that the efficient market hypothesis and the theory of reflexivity are alternative theories about the behavior of financial markets. The efficient market hypothesis does not fit the facts, and it is also questionable on theoretical grounds: the illusion that markets are always right is created by the reflexive interaction between the participating and cognitive functions. In fact, markets are almost always wrong but their bias is validated during both the self-fulfilling and the self-defeating phases of boom/bust sequences. Only at inflection points is the prevailing bias proven wrong.

It is an interesting question why such an unrealistic interpretation of financial markets as the efficient market hypothesis should have gained such widespread acceptance. The answer is to be found in the requirements of economic theory as a scientific pursuit. Scientific theories are supposed to have some predictive value, and the efficient market hypothesis seeks to meet that requirement, while the theory of reflexivity does not. On the contrary, it contends that the course of events is inherently unpredictable. Thus, the former qualifies as a scientific theory (albeit a false one) while the latter does not. I have acknowledged this fact by entitling my book *The Alchemy of Finance*, as distinct from science.

It would be difficult for a nonscientific theory to falsify a scientific one without a far-reaching reconsideration of scientific method as it applies to human affairs in general and financial markets in particular. I have attempted such a reevaluation in *The Alchemy of Finance*, but I cannot claim to have made much of an impression. I consider the issue so important for understanding not only financial markets but human affairs in general that I feel obliged to try again.

The Human Uncertainty Principle

We live in the real world, but our view of the world does not correspond to the real world. The theory of rational expectations itself provides a striking example of how far our interpretation can stray from the real world. Yet our view of the world is part of the real world—we are participants. And the gap between reality and our interpretation of it introduces an element of uncertainty into the real world. Again, this sounds like circular reasoning, but it accurately describes situations with thinking participants.

I can now define the element of uncertainty better than I did in the original edition of *The Alchemy of Finance*. Invoking both the correspondence and coherence theories of truth, I can proclaim what I call the "human uncertainty principle." That principle holds that people's understanding of the world in which they live cannot correspond to the facts and be complete and coherent at the same time. Insofar as people's thinking is confined to the facts, it is not sufficient to reach decisions; and insofar as it serves as the basis of decisions, it cannot be confined to the facts. The human uncertainty principle applies to both thinking and reality. It ensures that our understanding is often incoher-

ent and always incomplete and introduces an element of genuine uncertainty—as distinct from randomness—into the course of events.

The human uncertainty principle bears a strong resemblance to
Heisenberg's uncertainty principle, which holds that the position and momentum of quantum particles cannot be measured at the same time. But
there is an important difference. Heisenberg's uncertainty principle does
not influence the behavior of quantum particles one iota; they would behave the same way if the principle had never been discovered. The same is
not true of the human uncertainty principle. Theories about human behavior can and do influence human behavior. Marxism had a tremendous
impact on history, and market fundamentalism is having a similar influence today. A phrase like "the axis of evil" can alter the course of history,
and calling the estate tax "the death tax" can influence public policy. My
own actions—and my performance in the financial markets—would have
been different if they had not been based on the human uncertainty principle (although I had not yet given it that name).

Just as quantum physics is subject to alternative interpretations—
quanta can be described as particles or as waves—so it is with the human uncertainty principle. We may speak of imperfect understanding
but it may be more appropriate to speak of human creativity. Imperfect
understanding has a negative sound; creativity is more inspiring. If perfect understanding were possible, there would be no room for creativity.
As it is, the world in which we live is, to some extent, our own creation.

The extent to which people's thinking shapes reality requires further
examination. There is a tendency to deconstruct reality into people's perception of reality. This is an overreaction to a previous tendency to interpret reality as being governed by the inexorable laws of science, which
are capable of being discovered and prevail irrespective of what anybody
thinks. Reality is more complicated. To understand it properly, we must
distinguish between natural phenomena that are impervious to what
people think and social phenomena that contain thinking participants.

The laws that apply to natural phenomena operate independently
of what anybody thinks—although the formulation of the laws and the
selection of the phenomena to which they apply are very much influenced by prevailing areas in science. The availability of an independent
criterion by which the validity of scientific hypotheses can be judged
has been a boon to scientific method. Natural science has, in fact, produced many more amazing results than those wrought by magic, superstition, or religious beliefs.

When it comes to events that have human participants, scientific knowledge is more difficult to attain, and thinking plays a more active, creative role, both in understanding them and in shaping them. As we have seen, people base their actions not on reality but on their view of the world, and the two are not identical. As a result even past history cannot be treated in the same way as natural phenomena because it does not consist only of hard facts like the birth and death of kings. Social situations like revolutions or political compromises have different meanings for different participants, and even after the event they are subject to different interpretations.[2] Myths about the past have a bearing on the future. The battle of Kosovo in 1389 loomed large in the recent breakup of Yugoslavia. This poses problems for scientific method, but at the same time renders scientific knowledge less important in the understanding and shaping of human affairs. History is a story, and there is plenty of room for magic, superstition, religion, and other beliefs.

Since people's decisions are not based on knowledge, outcomes are liable to diverge from expectations. Events that have thinking participants cannot be understood without taking that divergence into account. In the case of natural phenomena, events unfold irrespective of what anybody thinks—although what people choose to notice is influenced by the prevailing paradigm. In the case of social events, the influence of thinking is more pervasive: it can affect the course of events. This has far-reaching implications for scientific method.

Social versus Natural Science

The standards and criteria of scientific method are based on the achievements of natural science. Karl Popper—who has greatly influenced my thinking—proclaimed the doctrine of the unity of science: the same standards and criteria apply to both the natural and the social sciences.[3] And he was not alone. The achievements of the natural sciences were so impressive that the social sciences sought to imitate them. Not all of the social sciences—for instance, anthropology insists on telling stories rather than establishing universally valid theories—but economic theory in particular has made a valiant effort to imitate natural science.

I disagree with my mentor, Karl Popper, on the doctrine of the unity of science. There are two fundamental differences between the social and the natural sciences. One relates to the subject matter, the other to the role of the scientist. First, reflexivity and the human uncertainty principle interfere with the predictability of human behavior; second, theories about human behavior can and do influence human behavior.

Given these handicaps, imposing the standards and criteria of natural science on the human sciences gives rise to false claims and misleading results. It encourages theories such as rational expectations that do not correspond to reality, and it disqualifies the theory of reflexivity because it does not yield the predictions expected of scientific theory. Yet if there is an element of uncertainty in the underlying phenomena, it ought to be reflected in the theories that deal with them.

Heisenberg's uncertainty principle did not undermine the status of natural science because natural science had produced some truly amazing results before the uncertainty inherent in quantum physics was encountered. In the light of those discoveries, Heisenberg's uncertainty principle appears as a crowning achievement of scientific method. The human sciences find themselves in a much more unfavorable position because they encounter the element of uncertainty inherent in the participants' thinking at the very beginning of their enquiry, not when their quest is already well-advanced. They can postpone the day of reckoning, as economics has done, by building their theories on postulates that deliberately exclude that uncertainty, but by doing so they are doing violence to their subject matter.

Why did Popper embrace the doctrine of the unity of science when he was at least as aware of the principle of human uncertainty as I am? I believe he did so because he wanted to show that Marxism is unscientific and he needed the doctrine to make the argument stick. But that does not mitigate the fact that he employed the wrong argument. It would have been much better to establish that the social sciences cannot meet the standards and requirements of natural science because of the two handicaps I have identified; therefore, those social theories that base their claim to validity on their scientific status are making a false claim. That is not to say that social theories cannot be valid, but they must establish their claim to validity on their own merit and not by parading in the false feathers of natural science.

This is not an arcane theoretical argument. It has great practical relevance right now. The same critique that Popper raised against Marxism can be applied to mainstream economics. Many economic theories such as the theory of perfect competition cannot be disproved, because they are based on certain specified assumptions and the conclusions follow from the assumptions by deductive logic. Many thoughtful economists have made this point perfectly clear, but market fundamentalists have found it convenient to ignore the difference between the artificial world created by those postulates and reality.

Today's ideology of market fundamentalism was known as *laissez faire* in the nineteenth century. It is once again very influential by virtue of its influence on the policies of the United States and the so-called Washington consensus. Its dominance cannot be compared with the paramount position that Marxism used to enjoy in the Soviet Union because the United States is a democratic country but the two ideologies have one feature in common: they both base their claim to validity on the authority of science. Without holding economic theory responsible for the sins of market fundamentalism, I must contest that claim.

I consider market fundamentalism a dangerous ideology—more dangerous today than Marxism because Marxism has been discredited while market fundamentalism is the ideology that underlies the globalization of financial markets. I have been at pains to point out the excesses and deficiencies of globalization, but every time I criticize market fundamentalism I have to go through the argument that I have presented here to show that financial markets do not tend toward a rational expectations equilibrium. That would not be necessary if the implications of reflexivity and the principle of human uncertainty were generally accepted.

SELF-CRITIQUE

Judging by the published reviews, the concept of reflexivity as presented in *The Alchemy of Finance* has not been properly understood. I should like to use this occasion to correct some of the shortcomings of the original presentation. Many reviews described reflexivity by saying that prevailing sentiments greatly influence market prices. If that were all, I would be indeed belaboring the obvious. What makes reflexivity interesting is that the prevailing bias has ways, via the market prices, to affect the so-called fundamentals that market prices are supposed to reflect. Only when the fundamentals are affected does reflexivity become significant enough to influence the course of events. It does not happen all the time, but when it does it gives rise to the boom/bust sequences and other far-from-equilibrium conditions that are so typical of financial markets.

Terminology

With the benefit of hindsight I have to admit that my terminology in expounding the theory of reflexivity is somewhat confusing. I use the term "reflexivity" to describe both the two-way feedback mechanism between the cognitive and participating functions and the boom/bust process in financial markets. Both uses are legitimate: the boom/bust process is a particular manifestation of a more general relationship. But it is not the only manifestation; it is only the most spectacular one. There are many other, more subtle reflexive connections and there are times when the reflexive connections are so feeble that they can be disregarded altogether.

Let me try to clarify matters. The relationship between the cognitive and participating functions is a universal condition; but the two-way interaction between the participants' bias and the fundamentals occurs only intermittently and it takes different forms at different times. In the book I identify such interactions but I do not have a good word to describe them. To speak of reflexivity is too weak because it can be taken to refer to a universal condition; to speak of initially self-reinforcing but eventually self-defeating processes is just too long; therefore I use the term "boom/bust" even where it is not, strictly speaking, appropriate. This is a source of confusion.

I do not have a ready solution. Since writing the book I have started speaking of "far-from-equilibrium" conditions as distinct from "near-equilibrium" situations. But this terminology is not entirely satisfactory either, because what characterizes a boom/bust process is exactly that it passes from near-equilibrium to far-from-equilibrium conditions and it is difficult to decide when the transition occurs. Nevertheless, I wish I had thought of these terms at the time I wrote the book. The lack of a suitable terminology affected not only the presentation but also the analysis. In retrospect I find that I laid too much emphasis on the boom/bust model. I identify some pure cases (see Chapter 1), and they are very convincing. But then I went on to develop a credit and regulatory cycle (Chapter 3) which is less satisfactory.

The underlying ideas of the latter are valid. There is a reflexive connection between the act of lending and the value of the collateral, and it is the liquidation of credit that gives the boom/bust model its asymmetric shape: slowly rising and abruptly falling. Similarly, there is a reflexive interaction between regulators and the economy they regulate, and financial crises usually lead to a tightening of regulations. Both these ideas are incorporated in the boom/bust model, but they do not add up to a grand pattern of credit and regulatory cycles. By looking for such a pattern I weakened my argument.

Reflexivity is the rule, not the exception. If that were not the case, the spectacular bubbles that occasionally occur would be difficult to explain. But reflexivity may also manifest itself in other forms. I discuss such non-boom/bust phenomena in the book. Freely floating exchange rates (Chapter 2) tend to produce wavelike patterns. Reagan's Imperial Circle (Chapter 6) was an initially self-reinforcing but eventually unsustainable process that did not follow a boom/bust pattern. And the mergermania that swept through the American corporate scene in the mid-1980s (Chapter 8) differed in character from the conglomerate boom described in Chapter 1. There were no boom/bust sequences during the real-time experiment I recorded in Part Three, yet I kept looking for it. This was a defect not only in the book but also in my investment decisions at the time. I might have avoided it with a different terminology. This is an example of how misconceptions can influence reality.

Power

I have discovered another shortcoming in the book recently after reading Mancur Olson's *Power and Prosperity*[4]: I did not give sufficient weight to power relations. My first objective in *The Alchemy of Finance* was to disprove the prevailing paradigm, the equilibrium model of financial markets. For this purpose, I accepted the economists' description of financial markets as a free exchange among willing participants. Using that starting point, I succeeded in showing that, far from tending to rational expectations equilibrium, financial markets lend themselves to initially self-reinforcing but eventually self-defeating processes. Changes in the political, institutional, and regulatory environment play a crucial role in these processes, particularly at inflection points. For instance, the conglomerate boom of the late 1960s reached its apogee when Saul Steinberg tried to take over Chemical Bank and the establishment united against him; the crash of 1929 led to the Glass-Steagal Act, and the bust beginning in March 2000 to the

Sarbanes-Oxley Act. These are political developments; they cannot be described as a free exchange among willing participants. While I took full notice of them in my description of individual boom/bust processes, I did not make it clear that more is involved in financial markets than free exchange: power and politics play an important role. This is a serious analytical defect that detracts from the theory of financial markets as presented in the book.

The neglect of power relations is especially noticeable when the book deals with the evolution of the global financial system: "The International Debt Problem" and "The Collective System of Lending" (Chapters 4 and 5). One of the major tenets of my recent book *On Globalization* (Public-Affairs, 2002) is the inherent disparity between center and periphery. The center consists of countries that can borrow in financial markets in their own currencies; the periphery is constituted by those countries that cannot. The disparity arises because the countries at the center control the international financial institutions: when threatened by recession, they themselves can follow countercyclical policies; but countries that depend on the support of the International Monetary Fund cannot indulge in such luxuries. The primary interest of the IMF is to protect the system; maintaining economic activity in the periphery countries comes second. While the disparity between center and periphery was subsumed in the discussion, it was never made explicit. As a result, *The Alchemy of Finance* does not provide a coherent analysis of globalization. This is particularly relevant to Part Two: Historical Perspective.

The globalization of financial markets was a market fundamentalist project. Its aim was to constrain the ability of national governments to interfere in the economy by making it easy for financial capital to move around internationally and making it difficult for national governments to tax it and regulate it. Financial capital is an essential ingredient of production, and it will seek to go where it is best rewarded. National governments must therefore compete to attract and retain international capital.

As a market fundamentalist project, globalization has been highly successful. The taxation and regulation of financial assets have in fact been greatly reduced, and the return on capital has been significantly increased. That engendered a global bull market that lasted—with minor interruptions—from the early 1980s to the year 2000. In the emerging markets, it came to an end earlier, in 1997. The greatest beneficiaries were the countries that initiated it: the United States and the United Kingdom. They earned a great deal of money by providing financial services to the world. They also attracted a significant portion of the world's savings, as witnessed by the large and increasing current account deficit of the United States: it now amounts to an amazing $500 billion a year.

Taking power relations into account would undermine the market fundamentalist case even more than showing that financial markets are inherently unstable. Market fundamentalists insinuate that markets have a moral quality about them by allowing the diligent and creative participants to come out ahead. This argument always suffered from neglecting the social injustice of unequal initial endowments; but it is entirely destroyed if financial markets do not merely permit free exchange but promote the dominance of the powerful. As I have pointed out elsewhere,[5] the distinguishing feature of financial markets is that they are amoral; that is one of the factors that make them so efficient. But society cannot exist without morality; therefore it cannot rely exclusively on market discipline. Market fundamentalism is a convenient ideology for the rich and powerful.

The omission of power relations also makes it impossible to understand the present moment in history. There is a dominant group within the Bush administration that believes that international relations are relations of power, not law, and the United States, being the most powerful state, has the right to impose its will on the rest of the world. They held this belief before September 11, 2001, and, to the extent they could, they acted upon it. They renounced international treaties and sought to make American military power absolute by militarizing space. But they were constrained by the lack of a clear political mandate from the voters. The terrorist attacks on September 11, 2001, changed that. The Bush administration can now claim to be acting in self-defense and carry the nation behind it.

The beliefs of this dominant group are incorporated in the Bush doctrine. It is built on two pillars: first, the United States must do whatever is necessary to maintain its unquestioned military dominance, and, second, the United States reserves the right to engage in preemptive strikes. I believe this is a dangerous doctrine. Carried to its logical conclusion, the Bush doctrine establishes two classes of sovereignty in the world: the sovereignty of the United States, which is sacrosanct and not subject to limitations imposed by international law, and the sovereignty of other states, which is subject to the Bush doctrine. This carries echoes of George Orwell's *1984*: all animals are equal but the pigs are more equal than the others. Even if, under the influence of September 11, the American public went along with the Bush doctrine, the rest of the world could never accept it. Therefore it will have to be enforced by the use of military power.

The attitude of this dominant group can be described as a crude form of social Darwinism: the survival of the fittest in a world characterized by the struggle for survival. In the markets, the struggle is among individuals and enterprises; in geopolitics it is among states. This is a distorted view of the world. It emphasizes competition to the exclusion of cooperation. Yet, without cooperation there would be no laws, no markets, no civilization. Until recently, I was inveighing against market fundamentalism, which I considered a greater current threat than Marxism. Now I regard the ideologues of American supremacy as even more dangerous than market fundamentalists. What I am afraid of is that the pursuit of American supremacy may be successful for a while because the United States in fact enjoys a dominant position in the world today. However, it will fail in the long run because the concept is flawed. If the Bush doctrine passes some early tests successfully, it may give rise to a boom/bust process with much more devastating consequences than a purely financial crash.[6]

A Negative Approach

By far the greatest shortcoming of the original book was that it was couched almost entirely in negative terms: imperfect understanding, human uncertainty, inability to match the achievements of natural science, and so on. It is easy to see why this should be so. I was trying to discredit a certain way of thinking by using the categories created by that way of thinking. No wonder that I had to take a negative view of those categories. I felt I had no alternative because the conceptual framework I was seeking to replace was so pervasive that there were no other categories available that would have been readily comprehensible to the reader.

When I speak of categories I could not avoid using, I have in mind the dichotomy between statements and facts, thinking and reality. Using these dichotomies is appropriate to natural phenomena, which occur independently of what anybody thinks or says, but not to social phenomena in which the participants' thinking plays a formative role.

Nevertheless these dichotomies have become so deeply ingrained in our way of thinking that it is difficult to avoid them.

The distinction between statements and facts is a very fruitful one. It is the foundation of logic because it creates an independent criterion by which the truth of statements can be judged. It also plays a very important role in the acquisition of scientific knowledge, although that role has been exaggerated. The distinction applies only in natural science where facts and statements do indeed belong to separate universes; in the case of social science it distorts reality.

In natural science thinking is supposed to play a purely passive role. The universe of facts is supposed to be governed by laws of universal validity, and the task of science is to discover them. Karl Popper has shown that this is not, strictly speaking, true because the laws of science are hypothetical in character and there is an element of intuition or invention in the formulation of hypotheses. Nevertheless it is accurate to say that the role of thinking in natural science is purely passive in the sense that statements can only reflect (or fail to reflect) the facts; they cannot affect them.

The universe that forms the subject matter of social science is different. It has participants whose thinking both reflects and affects the situation in which they participate. Thinking and reality cannot be treated as separate categories, because they are interconnected in a reflexive fashion: thinking is part of the reality people have to think about. The subject is also the object, as in certain French verbs (e.g., *il se lave*), which are called reflexive.

Reflexivity has been strangely neglected in economic theory. By taking the demand supply curves as given, economic theory can treat market prices as a mere reflection of the underlying fundamentals (i.e., supply) and the participants' preferences (i.e., demand). This leaves out of account the active, creative, and distortive effect of the participants' imperfect understanding. It gives a very misleading picture of financial markets. For instance, it implies that investors base their decisions on the fundamentals, whereas the goal of market participants is to make money. Only if market prices reflected the fundamentals accurately would it make sense for them to be guided by those fundamentals—and in that case, nobody could make more money than anybody else and everyone ought to invest in index funds. This is an absurd conclusion, yet it is still widely accepted.

Criticizing the prevailing paradigm is not enough. The theory of reflexivity ought to provide some positive insight into the way financial markets work in order to serve as the basis of a new paradigm.

THE NEW PARADIGM

I have used the term reflexivity to indicate that understanding and participating are interconnected. So far I have focused on the negative implications of reflexivity, explaining how the two functions interfere with each other. Now I must face up to the challenge of exploring how the two functions can be best performed in the light of that interference. That means finding a positive way of studying social situations—and even more importantly, of participating in them—as opposed to explaining why they cannot be treated in the same way as natural phenomena. It requires a new paradigm that differs from the old one in acknowledging that the separation between thinking and reality is not as watertight as in natural science.

The new paradigm cannot treat facts as if they constituted reality and statements as if they constituted thinking. Instead of drawing dichotomies between thinking and reality, we must recognize that thinking forms part of reality instead of being separate from it. This integrated reality cannot be described by statements that are separate and independent of it. Such statements would immediately accrue to the subject matter, enlarging it and requiring additional statements to correspond to it. The dichotomy between thinking and reality is itself something that was not discovered but rather invented by us in our attempt to understand reality; as such, it became part of reality and rendered reality more difficult to understand. In other words, reality always exceeds our capacity to understand it. Gödel's theorem provides a proof of this point for arithmetics. The method Gödel used was to assign so-called Gödel numbers to all arithmetic truths. He was then able to show that the number of arithmetic truths is always greater than the number of proofs. Arithmetical reality exceeds our capacity to understand it. A neat theorem![7]

Now that we have come to understand this point, we need to invent a new way of dealing with reality or more exactly that part of reality that has thinking participants. The dichotomy between statements and facts proved very fruitful in the study of natural phenomena, which consist of nothing but facts. We must take a different approach in the study of reflexive phenomena, which contain both statements and facts. Since thinking and reality are interconnected, it seems advisable to take an integrated rather than an analytical approach. By that I mean that instead of looking for timelessly and universally valid laws that govern social situations, we should accept that we, with our imperfect understanding, play a role in governing them. Our participation gives reality a different character from the one with which we are familiar from natural science.

To establish the new paradigm I could take two avenues. One is to approach reality from the position of a detached observer; the other is to approach it from the inside, as a market participant. I shall explore both avenues. The first approach can be described as an attempt to reduce an infinitely complex reality to something comprehensible. What makes the attempt difficult, and reality infinitely complex, is that the various attempts to accomplish that task are themselves part of reality. The second approach leads to some interesting revelations about managing a hedge fund, and it is an easy read.

Having already tried the patience of the reader with my philosophical musings and meanderings, I would have preferred to give you the inside scoop on financial markets first. But there is more to be said from the point of view of the detached observer; so be prepared for another dose of philosophy. I realize that I may be losing you; in that case, please turn to page 35 where I return to the financial markets.

The "Shoelace" and "Zip-Lock" Theories

Obviously, the new paradigm has to be based on reflexivity and the human uncertainty principle.[8] To enable the principle to play that role it must be converted from a negative statement into a positive assertion. That can be accomplished by replacing the *lack of correspondence* between people's views and the actual state of affairs with the assertion that there is a *divergence* between the two. This renders the assertion operational: it gives us two variables—the *ex-ante* expectations and the *ex-post* outcome—and it directs us to study the relationship between them. The divergence between expectations and outcomes provides the key to understanding history—and I interpret financial markets as a historical process. There are as many expectations as there are participants, but there is only one outcome. It is that outcome that constitutes reality, and it is reality that needs to be understood. It cannot be understood, however, without taking into account expectations, both in lead-ing up to the outcome and in being part of that outcome.

The benefit of this approach is that it focuses our attention on the divergence between outcomes and expectations. Outcomes are affected but not determined by expectations. There is a two-way feedback loop between them: the cognitive function runs from outcomes to expecta-tions, the participating function from expectations to outcomes. Both functions operate continuously and in opposite directions. The arrow of causation does not run from one set of outcomes to the next; it crisscrosses from outcomes to expectations and vice versa. I have called this the "shoelace theory of history."

I need to specify what I mean by outcomes in this context. Nor-mally, outcomes are meant to be observable, that is to say objective, facts. If one adopted that definition, the "shoelace" would connect the objective and subjective aspects of reality. I do not think that gives an accurate picture of the relationship between thinking and reality be-cause it puts too much emphasis on the objective aspect. Thinking is not confined to observable facts. People think of all aspects of reality, not only the objective one and they care a lot about what others think. To give a more accurate picture, the outcome should include not only observable facts but all aspects of reality including the think-ing of the participants.

We can achieve this effect by qualifying everything that is *ex-post* as a fact whether it is directly observable or not. That means including the participants' thinking among the facts. I believe that is a legitimate use of the word, as the expression *ex-post facto* attests. We may not be able to tell what people think but as long as it is *ex-post facto*, it is uniquely de-termined: people cannot think anything different as of that moment. That means that the distinction is not between the subjective and ob-jective aspects of reality but between *ex-ante* and *ex-post*. *Ex-ante* there is a range of possibilities that people can contemplate; *ex-post* there is only one situation that has actually prevailed. Instead of a shoelace the-ory of history, which implies that the two sides that are connected are somehow symmetrical, it would be better to speak of a "zip-lock the-ory of history": the past is closed; the future is open. Needless to say, neither theory claims that history can ever be fully known. Calling them theories is an exaggeration.

This way of looking at reality will be difficult to get used to be-cause we have been conditioned to think differently. We have learned to distinguish between facts and statements, reality and ideas. Now we are required to think of reality as incorporating ideas and facts as including statements; yet to make sense of such a reality we still need to draw a distinction between the facts and the statements that relate to them. It is the dual role of thinking as both a fact and an interpretation of, or a statement about, facts that causes the difficulties.

I speak from personal experience. In my earlier attempts at formulating the concept of reflexivity I ended up with the version I am now rejecting, namely a connection between the objective and subjective aspects of reality. That is what led me to speak of the shoelace theory of history. The zip-lock theory is meant to correct that distortion by focusing on the temporal aspect, the difference between *ex-ante* and *ex-post*. It should be pointed out that the zip-lock theory is really just another way of saying that reality is path-dependent. Under that name the idea is much more familiar. However, the specific mechanism of path dependence, the reflexive feedback loop, is less well recognized.

Understanding Reality

The zip-lock theory has important implications for our ability to understand reality. Let's invoke Popper's model of scientific method. The model works with universally valid generalizations of a hypothetical character that can be tested by subjecting them to repeated experiments. Since the generalizations are timeless, explanations and predictions are symmetrical and reversible. This model is clearly not applicable to reflexive situations because of the asymmetry between *ex-ante* and *ex-post*. Experiments are not repeatable because even if all the observable facts are identical, the prevailing views of the participants are liable to be different when an experiment is repeated. The very fact that an experiment has been conducted is liable to change the perceptions of the participants. Yet, without testing, generalizations cannot be falsified. Moreover, generalizations cannot be used reversibly to provide explanations and predictions because history is path-dependent: *ex-post* is uniquely determined; *ex-ante* the range of possibilities is more open. Explaining ought to be easier than predicting.

I am slipping into a negative frame of mind again. Instead of specifying what cannot be done, I must explore what can be done. Situations can be explained because *ex-post facto* they are uniquely determined. There is also room for predictions as long as no claim is made that the future is predetermined. The range of possibilities is bounded by the present, which is uniquely determined, and the participants' decisions, which, we know, are based on biased views. Instead of looking for determinate equilibria surrounded by random walks, as economic theory has done, it is this range of possibilities that needs to be explored. Most importantly, the zip-lock theory of history holds open the possibility of changing the world in which we live. Social alchemists can succeed where the original alchemists failed. This possibility poses a danger to scientific method, but it offers hope for mankind.

The divergence between thinking and reality has emerged as an important factor in determining the course of events. The divergence varies from time to time, person to person and case to case. In some situations it is so minimal that it can be disregarded altogether. That is the case in humdrum, everyday situations like driving to work or shopping at the supermarket. In other situations, the divergence takes on great significance. Not only are the participants' views far removed from reality, but they also manage to move reality further away from what it would be in the absence of a divergence. For instance, President Bush, by rejecting South Korean president Kim Dae Jung's sunshine policy, precipitated a crisis with North Korea and led many South Koreans to think that the United States is more of an aggressor than North Korea—which is even further removed from reality than President Bush's statement about the "axis of evil."

We may therefore draw a distinction between humdrum and historic events, depending on the impact that the participants' misconceptions have on the course of events. In humdrum, everyday events the effect is negligible; in historic events, the impact is significant enough to alter the participants' perceptions. I call those misconceptions that influence the course of history "fertile fallacies." We can then assert that fertile fallacies and other misconceptions provide the key to history. Needless to say, this is a tautology: first we distinguish between humdrum and historic events according to the participants' misconceptions and then we claim that those misconceptions are the source of historic change. Nevertheless, the tautology is useful in directing our attention to the role of misconceptions and fertile fallacies.

The new paradigm can be formulated in purely abstract terms by asserting that *all human constructs are fallible*. The term "constructs" includes both thinking and reality: institutions as well as conceptual frameworks, theories, and points of view. The term "fallible" refers to something more than the possibility that our constructs may be flawed; it asserts that most of our constructs are, in fact, flawed.

Reality is full of flawed constructs. The fact that a certain way of thinking prevails does not mean that it is valid; the fact that an institution exists does not mean that it is well constructed. That is what sets social constructs like governments or religions apart from physical constructs like bridges or automobiles. A badly designed car will not run while social institutions or ideologies can be badly flawed and still persist.

The new paradigm should protect us from what may be called the "fundamentalist fallacy": the argument that just because a construct has proved flawed, its opposite is bound to be flawless. The fundamentalist fallacy, combined with the efficient market hypothesis, has given rise to market fundamentalism. To keep things in perspective, the same fundamentalist fallacy can be detected also in communism and among antiglobalization activists.

Financial Markets as Laboratory

The trouble with this way of presenting the new paradigm is that it is too abstract. That is why we must now turn to the financial markets for a practical demonstration. *The Alchemy of Finance* explores a variety of specific examples; here I want to focus on the role of flaws and misconceptions in general terms, but I use the financial markets to make the discussion less abstract.

I contend that the application of the concept of equilibrium to the financial markets is itself a misconception. It came about because of the success of natural science. Economic theory sought to mimic Newtonian physics. It tried to establish universally valid generalizations about the conditions of equilibrium, and to a large extent it succeeded. As long as the analysis was confined to physical goods, no great distortion was involved. Both the supply and demand curves could be taken as independently given, and the equilibrium was determined by the intersection of the two curves. The distortion became more pronounced when credit was introduced into the analysis.

Credit cannot be treated as if it were merely a passive reflection of the underlying fundamentals, since it also plays an active role in shaping those fundamentals. This can be seen when we consider the relationship between the act of lending and the value of the collateral. Banks base their lending on the value of the collateral; but the act of lending can also influence that value. When people are eager to borrow and the banks are willing to lend, the value of the collateral rises in a self-reinforcing manner and vice versa. Thus the act of lending activates a reflexive relationship that is absent in pure exchange. This was particularly noticeable in the great sovereign lending boom of the 1970s, which forms the subject of Chapters 4 and 5.

In a pure exchange, equilibrium has a clearly defined meaning: it is the price that clears the markets. When it is applied to financial markets, equilibrium becomes more like a theological concept: it is the price that ought to clear the markets if market prices did not have any effect on the participants' attitudes and/or the fundamentals. But it is in the nature of financial markets that they do have such effects. Consequently financial markets often develop boom/bust sequences and other far-from-equilibrium conditions.

Flaws and misconceptions play a crucial role in individual boom/bust sequences. Usually they involve a failure to recognize that a relationship is reflexive. In the great sovereign lending boom of the 1970s, the mistake was not to recognize that the banks' willingness to lend enhanced the various debt ratios by which the banks measured the borrowers' creditworthiness. In the conglomerate boom the error was the willingness of investors to put a high value on earnings growth generated by acquisitions that reinforced the overvaluation of conglomerates. The misconception in the recent technology boom was even more egregious. Investors valued top-line revenue growth disregarding that the business models could be sustained only as long as companies could sell stock at inflated prices. In other far-from-equilibrium situations the flaws take other forms. Reagan's Imperial Circle (Chapter 6) arose out of an internal contradiction between monetarism and supply-side economics; mergermania (Chapter 8) was facilitated by the tax deductibility of interest on corporate loans and the hefty fees earned by the intermediaries.

In the absence of such flaws and misconceptions, market excesses tend to correct themselves in short order; but when the so-called fundamentals are susceptible to such influences the self-correcting mechanism of the markets is impaired and an initially self-reinforcing but eventually self-defeating process is set in motion. Self-correcting markets are humdrum, everyday events; boom/bust sequences are historic

in the sense that neither the fundamentals nor the participants' perceptions remain the same as they were at inception. In these cases it makes
no sense to speak of equilibrium; that is what makes the expression
"far-from-equilibrium conditions" so apt.

In the absence of equilibrium, it is the task of the authorities to
prevent or correct market excesses. But they, too, are fallible. Although
they are supposed to be above the fray, they are also participants with
their own institutional interests and biases. The result is a reflexive interaction between regulators and markets, a kind of cat and mouse
game, which occasionally deteriorates into a boom/bust sequence due
to the regulators' failure to prevent it from happening.

In the book I tried to develop a regulatory and credit cycle but it
fell short of a full-fledged theory. That is just as well. In retrospect I feel
I went too far in trying to impose a cyclical pattern on history. As we
have seen, the boom/bust pattern is only one of many possibilities.
There are other far-from-equilibrium situations; there are also long
stretches of humdrum, everyday events and self-correcting misconceptions. The boom/bust pattern provides a very dramatic spectacle, and it
is easy to be impressed by it. I am guilty of making too much of it in
the book. Instead of interpreting history in terms of credit and regulatory cycles, I should have emphasized the role of flaws and misconceptions as a key to understanding historical developments. That is what I
am doing now.

My starting point is that financial transactions do not take place in a
vacuum in accordance with timelessly valid laws; there are actual laws
and institutions at work that evolve over time and provide a historical
context within which the timelessly valid generalizations operate.
When we apply the timelessly valid concept of fallibility to this institutional framework we arrive at the proposition that whatever regime or
arrangement prevails, it is bound to be flawed.

I have actually demonstrated that proposition in the book with regard to currency markets, and events since then have reinforced my
thesis. Jokingly, I compare the exchange rate regimes to matrimonial
regimes: whatever regime prevails, its opposite appears more attractive.
Fixed exchange rates are too rigid, and freely floating exchange rates
lend themselves to long-lasting, self-validating trends that eventually
become unsustainable. We are currently (March 2003) at a point where
the strong dollar may have become unsustainable. Currency pegs were
discredited by the emerging markets crisis of 1997–1998, and for a time

it was believed that the answer was to be found at either extreme: a currency board or a free float. This belief did not survive long; it was put to rest by the Argentine default. Dirty floats remain out of favor, yet I believe it is the right prescription for Brazil.[9] (Dirty float is a floating exchange rate regime that includes *ad hoc* government intervention to influence a currency's directions.)

It can be seen that whatever currency regime prevails, it is flawed. The fact that a regime is flawed makes its opposite more attractive, but that does not render its opposite flawless; the flaws will become apparent when the opposite regime prevails. This sounds discouraging, but it can also be interpreted in a positive way: there is infinite room for improvement. Since perfection is unattainable, future generations will not be deprived of the opportunity to improve the world in which they live. But there are no universally valid solutions; all improvements have to be considered in the context of the prevailing arrangements. Reforms that may work in a particular context may be inappropriate at another time. Those who claim to be in possession of timelessly valid solutions are making a false claim. That is not to say that we cannot make universally valid generalizations—the human uncertainty principle is such a generalization—only that such generalizations do not and should not determine reality.

In my investment career I operated on the assumption that all investment theses are flawed. This proposition itself is flawed: it does not follow from the human uncertainty principle that all theories are flawed. But it is a very useful assumption to work with. The fact that a thesis is flawed does not mean that we should not invest in it as long as other people believe in it and there is a large group of people left to be convinced. The point was made by John Maynard Keynes when he compared the stock market to a beauty contest where the winner is not the most beautiful contestant but the one whom the greatest number of people consider beautiful. Where I have something significant to add is in pointing out that it pays to look for the flaws; if we find them, we are ahead of the game because we can limit our losses when the market also discovers what we already know. It is when we are unaware of what could go wrong that we have to worry.

It hardly needs stressing that this approach is in contradiction with the efficient market hypothesis and the theory of rational expectations. The latter claims that the markets are always right; my proposition is that markets are almost always wrong but often they can validate themselves.

As the real-time experiment demonstrates, this interpretation of how financial markets operate can be much more profitable than the rational expectations theory would permit.

Whether the approach works outside the financial markets is another question. I contend that it works as far as understanding a situation is concerned. I have used it in understanding and anticipating events connected with the collapse of the Soviet system and I can claim some success.[10] I am currently using it in interpreting the Bush doctrine.[11] But when it comes to influencing the course of events a critical mode of thinking may be more of a hindrance than help. People do not like to hear when they are wrong, and they like to follow leaders who can convince them that they know what they are doing. Those who admit their mistakes or their doubts do not stay leaders very long. This may be one reason why markets are more efficient than politics.

There is a difference between what is successful and what is true. That is one of the great insights that the theory of reflexivity has to offer and it applies both to the financial markets and politics. It is a lesson that still needs to be learned. Our society worships success as if it combined truth and virtue. This view, which is dominant in present-day America, is false.

The Search for Second-Best Solutions

Where does this leave the study of social phenomena in general and economic theory in particular? A strong case can be made that the slavish imitation of natural science has led economic theory down the wrong path. In their search for universally valid generalizations, economists largely ignored the complexities and uncertainties of the real world and constructed an elegant axiomatic structure based on unrealistic assumptions. The assumptions underlying perfect competition include perfect information, homogeneous commodities, a large number of participants engaged in profit-maximizing behavior, and no transaction costs. The contention that unregulated financial markets lead to the optimum allocation of resources rests on the assumption that participants base their decisions on rational expectations. None of these assumptions prevail in the real world.

The edifice that has been erected on these unsound foundations is extremely fragile. General equilibrium prevails only under optimum conditions when all the assumptions are met. Remove even a few of the assumptions, and the edifice comes crashing down. It is not enough for some of the participants to act on the basis of rational expectations; they must all do so—otherwise it is irrational for any of them to do so. And if the optimum is unattainable, it is not at all certain that unregulated markets offer the second best solution. For instance, it might have been good public policy to dampen the "irrational exuberance" of the information technology boom by raising margin requirements; or it may be preferable to increase the supply of public goods. Since the optimum is ruled out by the principle of fallibility and only the second best is available, the prevailing paradigm is not only unrealistic but actually misleading because it is used to buttress market fundamentalist policies.

I am of course not advocating demolishing the edifice of economic analysis. That would be another example of the fundamentalist fallacy: just because the results are found wanting, the method that produced them has to be abandoned. In fact, the same method that produced equilibrium theory has also led to the questioning of that theory, and to the exploration of alternative approaches. Critics of *The Alchemy of Finance* reproached me for not being up-to-date on recent developments in economic theory, and their criticism was justified. While I still cannot claim full familiarity with the literature, I see some merit in behavioral economics and even more merit in evolutionary game theory. I consider the latter a practical exploration of reflexivity.

Adaptive Behavior

A new paradigm seems to be gradually emerging. It consists of replacing the assumption of rational behavior with the concept of adaptive behavior. The two concepts are very different in character. Rational behavior is a postulate that lends itself to deductive logic and an axiomatic system. Adaptive behavior is an empirical concept and it does not lead to any a priori conclusions. It is what it is—a subject for exploration. The exploration has led to evolutionary game theory and evolutionary systems theory—both of which treat behavior as path-dependent and not necessarily internally consistent. Both disciplines are capable of producing determinate results. For instance, in repeated prisoners' dilemma games tit for tat proves to be the best strategy. But not all results are determinate. For instance, in most predator-prey relationships the outcome is constantly fluctuating, and only rarely is a stable equilibrium reached.

Does that mean that a new paradigm has superceded the old one and reflexivity has been recognized in fact although not in name? Not quite. The old paradigm is far from abandoned. Indeed, it is more influential than ever when it comes to policy. And the new paradigm has not yet produced a coherent and comprehensive explanation of social phenomena. For instance, adaptive behavior is easier to reconcile with the recent technology boom than rational behavior, but it does not provide an adequate explanation of the course of events. What is missing is exactly a recognition of reflexivity and the consequent divergence between outcomes and expectations.

Reflexivity goes beyond the concept of adaptive human behavior and makes a claim about the situations in which adaptive humans participate. The claim is that adaptive behavior helps create what may be called, for lack of a better name, an "adaptive environment," and the two are interconnected in a reflexive manner. This means that participants have to adapt to constantly changing situations and the process will never be complete. The idea is implicit in the predator-prey relationship: one party is the other party's environment. Reflexivity makes the idea explicit. If the claim is valid, the prevailing paradigm cannot be valid: equilibrium may never be reached, because the attempt to reach it moves the target.

The concept of adaptive behavior is equally applicable both to biology and to the social sciences. There is something reassuring about that, because it blurs the sharp dividing line that I have drawn between the natural and social sciences. Dichotomies are characteristic of our attempts at understanding reality, not of reality itself. It is reassuring to have a bridge across the divide. Yet there must be a deficiency in the concept of adaptive behavior because it fails to identify what is different between biology and human affairs. That deficiency is corrected by introducing the concept of reflexivity. The divergence between outcomes and expectations is specific to human behavior. While it may be appropriate to assign expectations and intentions to some animals, only in the case of humans are we in a position to study them.

The mechanism through which adaptive behavior manifests itself is different in biology and the social sciences. In biology it operates through mutation and manifests itself in the propagation of particular genes within the species. In human affairs flaws and misconceptions play the same role as mutation does in biology, but it is ideas and behavior patterns that are being propagated, not genes. My success in the financial markets will have no effect on the gene pool of future hedge fund managers, but the success of trend-following behavior in currency markets can increase the crowd of trend-following speculators.

Behavioral economics and evolutionary game theory were far less advanced when I wrote *The Alchemy of Finance* than they are today. These disciplines are potentially compatible with reflexivity, and I hope they will make the concept more acceptable. Nevertheless I contend that the concept of reflexivity is needed in order to establish a new paradigm. It is needed, first, to debunk the theory of rational expectations and the efficient market hypothesis; second, to give the proper foundations to behavioral economics and evolutionary game theory.

It may be questioned whether we need a new paradigm. Why not let a thousand flowers bloom? I am sympathetic to this point of view. The best response to fallibility is pluralism. The main merit of a market economy is not that it assures the optimum allocation of resources but that it allows people to have a choice and to learn from their mistakes. But fallibility cannot be used to justify false theories. Reflexivity and rational expectations are incompatible, and we therefore do have to make a choice.

I trust that enough has been said to make the choice clear. Rational expectations theory could prevail only under conditions so extreme as to be unsuitable for human habitation. By contrast, the theory of reflexivity does not provide the rigorous results we have come to expect from scientific theories, but it does fit the actual behavior of financial markets much better. There ought to be no contest.

The Boom/Bust Model

What about the second part of a paradigm shift: the establishment of a new paradigm? Let us see how my boom/bust model stands up to critical examination. Robert Solow criticized it for incorporating so many escape clauses that it cannot possibly be falsified.[12] He is both right and wrong. He is right in the sense that the boom/bust model is not a falsifiable theory. He is wrong in the sense that it was never proposed as a falsifiable theory but rather as an illustration, a prototype of how reflexivity works in financial markets. Reflexivity is a meta-theory, a paradigm, like the utility maximizing model of neoclassical economics; neither is directly testable.

As a prototype, the boom/bust model is perhaps even more relevant today than it was when originally published. We have just lived through the biggest boom/bust cycle since World War II. The cycle bears a remarkable similarity to the conglomerate boom of the late 1960s on which the boom/bust model described in *The Alchemy of Finance* was based. It will be instructive to identify the similarities and the differences.

The main similarity lies in a self-reinforcing process whereby inflated stock prices can accelerate an underlying trend, which in turn enhances expectations and inflates stock prices until the outcomes fail to sustain expectations and there is a crash. In the conglomerate boom the process had to do with using inflated stock for acquisitions. In the Internet and telecom boom, inflated stock prices accelerated the introduction of new technologies. In each case, there was a misconception involved. In the conglomerate boom investors put the same value on per-share earnings irrespective of how they were achieved; in the technology boom the error was more egregious: stocks were valued at a multiple of revenues, not earnings, and growth was financed by selling stock, not by following sound business plans. In each case the misconceptions were reinforced by positive changes in the fundamentals: earnings and revenue growth accelerated. Expectations were inflated until they became unsustainable, but before that happened the process had withstood some difficult tests.

Eventually, a turning point was reached. In the conglomerate boom it came when Sol Steinberg was unsuccessful in taking over Chemical Bank. In the technology boom the critical event was the auctioning of 3G licenses in Europe. Telecom companies were obliged to make inflated bids in order to justify their inflated stock prices. Until then, inflated stock prices had been a source of cash; on that occasion they turned into a cash drain. As stocks began to decline the trend became self-reinforcing in the opposite direction. The excesses that could be concealed while stock prices were rising started to surface. During the boom, corporations had used every avenue at their disposal to boost earnings, and when they ran out of legitimate devices, some corporations turned to illegitimate ones. When the market turned, some of these illegitimate practices were exposed. The coup de grace was delivered when Enron went bust. Enron, like many companies, used special purpose entities (SPEs) to keep debts off its balance sheets. But unlike many other companies, it used its own stock to guarantee the debt of its SPEs. When the price of Enron fell, the scheme unraveled, exposing a number of other financial misdeeds the company had committed. The Enron bankruptcy reinforced the downtrend in the stock market, which led to further bankruptcies and news of further corporate and individual misdeeds. Both the downtrend and the clamor for corrective action gathered momentum in a self-reinforcing fashion—just as the boom/bust model envisions.

There was nothing surprising about this course of events. It has happened many times before. The real surprise was that people were surprised. After all, many of the practices that were subsequently condemned were carried on quite openly. Everybody knew that the best companies, such as General Electric and Cisco Systems, were massaging their numbers to maintain the appearance of a steady progression of earnings. Indeed, investors put a premium on management's ability to do just that. SPEs could be bought off the shelf, and investment banks maintained structured finance departments to provide custom-made designs. The management of Tyco International Ltd. proudly proclaimed that they could generate earnings growth by acquiring companies and moving them to Bermuda where their earnings were tax exempt, and Tyco was accorded a high earnings multiple. Stock options were not only accepted but considered a useful device for boosting shareholders' values since they provided executive compensation without incurring any costs and encouraged management to focus on the stock price above all other considerations. A similar change of attitudes had occurred in the conglomerate boom/bust sequence. During the boom phase investors idolized managements. After the bust, the president of Ogden Corporation told me ruefully at lunch that "I have no audience to play to."

The major difference between the two instances is a difference in the pervasiveness of the boom/bust process and in the extent of the malfeasance involved. The conglomerate boom affected only a segment of the stock market—the conglomerates and the companies they acquired—and a segment of the investing public, spearheaded by the so-called "go-go" funds. When the conglomerates began to threaten the overall financial establishment, that establishment closed ranks against them. By contrast, the recent boom encompassed the entire corporate and investment community, and today's establishment, including the political establishment, was fully complicit. Enron, WorldCom, and Arthur Andersen could not have gotten away with their nefarious activities without encouragement and active reinforcement from virtually all sectors of American society—their corporate peers, investment professionals, politicians, the media, and the public at large. Whereas the conglomerate boom ended because of resistance from the establishment, in this case the boom was allowed to run its course, and the search for corrective measures started only after the collapse. Even after the crash, a probusiness administration was trying to downplay the damage. The head of the Securities and Exchange Commission (SEC), Harvey Pitt, was so lax on enforcement that it fell to Eliot Spitzer, the Attorney General of New York State, to investigate the malpractices of New York investment bankers. Eventually Harvey Pitt had to resign.

Most of the misdeeds of the recent boom fall into two categories: a decline in professional standards and a dramatic rise in conflicts of interest. And both are really symptoms of the same broader phenomenon: the glorification of financial gain irrespective of how it is achieved. The professions—lawyers, accountants, auditors, security analysts, corporate officers, and bankers—allowed the pursuit of profit to take precedence over long-standing professional values. Security analysts promoted stocks in order to gain investment-banking business; bankers, lawyers, and auditors aided and abetted deceptive practices for the same reason. Similarly, conflicts of interest were ignored in the mad dash for profits.

While only a small number of people committed acts that actually qualify as criminal, many more engaged in activities that in retrospect appear dubious and misleading. They did so thanks to reassuring legal opinions, Generally Accepted Accounting Principles (GAAP), and the comforting knowledge that everybody else was doing the same. When broad principles are minutely codified—as they are in GAAP—the rules paradoxically become easier to evade. A whole industry was born, called structured finance, largely devoted to rule evasion. Once a financial innovation was successfully introduced it was eagerly imitated, and the limits of the acceptable were progressively pushed out by aggressive and unscrupulous practitioners. A process of natural selection was at work: those who refused to be swayed were pushed to the sidelines; those leading the process could not see the danger signs because they were carried away by their own success and the reinforcement they received from others. As the *Financial Times* reported, "They couldn't see the iceberg because they were standing on top of it."[13] Underlying this indiscriminate pursuit of financial success was a belief that the common interest is best served by allowing people to pursue their narrow self-interest—or market fundamentalism, for short.

Market fundamentalism is a false and dangerous ideology. It is false on at least two counts. First, it profoundly misapprehends the way financial markets operate. It assumes that markets tend toward an equilibrium that assures the optimum allocation of resources. Second, by equating private interests with the public interest, market fundamentalism endows the pursuit of self-interest with a moral quality. The second fallacy is even more dangerous than the first one. It accounts for the widespread abuses that characterized the recent bust as compared to the earlier one.

It can be seen that the boom/bust model has withstood the test of time. The fact that people have been surprised by what happened indicates that the model, far from belaboring the obvious, still has some explanatory power. At the same time, it can also be seen that the model emphasizes one aspect of reality, the cyclical, at the expense of another, the unique. The technology boom was more pervasive and the abuses more widespread than in the case of the conglomerate boom. I attribute this unique feature to the spread of market fundamentalism. The fact that the pursuit of success has taken precedence over moral considerations is a source of instability. I have explored the subject in greater depth in my book *Open Society: Reforming Global Capitalism* (PublicAffairs, 2000).

Toward a New Paradigm

The fact remains that the boom/bust model does not qualify as a scientific theory because it cannot be falsified. Reflexivity may or may not give rise to a boom/bust sequence and the process may be aborted at any time. Each case contains unique features. The model has some predictive power—for instance, a bust could never precede a boom, and the magnitude of the bust tends to be proportionate to the boom that preceded it—but it is minimal. The model can be used to predict practically anything, and if it turns out to be false the error can be ascribed to the particular prophesy, not to the model. It will be recalled that I predicted imminent catastrophe in *The Crisis of Global Capitalism: Open Society Endangered* (BBS/PublicAffairs, 1998).

Rational expectations theory cannot be directly falsified, either. The postulated conditions are never met, and any deviation from the expected results can be ascribed to extraneous shocks. Its main conclusion, however, that it is impossible to consistently outperform the averages, has been falsified by many outstanding performers, including me—and I was not even familiar with the theory. These performance records could not possibly be considered random walks; yet the theory has not been abandoned.

As mentioned before, reflexivity is a meta-theory, a conceptual framework. In considering its suitability to serve as a paradigm for the financial markets and even more broadly for human affairs the lack of falsifiability does matter. I am inclined to argue that it is inevitable, due to the unpredictability of the subject matter, but I am on weak grounds here. It may be that I have just not found the right methodology.

I am forced to conclude that the theory of reflexivity as it stands today cannot serve as a new paradigm. It is a philosophical theory, not a scientific one. It can, however, be combined with the new departures in economic research that are compatible with it, such as behavioral economics and evolutionary game theory. The recognition of reflexivity may inspire other new approaches. Together, they can form a new paradigm: the theory of reflexivity undermines the old paradigm, while the new disciplines help to build a new one.

There is also more to be found out about boom/bust and other far-from-equilibrium conditions than I have done so far. Accepting that each sequence is unique, there are more specific facts that could be adduced with regard to each sequence. There are also more common features that could be established by comparative studies. The theory of reflexivity imposes certain limitations on what can be accomplished, but I am very far from pushing against those limits. A closer study of boom/bust processes could also produce some testable generalizations similar to the tit-for-tat solution for repeated prisoners' dilemma games.

All this could be done, but not by me. I have taken the argument as far as I could. Now that my attention has veered from the financial markets to other pursuits I have neither the energy nor the interest to take it any further. (I also lack the qualifications. I have never been good at math. As a student, I started questioning the assumptions of economic theory because I had difficulty practicing it.) I am putting my faith in the emerging new disciplines I have already mentioned. They seem to possess the methodology that the new paradigm needs: nonlinear programming and empirical testing. The old paradigm relied on solving equations; the new paradigm is likely to rely on running scenarios on computers and experiments in real life.

Many professional economists do not feel the need for a new paradigm. Fifteen years ago they could dismiss my attack on the old paradigm on the grounds that I did not understand it; now they can claim that reflexivity is already incorporated in the latest advances in economic analysis. It is true that some progress has been made in that direction, but it is mostly at the margin. More importantly, public discourse is still dominated by the old paradigm, and that stands in the way of some much-needed improvement in public policy. Recognizing reflexivity could definitely improve public policy. The management of currencies would benefit from a greater willingness to modify the prevailing regime when its deficiency becomes apparent; and a better understanding of the boom/bust process could help the authorities to prevent it from getting out of hand.

At the same time, I have to admit that the boom/bust model as it stands today is of limited use to market participants. It has not even always helped me to make money. For instance, I managed to lose money in the technology boom by selling short Internet stocks too soon. How to convert theory into practice is the next subject to be discussed.

SECRETS OF A SUCCESSFUL SPECULATOR

Theories about financial markets look at them from the perspective of the outside observer. I should now like to change the perspective and describe what it is like to be an active participant. This will not change any of the conclusions I have reached so far because the theory of reflexivity was designed to illuminate the role of the active participant, but it will shed some additional light on the subject. The book contains a real-time experiment, a sequence of investment decisions recorded at the time they were made. Here I shall go a step further and give a subjective account of my decision-making process. In other words, I shall try to reveal "the secret of my success." Needless to say, I leave behind any pretense of scientific objectivity.

As a money manager I was emotionally engaged in managing my fund. I managed it as if my existence depended on it, as indeed it did. I relied on my instincts and intuition as well as my conceptual framework to guide me through uncertainty. A number of factors conspired to increase my dependence on emotions. For one thing, I had less knowledge and information at my disposal than most other fund managers. I had never studied security analysis, I was not part of a team, and I was ready to engage in a much broader range of activities than most others. I was not well positioned to perform better than others if I had tried to play the market by a particular set of rules; my competitive advantage lay in recognizing changes in the rules of the game. I started with hypotheses relating to individual companies; with the passage of time my interests veered increasingly toward macroeconomic themes. This was due partly to the growth of the fund and partly to the growing instability of the macroeconomic environment. For instance, exchange rates were fixed until 1973; subsequently, they became a fertile field for speculation.

Specializing in reflexive change put me under tremendous time pressure. I had to familiarize myself with particular industries or countries at short notice, and having done so I did not have the luxury of keeping up-to-date. I used to claim, only half jokingly, that it took me 48 hours to become an expert on any subject; if I spent any more time on it my judgment would be clouded by the facts. Specialists often develop a vested interest in their subject; the information they collect is never enough for them. I was only interested in the information that was sufficient to make a decision; the rest would merely confuse the issues. I called it "going for the jugular."

I also developed the practice of "investing first and investigating later." It worked very well because if an idea was appealing enough to attract me on first hearing, it was likely to have the same effect on others. If, on further investigation, I found it to be flawed I could always turn around and liquidate my position with a profit provided I was not the last one to hear it. If the idea checked out, I was better situated to increase my position because I had already bought at a lower price or sold short at a higher one.

The fact that I was managing a hedge fund also contributed to my emotional engagement. The use of leverage adds an additional dimension of risk to an investment portfolio. A portfolio without leverage is flat, as its name indicates. It can get larger or smaller but it cannot be subject to margin calls and disappear altogether. The use of credit, whether on the long or the short side, makes a hedge fund three-dimensional. The equity base can support more or less leverage, and if the structure is not properly balanced it can collapse. This made the uncertainty with which all fund managers have to contend existential. The very survival of the fund depended on me. At the same time, my reward was directly tied to the performance of the fund.

I was well qualified to deal with existential uncertainty. If I had to sum up my qualifications, I would use one word: survival. When I was an adolescent, the Second World War gave me a lesson in survival that I have never forgotten. I was fortunate enough to have a father who was a grand master in the art of survival, having lived through the Russian revolution as an escaped prisoner of war. Under his tutelage the holocaust in Hungary served as an advanced course at a tender age.[14] I have no doubt that my experiences as an adolescent played a major role in my subsequent success as a hedge fund manager. So did my conceptual framework.

Those who want to belittle the theory of reflexivity deny that it has had much, if anything, to do with my financial success. They attribute my performance to an uncanny intuition, and they treat the theory as the self-indulgence of a successful speculator. My biographer quotes my son Robert as saying:

> My father will sit down and give you theories to explain why he does this or that. But I remember seeing it as a kid and thinking, Jesus Christ, at least half of this is bullshit. I mean, you know the reason he changes his position on the market or whatever is because his back starts killing him. It has nothing to do with reason. He literally goes into a spasm, and it's this early warning sign.[15]

My son is right about the backache. I used to treat it as a warning sign that something was wrong in the portfolio. It used to occur before I knew what was wrong, often even before the fund began to decline in value. That is what made it so valuable as a signal. It would be wrong, however, to dismiss the theory on that account, because it was the theory that made me take the signal seriously. I knew that I did not act on the basis of knowledge; I was acutely aware of uncertainty and I was always on the lookout for mistakes. As I mentioned earlier, it is when I did not know the flaws in my positions that I had to worry. When I finally discovered what was wrong my backache usually went away.

The major insight I gained from the theory of reflexivity and what I now call the human uncertainty principle is that all human constructs (concepts, business plans or institutional arrangements) are flawed. The flaws may be revealed only after the construct has come into existence. That is the key to understanding reflexive processes. Recognizing the flaws that are likely to appear when a hypothesis becomes reality puts you ahead of the game.

The existential uncertainty, the close connection to my own fortunes, and the three-dimensional structure of the fund made me treat it as a living organism that was tied to me like a Siamese twin. This was more than a figure of speech; it was intensely felt. The fund was draining me and feeding me at the same time. Conversely, I endowed the fund with the attributes of a living organism.

The thinking in which a living organism engages is very different from the kind of thinking envisioned by the theory of rational expectations. The latter is akin to the thinking of an outside observer. It involves information processing with the assumed objective of maximizing self-interest. The former involves emotions as well as reason. Indeed, emotions often take precedence over reason because of the time element: decisions often have to be taken in a hurry, and the less time there is to weigh all the relevant considerations the greater the role of instincts and primal emotions. Perhaps I did not make this point sufficiently clear when I spoke of the cognitive function; it might be better to speak of precognition, which is carried on in different parts of the brain and the cortex than rational thought. Precognition predates the evolution of reason. It is more like animal behavior. Indeed, descriptions of the financial markets are full of animal imagery: bulls, bears, herd instinct. And scientific theories have remarkably little traction among practitioners. That does not mean that there is no room for reason. Reason and emotion are intricately interwoven, and human behavior cannot be properly understood as wholly rational. I relied on reason more than most practitioners and I prided myself on a conceptual framework that recognized the role of emotions and the limitations of reason.

The thinking of the active participant is very different from that of the outside observer. We may call it "organic" as distinct from rational. Scientists are interested in timeless generalizations and statistical probabilities; participants need to focus on the one particular case in which they are participating. Probabilities and generalizations can be useful, but they are misleading if they are based on the viewpoint of the outside observer. That is what happened in economic theory.

Classical economics allotted a purely passive role to the participants' thinking. That made it possible to postulate perfect knowledge, which was, in turn, the foundation of perfect competition. The concept has undergone an intricate evolution in which the assumption of perfect knowledge was replaced by the assumption of perfect information, and it was supplemented by a so-called methodological convention, which took the supply and demand curves as independently given. This convention managed to exclude the reflexive feedback mechanism whereby market prices can affect those curves. More recently, deviations from the equilibrium position have been attributed to asymmetric information. It may seem as if the theoretical framework has been gradually brought closer to reality; in fact, it has become ever further removed from it because the active, participating function has not been taken into account. By contrast, the theory of reflexivity takes the active participants as its starting point. Therefore, it can provide them with a useful conceptual framework, and I have used it in that capacity. What it cannot do is to enable the participant to occupy the position of a detached observer.

I have, in fact, tried to put myself into the position of an outside observer and remain as detached as possible. I realize that it is impossible to rid oneself of emotions, yet it is important to keep one's emotional state as stable as possible in order to have a solid platform from which changes in the outside world can be evaluated. If the platform itself is responding to different emotions than the market, it becomes difficult to observe changes in the market. The task is easier if the participant is moved by the same emotions. That is what I sought to achieve by identifying myself with my fund. It should be recognized, however, that the process involves something very different from rational thought; it is better described as empathy. The participant enters into the mind of the market and tries to understand it from the inside. I found the task easier than most other investors, partly because of my conceptual framework and partly because I identified myself with my hedge fund so intimately. I assumed that the market felt the same way as I did, and by keeping myself detached from other personal feelings I could sense changes in its mood. This was a hard discipline. It meant subordinating my own emotions to those of the market. It made it difficult to maintain other emotional involvements. My family had good reason to resent it. I looked on myself as an athlete or a boxer in training who had to sacrifice many other things for the sake of success. Managing a hedge fund requires single-minded devotion. When I became engaged in setting up a foundation network, I found that my philanthropy did not mix well with managing a hedge fund. The trouble was not only the amount of time it took but, even more, the conflicting emotional signals. It was confusing to feel good about something I was doing in philanthropy when I ought to feel bad about

the way I was positioned in the market, or vice versa. I resolved the conflict by giving up the active management of my fund. I ceased to be a boxer in training and became the coach.

I should clarify what I meant when I said that I felt the same way the market did. I was referring to the mood of the market, not to the content of the hypotheses I formulated. On the contrary, I was acutely aware that I was operating with a conceptual framework that was at loggerheads with the prevailing wisdom. I made a conscious effort to find investment theses that were at odds with the prevailing opinion because that is where the best profit opportunities are to be found. I defined my task as engaging in an arbitrage between my own judgment and the prevailing view. Both my conceptual framework and my animal instincts formed part of what I have called "organic thinking." When I identified the makings of a self-reinforcing process, I could almost feel my mouth water like one of Pavlov's dogs.

It is an interesting question whether I would still enjoy a competitive advantage if I were an active participant. My conceptual framework has become common knowledge. It used to be easy to write circles around institutional investors, but they have become much more sophisticated; hedge funds have proliferated, and methods of risk control have greatly improved. Nevertheless, I have a sneaking suspicion that I would still be able to discover some flaws that can be exploited. For instance, the prevailing methods of risk control are built on the old paradigm, and they are bound to break down from time to time. But to take advantage of the flaws I would have to learn how the risk control systems work. It would be like learning how to play against a chess machine: empathy would be less useful, and some knowledge of mathematics—which is not my long suit—would probably be unavoidable. I had the luxury of ignoring rational expectations theory; I could not ignore modern risk and performance management techniques even if I consider them flawed. I would have to understand how they work because, in contrast to rational expectations theory, they do influence investor behavior.

In my view, risk management techniques cannot account for the element of genuine uncertainty introduced by the improved techniques—although it is possible to make allowances for it by so-called stress testing. But the past is an unreliable guide to the future. I used to take a much more primitive, organic view of risk and uncertainty. Two days—one up day and one down day—were sufficient to tell me whether my fund was well positioned. Usually this gave me timely notice to make some adjustments. I was willing to risk only my gains, not my capital. This gave the fund its own momentum: picking up speed when the wind was behind us and trimming sails in stormy weather. My favorite saying was: "He who runs away lives to fight another day." I refused to be bound by the calendar in deciding what counts as profit and what is principal. After a good run, I was willing to give back a portion of the gains even if it pushed me into negative territory in a new year. As a result, we had multiyear runs. I find it amusing that most hedge funds today do not use these simple guidelines. With their help, I managed—with one exception—to confine declines to within 20% of the highest point reached by the fund, calculated on a daily basis. There were no similar limitations on the upside.

Where I have doubts whether I would be able to perform as I used to is in the currency markets, particularly in the euro. Currencies used to be like lakes with a few rivers feeding into them; by going upriver it used to be possible to anticipate the level of the lakes. Now the lakes are interconnected, and there are just too many tributaries to consider to be able to predict currency movements.

The symbiotic relationship between me and my fund gave rise to some serious identity problems. When I first started managing the fund, I identified with it completely. I came from the trading and sales side, where I had made it a point of keeping myself scrupulously insulated from my work. I had had some experience as a salesman before entering the securities business. After finishing college in England I joined as management trainee a firm making and selling handbags, custom jewelry, and fancy goods, and I ended up as a salesman. I developed a theory of salesmanship based on the principle that one must not on any account identify oneself with the merchandise one is selling. Selling is a game where you score when you make a sale. If you allow your ego to be involved, the customer can brush you off and you lose; but if you do not identify yourself with your work you will be able to redouble your efforts when you are rejected, and if you make a sale you come out the winner. I carried this principle over into the securities business, so it came as a great relief when I switched from the sell to the buy side and I could finally identify myself with my merchandise.

I soon discovered that running a hedge fund is a deadly serious game: once you identify with your portfolio, your survival is at stake. That is what makes financial markets such a good laboratory for testing your ideas: failing a test can be very painful; passing a test brings relief. The objective evidence is reinforced by emotions. Short on knowledge, I relied heavily on the pain mechanism. There was also a positive side to it: the sense of mastery that comes with success. I remember a moment in time when I stood back and looked at myself with awe: I saw a perfectly honed machine. Whatever happened in the world—economists call them exogenous shocks—I could immediately put them into perspective and relate them to everything else. I was operating in a state of heightened awareness.

The fund performed well, but the bigger it grew the more money I had to manage and the greater the pressures became. I remember an occasion when I urgently had to find some new bank credit lines. I was walking along Leadenhall Street in the City of London and I thought I was going to have a heart attack. It made me realize that if I died I would be the loser, and the insight undermined the identity of interests between me and my fund. I decided to pay more attention to myself and less to the fund. I relaxed the reins. Amazingly, the fund performed even better. Evidently I had been too cautious and controlling, replacing one investment thesis with another too soon. When I let the reins loose, the fund rose nearly four-fold in the space of two years. I was enjoying myself *and* the success of the fund but the identity problem remained unresolved. I was aware that the underlying position of the fund was gradually deteriorating because I was depleting my store of investment ideas; it was only a matter of time before we would run into trouble.

Eventually the internal conflict came to a head. I posed myself the question, who is more important: I or my fund? Am I the master of my destiny or the slave of my own creation? I resolved the question in favor of myself: I won, but my fund lost—the only occasion when the loss exceeded 20%; it was 22.9% in 1981, to be precise. I informed my shareholders of the identity crisis, and many of them redeemed their shares. The size of the fund was cut in half. I withdrew from active management while I reflected on what I really cared about. Out of this soul-searching came the Open Society Foundation and this book. To engage in the real-time experiment I had to go back to active management of the fund. The experiment held my attention and the fund exceeded its previous performance. I was well rewarded for writing this book.

It can be seen that I care for my conceptual framework more than I care about making money. (That framework also includes the concept of open society and the foundation network devoted to it, which I do not discuss in detail here.) The fact is, I have a passionate interest in the truth, but I do not care much for money; otherwise I would not give so much of it away. To be truthful, my interest in the truth takes precedence over even my interest in humanity—it is through my philosophy that I arrived at my philanthropy. I am glad I did because my philanthropy rescued me from the isolation to which my pursuit of profit consigned me. I am much happier identifying with my foundation network than I ever was identifying with my hedge fund—but the pursuit of truth takes precedence over both, as this admission demonstrates.

I note this as a fact, not as something I can explain. I could hazard a guess, but that would take me too deeply into my personal history. It is not at all self-evident that the pursuit of truth should take precedence over other considerations. My love of truth is something personal. I did not sacrifice everything for its sake, as my adventures as a salesman attest, but I feel happy when I can indulge in it.

Taking my passionate interest in the truth as a starting point, I can build a couple of interesting arguments on it. One will establish the merits of financial markets as a laboratory for the pursuit of truth, and the other will extoll the merits of philosophy.

Financial Markets as Laboratory

First, the financial markets offer an excellent laboratory for the pursuit of truth. The reason is to be found not only in the quantitative and public character of the data but even more in the emotional reality of financial markets. This will come as a surprise to many who regard financial markets as far removed from reality, but it is their concept of reality that is far removed, not the financial markets. Playing the markets is about as real as a game can get. There is, of course, a divergence between expectations and outcomes, but the outcome has an inexorable quality about it. In most social situations—in politics and in personal and business relations—it is possible to deceive oneself and others. In the financial markets, the actual results do not leave much room for illusions. The financial markets are very unkind to the ego: those who have illusions about themselves have to pay a heavy price in the literal sense. It turns out that a passionate interest in the truth is a good qualification for financial success.

How does the actual course of events relate to the truth? The relationship is not as straightforward as it may appear at first sight. Decisions have unintended consequences; so a successful outcome does not assure that the initial decision was based on correct understanding. Financial markets may reinforce illusions, after all; that is how boom/bust processes are generated. But the process eventually becomes unsustainable and the moment of truth dawns. So the truth lies somewhere beneath the surface of reality as expressed in market prices, and financial success serves as a rather unreliable indicator of true understanding. This point is well made in Part Four: Evaluation.

Testing theories in the financial markets is a useful substitute for scientific testing. The tests are not as reliable as scientific ones but at least the participant has a powerful incentive not to deceive him- or herself about the results because of the financial and emotional costs involved. If I were deceiving myself in the real-time experiment, I could not have performed as well as I did. Admittedly, the 32-year performance record of Quantum Fund cannot be attributed solely to my conceptual framework, especially as I was not personally in charge over the entire period; but the theory of reflexivity undoubtedly played some part in it—how big a part I shall leave to those who are better versed in regression analysis than I.

Once you leave the confines of scientific method you are in constant danger of getting lost in a world of your own creation and leaving reality far behind. It has happened before, in medieval theology and in nineteenth-century German metaphysics. I have experienced it personally in my earlier philosophical endeavors. That is why testing your ideas in the financial markets can be so useful: the markets provide a merciless reality check. Again, I speak from personal experience. I used to be able to write much better whenever I was actually engaged in money management. Now that my moneymaking days are over, I sorely miss the reality check that playing the markets used to impose.

The Case for Philosophy

I should like to end with an impassioned plea for reinstating philosophy as the source of all knowledge and wisdom. Obviously I have a passionate interest in the pursuit of truth; I have established it as a fact. Now I want to make a case for it.

Philosophy has fallen out of favor. Without the constraints imposed by scientific method, the philosophers of the nineteenth century lost contact with the physical world and became immerged in the metaphysics of their own creation. Encouraged by the success of natural science, logical positivists launched a frontal attack on metaphysics. Logical positivism did not survive long—Ludwig Wittgenstein himself abandoned the conclusions of his *Tractatus Logico-Philosophicus* in favor of language analysis—but old-fashioned philosophy that seeks to address real problems as opposed to the problems of language never recovered from the onslaught. Analytical philosophy, which has come to dominate the philosophy departments, is a branch of knowledge, not the source of all knowledge. That is not satisfactory. Our knowledge is not so securely based that we can afford to stop asking the eternal questions about the relationship between thinking and reality, the meaning of meaning, and so on, even if we cannot find satisfactory answers to them, or, more exactly, even if the answers always raise new questions. We are fed up with philosophy because the questions never end. But the questions are inherent in the human uncertainty principle. If the principle is valid, we must never stop questioning. A critical mode of thinking is indispensable to a better understanding of the world and also for making the world a better place. It is the foundation of an open society.

I contend that the human uncertainty principle is a step forward in understanding the human condition. It tells us that all human constructs are flawed, philosophy included. But that is not a valid reason for abandoning philosophy; we must just learn to watch out that the never-ending questions should not lead to answers that become ever more removed from reality. The theory of reflexivity is a philosophical theory, not a scientific one. It should not be dismissed on that account, but it should be held to the test of reality. What better laboratory could we find for it than the financial markets, which brook no excuses?

There was a famous discussion between Karl Popper and Ludwig Wittgenstein in Cambridge, England, that became the subject of a popular book, *Wittgenstein's Poker*.[16] Popper argued that philosophy ought to address real problems, while Wittgenstein took the position that it can address only problems of language. I am testifying on behalf of Popper.

Part One

THEORY

1

Reflexivity in the Stock Market

I n trying to develop a theory of reflexivity, I shall start with the stock
market. For one thing, it is the market I am most familiar with: I have
been a professional investor for more than twenty-five years. For another, the stock market provides an excellent laboratory for testing theories: changes are expressed in quantitative terms and the data are easily
accessible. Even the participants' views are usually available in the form
of brokers' reports. Most important, I have actually tested my theory in
the stock market and I have some interesting case studies to present.

As I mentioned in the Introduction, I did not develop my ideas
on reflexivity in connection with my activities in the stock market.
The theory of reflexivity started out as abstract philosophical speculation and only gradually did I discover its relevance to the behavior
of stock prices. I was singularly unsuccessful in formulating my theory at the level of abstraction at which I conceived it: my failure as a
philosopher stands in stark contrast with my career as an investment
professional. I hope that by presenting my ideas in the reverse order
from the one in which I arrived at them I may be able to avoid getting lost in arcane abstractions.

There is yet another reason why the stock market may provide the
best entry point for the study of reflexive phenomena. The stock market comes as close to meeting the criteria of perfect competition as any
market: a central marketplace, homogeneous products, low transaction

49

and transportation costs, instant communications, a large enough crowd of participants to ensure that no individual can influence market prices in the ordinary course of events, and special rules for insider transactions as well as special safeguards to provide all participants with access to relevant information. What more can one ask for? If there is any place where the theory of perfect competition ought to be translated into practice, it is in the stock market.

Yet there is little empirical evidence of an equilibrium or even a tendency for prices to move toward an equilibrium. The concept of an equilibrium seems irrelevant at best and misleading at worst. The evidence shows persistent fluctuations, whatever length of time is chosen as the period of observation. Admittedly, the underlying conditions that are supposed to be reflected in stock prices are also constantly changing, but it is difficult to establish any firm relationship between changes in stock prices and changes in underlying conditions. Whatever relationship can be established has to be imputed rather than observed. I intend to use the theory of reflexivity to criticize the preoccupation of economic theory with the equilibrium position. What better example could I find than the stock market?

Existing theories about the behavior of stock prices are remarkably inadequate. They are of so little value to the practitioner that I am not even fully familiar with them. The fact that I could get by without them speaks for itself.

Generally, theories fall into two categories: fundamentalist and technical. More recently, the random walk theory has come into vogue; this theory holds that the market fully discounts all future developments so that the individual participant's chances of over- or underperforming the market as a whole are even. This line of argument has served as theoretical justification for the increasing number of institutions that invest their money in index funds. The theory is manifestly false—I have disproved it by consistently outperforming the averages over a period of twelve years. Institutions may be well advised to invest in index funds rather than making specific investment decisions, but the reason is to be found in their substandard performance, not in the impossibility of outperforming the averages.

Technical analysis studies market patterns and the demand and supply of stocks. It has undoubted merit in predicting probabilities but not the actual course of events. For the purposes of this discussion it is of no particular interest, because it has little theoretical foundation other than the assertions that stock prices are determined by their supply and demand and that past experience is relevant in predicting the future.

Fundamental analysis is more interesting because it is an outgrowth of equilibrium theory. Stocks are supposed to have a true or fundamental value as distinct from their current market price. The fundamental value of a stock may be defined either in relation to the earning power of the underlying assets or in relation to the fundamental value of other stocks. In either case, the market price of a stock is supposed to tend toward its fundamental value over a period of time so that the analysis of fundamental values provides a useful guide to investment decisions.

The important point about this approach is that the connection between stock prices and the companies whose stocks are traded is assumed to be in one direction. The fortunes of the companies determine—however belatedly—the relative values of the various stocks traded in the stock market. The possibility that stock market developments may affect the fortunes of the companies is left out of account. There is a clear parallel with the theory of price where the indifference curve determines the relative amounts consumed, and the possibility that the market may influence the indifference curve is disregarded. The parallel is not accidental: the fundamentalist approach is based on the theory of price. But the omission is more glaring in the stock market than in other markets. Stock market valuations have a direct way of influencing underlying values: through the issue and repurchase of shares and options and through corporate transactions of all kinds—mergers, acquisitions, going public, going private, and so on. There are also more subtle ways in which stock prices may influence the standing of a company: credit rating, consumer acceptance, management credibility, etc. The influence of these factors on stock prices is, of course, fully recognized; it is the influence of stock prices on these factors that is so strangely ignored by the fundamentalist approach.

If there are any glaring discrepancies between prevailing stock prices and fundamental values, they are attributed to future developments in the companies concerned that are not yet known but are correctly anticipated by the stock market. Movements in stock prices are believed to precede the developments that subsequently justify them. How future developments ought to be discounted is the subject of an ongoing debate, but it is presumed that the market is doing the job correctly even if the correct method cannot be theoretically established.

This point of view follows naturally from the theory of perfect competition. It is summed up in the assertion that "the market is always right." The assertion is generally accepted, even by people who do not put much faith in fundamental analysis.

I take a totally opposite point of view. I do not accept the proposition that stock prices are a passive reflection of underlying values, nor do I accept the proposition that the reflection tends to correspond to the underlying value. I contend that market valuations are always distorted; moreover—and this is the crucial departure from equilibrium theory—the distortions can affect the underlying values. Stock prices are not merely passive reflections; they are active ingredients in a process in which both stock prices and the fortunes of the companies whose stocks are traded are determined. In other words, I regard changes in stock prices as part of a historical process and I focus on the discrepancy between the participants' expectations and the actual course of events as a causal factor in that process.

To explain the process, I take the discrepancy as my starting point. I do not rule out the possibility that events may actually correspond to people's expectations, but I treat it as a limiting case. Translating this assertion into market terms, I claim that market participants are always biased in one way or another. I do not deny that markets have a predictive or anticipating power that seems uncanny at times, but I argue that it can be explained by the influence that the participants' bias has on the course of events. For instance, the stock market is generally believed to anticipate recessions; it would be more correct to say that it can help to precipitate them. Thus I replace the assertion that markets are always right with two others:

1. Markets are always biased in one direction or another.
2. Markets can influence the events that they anticipate.

The combination of these two assertions explains why markets may so often appear to anticipate events correctly.

Using the participants' bias as our starting point, we can try to build a model of the interaction between the participants' views and the situation in which they participate. What makes the analysis so difficult is that the participants' views are part of the situation to which they relate. To make any sense of such a complex situation, we need to simplify it. I introduced a simplifying concept when I spoke of the participants' bias. Now I want to take the argument a step further and introduce the concept of a prevailing bias.

Markets have many participants, whose views are bound to differ. I shall assume that many of the individual biases cancel each other out, leaving what I call the "prevailing bias." This assumption is not appropriate to all historical processes but it does apply to the stock market and to other markets as well. What makes the procedure of aggregating individual perceptions legitimate is that they can be related to a common denominator, namely, stock prices. In other historical processes, the participants' views are too diffuse to be aggregated and the concept of a prevailing bias becomes little more than a metaphor. In these cases a different model may be needed, but in the stock market the participants' bias finds expression in purchases and sales. Other things being equal, a positive bias leads to rising stock prices and a negative one to falling prices. Thus the prevailing bias is an observable phenomenon.

Other things are, of course, never equal. We need to know a little more about those "other things" in order to build our model. At this point I shall introduce a second simplifying concept. I shall postulate an "underlying trend" that influences the movement of stock prices whether it is recognized by investors or not. The influence on stock prices will, of course, vary, depending on the market participants' views. The trend in stock prices can then be envisioned as a composite of the "underlying trend" and the "prevailing bias."

How do these two factors interact? It will be recalled that there are two connections at play: the participating and the cognitive functions. The underlying trend influences the participants' perceptions through the cognitive function; the resulting change in perceptions affects the situation through the participating function. In the case of the stock market, the primary impact is on stock prices. The change in stock prices may, in turn, affect both the participants' bias and the underlying trend.

We have here a reflexive relationship in which stock prices are determined by two factors—underlying trend and prevailing bias—both of which are, in turn, influenced by stock prices. The interplay between stock prices and the other two factors has no constant: what is supposed to be the independent variable in one function is the dependent variable in the other. Without a constant, there is no tendency toward equilibrium. The sequence of events is best interpreted as a process of historical change in which none of the variables—stock prices, underlying trend, and prevailing bias—remains as it was before. In the typical sequence the three variables reinforce each other first in one direction and then in the other in a pattern that is known, in its simplest form, as boom and bust.

First, we must start with some definitions. When stock prices reinforce the underlying trend, we shall call the trend self-reinforcing; when they work in the opposite direction, self-correcting. The same terminology holds for the prevailing bias: it can be self-reinforcing or self-correcting. It is important to realize what these terms mean. When a trend is reinforced, it accelerates. When the bias is reinforced, the divergence between expectations and the actual course of future stock prices gets wider and, conversely, when it is self-correcting, the divergence gets narrower. As far as stock prices are concerned, we shall describe them simply as rising and failing. When the prevailing bias helps to raise prices we shall call it positive; when it works in the opposite direction, negative. Thus rising prices are reinforced by a positive bias and falling prices by a negative one. In a boom/bust sequence we would expect to find at least one stretch where rising prices are reinforced by a positive bias and another where falling prices are reinforced by a negative bias. There must also be a point where the underlying trend and the prevailing bias combine to reverse the trend in stock prices.

Let us now try to build a rudimentary model of boom and bust. We start with an underlying trend that is not yet recognized—although a prevailing bias that is not yet reflected in stock prices is also conceivable. Thus, the prevailing bias is negative to start with. When the market participants recognize the trend, this change in perceptions will affect stock prices. The change in stock prices may or may not affect the underlying trend. In the latter case, there is little more to discuss. In the former case we have the beginning of a self-reinforcing process.

The enhanced trend will affect the prevailing bias in one of two ways: it will lead to the expectation of further acceleration or to the expectation of a correction. In the latter case, the underlying trend may or may not survive the correction in stock prices. In the former case, a positive bias develops causing a further rise in stock prices and a further acceleration in the underlying trend. As long as the bias is self-reinforcing, expectations rise even faster than stock prices. The underlying trend becomes increasingly influenced by stock prices and the rise in stock prices becomes increasingly dependent on the prevailing bias, so that both the underlying trend and the prevailing bias become increasingly vulnerable. Eventually, the trend in prices cannot sustain prevailing expectations and a correction sets in. Disappointed expectations have a negative effect on stock prices, and faltering stock prices weaken the underlying trend. If the underlying trend has become overly dependent on stock prices, the correction may turn into a total reversal. In that case, stock prices fall, the underlying trend is reversed, and expectations fall even further. In this way, a self-reinforcing process gets started in the opposite direction. Eventually, the downturn also reaches a climax and reverses itself.

Typically, a self-reinforcing process undergoes orderly corrections in the early stages, and, if it survives them, the bias tends to be reinforced, and is less easily shaken. When the process is advanced, corrections become scarcer and the danger of a climactic reversal greater.

I have sketched out a typical boom/bust sequence. It can be illustrated by two curves that follow more or less the same direction. One represents stock prices, and the other, earnings per share. It would be natural to envision the earnings curve as a measure of the underlying trend, and the divergence between the two curves as an indication of the underlying bias. The relationship is much more complex. The earnings curve incorporates not only the underlying trend but also the influence of stock prices on that trend; the prevailing bias is expressed only partially by the divergence between the two curves—partially it is already reflected in those curves. Concepts that are only partially observable are extremely difficult to work with; that is why we have chosen variables that can be observed and quantified—although, as we shall see later, the quantification of earnings per share can be very misleading. For present purposes, we shall assume that the "fundamentals" in which investors are interested are properly measured by earnings per share.

A typical path for the two curves may be as follows. (See the figure on page 56.) At first, recognition of an underlying trend is lagging but the trend is strong enough to manifest itself in earnings per share (AB). When the underlying trend is finally recognized, it is reinforced by rising expectations (BC). Doubts arise, but the trend survives. Alternatively, the trend waivers but reasserts itself. Such testing may be repeated several times, but here I show it only once (CD). Eventually, conviction develops and it is no longer shaken by a setback in the earning trend (DE). Expectations become excessive, and fail to be sustained by reality (EF). The bias is recognized as such and expectations are lowered (FG).

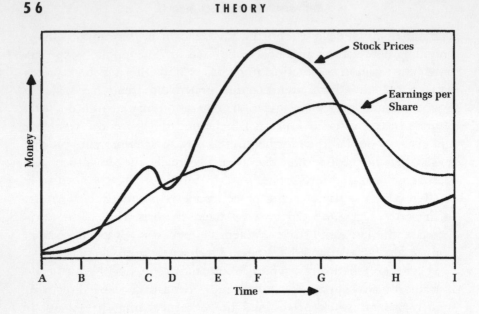

Stock prices lose their last prop and plunge (G). The underlying trend is reversed, reinforcing the decline (GH). Eventually, the pessimism becomes overdone and the market stabilizes (HI).

It should be emphasized that this is only one possible path that results from the interplay of a single underlying trend and a prevailing bias. There could be more than one trend at work and the prevailing bias could have many nuances, so that the sequence of events might require a totally different representation.

A few words about the theoretical construction of the model may be in order. We are interested in the interplay between the participants' bias and the actual course of events. Yet the participants' bias is not directly represented in our model; both curves denote the actual course of events. The prevailing bias is partially incorporated in the two curves and partially denoted by the divergence between them.

The great merit of this construction is that it uses variables that can be quantified. Stock prices serve as a convenient proxy for the situation to which the participants' bias relates. In other historical processes the situation that is interconnected with the participants' perception by the cognitive and participating functions is more difficult to identify and impossible to quantify. It is the availability of a convenient proxy that renders the stock market such a useful labora-tory for studying reflexivity.

Unfortunately, the model offers only a partial explanation of how stock prices are determined. The concept of an underlying trend has been introduced as a placeholder term, to denote changes in the "fun-damentals." What the fundamentals are has not been defined. Even the question of how the fundamentals are to be measured has not been an-swered. Earnings, dividends, asset value, free cash flow: all these yard-sticks are relevant, as well as many others, but the relative weight given to each depends on the investors' judgments and is therefore subject to their bias. We may use earnings per share for purposes of illustration, but that merely begs the question. It is a question security analysts have been struggling with for a long time. We do not need to answer it here in order to develop a theory of reflexivity.

Without knowing anything about the fundamentals we can make some worthwhile generalizations. The first generalization is that stock prices must have some effect on the fundamentals (whatever they are), in order to create a boom/bust pattern. Sometimes the connec-tion is direct, as in the examples I shall use in this chapter, but gener-ally it is indirect. Often it makes its effect felt through a political process, such as changes in taxation, or regulation, or attitudes toward saving and investment.

It is possible to have a reflexive connection between stock prices and the prevailing bias even if the fundamentals remain unaffected, but the connection becomes interesting only if the fundamentals are also in-volved. Without a change in fundamentals, the prevailing bias is likely to be corrected in short order, as we can observe in the daily fluctuations of stock prices. It would be quite in order to ignore the bias as mere noise. That is what the theory of perfect competition and the fundamentalist ap-proach to security analysis have done. By contrast, when the fundamentals are affected, the bias cannot be left out of account without serious distor-tion, because the bias gives rise to a self-reinforcing/self-defeating process that leaves neither stock prices, nor the fundamentals, nor the participants' views the same as they were before.

The second generalization is that there is bound to be a flaw in the participants' perception of the fundamentals. The flaw may not be ap-parent in the early stages but it is likely to manifest itself later on. When it does, it sets the stage for a reversal in the prevailing bias. If the change in bias reverses the underlying trend a self-reinforcing process is set in motion in the opposite direction. What the flaw is and how and when it is likely to manifest itself are the keys to understanding boom/bust sequences.

The model I presented above is built on these two generalizations. It hardly needs emphasizing how crude the model is. Nevertheless, it is valuable in identifying the crucial features of a typical boom/bust sequence. These are the unrecognized trend; the beginning of a self-reinforcing process; the successful test; the growing conviction, resulting in a widening divergence between reality and expectations; the flaw in perceptions; the climax; a self-reinforcing process in the opposite direction. Just by identifying these features we can gain some insight into the behavior of stock prices. We cannot expect much more from our rudimentary model.

In any case, a reflexive model cannot take the place of fundamental analysis: all it can do is to provide an ingredient that is missing from it. In principle, the two approaches could be reconciled. Fundamental analysis seeks to establish how underlying values are reflected in stock prices, whereas the theory of reflexivity shows how stock prices can influence underlying values. One provides a static picture, the other a dynamic one.

A theory that offers a partial explanation of stock price movements can be very useful to the investor especially if it illuminates a relationship that other investors fail to grasp. Investors operate with limited funds and limited intelligence: they do not need to know everything. As long as they understand something better than others, they have an edge. The trouble with any kind of specialized knowledge is that one's area of expertise may not be especially interesting, but the theory of reflexivity serves to identify historically significant price movements, so it goes right to the heart of the matter.

The rudimentary model I have outlined above has proved extremely rewarding in my career as an investor. That may seem surprising because the model is so simple and it fits a well-trodden stock market pattern so well that one would expect every investor to be familiar with it. Yet, that is not the case. Why? Part of the answer must be that market participants have been misguided by a different theoretical construction, one derived from classical economics and, even more important, from the natural sciences. The ingrained attitude is that stock prices are the passive reflection of some underlying reality and not an active ingredient in the historical process. This view is simply false. It is remarkable that the error has still not been fully recognized. Nevertheless, investors do recognize the sequence I have described and do respond to it, only they respond later than someone who is working with the appropriate model and is on the lookout for the crucial features that define the shape of the price curve. That is what has given me my edge.

The first time I used the model systematically was in the conglomerate boom of the late 1960s. It enabled me to make money both on the way up and on the way down.

The key to the conglomerate boom was a prevailing misconception among investors. Investors had come to value growth in per-share earnings and failed to discriminate about the way the earnings growth was accomplished. A few companies learned to produce earnings growth through acquisitions. Once the market started to reward them for their performance, their task became easier because they could offer their own highly priced stock in acquiring other companies.

In theory, the process works as follows. Let us assume that all of the companies involved have the same intrinsic growth in earnings but the stock of the acquiring company sells at twice the earnings multiple of the acquired ones; if the acquiring company manages to double its size, its earnings per share jump by 50%, and its growth rate increases accordingly.

In practice, the early conglomerates started out with high intrinsic growth rates that were rewarded by high multiples. Several of the pathbreakers were high-technology companies with a strong defense component whose managements recognized that their historic growth rate could not be sustained indefinitely: Textron, Teledyne, Ling-Temco-Vought (later LTV), to mention a few. They started to acquire more mundane companies, but, as their per-share earnings growth accelerated, the multiples expanded instead of contracting. Their success attracted imitators and later on even the most humdrum companies could attain a high multiple by going on an acquisition spree. For instance, the bulk of Ogden's earnings was derived from trading scrap metal; nevertheless, the stock sold at more than twenty times earnings at its peak. Eventually, a company could achieve a high multiple just by promising to put it to good use by making acquisitions.

Managements developed special accounting techniques that enhanced the impact of acquisitions. They also introduced changes in the acquired companies, streamlining operations, disposing of assets, and generally focusing on the bottom line, but these changes were less significant than the impact on per-share earnings of the acquisitions themselves.

Investors responded like Indians to firewater. At first, the record of each company was judged on its own merit, but gradually conglomerates became recognized as a group. A new breed of investors emerged, the so-called go-go fund managers, or gunslingers, who developed a special affinity with the managements of conglomerates. Direct lines of communication were opened between them and conglomerates would place so-called "letter stock" directly with investors. Eventually, conglomerates learned to manage their stock prices as well as their earnings.

Events followed the sequence described in my model. Multiples expanded and eventually reality could not sustain expectations. More and more people realized the misconception on which the boom rested even as they continued to play the game. Acquisitions had to get larger and larger in order to maintain the momentum, and in the end they ran into the limits of size. The climactic event was the attempt by Saul Steinberg to acquire Chemical Bank: it was fought and defeated by the establishment.

When stock prices started to fall, the decline fed on itself. The favorable impact of acquisitions on per-share earnings diminished and eventually it became impractical to make new acquisitions. The internal problems that had been swept under the carpet during the period of rapid external growth began to surface. Earnings reports revealed unpleasant surprises. Investors became disillusioned and managements went through their own crises: after the heady days of success, few were willing to buckle down to the burdens of day-to-day management. The situation was aggravated by recession, and many of the high-flying conglomerates literally disintegrated. Investors were prepared to believe the worst and in some cases the worst actually occurred. In others, reality turned out to be better than expectations and eventually the situation stabilized with the surviving companies, often under new management, slowly working themselves out from under the debris.

The conglomerate boom is particularly well suited to serve as an illustration of my rudimentary model because the "fundamentals" are readily quantified. Investors based their valuations on reported per-share earnings. However meaningless the figures, they provide charts that closely conform to my theoretical prototype. Here they are:

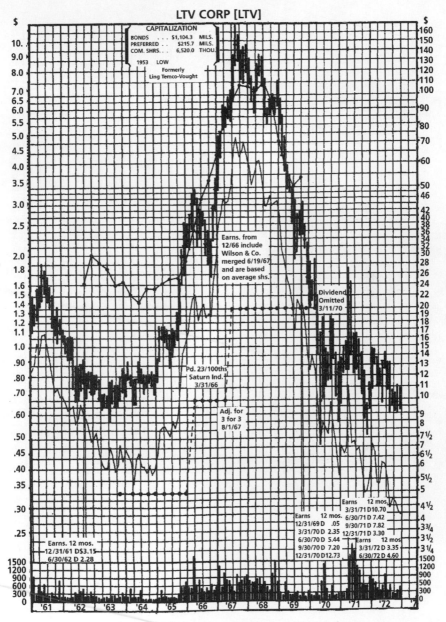

LTV CORP [LTV]

CAPITALIZATION
BONDS . . . $1,104.3 MILS.
PREFERRED . . $215.7 MILS.
COM. SHRS. . . 6,520.0 THOU.

1953 LOW

Formerly
Ling Temco-Vought

Earns. from
12/66 include
Wilson & Co.
merged 6/19/67
and are based
on average shs.

Dividend
Omitted
3/11/70

Pd. 23/100ths
Saturn Ind.
3/31/66

Adj. for
3 for 3
8/1/67

Earns. 12 mos.
3/31/71 D 10.70
6/30/71 D 7.42
9/30/71 D 7.82
12/31/71 D 3.30

Earns. 12 mos.
12/31/69 D .05
3/31/70 D 2.35
6/30/70 D 5.44
9/30/70 D 7.20
12/31/70 D 12.73

Earns. 12 mos
3/31/72 D 3.35
6/30/72 D 4.60

Earns. 12 mos.
12/31/61 D $3.15
6/30/62 D 2.28

'61 '62 '63 '64 '65 '66 '67 '68 '69 '70 '71 '72

(Courtesy of Securities Research Company, a Division of
Babson-United Investment Advisors, Inc., 208 Newbury St., Boston, MA 02116.)

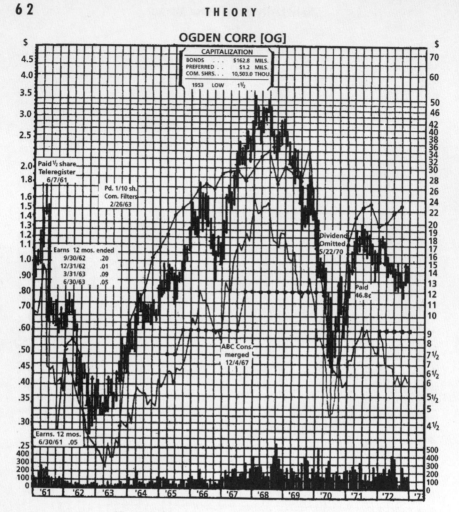

*(Courtesy of Securities Research Company, a Division of
Babson-United Investment Advisors, Inc., 208 Newbury St., Boston, MA 02116.)*

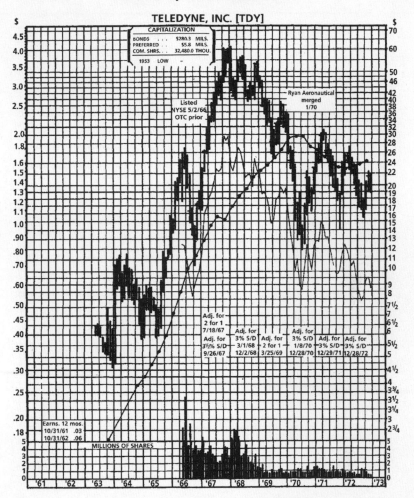

(Courtesy of Securities Research Company, a Division of
Babson-United Investment Advisors, Inc., 208 Newbury St., Boston, MA 02116.)

My best documented encounter with a boom/bust sequence is that of Real Estate Investment Trusts. REITs, as they are called, are a special corporate form brought into existence by legislation. Their key feature is that they can distribute their income free of corporate taxation, provided they distribute all the income they receive. The opportunity created by this legislation remained largely unexploited until 1969 when a large number of REITs were founded. I was present at the creation and, fresh from my experience with conglomerates, recognized their boom/bust potential. I published a research report whose key part reads as follows:

THE CASE FOR MORTGAGE TRUSTS
(February 1970)

THE CONCEPT

Superficially, mortgage trusts seem to resemble mutual funds designed to provide high current yields. But the analogy is misleading. The true attraction of mortgage trusts lies in their ability to
generate capital gains for their shareholders by selling additional
shares at a premium over book value. If a trust with a book value
of $10 and a 12% return on equity doubles its equity by selling
additional shares at $20, the book value jumps to $13.33 and per-
share earnings go from $1.20 to $1.60.

Investors are willing to pay a premium because of the high
yield and the expectation of per-share earnings growth. The
higher the premium, the easier it is for the trust to fulfill this expectation. The process is a self-reinforcing one. Once it gets under
way, the trust can show a steady growth in per-share earnings despite the fact that it distributes practically all its earnings as dividends. Investors who participate in the process early enough can
enjoy the compound benefits of a high return on equity, a rising
book value, and a rising premium over book value.

ANALYTICAL APPROACH

The conventional method of security analysis is to try and predict
the future course of earnings and then to estimate the price that
investors may be willing to pay for those earnings. This method is
inappropriate to the analysis of mortgage trusts because the price
that investors are willing to pay for the shares is an important factor in determining the future course of earnings.

Instead of predicting future earnings and valuations separately, we shall try to predict the future course of the entire self-
reinforcing process. We shall identify three major factors which
reinforce each other and we shall sketch out a scenario of the
probable course of development. The three factors are:

1. The effective rate of return on the mortgage trust's capital
2. The rate of growth of the mortgage trust's size

3. Investor recognition, i.e., the multiple investors are willing to pay for a given rate of growth in per-share earnings

THE SCENARIO

Act One: At present, the effective yield on construction loans is at an optimum. Not only are interest rates high but losses are at a relatively low level. There is a pent-up demand for housing and new houses readily find buyers. There is a shortage of funds so that the projects which do get off the ground are economically well justified. Builders who are still in business are more substantial and more reliable than at the tail end of a boom. Moreover, they do their utmost to complete the construction phase as fast as possible because money is so expensive. Shortages of labor and material do cause defaults and delays but rising costs permit mortgage trusts to liquidate their commitments without loss.

Money is tight and alternative sources of interim financing are in short supply. Investor recognition of the mortgage trust concept has progressed far enough to permit the formation of new trusts and the rapid expansion of existing ones. The self-reinforcing process gets under way.

Act Two: If and when inflation abates, the effective yield on construction loans will decline. On the other hand, there will be a housing boom and bank credit will be available at advantageous rates. With higher leverage, the rate of return on equity can be maintained despite a lower effective yield. With a growing market and growing investor recognition, the premium over book value may continue to increase. Mortgage trusts are likely to take full advantage of the premium and show a rapid rise in both size and per-share earnings. Since entry into the field is unrestricted, the number of mortgage trusts will also increase.

Act Three: The self-reinforcing process will continue until mortgage trusts have captured a significant part of the construction loan market. Increasing competition will then force them to take greater risks. Construction activity itself will have become more

(Continued)

speculative and bad loans will increase. Eventually, the housing boom will slacken off and housing surpluses will appear in various parts of the country, accompanied by a slack real estate market and temporary declines in real estate prices. At this point, some of the mortgage trusts will be bound to have a large number of delinquent loans in their portfolios and the banks will panic and demand that their lines of credit be paid off.

Act Four: Investor disappointment will affect the valuation of the group, and a lower premium coupled with slower growth will in turn reduce the per-share earnings progression. The multiple will decline and the group will go through a shakeout period. After the shakeout, the industry will have attained maturity: there will be few new entries, regulations may be introduced, and existing trusts will settle down to a more moderate growth.

EVALUATION

The shakeout is a long time away. Before it occurs, mortgage trusts will have grown manifold in size and mortgage trust shares will have shown tremendous gains. It is not a danger that should deter investors at the present time.

The only real danger at present is that the self-reinforcing process may not get under way at all. In a really serious stock market decline investors may be unwilling to pay any premium even for a 12% return on equity. We doubt that such conditions would arise; we are more inclined to expect an environment in which a 12% return is more exceptional than it has been recently and in which the self-reinforcing processes of the last few years, notably conglomerates and computer leasing companies, are going through their shakeout period. In such an environment there should be enough money available for a self-reinforcing process which is just starting, especially if it is the only game in town.

If the process fails to get under way, investors would find downside protection in the book value. The new trusts are coming to the market at book value plus underwriting commission (usually 10%). Most recently formed trusts are selling at a premium which is still modest. It will be recalled that when their assets are fully employed in interim loans, mortgage trusts can earn 11% on their book without leverage and 12% with a 1:1 leverage. A modest premium over book value would seem justified even in the absence of growth.

If the self-reinforcing process does get under way, shareholders in well-managed mortgage trusts should enjoy the compound benefits of a high return on equity, a rising book value, and a rising premium over book value for the next few years. The capital gains potential is of the same order of magnitude as at the beginning of other self-reinforcing processes in recent stock market history.

My report had an interesting history. It came at a time when go-go fund managers had suffered severe losses in the collapse of the conglomerates. Since they were entitled to share in the profits but did not have to share in the losses of the funds they managed, they were inclined to grasp at anything that held out the prospect of a quick profit. They instinctively understood how a self-reinforcing process works since they had just participated in one and they were anxious to play. The report found a tremendous response whose extent I realized only when I received a telephone call from a bank in Cleveland asking for a new copy because theirs had gone through so many Xerox incarnations that it was no longer legible. There were only a few mortgage trusts in existence at the time but the shares were so eagerly sought after that they nearly doubled in price in the space of a month or so. Demand generated supply and there was a flood of new issues coming to market. When it became clear that the stream of new mortgage trusts was inexhaustible, prices fell almost as rapidly as they had gone up. Obviously the readers of the report failed to take into account the ease of entry and their mistake was corrected in short order. Nevertheless their enthusiastic reception helped to get the self-reinforcing process described in the report under way. Subsequent events took the course outlined in the report. Mortgage trust shares enjoyed a boom that was not as violent as the one that followed the publication of the report but turned out to be more enduring.

I had invested heavily in mortgage trusts and took some profits when the reception of my study exceeded my expectations. But I was sufficiently carried away by my own success to be caught in the down-draft with a significant inventory. I hung on and even increased my positions. I followed the industry closely for a year or so and sold my holdings with good profits. Then I lost touch with the group until a few years later when problems began to surface. I was tempted to establish a short position but was handicapped in that I was no longer familiar with the terrain. Nevertheless, when I reread the report I had written several years earlier, I was persuaded by my own prediction. I decided to sell the group short more or less indiscriminately. Moreover, as the shares fell I maintained the same level of exposure by selling additional shares short. My original prediction was fulfilled and most REITs went broke. The result was that I reaped more than 100% profit on my short positions—a seeming impossibility since the maximum profit on a short position is 100%. (The explanation is that I kept on selling additional shares.)

Self-reinforcing/self-defeating cycles like the conglomerate boom and the REITs do not occur every day. There are long fallow periods when the specialist in such cycles remains unemployed. He need not starve, however. The divergence between underlying trends and investor recognition persists at all times and the astute investor can take advantage of it. New industries arise, or old ones come back into favor. Typically, they are inadequately followed at first. For instance, when defense spending started to rise in the early 1970s after a long decline, there were only two or three analysts left who followed the industry, although it still represented a substantial portion of the economy. Those who were left were too demoralized to recognize the beginning of a major new trend. That was a wonderful time to invest in defense stocks. There were high-tech defense stocks that had never been visited by an analyst, like E-Systems, Inc., and well-established companies that had fallen on evil days trying to diversify out of defense, like Sanders Associates, or getting caught up in scandals trying to sell airplanes through bribery, like Northrop and Lockheed.

In the case of defense stocks, there was no self-reinforcing process involved but investor recognition certainly helped the price of the stocks. Actually, it is a rare case where the investors' bias leaves the fundamentals totally unaffected. Even with defense stocks the prevailing bias played a role, but it was a negative one. Lockheed had to be bailed out by the government and companies like Sanders Associates had to restructure their debt by offering convertible bonds at prices that turned out to be very low in retrospect. Only when the negative bias was corrected was there very little further feedback: companies had little need for additional capital, and managements, having been burned once before, were leery of diversifying out of defense. There were exceptions, like United Aircraft, but investors' bias never turned positive enough to allow a self-reinforcing process to get under way: many of United Aircraft's acquisitions were for cash and those that involved stock did not enhance earnings significantly. The result was a larger, diversified company, but no boom and bust in the stock.

Perhaps the most interesting case of negative bias occurred in technology stocks. After the stock market debacle of 1974, investors were leery of any company that needed to raise equity capital from outside sources. Distributed data processing was in the early stages of its development. New companies like Datapoint and Four-Phase were in the vanguard with IBM lagging badly. The market was practically exploding but these little companies were hamstrung by their inability to raise capital. The stocks were selling at very low multiples of anticipated earnings and the main argument against them was that they would not be able to grow fast enough to meet the demand and eventually IBM would move into the market. The argument turned out to be valid, but not before these companies became large and prosperous and investors became eager to throw money at them at high multiples. Those who had been willing to fight the negative bias were amply rewarded.

As the various niches occupied by these small companies converged to form a large market, most of them were absorbed by larger companies and those that stayed independent fell on evil days. Datapoint is currently looking for a home at a much reduced multiple. Four-Phase was recently acquired by Motorola, which proceeded to lose its shirt on it. If the initial market reaction to distributed data-processing companies had been more positive, it is possible that some of the early starters might have grown fast enough to survive, just as the earlier wave of microcomputer manufacturers did spawn a few enduring companies like Digital Equipment and Data General.

The negative bias of the 1975–1976 period gave way to the opposite extreme. It found expression in a venture capital boom that culminated in the second quarter of 1983. The sequence of events is not as clear cut as in the case of REITs, but that is only because high technology is not as homogeneous an industry. The same reflexive interaction between stock prices, prevailing bias, and fundamentals can be observed but much more specific knowledge is required to trace the course of events.

The availability of venture capital on attractive terms led to a proliferation of new ventures. Every new company needed equipment, as well as inventory, so that electronic equipment manufacturers enjoyed a boom, and so did the manufacturers of products and components. The electronics industry is a large customer of its own products so that the boom was self-reinforcing. But the proliferation of companies intensified competition. Industry leaders lost their market position as a new generation of products was introduced because the individuals who were responsible for developing them left their companies and set up new ones. Instead of companies growing in step with their industry, the industry grew by the multiplication of companies. Investors failed to recognize this trend; as a result, technology stocks in general and new issues in particular became substantially overvalued.

The new issue boom culminated in the second quarter of 1983. When prices started to decline, fewer issues could be sold and eventually venture capitalists became less venturesome. As fewer companies were formed and the existing ones depleted their cash, the market for technology products softened. Competition intensified and profit margins deteriorated. The process started to feed on itself and the low point has probably still not been reached.★

The venture capital boom was not the only cause of the subsequent shakeout—the strong dollar and the rise of Japanese competition were at least as important—but it is clear that stock prices had an impact on the "fundamentals" in both directions.

What distinguishes the conglomerate and REIT sequences from the venture capital boom is that in the first two cases the underlying trend itself was based on the exploitation of the investors' bias while in the third it was not. In the case of conglomerates the idea was to acquire other companies with inflated paper; in the case of REITs the idea was equity leveraging. The idea behind the latest generation of technology products had nothing to do with the stock market.

To understand the ups and downs of technology stocks we must know something about the underlying trends in technology; in the case

★P.S., February 1987: No longer true after the current explosive rally.

of conglomerates and REITs we need to know little else than the theory of reflexivity.

It is important to realize, however, that knowing everything about underlying trends in technology is not sufficient to explain the ups and downs of technology stocks: the reflexive interaction between underlying trends, prevailing biases, and stock prices also needs to be understood. Combining the two kinds of understanding is extremely difficult. Those who want to be familiar with technology must follow the industry closely and continuously; those who want to exploit the divergence between perception and reality must move from group to group. Most technology experts are ignorant of reflexivity and tend to remain fully invested at all times. Their popularity and influence wax and wane in a reflexive fashion. After the recent decline in technology stocks, a new breed of analysts seems to be emerging who are overly sensitive to the importance of investors' perceptions. After a decent interval it may be once again profitable to go against the prevailing bias and invest in technology stocks on the basis of fundamental trends.

I have always had a lot of difficulty investing in technology stocks because of the specialized knowledge required. Finally, I managed to gain a good insight into the computer industry during the 1975–1976 period and profited from the prevailing negative bias. I held on to my positions for a few years but then I sold them and lost my grip on the industry. In 1981 I made the mistake of not participating in a venture capital fund operated by one of the most successful venture capitalists of the period in the belief that the boom could not last long enough to allow investors to exit in time. In this, I was undoubtedly influenced by misgivings about the larger picture. In any event, his investors realized a good profit in 1983. By that time I was totally out of touch with technology stocks and the boom passed me by.

Even the conglomerate and REIT sequences were not totally self-contained. Extraneous developments, such as the level of economic activity, regulation, or specific events (e.g., the attempted takeover of Chemical Bank), played a crucial role in the conglomerate boom. In less "pure" sequences the importance of outside influences is even greater.

We are currently in the midst of another self-reinforcing/self-defeating cycle that will go down in history as the mergermania of the 1980s. Instead of inflated paper, it is cash that serves as the currency. The scale of transactions already dwarfs the conglomerate boom. Merger-mania is but an element in a much larger ongoing historical drama whose ramifications reach far beyond the stock market and involve politics, exchange rates, monetary and fiscal policies, quirks of taxation, international capital movements, and many other developments.

I shall make an attempt at unraveling the ongoing historical drama, but that is not as simple as analyzing a more or less self-contained boom/bust sequence. The larger picture is full of reflexive interactions as well as nonreflexive fundamental trends. We need a more complex model that allows for the transition from one boom/bust sequence to another and for the coexistence of several reflexive processes at the same time.

Before I embark on such an ambitious project, I want to examine another market that is characterized by vicious and benign circles: the currency market.

2

Reflexivity in
the Currency Market*

While reflexive interactions are intermittent in the stock market, they are continuous in the market for currencies. I shall try to show that freely floating exchange rates are inherently unstable; moreover, the instability is cumulative so that the eventual breakdown of a freely floating exchange rate system is virtually assured.

The traditional view of the currency market is that it tends toward equilibrium. An overvalued exchange rate encourages imports and discourages exports until equilibrium is reestablished. Similarly, an improvement in competitive position is reflected in an appreciating exchange rate that reduces the trade surplus so that equilibrium is again reestablished. Speculation cannot disrupt the trend toward equilibrium—if speculators anticipate the future correctly, they accelerate the trend; if they misjudge it, they will be penalized by the underlying trend that may be delayed but will inexorably assert itself.

Experience since floating exchange rates were introduced in 1973 has disproved this view. Instead of fundamentals determining exchange rates, exchange rates have found a way of influencing the fundamentals. For instance, a strong exchange rate discourages inflation: wages remain stable and the price of imports falls. When exports have a large import component, a country can remain competitive almost indefinitely in

*This chapter was written in April/May 1985 and revised in December 1986.

spite of a steady appreciation of its currency, as Germany demonstrated in the 1970s.

The fact is that the relationship between the domestic inflation rate and the international exchange rate is not unidirectional but circular. Changes in one may precede changes in the other, but it does not make sense to describe one as the cause and the other as the effect because they mutually reinforce each other. It is more appropriate to speak of a vicious circle in which the currency depreciates and inflation accelerates or of a benign circle where the opposite happens.

Vicious and benign circles are a far cry from equilibrium. Nevertheless, they could produce a state of affairs akin to equilibrium if the reflexive, mutually self-reinforcing relationship could be sustained indefinitely. But that is not the case. The self-reinforcing process tends to become more vulnerable the longer it lasts and eventually it is bound to reverse itself, setting in motion a self-reinforcing process in the opposite direction. A complete cycle is characterized by wide fluctuations not only in the exchange rate but also in interest rates, inflation, and/or the level of economic activity.

The participants' bias introduces an element of instability into the system. If the system had an innate tendency toward equilibrium the participants' bias could not disrupt it; at worst, it could introduce some random, short-term fluctuations. But when the causal connections are reflexive, the participants' bias may engender, sustain, or destroy a vicious or benign circle. Moreover, the prevailing bias takes on a life of its own as one of the constituent parts in a circular relationship. It finds expression in speculative capital movements that may serve as a counterweight to an imbalance in trade, allowing a trade surplus or deficit to exceed, both in size and in duration, the level that could have been sustained in its absence. When that happens speculation becomes a destabilizing influence.

International capital movements tend to follow a self-reinforcing/self-defeating pattern similar to the one we identified in the stock market. But the model we used for stock price movements cannot be applied to currency markets without substantial modifications. In the stock market we focused on the reflexive relationship between two variables: stock prices and a single underlying trend. We were trying to build the simplest possible model and we were willing to simplify a much more complex reality to serve our purpose. In the currency market we cannot get by with two variables; even the simplest model will need seven or eight. We have selected four rates and four quantities, namely:

e nominal exchange rate (number of foreign currency units for one domestic currency unit; $\uparrow e$ = strengthening)

i nominal interest rate

p domestic versus foreign price level ($\uparrow p$ = increase in domestic prices faster than in foreign prices and vice versa)

v level of economic activity

N nonspeculative capital flow $\left.\right\}$ $\uparrow$ = increased outflow

S speculative capital flow $\downarrow$ = increased inflow

T trade balance $\left.\right\}$ $\uparrow$ = surplus

B government budget $\downarrow$ = deficit

Our task is to establish how these variables relate to each other. We shall not attempt to explore all the relationships but only those that are necessary to build simple models. In other words, we are not aiming at a general theory, only at a partial explanation of currency movements. Our focus is the exchange rate and we bring in the other variables only when we need them. We shall not quantify any of the variables but only indicate direction ($\uparrow$, $\downarrow$) or order of magnitude ($>$, $<$).

Before we start, two general observations can be made. One is that relationships tend to be circular; that is, variables can serve as both cause and effect in relation to other variables. We shall denote the causal connection by a horizontal arrow ($\rightarrow$). The other point is that the relationship of the variables need not be internally consistent; it is the inconsistencies that make that entire situation move in a certain direction, creating vicious or benign circles. Equilibrium would require internal consistency; historical change does not. Describing historical change in terms of vicious and benign circles is, of course, merely a figure of speech. A circular movement between component parts when the entire system is in motion could also be described as a spiral. Moreover, what is benign and what is vicious are in the eye of the beholder.

Exchange rates are determined by the demand and supply of currencies. For present purposes, we can group the various factors that constitute demand and supply under three headings: trade, nonspeculative capital transactions, and speculative capital transactions. This gives us the simplest model of a freely floating exchange rate system:

$$(\downarrow T + \uparrow N + \uparrow S) \rightarrow \downarrow e$$

In other words, the sum of the currency transactions under the three headings determines the direction of the exchange rate.

Our primary interest is in investigating the role that the participants' bias plays in exchange rate movements. To facilitate the investigation, we shall assume that the bias finds expression only in speculative capital transactions (S), while trade (T) and non-speculative capital flows (N) are independent of expectations: they constitute the "fundamentals." In reality, the "fundamentals" are also influenced by the participants' expectations about the future course of exchange rates. Trade figures are notoriously distorted by leads and lags in payment, not to mention the effect of expectations on the inventory policy of exporters and importers. As far as capital movements are concerned, perhaps the only transaction that is totally independent of expectations is the payment of interest on accumulated debt; the reinvestment of interest receipts already qualifies as a speculative transaction. The repatriation of bank debt from less developed countries is probably best described as nonspeculative, although speculative considerations come into play if and when the assets are redeployed. What about direct investment? If managements were interested only in the total rate of return, it ought to be classified as speculative, but often there are overriding industrial considerations. It can be seen that there are many gradations between speculative and nonspeculative transactions; but we do not do any great violence to reality by putting them into these two broad categories.

We shall focus on speculative capital transactions because that is where the participants' bias finds expression. Speculative capital moves in search of the highest total return. Total return has three elements: the interest rate differential, the exchange rate differential, and the capital appreciation in local currency. Since the third element varies from case to case we can propose the following general rule: speculative capital is attracted by rising exchange rates and rising interest rates.

$$\uparrow (e + i) \rightarrow \downarrow S$$

Of the two, exchange rates are by far the more important. It does not take much of a decline in the currency to render the total return negative. By the same token, when an appreciating currency also offers an interest rate advantage, the total return exceeds anything that a holder of financial assets could expect in the normal course of events.

That is not to say that interest rate differentials are unimportant; but much of their importance lies in their effect on exchange rates and that depends on the participants' perceptions. There are times when relative interest rates seem to be a major influence; at other times they are totally disregarded. For instance, from 1982 to 1986 capital was attracted to the currency with the highest interest rate, namely, the dollar, but in the late 1970s Switzerland could not arrest the influx of capital even by imposing negative interest rates. Moreover, perceptions about the importance of interest rates are often wrong. For instance, until November 1984 the strength of the dollar was widely attributed to high interest rates in the United States. When interest rates declined without the dollar weakening this view was discredited and the dollar went through the roof.

Expectations about exchange rates play the same role in currency markets as expectations about stock prices do in the stock market: they constitute the paramount consideration for those who are motivated by the total rate of return. In the stock market that covers practically all investors, in currency markets all speculative transactions.

In the stock market we used a model that focused on stock prices and disregarded dividend income. No great distortion was involved because in the kind of boom/bust sequences we were considering stock price movements far outweigh dividend income. Similar conditions prevail in currency markets: expectations about future exchange rates constitute the main motivation in speculative capital transactions.

The major difference between the stock market and the currency market seems to be the role played by the fundamentals. We have seen that the "fundamentals" were rather nebulous even in the case of stocks but at least we had no reason to doubt that stock prices were somehow connected to the fundamentals. In the case of currencies the trade balance is clearly the most important fundamental factor, yet the dollar strengthened between 1982 and 1985 while the trade balance of the United States was deteriorating. It would seem that the fundamentals are even less relevant in determining price trends than in the stock market. We do not need to look far afield for an explanation: it is to be found in the relative importance of speculative capital movements.

As we have seen, speculative capital is motivated primarily by expectations about future exchange rates. To the extent that exchange rates are dominated by speculative capital transfers, they are purely reflexive: expectations relate to expectations and the prevailing bias can validate itself almost indefinitely. The situation is highly unstable: if the opposite bias prevailed, it could also validate itself. The greater the relative importance of speculation, the more unstable the system becomes: the total rate of return can flip-flop with every change in the prevailing bias.

In our discussion of the stock market we identified certain sequences such as the conglomerate boom where the prevailing bias formed an important part of the underlying trend, but we concluded that such pure examples of reflexivity are exceptional. By contrast, in a system of freely fluctuating exchange rates reflexivity constitutes the rule. Of course, there is no such thing as a purely reflexive situation. Speculation is only one of the factors that determine exchange rates and the other factors must also be taken into account in formulating one's expectations. Thus, expectations cannot be totally capricious: they must be rooted in something other than themselves. How a prevailing bias becomes established and, even more important, how it is reversed are the most important questions confronting us.

There are no universally valid answers. Reflexive processes tend to follow a certain pattern. In the early stages, the trend has to be self-reinforcing, otherwise the process aborts. As the trend extends, it becomes increasingly vulnerable because the fundamentals such as trade and interest payments move against the trend, in accordance with the precepts of classical analysis, and the trend becomes increasingly dependent on the prevailing bias. Eventually a turning point is reached and, in a full-fledged sequence, a self-reinforcing process starts operating in the opposite direction.

Within this general pattern each sequence is unique. It is the characteristic feature of a reflexive process that neither the participants' perceptions nor the situation to which they relate remain unaffected by it. It follows that no sequence can repeat itself. Not even the variables that interact in a circular fashion need be the same; certainly they will not carry the same weight on different occasions.

We have had two major reflexive moves in the dollar since the breakdown of the Bretton Woods system and at least that many in sterling. It is instructive to compare the two big moves in the dollar because the interaction between the trade balance and capital movements was radically different in the two instances.

In the late 1970s the dollar got progressively weaker, especially against the continental currencies, while in the 1980s it got progressively stronger. We shall call the first move Carter's vicious circle and the second Reagan's benign circle. We can build simple models to show how different the two trends were.

In the case of Germany in the late 1970s, the German mark was strong ($\uparrow e$). Speculative purchases played a major role in making it stronger ($\downarrow S$) and sustaining the benign circle. Germany started with a trade surplus and the strength of the currency helped to keep the price level down. Since exports had a large import content the real exchange rate, as opposed to the nominal, remained more or less stable ($\updownarrow ep$) and the effect on the trade balance was negligible ($\updownarrow T$). With the speculative inflow predominating ($\downarrow S > \updownarrow T$), the benign circle was self-reinforcing:

$$\uparrow e \to \downarrow p \to \updownarrow (ep) \to (\updownarrow T < \downarrow S) \to \uparrow e$$

The fact that the rate of currency appreciation exceeded the interest rate differential made it very profitable to hold German marks, so that the speculative inflow was both self-reinforcing and self-validating.

What was a benign circle for Germany was a vicious circle for the United States. As the exchange rate depreciated, inflation accelerated. Despite rising nominal interest rates, real rates remained very low, if not negative. Various measures were tried to compensate for the outflow of capital, of which the issue of so-called Carter bonds denominated in German marks and Swiss francs was the most dramatic, but nothing seemed to work until the Federal Reserve embraced a strict monetarist policy. Then came the election of Ronald Reagan to the presidency and the dollar embarked on a sustained rise.

During Reagan's benign circle the strong dollar caused a sharp deterioration in the trade balance of the United States. In contrast to Germany in the late 1970s, the United States did not have a trade surplus to start with. Moreover, the appreciation in the currency was not matched by inflation rate differentials. The inflation rate declined in the United States but it remained low in other countries as well. As a consequence, the United States developed an unprecedented trade deficit as well as an unprecedented interest rate differential in favor of the dollar. It was extremely attractive to hold dollars as long as the dollar remained firm, and the dollar remained firm as long as the deficit on current account was fully matched by a surplus on capital account. In our notation:

$$(\uparrow e + \uparrow i) \rightarrow (\downarrow S > \downarrow T) \rightarrow \uparrow e \rightarrow (\downarrow S > \downarrow T)$$

The models are obviously oversimplified. We shall explore Reagan's benign circle in greater depth later. The point we are trying to make here is that different sequences have totally different structures. In the case of Germany in the late 1970s the appreciation of the currency was sustained by the inflation rate differential and the balance of trade was largely unaffected. Reagan's benign circle was sustained by a differential in interest rates rather than inflation rates and there was an ever-growing trade deficit which was matched by an ever-growing inflow of capital. While in the first case it was possible to claim some kind of equilibrium, in the second case the disequilibrium was palpable. The inflow of capital depended on a strong dollar and a strong dollar depended on an ever-rising inflow of capital which carried with it ever-rising interest and repayment obligations ($\downarrow N$). It was obvious that the benign circle could not be sustained indefinitely. Yet, while it lasted, any currency speculator who dared to fight the trend had to pay dearly for it. Speculation did not serve to reestablish equilibrium. On the contrary, it reinforced the trend and thereby increased the disequilibrium, which would eventually have to be corrected.

Although each self-reinforcing circle is unique, we can make some universally valid generalizations about freely fluctuating exchange rates. First, the relative importance of speculative transactions tends to increase during the lifetime of a self-reinforcing trend. Second, the prevailing bias is a trend-following one and the longer the trend persists, the stronger the bias becomes. The third is simply that once a trend is established it tends to persist and to run its full course; when the turn finally comes, it tends to set into motion a self-reinforcing process in the opposite direction. In other words, currencies tend to move in large waves, with each move lasting several years.

These three tendencies are mutually self-validating. It is the growth in speculative capital flows moving in a trend-following fashion that makes the trend so persistent; it is the persistence of the trend that makes a trend-following bias so rewarding; and it is the rewards reaped by speculation that attract increasing amounts of capital.

The longer a benign circle lasts, the more attractive it is to hold financial assets in the appreciating currency and the more important the exchange rate becomes in calculating total return. Those who are inclined to fight the trend are progressively eliminated and in the end only trend followers survive as active participants. As speculation gains in importance, other factors lose their influence. There is nothing to guide speculators but the market itself, and the market is dominated by trend followers. These considerations explain how the dollar could continue to appreciate in the face of an ever-rising trade deficit. Eventually, a crossover point would have been reached, even without the intervention of the authorities, when the inflow of speculative funds could not keep pace with the trade deficit and with rising interest obligations, and the trend would have been reversed. Since the predominating bias is trend following, speculative capital would then have started moving in the opposite direction. If and when that happened, the reversal could easily have accelerated into a free fall. For one thing, speculation and "fundamental" flows would then have worked in the same direction. Even more important, when a change in trend is recognized, the volume of speculative transactions is likely to undergo a dramatic, not to say catastrophic, increase. While a trend persists, speculative flows are incremental; but a reversal involves not only the current flow but also the accumulated stock of speculative capital. The longer the trend has persisted, the larger the accumulation. There are, of course, mitigating circumstances. One is that market participants are likely to recognize a change in trend only gradually. The other is that the authorities are bound to be aware of the danger and do something to prevent a crash. How the drama actually unfolded will be the subject of a later chapter. Here we are trying to establish a general proposition.

Taking the three generalizations together, it can be asserted that speculation is progressively destabilizing. The destabilizing effect arises not because the speculative capital flows must be eventually reversed but exactly because they need not be reversed until much later. If they had to be reversed in short order, capital transactions would provide a welcome cushion for making the adjustment process less painful. If they need not be reversed, the participants get to depend on them so that eventually when the turn comes the adjustment becomes that much more painful.

It is quite likely that the generalization about the progressive accumulation of hot money holds true not only within a cycle but also from one cycle to another, although the history of fluctuating exchange rates is too short to provide reliable evidence. It has certainly been true so far—the size of speculative capital movements was far greater in Reagan's benign circle than it was during Carter's vicious circle. Empirical studies of the 1930s also showed a cumulative growth in "hot money" movements,[1] although circumstances were somewhat different because currencies were not freely floating.

We can see why hot money should continue to accumulate as long as real interest rates are high and the return on physical investments low: keeping capital in liquid form in an appreciating currency is more rewarding than investing it in physical assets. What is needed to give the generalization universal validity is an argument that would show that fluctuating exchange rates are associated with high returns on financial assets and low returns on physical investments. Let me try. We have seen that hot money can earn exceptional returns if it gets the trend right; since it sets the trend, that is likely to be the case. Physical assets represent the opposite side of the coin: they cannot move to take advantage of the trend. The tradable goods sector is bound to suffer when a currency appreciates. Of course, a depreciating currency brings windfall profits to exporters, but having been hurt before, exporters are loath to invest on the basis of a temporary advantage: they prefer to hold their profits in financial assets, contributing to the growth of hot money. The process can be most clearly observed in the United Kingdom, where exporters refused to expand when sterling fell below $1.10 in 1985, despite record profits. How right they were! Sterling rose above $1.50 by April 1986. Thus, both an appreciating currency and a depreciating currency discourage physical investment and foster the accumulation of "hot money."

We can attempt yet another tentative generalization. When a

long-term trend loses its momentum, short-term volatility tends to rise. It is easy to see why that should be so: the trend-following crowd is disoriented. The generalization is tentative because it is based on inadequate evidence. It certainly was true when the dollar reversed its trend in 1985.[2]

If these generalizations are indeed valid, the eventual demise of a system of freely fluctuating exchange rates is inevitable. Fluctuations become so wild that either the system has to be modified by some kind of government intervention or it is bound to break down. Currency markets thus provide the best support for my contention that financial markets are inherently unstable. There is no built-in tendency toward equilibrium: to the extent that we need stability we must introduce it by deliberate policy measures.

These conclusions may not strike the reader as particularly revolutionary at the present time, but they certainly contradicted the prevailing wisdom at the time they were written in April/May 1985. There was widespread malaise about the instability of exchange rates, but belief in the magic of the market was still running strong, and the famous Plaza agreement in September 1985 came as something of a shock to market participants. Even today, there is no theoretical underpinning for the contention that a freely floating exchange rate system is cumulatively destabilizing. That is what I hope to have provided here.

I have been speculating in currencies ever since they started floating, but I have failed to make money on a consistent basis. On balance, I traded profitably through 1980 and then chalked up losses between 1981 and 1985. My approach has been tentative, based more on intuition than on conviction. By temperament, I have always been more interested in picking the turning point than in following a trend. I managed to catch both the rise and fall of European currencies against the dollar until 1981, but I traded myself out of my positions too soon. Having lost the trend, I found it too demeaning to start following the trend-followers; I tried to pick the reversal point instead—needless to say, without success. I had some temporary profits in the early part of 1984, but I gave them all back. I was again engaged in a speculation against the dollar at the time I wrote this chapter (April/May 1985). Writing it has undoubtedly helped to clarify my thoughts.

The real-time experiment recorded in Part III may be regarded as a practical test of the theory propounded here. Admittedly the theory is far too abstract to be of much use in making concrete predictions. Specifically, the turning point cannot be determined until it has actually occurred. But, as we shall see, the theory can be very useful in interpreting events as they unfold.

3

The Credit and Regulatory Cycle*

There seems to be a special affinity between reflexivity and credit. That is hardly surprising: credit depends on expectations; expectations involve bias; hence credit is one of the main avenues that permit bias to play a causal role in the course of events. But there is more to it. Credit seems to be associated with a particular kind of reflexive pattern that is known as boom and bust. The pattern is asymmetrical: the boom is drawn out and accelerates gradually; the bust is sudden and often catastrophic. By contrast, when credit is not an essential ingredient in a reflexive process, the pattern tends to be more symmetrical. For instance, in the currency market it does not seem to make much difference whether the dollar is rising or falling: the exchange rate seems to follow a wavelike pattern.

I believe the asymmetry arises out of a reflexive connection between loan and collateral. In this context I give collateral a very broad definition: it will denote whatever determines the creditworthiness of a debtor, whether it is actually pledged or not. It may mean a piece of property or an expected future stream of income; in either case, it is something on which the lender is willing to place a value. Valuation is supposed to be a passive relationship in which the value reflects the underlying asset; but in this case it involves a positive act: a loan is made.

*Written in August 1985.

8 5

The act of lending may affect the collateral value: that is the connection that gives rise to a reflexive process.

It will be recalled that we have analyzed reflexivity as two connections working in opposite directions: the "normal" connection where a value is placed on future events, as in the stock market or banking—we have called it the cognitive function; and a "perverse" connection in which expectations affect that which is expected—we have called it the participating function. The participating function is perverse because its effect is not always felt, and when it does operate its influence is so difficult to disentangle that it tends to go unrecognized. The prevailing view of how financial markets operate tends to leave the participating function out of account. For instance, in the international lending boom, bankers did not recognize that the debt ratios of borrowing countries were favorably influenced by their own lending activity. In the conglomerate boom, investors did not realize that per-share earnings growth can be affected by the valuation they place on it. At present, most people do not realize that the erosion of collateral values can depress the economy.

The act of lending usually stimulates economic activity. It enables the borrower to consume more than he would otherwise, or to invest in productive assets. There are exceptions, to be sure: if the assets in question are not physical but financial ones, the effect is not necessarily stimulative. By the same token, debt service has a depressing impact. Resources that would otherwise be devoted to consumption or the creation of a future stream of income are withdrawn. As the total amount of debt outstanding accumulates, the portion that has to be utilized for debt service increases. It is only net new lending that stimulates, and total new lending has to keep rising in order to keep net new lending stable.

The connection between lending and economic activity is far from straightforward (that is, in fact, the best justification for the monetarists' preoccupation with money supply, to the neglect of credit). The major difficulty is that credit need not be involved in the physical production or consumption of goods and services; it may be used for purely financial purposes. In this case, its influence on economic activity becomes problematic. For purposes of this discussion it may be helpful to distinguish between a "real" economy and a "financial" economy. Economic activity takes place in the "real" economy, while the extension and repayment of credit occur in the "financial" economy. The reflexive interaction between the act of lending and the value of the collateral may then connect the "real" and the "financial" economy or it may be confined to the "financial" economy. Here we shall focus on the first case.

A strong economy tends to enhance the asset values and income streams that serve to determine creditworthiness. In the early stages of a reflexive process of credit expansion the amount of credit involved is relatively small so that its impact on collateral values is negligible. That is why the expansionary phase is slow to start with and credit remains soundly based at first. But as the amount of debt accumulates, total lending increases in importance and begins to have an appreciable effect on collateral values. The process continues until a point is reached where total credit cannot increase fast enough to continue stimulating the economy. By that time, collateral values have become greatly dependent on the stimulative effect of new lending and, as new lending fails to accelerate, collateral values begin to decline. The erosion of collateral values has a depressing effect on economic activity, which in turn reinforces the erosion of collateral values. Since the collateral has been pretty fully utilized at that point, a decline may precipitate the liquidation of loans, which in turn may make the decline more precipitous. That is the anatomy of a typical boom and bust.

Booms and busts are not symmetrical because, at the inception of a boom, both the volume of credit and the value of the collateral are at a minimum; at the time of the bust, both are at a maximum. But there is another factor at play. The liquidation of loans takes time; the faster it has to be accomplished, the greater the effect on the value of the collateral. In a bust, the reflexive interaction between loans and collateral becomes compressed within a very short time frame and the consequences can be catastrophic. It is the sudden liquidation of accumulated positions that gives a bust such a different shape from the preceding boom.

It can be seen that the boom/bust sequence is a particular variant of reflexivity. Booms can arise whenever there is a two-way connection between values and the act of valuation. The act of valuation takes many forms. In the stock market, it is equity that is valued; in banking, it is collateral. It is possible, although unlikely, that a boom could be generated without any credit expansion. The two examples we studied in the stock market, the REIT and conglomerate booms, could, in theory, have unfolded without the stocks being used as collateral, although in practice there was a lot of credit involved. In the absence of credit the reversal would be a more gradual process. The contraction would not be a mirror image of the expansion for the reason mentioned earlier—the reflexive element in valuations is greater at the time of reversal than at the inception of a trend—but the compression that is characteristic of busts would be absent.

Both the boom/bust pattern and its explanation are almost too obvious to be interesting. The amazing thing is that the reflexive connection between lending and collateral has not been generally recognized. There is an enormous literature on the trade cycle, but I have not seen much awareness of the reflexive relationship described here. Moreover, the trade cycles that are generally discussed in textbooks differ in duration from the credit cycle I am discussing here: they are short-term fluctuations within a larger pattern. There is an awareness of a larger cycle, usually referred to as the Kondratieff wave, but it has never been "scientifically" explained. At present, there is much concern that we may be approaching another recession but the general assumption is that we are dealing with a recession just like any other; the fact that we are in the declining phase of the larger cycle is usually left out of account. I contend that all previous recessions since the end of World War II occurred while credit was expanding, while the one we may or may not be facing now would occur when borrowing capacity in the real economy is contracting. This creates a situation that has no precedent in recent history.

Exactly where we are in the larger cycle is difficult to determine. I must confess I have been confused on the issue since 1982. The reason for my confusion is that while the boom has clearly run out of steam, the bust has not taken place.

Busts can be very disruptive, especially if the liquidation of collateral causes a sudden compression of credit. The consequences are so unpleasant that strenuous efforts are made to avoid them. The institution of central banking has evolved in a continuing attempt to prevent sudden, catastrophic contractions in credit. Since a panic is hard to arrest once it has started, prevention is best practiced in the expansionary phase. That is why the role of central banks has gradually expanded to include the regulation of the money supply. That is also why organized financial markets regulate the ratio of collateral to credit.

Until now, the authorities have been able to prevent a bust. We find ourselves in a twilight zone where the "normal" process of credit expansion culminated long ago but the "normal" process of credit contraction has been prevented by the authorities. We are in uncharted territory because the actions of the authorities have no precedent.

The fact that banks and organized financial markets are regulated complicates the course of events tremendously. Financial history is best interpreted as a reflexive process in which there are two sets of participants instead of one: competitors and regulators.

Such a system is much more complex than the case we studied in the stock market. There, the regulatory environment was more or less fixed: it was the backdrop against which the drama was acted out. Here, the regulatory environment is an integral part of the process.

It is important to realize that the regulators are also participants. There is a natural tendency to regard them as superhuman beings who somehow stand outside and above the economic process and intervene only when the participants have made a mess of it. That is not the case. They also are human, all too human. They operate with imperfect understanding and their activities have unintended consequences. Indeed, they seem to adjust to changing circumstances less well than those who are motivated by profit and loss, so that regulations are generally designed to prevent the last mishap, not the next one. The deficiencies of regulation tend to be more noticeable when conditions are rapidly changing, and conditions tend to change more rapidly when the economy is less regulated.

We begin to discern a reflexive relationship between the regulators and the economy they regulate. It gives rise to a process that takes place concurrently with the process of credit expansion and contraction and interacts with it. It is no wonder that the result is so complex and perplexing!

The regulatory cycle does not have the asymmetric character of the credit cycle. It seems to fit the wave pattern we developed for the currency market better than the boom and bust pattern of the credit cycle. Just as freely floating currencies tend to fluctuate between over- and undervaluation, so market economies tend to fluctuate between over- and underregulation. The length of the cycle seems to be correlated with the credit cycle and one can sense intuitively why that should be so. Credit expansion and contraction have much to do with changes in the economy, which in turn have a bearing on the adequacy of regulations. Conversely, the regulatory environment influences not only how fast credit can expand but also how far. Clearly, there is a two-way connection between credit and regulation, but it is far from clear to me at this stage of the investigation what pattern, if any, the interaction follows. That is the main source of my confusion.

We have identified a credit cycle that follows a boom/bust pattern: a regulatory cycle that is more wavelike, and an interplay between the two whose pattern is unclear. There are, of course, many secular developments involved as well, some of which relate to credit, some to regulation, and some to both. We have mentioned that central banks tend to get stronger after each crisis; that is a secular development that renders each cycle unique. In the Great Depression both the banking system and the international trading system collapsed, making the contraction of credit and economic activity much more severe than it would have been otherwise. We can be certain that every effort will be made to avoid a similar collapse in this cycle. We did not dwell on the information revolution or on the improvements in transportation that have helped the development of an integrated world economy. The outcome of all these influences is a unique course of events that is easier to explain than to predict.

Looked at from this perspective, the entire postwar period is part of a large expansionary boom that is now well advanced and ripe for a bust. The bust has been avoided, however, by the intervention of the authorities at crucial moments. The interplay between government actions and the market mechanism has given rise to a unique constellation that I have called Reagan's Imperial Circle. We are now at the crucial moment where the Imperial Circle is beginning to unwind and the authorities must invent another solution to forestall a bust.

The same postwar period has also seen an almost complete swing from government regulation to unrestrained competition. We are now at a curious moment where the bias in favor of deregulation is still on the rise yet the need for government intervention in specific areas is beginning to reassert itself. The banking industry, for one, is already on the way to becoming more regulated.

One could try and write a history of the postwar era in these terms. The present credit cycle started after the end of World War II; the origins of the regulatory cycle go back even farther to the New Deal, although the creation of the Bretton Woods system can be taken as the starting point as far as the world economy is concerned. The expansion that followed was intimately related to the removal of restrictions on international trade and investment. But international capital movements created problems for the Bretton Woods system that were never anticipated and remain unresolved.

I shall not attempt to present the complete story here. I shall start at the point where I became actively involved and I shall follow the path of my own involvement. This will give the investigation a more experimental character.

My experiences began after the breakdown of the system of fixed exchange rates in 1973. Relationships that had been fixed became subject to reflexive influences and my interest veered from specific companies and industries to macroeconomic processes. My study of "growth banks" in 1972 constituted a transition point, although I did not know it at the time.

With the passage of time I found the instability of macroeconomic trends increasingly disturbing in both a subjective and an objective sense and I decided to distance myself from active investing in 1981. After the crisis of 1982 I made a theoretical study of the international debt problem. I was under the mistaken impression that the crisis of 1982 constituted the climax in the process of credit expansion. I thought that the authorities were not doing enough to prevent a bust; I failed to realize that they were doing too much. They actually kept credit expanding, albeit on a more unsound basis than ever. The United States replaced less developed countries as the "borrower of last resort" and commercial banks tried to grow their way out of the loans made to less developed countries by aggressively expanding in other directions. This led to another series of crises in 1984 that constituted the real turning point for the banking and thrift industries. We are now suffering from the aftereffects of that climax. The United States government continues to borrow on an ever-increasing scale, but here, too, a turning point is at hand. The dollar has begun to decline and foreigners are going to be repaid in a depreciating currency. Perhaps the last great engine of credit creation that is still going full blast is in the stock market where mergermania is at its peak; but it does not have a stimulating effect on the real economy.

The theoretical framework of an interrelated credit and regulatory cycle became somewhat clearer to me in the course of writing this book, although I cannot claim that the process of clarification is complete. Nevertheless, I felt it was appropriate to summarize it at this point. I shall now use the theoretical framework outlined here to explain the course of events since 1972. The reader should be advised that the writing of the explanation predates the formulation of this admittedly tentative theoretical framework.

P.S., DECEMBER 1986

Having completed the explanation, I engaged in a real-time experiment from August 1985 to the end of 1986, trying to predict the evolution of the credit and regulatory cycle. I came to a strange conclusion. It appears that the cycle got stuck in 1982. If it had not been for the successful intervention of the monetary authorities, the international debt crisis would have led to a collapse of the banking system. As it is, the collapse has been avoided, but the genuine trend reversal which it would have ushered in also failed to take place. We now live in a system where we continually go to the brink and then recoil when we see the abyss opening up at our feet. The cohesion we manage to muster in the sight of a disaster tends to disintegrate as soon as the danger recedes, and the process then repeats itself in different forms. We can observe it in international lending; in the U.S. budget deficit; in the international monetary system; in OPEC; in the banking system; in financial markets; and 1987 will undoubtedly be the year when protectionism drives the international trade system to the brink of collapse but probably not beyond it.

Part Two

HISTORICAL PERSPECTIVE

4

The International
Debt Problem

The greatest problem in reflexivity analysis is to decide what elements to single out for attention. In dealing with a financial market the problem is relatively simple. The critical variable is the market price and the elements that need to be considered are those that influence market prices. But even here the number of factors that may come into play is almost infinite. Using just one underlying trend and one predominant bias is an oversimplification that may be useful in demonstrating the dynamics, not to say dialectics, of a historical process, but it is totally inadequate to explain, let alone predict, the actual course of events.

When we venture outside the confines of a particular market, the problem of selection is even more complex. We need a set of interacting components that can explain the phenomenon we are dealing with. But there may be different sets that could explain the same phenomenon and we can have no assurance that we have selected the right one. The plethora of potential components is particularly troubling when we try to predict the future course of events: we do not know which one will become significant.

The boom and bust in international lending is a case in point. It is an indispensable element in the current economic situation. Taken by itself, it constitutes an almost perfect example of a boom/bust sequence. Looked at in the context of the overall situation, it is just one of many elements that need to be taken into account. To complicate matters, the international debt problem has played a crucial role in the evolution of the banking system, and the evolution of the banking system is also a reflexive process that is significant in itself as well as being a significant element in the overall situation.

What is, then, the best way to deal with international lending? One has to consider the subject from at least three points of view: as a reflexive phenomenon in its own right; as a factor in the evolution of the banking system; and as part of the current economic situation. I shall try to consider all three at the same time because that is the only way to avoid undue repetition. By choosing this route, I shall also provide a practical demonstration of the complexity of reflexive processes in the real world. It goes without saying that the analysis is not an easy one to follow; but I shall try to keep the three points of view separate as we go along. Some degree of distortion is inevitable: since we are interested in the evolution of the banking system, we shall pay more attention to the lenders than the borrowers. If we wanted to explore the fate of the less developed countries, we would have to shift our focus.

The origins of the international lending boom go back at least as far as the first oil shock in 1973; but to discuss the evolution of the banking system we have to go back even farther, and to understand the economic cycle that has dominated recent history we ought to start with the breakdown of the Bretton Woods system in 1971. That would take us too far back; so I shall take early 1972 as my starting point, and I shall begin by looking at the banking system in the United States. As it happens, that is the date of a stock market report I wrote entitled "The Case for Growth Banks."

Banks at the time were considered the stodgiest of institutions. Managements had been traumatized by the failures of the 1930s and safety was the paramount consideration, overshadowing profit or growth. The structure of the industry was practically frozen by regulation. Expansion across state lines was prohibited and in some states even branch banking was outlawed. A dull business attracted dull people and there was little movement or innovation in the industry. Bank stocks were ignored by investors looking for capital gains.

Underneath the calm surface, changes were brewing. A new breed of bankers was emerging who had been educated in business schools and thought in terms of bottom-line profits. The spiritual center of the new school of thinking was First National City Bank of New York, and people trained there were fanning out and occupying top spots at other banks. New kinds of financial instruments were being introduced, and some banks were beginning to utilize their capital more aggressively and putting together very creditable earnings performances. There were some acquisitions within state limits, leading to the emergence of larger units. The larger banks typically leveraged their equity 14 to 16 times, with the Bank of America running as high as 20 times. The better banks showed a return on equity in excess of 13%. In any other industry, such a return on equity, combined with per-share earnings growth of better than 10%, would have been rewarded by the shares selling at a decent premium over asset value, but bank shares were selling at little or no premium. Analysts of bank shares were aware of this relative under-valuation but they despaired of seeing the situation corrected because the underlying changes were too gradual and the prevailing valuation too stable. Yet, many banks had reached the point where they were pushing against the limits of what was considered prudent leverage by the standards of the time. If they wanted to continue growing they would need to raise additional equity capital.

It was against this background that First National City hosted a dinner for security analysts—an unheard of event in the banking indus-try. I was not invited but it prompted me to publish a report that rec-ommended purchase of a bouquet of the more aggressively managed banks. It documented the situation I have described here and it argued that bank stocks were about to come alive because managements had a good story to tell and they had started telling it. "Growth" and "banks" seemed like a contradiction in terms, I wrote, but the contradiction was about to be resolved by bank shares being awarded growth multiples.

Banks stocks did, in fact, have a good move in 1972 and we made about 50% on our bouquet. Some of the more alert banks managed to raise some capital. If the process of raising capital at a premium over book value had become established, banks could have expanded on a sound basis and the evolution of the banking system would have taken a different course. As it happened, the process had hardly started when inflation accelerated, interest rates rose, and a 13% return on capital was no longer sufficient to enable banks to sell shares at a premium.

Then came the aftermath of the first oil shock and a tremendous increase in the flow of funds to the oil-producing countries. These countries did not know what to do with the money and it piled up in the banks. A point was reached when some banks, like Bankers Trust, felt obliged to turn away deposits. How to recycle these so-called petrodollars became a major problem. There were active discussions about intergovernmental schemes but nothing much came out of them except for some increased Saudi contributions to the IMF and the World Bank. The governments of the industrialized world failed dismally to rise to the occasion and it was by default that the recycling of petrodollars was left to the banks.

The banks stepped into the breach and fulfilled their function all too well. Flush with funds, they became aggressive lenders, and they found plenty of takers. Less developed countries without oil sought to finance their deficits by running up large debts; those with oil embarked on ambitious expansion programs, which they financed by borrowing on the strength of their oil reserves. This was the time of détente, which meant that Eastern European countries borrowed huge amounts from Western banks in the hope of repaying them using the products of the factories they built with borrowed money. That is how the international lending boom began.

At first, the banks were recycling the OPEC surplus. As time passed, the oil-rich countries found other ways of utilizing their new-found wealth: acquiring the most sophisticated armaments, expanding their economy at a breakneck pace, buying diamonds and real estate, and making other long-term investments. Meanwhile, demand for bank financing continued to build. Increasingly, the banks became the source of credit. Each loan created deposits elsewhere so that the banks were able to generate the funds they were lending by their own activity. Since the Eurodollar market was not regulated, banks did not have to maintain minimum reserve requirements against the liabilities of their offshore affiliates. There was nothing to stop those affiliates from creating a seemingly unlimited supply of credit except self-restraint.

But international lending was too profitable to leave much room for caution. Business could be transacted on a large scale, the risk of adverse interest rate movements could be minimized by the use of floating rates, and administrative costs were much lower than in the case of corporate loans. Fierce competition kept spreads between borrowing and lending rates quite narrow; nevertheless, international lending became one of the easiest and most profitable forms of banking activity, attracting many banks with no previous experience in the field. The number of banks represented in London grew greatly during this period, and international lending became the fastest growing sector of the banking industry. Naturally, if banks had set up reserves that would have been appropriate in the light of subsequent experience, the business would not have been as profitable as it seemed at the time.

The external shape of the U.S. banking industry remained largely stagnant during this period. Expansion by way of mergers and acquisitions was strictly circumscribed by regulation. But the internal structure of banks underwent considerable transformation. The main corporate trend was the formation of bank holding companies. The change of format allowed additional leveraging at the holding company level so that the ratio of capital to total assets continued to deteriorate. Moreover, the so-called Edge Act subsidiaries escaped some of the regulatory restrictions imposed on banks. The greatest scope was abroad. Accordingly, most of the corporate moves were international with American banks expanding abroad and foreign banks establishing footholds in the United States. For instance, more than a quarter of Citicorp's earnings came from Brazil.

It was also a time of rapid technological innovations. The use of computers speeded up activities and permitted operations that would have been previously inconceivable. Many new financial instruments and financing techniques were invented and banking became a much more sophisticated business than it had been only a decade ago. These trends continue at an accelerating pace to the present day.

The task of the regulators was complicated both by the pace of innovation and by the international character of the competition. It is not unfair to say that the regulators were always lagging a step behind the practitioners and the industry became adept at finding a way around whatever regulations were imposed.

In the international arena the authorities did not want to hinder their own industry from competing on equal terms. With no regulatory constraints and individual banks competing for market share, the market as a whole grew by leaps and bounds. Banks were so anxious to obtain business that they asked very few questions. It is amazing how little information borrowing countries had to supply in order to obtain loans. Lending banks did not even know how much money the countries in question were borrowing elsewhere.

Debtor countries preferred to deal with commercial banks rather than go to the International Monetary Fund when they were in balance-of-payments difficulties. Unwittingly, commercial banks took over one of the functions that the Bretton Woods institutions— the IMF and the World Bank—had been designed to fulfill. They tranferred resources to less developed countries on a much larger scale than the Bretton Woods institutions would have been willing to countenance, and with much less interference in the debtor coun- tries' affairs. No wonder that less developed countries stayed away from the IMF! Mainly industrialized countries like the United King- dom asked for support from the IMF; developing countries could do better with commercial banks. There was a veritable explosion of in- ternational credit between 1973 and 1979. It was the foundation of the worldwide inflationary boom of the 1970s, which eventually culminated in the second oil shock.

In retrospect it is obvious that the borrowers spent the money un- wisely. At best they built white elephants like the Itaipu Dam in Brazil; at worst they spent it on armaments or used it to maintain unrealisti- cally high exchange rates as in the "southern cone" countries of Ar- gentina and Chile. At the time, the folly was not recognized. Indeed, Brazil was regarded as an economic miracle and Chile was praised as a paragon of monetarist virtue.

International lending grew so rapidly that the banks involved be- came overextended: their capital and reserves could not keep pace with the growth of their balance sheets. But the quality of their loan portfolios remained sound—at least outwardly. Indeed, one of the most striking features of the situation was that the borrowing coun- tries continued to meet the traditional yardsticks used to determine their creditworthiness even as their overall debt burden grew at an alarming rate.

Banks use ratios—such as external debt as a percentage of exports, debt service as a percentage of exports, and current deficits as a per- centage of exports—to measure creditworthiness. The international lending activity of the banks set in motion a self-reinforcing and self- validating process that increased the debt-servicing ability of the debtors, as measured by these ratios, almost as fast as their debt.

The key to the process is to be found in the very low and, even- tually, negative real interest rates that prevailed during the 1970s. Since the Eurocurrency market was outside the control of the central banks, its growth did not directly influence monetary policy in any country. As the banks graduated from recycling OPEC surpluses to creating credit, the monetary policy of the United States remained relaxed. The dollar started to depreciate, and interest rates failed to keep up with the rise in prices. The decline in real interest rates lowered the cost of debt service and rendered the borrowing countries more creditworthy. It also made them more eager to borrow. The expansion of credit stimulated the world economy and helped export performance all around. The less developed countries enjoyed strong demand for the commodities they exported; thus their terms of trade also tended to improve. The combination of declining real interest rates, expanding world trade, improving commodity prices, and the depreciating dollar enabled and encouraged the debtor countries to increase their indebtedness.

The self-validating process of credit expansion—inflation for short—was unsound in more ways than one. Prices and wages rose at accelerating rates. Balance-of-payments deficits and surpluses were perpetuated. The balance sheets of the banks deteriorated. Much of the investment activity financed by bank lending was misdirected. The creditworthiness of the debtors was illusory. Yet, as long as the process validated itself, the world economy prospered. Consumption remained high while saving was discouraged by low or negative interest rates. Investment was stimulated by the availability of cheap loans, and there was a flight from monetary to real assets. The combination of high consumption, high inventories, and strong investment activity created boom conditions.

The boom kept the demand for energy growing. The OPEC countries grew richer and less in need of current income, while negative real interest rates made it more attractive to keep oil in the ground than cash in the bank. This provided the setting in which the disruption of Iranian production in 1979 caused a second crisis and a second jump in the price of oil.

This time the response was different. Inflation had become a dominant concern, especially in the United Kingdom and the United States. Continental Europe and Japan had escaped the ravages of inflation by following a more restrictive monetary policy and allowing their currencies to appreciate. Since the price of oil is fixed in dollars, the cost of oil to Europe and Japan fell, and, in the absence of inflation, their exports remained competitive despite the appreciation of their currencies. The United Kingdom and the United States, by contrast, developed large budgetary and trade deficits, and inflation became a serious problem. Britain had to turn to the IMF for help. The United States, controlling as it did the reserve currency of the world, could inflate with impunity; nevertheless, the domestic and international consequences of inflation led to a shift in political preferences. The specter of accelerating inflation took precedence over the fear of recession. In response to the second oil shock, monetary policy turned restrictive and remained so even after the economy started to decline.

Monetarism became the doctrine that guided economic policy. Previously, central banks sought to influence economic activity by controlling interest rates; now the emphasis shifted to controlling the quantity of money. Interest rates were allowed to find their own level. Unfortunately, the level they found was inordinately high. The main reason was that fiscal policy remained stimulative, and it required a highly restrictive monetary policy to keep the growth in money supply in check.

Fiscal policy was influenced by supply-side economics. It was believed that lower tax rates would stimulate economic activity to such an extent that the impact on the budget would be neutralized. The deficit could then be reduced by cutting government spending. But the decision to increase defense expenditures at the same time as taxes were cut made a balanced budget unattainable. The interaction between a swelling budget deficit and strict monetary targets sent interest rates sky high. High interest rates swamped the stimulative effect of the tax cuts. The budget deficit widened, and the economy plunged into a deep recession.

The impact on the rest of the world was awesome. The debtor countries were hit by a threefold increase in oil prices, plunging commodity prices, soaring interest rates, a strong dollar, and a worldwide recession. They engaged in a final binge of borrowing that increased their total debt outstanding another 30%, but the ratios measuring their creditworthiness rapidly deteriorated. The situations in Poland and in the Falklands helped to undermine confidence. There was a twilight period during which banks continued to lend, but reluctantly. Maturities were shortened, and some countries developed liquidity problems. Then the Mexican debt crisis erupted in 1982, and voluntary lending to the heavily indebted countries came to a virtual standstill. The position of the debtors was much worse than most bankers had realized. For instance, Brazil was using the interbank market to finance its balance-of-payments deficit, unbeknownst to the correspondent banks. The international lending boom turned into a bust.

We shall pause at this point to analyze the international lending boom as a reflexive process in its own right. The above description contains all the necessary ingredients of a boom/bust sequence. What are they? First, there must be a reflexive connection between the underlying trend and the participants' perception. Second, there must be a flaw in the participants' perception that influences the underlying trend through a reflexive connection. The trend reinforces the bias until a point is reached where they both become unsustainable. Typically, the trend appears to be sound when it is first established and the flaws become apparent only when the trend is already well advanced. There is a twilight period during which the participants grow increasingly leery and reluctant, and the trend loses momentum. Eventually, the realization that the trend is unsound and unsustainable comes crashing in. The prophecy is self-fulfilling and the trend is reversed, often with catastrophic consequences.

In the case of international lending, there are a number of reflexive connections between the banks and the debtor countries. Banks use debt ratios to measure a country's capacity to borrow. These ratios were generally considered to be objective measurements, whereas in fact they are reflexive. As we have seen, both exports and GNP are influenced by the volume of international lending in a number of ways. Moreover, debt ratios measure only a debtor country's capacity to pay, not its willingness. To measure willingness a different calculation is needed which is essentially political in character. The critical variable is not debt service but net resource transfer, that is, the difference between debt service and the inflow of new credit. As long as debtor countries can borrow freely their willingness to pay is not in doubt: they can always borrow the money they need to pay the interest. But as soon as the flow of credit is interrupted, the willingness to pay becomes the critical issue. Bankers refused to face the issue during the great lending boom. Walter Wriston of Citicorp asserted that "sovereign nations don't go bankrupt."[1]

As we have seen, debt ratios remained largely satisfactory until the second oil shock, and banks were eager to lend. When debt ratios finally began to deteriorate, the banks started to worry and their willingness to lend was impaired, precipitating the crisis of 1982. The crisis brought the reflexive connection between net resource transfers and willingness to pay into play, leading to a permanent breakdown in voluntary lending. What happened afterward will be the subject of the next chapter. Here we are concerned with analyzing the system that prevailed until 1982.

Why the commercial banks were willing and able to sustain such explosive growth in their international loan portfolios is a fascinating question that will be hotly debated for years to come. Part of the answer is that banks did not consider themselves responsible for the soundness of the system. Banking is an intensely competitive business, which is, however, subject to regulation.

It is the job of the central banks to prevent excesses. Commercial banks operate under a protective umbrella; they seek to maximize their profits within the framework of existing regulations and they cannot afford to pay too much attention to the systemic effects of their activities. A commercial banker who refuses to go after what seems like profitable business is liable to be pushed to the side, and even if a bank decided to abstain there are many others anxious to take its place. Thus, even those who realized that the international lending boom was unsound found themselves obliged to participate or lose their places.

There is an important lesson here: participants are not in a position to prevent a boom from developing even if they recognize that it is bound to lead to a bust. That is true of all boom/bust sequences. Abstaining altogether is neither possible nor advisable. For instance, in my analysis of mortgage trusts I clearly predicted a bad end, yet my advice was to buy now because the shares would have to rise substantially before they crashed. As it happened, a certain class of investors responded with alacrity. But even if they had not done so, the boom/bust sequence would have occurred, albeit more slowly.

The best that a participant can do is to cease to be a participant at the right time. But that may not always be possible. For instance, in a system of fluctuating exchange rates, holders of financial assets have an existential choice in deciding what currency to hold: they cannot avoid holding some currency, except by buying options. In the case of international lending, Citicorp deliberately reduced its market share in the later stages of the boom; but that did not stop the drama from unfolding and Citicorp from being caught up in it. Toward the end most banks knew that the position of the debtor countries was rapidly deteriorating, yet they could not disengage themselves.

The lesson to be learned is that financial markets need to be supervised. Only some kind of intervention, be it legislative, regulatory, or a gentle hint from a central bank, can prevent boom/bust sequences from getting out of hand.

The history of central banking is a history of crises followed by institutional reform. It is truly surprising that the lessons of the international debt crisis have still not been learned. The champions of unregulated competition are more vocal, and more influential, than ever. They base their case on the inefficiency of regulators and it must be admitted that they have a point. The participants could not have prevented the international lending boom from getting out of hand, but the monetary authorities could have. Why did they fail to do so?

There is no clear answer to this question. Central banks were aware of the explosive growth of the Eurodollar market, although they lacked reliable statistics. They recognized their responsibilities as lenders of last resort and mapped out their respective spheres of responsibility as early as 1975, but they did not deem it necessary to regulate the growth of Eurodollar lending. Why? The question requires more thorough historical research than it has received so far. I shall hazard two tentative hypotheses.

One is that the central banks themselves were influenced by the competitive pressures that affected the commercial banks under their aegis. Had they imposed regulatory restrictions, the banks under their supervision would have lost business to others. Only concerted action by all the central banks could have brought the burgeoning Eurodollar market under control. That would have required institutional reform, and the monetary authorities did not recognize the need for reform. Reform usually occurs after a crisis, not before.

That is where the second hypothesis comes into play. I contend that the central banks were acting under the influence of a false ideology. It was a time when monetarism was gaining ground among central bankers. Monetarism holds that inflation is a function of money and not of credit. If monetarism is valid, the growth of money supply needs to be regulated, not the growth of credit. Accordingly, there was no need to interfere with the Eurodollar market: as long as the central banks regulate their own money supply, the market will regulate itself.

The issue is arcane and I cannot claim to understand it fully. Money shows up on one side of the balance sheet of banks and credit on the other. Milton Friedman tells us that it is the money side that counts because the other side is determined by the money side.[2] The theory of reflexivity leads me to believe that his theory is wrong. I would expect that the two sides influence each other in a reflexive fashion, and his dream of controlling the money supply is impractical. I lack sufficient expertise to take him on directly, but I can point to the empirical evidence that shows that the money supply always fails to behave in accordance with the regulators' wishes.

What role the growth of the Eurodollar market has played in the worldwide inflation of the 1970s has never been decided. For that matter, we do not know the extent to which the contraction of international lending is responsible for the deflationary pressures that seem to dominate the world economy at present. I firmly believe that both the expansion and the contraction of international lending have been important influences on the world economy, but my view is far from being generally accepted, and the issue remains unresolved to this day. If my view is correct, the volume of international credit ought to be an important consideration in setting economic policies. Monetary authorities committed a serious error in allowing it to get out of hand during the late 1970s. The crisis of 1982 is as much a failure of regulation as a failure of the free market.

We shall return to this issue again later. The imperfection of both regulated and free markets is one of the main themes of this book. Now we have to deal with the new system of international lending that evolved in response to the crisis of 1982.

5

The Collective System of Lending

There can be no doubt that without the active and imaginative intervention of the authorities the international debt crisis would have led to the collapse of the banking system, with disastrous consequences for the world economy. The last time such a collapse occurred was in the 1930s. Because of that experience, an institutional framework was established with a mandate to prevent a recurrence. Therefore it is inconceivable that events would have been allowed to unfold without intervention. It is the form that the intervention took that created a situation without parallel in history.

The institutional setup gives central banks the authority, and obligation, to act as lenders of last resort. But the debt problem was too big to be handled by providing liquidity to the banks. The amounts involved far exceeded the banks' own capital; if the countries in question had been allowed to go into default, the banking system would have become insolvent. Accordingly, the central banks exceeded their traditional role and banded together to bail out the debtor countries.

A precedent of sorts had been established in England in 1974, when the Bank of England decided to bail out the so-called fringe banks that were outside its sphere of responsibility rather than to allow the clearing banks, from whom the fringe banks had borrowed heavily, to come under suspicion. But the crisis of 1982 was the first time that the strategy of bailing out the debtors was applied on an international scale.

The central banks did not have sufficient authority to execute such a strategy, and makeshift arrangements had to be made in which the governments of all the creditor countries participated and the IMF played a key role. A rescue package was put together for one country after another. Typically, commercial banks extended their commitments, the international monetary institutions injected new cash, and the debtor countries agreed to austerity programs designed to improve their balance of payments. In most cases, the commercial banks also had to come up with additional cash enabling the debtor countries to stay current on their interest payments. The rescue packages constituted a remarkable achievement in international cooperation. The participants included the International Monetary Fund, the Bank for International Settlements, a number of governments and central banks, and a much larger number of commercial banks. In the case of Mexico, for instance, there were more than 500 commercial banks involved. I shall refer to the participants as "the Collective."

The process was repeated several times over a short period of time. The story of what actually happened would make fascinating reading, but here we must confine ourselves to examining the outcome.

The system of lending that emerged from the crisis is in many ways the opposite of the system that broke down in 1982. The prior system was competitive: banks were lending willingly, in pursuit of profit and in sharp competition with each other. The new system is cooperative: banks are lending under duress, in the hope of protecting their already committed assets, and they act jointly with other banks to this end. The prior system was reflexive in a positive direction: the banks' willingness and ability to lend were both reinforcing the debtor countries' ability and willingness to pay, and vice versa. In the present situation, reflexivity works in the opposite direction: it is the banks' inability and unwillingness to lend and the debtor countries' inability and unwillingness to pay that are mutually self-reinforcing. The system could not survive without the various participants actively cooperating to prevent a collapse. Action by the lenders takes the form of extending new credit in order to enable debtor countries to service their existing debt; action by the borrowers consists of accepting austerity programs that keep the amount of new credit needed to a minimum. What that minimum is depends on delicate negotiations between lenders and borrowers. The IMF has taken the lead in conducting these negotiations, although debtor countries are generally reluctant to allow the IMF a permanent role in monitoring the agreements.

The system is highly precarious because it requires both lenders and borrowers to override their narrow self-interest for the sake of remaining part of the system. In the case of debtors, the sacrifice is measured by negative resource transfers; in the case of the banks, by the amount of new credit extended. The sacrifice is not symmetrical, however, because the borrowers pay interest on the newly extended credit, while the lenders receive it. Only if the banks forgave some of the interest or principal would they suffer an actual loss. But the Collective system of lending is based on the principle that the integrity of the debt must be preserved—that is the principle that holds the Collective together. Unfortunately, it leaves a crucial problem unresolved: debtor countries need concessions to service their debt, but each concession adds to their future obligations. Recognizing the problem, banks are building bad debt reserves; but no way has been found to pass these reserves on to the debtor countries without destroying the principle that holds the Collective together.

The Collective system of lending came into existence unplanned and unannounced. It has been transitional from its inception and it is bound to lead to something else. The most interesting question that can be asked about it is what its eventual outcome will be. Unfortunately, this is not a question that can be satisfactorily answered. For one thing, reflexive processes do not have a predetermined outcome: the outcome is determined in the course of the process. For another, the prediction itself can influence the outcome. In this case, the hope that the Collectives will accomplish their mission is one of the main forces holding them together; any statement that has a bearing on that hope immediately becomes a part of the situation to which it refers, so that it is impossible to keep the discussion objective. Nevertheless, the question is pressing. Can the approach I have taken help to provide an answer? And can an answer help to develop a theory of reflexivity?

I published two papers[1]—one in July 1983 and one in March 1984—in which I tried to analyze the international debt problem using a theory of reflexivity but not spelling it out. This is what I said (with minor modifications):

> For heavily indebted countries, the collapse of voluntary lending has forced a drastic readjustment. The readjustment can be divided into

four phases. In the first phase, imports decline; in the second, exports increase. During the first two phases, domestic economic activity slows. In the third, domestic economic activity recovers and both imports and exports rise. In the fourth phase, the advance in GDP and exports exceeds the increase in debt service requirements and the adjustment is complete.

The first phase is involuntary. When the flow of credit is cut off, the trade deficit is automatically eliminated by a cut in imports. Living standards are reduced, the production process may be disrupted, and the country is plunged into depression. The amount of lending required of the Collective is determined by the inability of the debtor country quickly to generate a trade surplus sufficient to cover debt service requirements.

It is in the second phase that the real adjustment begins. The currency is devalued in real terms, and productive resources, idled by the reduction in domestic demand, are reoriented toward exports. The trade balance improves, and the ability to service the debt improves with it.

It is at this point that the willingness to pay and the willingness to lend become crucial. The country in question must increase its imports in order to support a domestic recovery. That means a reduction in the amount available for negative resource transfer. If the hurdle is passed, the third phase begins. Domestic recovery renders negative resource transfer more palatable. As the economy expands, the creditworthiness of the country begins to improve, provided that exports grow faster than the GDP. When that happens, the adjustment process has been accomplished.

On the lending side, Collectives operate with a chronic shortage of resources. Commercial banks can be divided into two categories: those whose very survival is at stake and those who are only marginally involved. The first category constitutes the core of the Collectives. They can be counted upon to participate, but their capacity to do so is limited. Marginal members need more persuasion. As the sense of urgency diminishes, the marginals wish to withdraw, leaving only majors to provide the flow of fresh credit. The categories are flexible. The large U.S., U.K., and Japanese banks will always remain core members; U.S. regionals and many continental banks are marginal to start with. In between the two groups there are many banks whose existence is at stake today but who may be able to build up sufficient reserves over a period of time to qualify as marginal in the future.

Because of the actual or potential shrinkage of membership, the resources of the Collectives are liable to remain fully stretched. The Collectives cannot meet the demands made upon them without the injection of additional funds from international lending institutions, but the institutions also are fully stretched. Thus, the Collectives are bound to push for the maximum resource transfers, making the hurdle between Phase 2 and Phase 3 difficult to pass.

I concluded that the Collective system of lending "is a system born of emergency. It needs emergency conditions to survive, and it is so constructed as to generate the emergency conditions that are needed to keep it in existence."

By and large, this analytical framework stood the test of time, although in retrospect I did make two serious mistakes. First, I argued that debtor countries were willing to tolerate negative resource transfers for two reasons: (1) to maintain access to capital markets and (2) to avoid seizure of assets. I neglected to consider what turned out to be the most important reason: (3) to maintain access to export markets. With domestic markets in shambles, the threat that export markets might be closed off was a potent one. Argentina was relatively the best situated to overcome an embargo because most of its exports were fungible commodities, but even Argentina sells many items, such as shoes and steel, that are destined for specific markets. Moreover, the newly elected Argentine government did not want to be isolated from the Western world. It was determined to avoid an "economic Falklands." As a result, the threat of default never became as serious as I expected.

In my analysis I did not put much store in the first two inducements. As regards free access to capital markets, I maintained that the system of lending that prevailed prior to 1982 had broken down for good. It had been based on certain misconceptions which had been recognized as such. The positive bias had been replaced by a negative one, and it would take a long time to overcome it. Events have borne out this analysis: bank lending to less developed countries is far below projections. As regards the seizure of assets, I dismissed it as a more or less empty threat. Since then this point of view has been fully documented.[2] Having ignored the third and most potent inducement, I concluded that "the only way to ensure that the debtor countries will honor their debt is to make credit available in quantities that approximate their debt service obligations."

This conclusion was false. In 1984 less than half the interest had to be advanced in the form of new credit, and much of the new credit came from sources other than the commercial banks. As a result, the cash drain on commercial banks was less severe than I had envisioned, and the strain between core members and marginal members never reached the breaking point. In fact, even core members have been able to begin building reserves against bad debts and improving their capital ratios.

The second mistake I made was to underestimate the ability of debtor countries to increase exports. The world economy turned out to be much stronger than I expected, for reasons that will be discussed in the next chapter. Brazil, in particular, produced a much larger trade surplus than I had expected. The official target for 1984 was $9 billion; the actual figure exceeded $12 billion. The strength in exports led to a modest domestic recovery and enabled Brazil to enter Phase 3.

These two mistakes together were sufficient to render my analysis unduly pessimistic. In February 1984 I asserted that "it is increasingly unlikely that much progress can be made in Phase 3, and Phase 4 appears increasingly unattainable under the present system." Yet by 1985 several of the major debtors had entered Phase 3, and the worst seemed to be over. Then came the precipitous drop in oil prices in 1986, and Mexico became a casualty. The emergency could be attributed to external causes, but recent developments in Brazil are much more ominous. As a result of the Cruzado Plan the economy became overheated in no time and the international trade balance deteriorated dangerously. As soon as the government was reelected in a landslide victory, it started to rein in the economy. Even so, it is clear that domestic political considerations take precedence over international debt obligations, and 1987 is likely to be a year of crisis in Brazilian debt negotiations.

Positions have softened considerably on the part of the creditor countries. U.S. Treasury Secretary James Baker recognized the need for domestic growth in the debtor countries in the plan he launched at the Seoul meeting of the World Bank in October 1985. Subsequently, the Bradley Plan expressly advocated forgiving a portion of the interest and principal on the accumulated debt. The fact is that the trade surpluses of the debtor countries have become troublesome for the United States. The banks are better reserved than they were a few years ago, so that 1987 may well bring some measure of protection coupled with some measure of loan forgiveness. If the experience of the last five years is any guide, the changes will not be radical enough to cause a breakdown of the system.

Although it was faulty in its details, my analytical framework remains valid in its broad outlines. It is not a blueprint for successful adjustment but rather a model for surviving failure. As we have seen, the Collective system is held together only by the threat of a breakdown. As we shall see, this is a characteristic of many arrangements which have prevailed since 1982.

6

Reagan's Imperial Circle*

t the time of the international debt crisis I was working with a
rather crude and inarticulate model of credit expansion and credit
contraction similar to a boom/bust sequence in the stockmarket. I
thought that 1982 was the end of a period of worldwide credit expansion and failed to anticipate the emergence of the United States as the
"borrower of the last resort."

The large and growing U.S. budget deficit emerged as the unintended consequence of conflicting policy objectives. On the one hand,
President Reagan sought to reduce the role of the federal government
in the economy by reducing taxes; on the other, he wanted to assume a
strong military posture in confronting what he considered the Communist menace. These two objectives could not be pursued within the
constraints of a balanced budget.

To make matters worse, fiscal and monetary policies were dominated by two conflicting schools of thought. Fiscal policy was influenced by "supply-side" economics, whereas monetary policy was
guided by the precepts of monetarism.

The supply-siders believed that a tax cut would have such a stimulating effect both on output and on willingness to pay taxes that the economy could grow at a rapid rate without exacerbating inflation and the
budget would be brought back into balance by higher tax receipts. It was
a thoroughly reflexive line of reasoning, and it contained serious flaws, as

*This chapter, finished in August 1985, has not been updated. Developments since then are dealt
with in the real-time experiment (Part Three).

such reasoning usually does. Its validity hinged on its being universally accepted; therefore, it was an all or none proposition. In a democracy that functions by compromise, such propositions rarely prevail. In this case, the chances of success were particularly poor because there was another major school of thought influencing government policy.

Monetarists believed that the primary objective was to bring inflation under control and to that end the money supply must be strictly regulated. Instead of controlling short-term interest rates, as it had done hitherto, the Federal Reserve fixed targets for money supply and allowed the rate on federal funds to fluctuate freely. The Federal Reserve's new policy was introduced in October 1979, and interest rates were already at record levels when President Reagan took office. In his first budget, he cut taxes and increased military spending simultaneously. Although a concerted effort was made to reduce domestic spending, the savings were not large enough to offset the other two items. The path of least resistance led to a large budget deficit.

Since the budget deficit had to be financed within the limits of strict money supply targets, interest rates rose to unprecedented heights. Instead of economic expansion, the conflict between fiscal and monetary policy brought on a severe recession. Unexpectedly high interest rates combined with a recession to precipitate the international debt crisis of 1982. Henry Kaufman had long warned that government deficits would drive other borrowers out of the market.[1] He proved to be right but it was the foreign governments that were driven out first, not the domestic users of credit.

The Federal Reserve responded to the Mexican crisis of August 1982 by relaxing its grip on the money supply. The budget deficit was just beginning to accelerate. With the brakes released, the economy took off and the recovery was as vigorous as the recession had been severe. It was aided by a spending spree by both the private and the corporate sectors and it was abetted by the banking system. Military spending was just gearing up; the private sector enjoyed rising real incomes; the corporate sector benefited from accelerated depreciation and other tax concessions. Banks were eager to lend because practically any new lending had the effect of improving the quality of their loan portfolios.

The demand emanating from all these sources was so strong that interest rates, after an initial decline, stabilized at historically high levels and eventually began to rise again. Banks bid for deposits aggressively and holders of financial assets could obtain even higher returns from the banks than from holding government obligations. Foreign capital was attracted, partly by the high return on financial assets and partly by the confidence inspired by President Reagan. The dollar strengthened and a strengthening currency combined with a positive interest rate differential made the move into the dollar irresistible. The strong dollar attracted imports, which helped to satisfy excess demand and to keep down the price level. A self-reinforcing process was set into motion in which a strong economy, a strong currency, a large budget deficit, and a large trade deficit mutually reinforced each other to produce noninflationary growth. I have called this circular relationship Reagan's Imperial Circle because it finances a strong military posture by attracting both goods and capital from abroad. This makes the circle benign at the center and vicious at the periphery.

It can be seen that the Imperial Circle was built on an internal contradiction between monetarism and supply-side economics. The outcome was not intended or even anticipated. Many momentous historical developments occur without the participants fully realizing what is happening. The tremendous transfer of resources to less developed countries that occurred between 1974 and 1982 could not have taken place in a planned and organized manner, and, as we have seen, the Collective system of lending came into existence unintended and unannounced.

Most professional economists did not consider the emergence or the survival of a benign circle possible, but President Reagan, despite his intellectual limitations, seems to have had a better understanding of what was possible than did his economic advisers. After all, the reflexive process of the Imperial Circle fitted well with his concept of leadership—which is, of course, a reflexive concept par excellence. He was therefore content to pay lip service to the desirability of balancing the budget, ignored and eventually got rid of Martin Feldstein, and left the deficit well enough alone. Europeans complained about the strong dollar—although it is not quite clear why—but the U.S. administration insisted on a policy of benign neglect.

A benign circle for the United States is a vicious circle for the debtor nations. The trade deficit of the United States is mirrored by trade surpluses in other countries. To the extent that a strong export performance has enabled heavily indebted countries to become

current on their interest payments, the effect may be judged beneficial; but, even here, the benefit accrues to the lenders. For the rest,
the debtor nations have been laboring under high real interest rates
and very unfavorable terms of trade. Dollars are cheap when they are
borrowed, but expensive when the interest has to be paid. The
scramble to export depresses the prices of the commodities exported. Although the external performance of the debtor countries
has exceeded most expectations, the internal performance is much
less satisfactory. There are some that have shown practically no recovery, and even among the more successful ones per capita income
has been lagging; now that it has begun to rise the trade surplus is
beginning to deteriorate. Some of the weakest countries have en-
dured a downward spiral in which both their domestic economies
and their abilities to service their debts have deteriorated to the van-
ishing point. This group comprises a large part of Africa and some
Latin American and Caribbean countries like Peru and the Domini-
can Republic.

As far as the more developed countries are concerned, rising exports to the United States have had a stimulating effect but the response has been very subdued. Corporations have been reluctant to
add to capacity because they are afraid, and justifiably so, that the dollar will decline just when their capacity comes on stream. By contrast,
holding financial assets in dollars exerts an almost irresistible attraction. The phenomenon is particularly noticeable in Britain, where
currency swings have been especially wild. The whole of Europe has
been languishing with high unemployment and little growth, and it
has become fashionable to speak of "Eurosclerosis." The Far East has
shown much greater dynamism under the impetus of the newly industrialized countries and the opening up of China. Japan has been
the greatest beneficiary of the present state of affairs. Its position is almost the mirror image of that of the United States, with a large export surplus and strong domestic savings counterbalanced by the
export of capital.

Let us try to analyze Reagan's Imperial Circle with the help of the
analytical tools we have developed so far. We shall use the notation
adopted in Chapter 2. The four key elements are a strong economy
($\uparrow v$), a strong currency ($\uparrow e$), a growing budget deficit ($\downarrow B$), and a
growing trade deficit ($\downarrow T$). At first sight, there are some obvious contradictions between these four variables. Conventional economics tells

us that a growing trade deficit ($\downarrow T$) tends to depress both the exchange rate ($\downarrow e$) and the level of domestic activity ($\downarrow v$):

(1)

But the Imperial Circle managed to overcome these causal relationships with the help of two other variables: the budget deficit and capital inflows.

The economy strengthened because the stimulus of the budget deficit outweighed the drag of the trade deficit. Economic activity is, of course, influenced by many other factors. To bring them all into the picture would complicate the argument unduly. What matters is the end result: a strong economy. To keep the picture simple, we shall denote the net effect of all other factors with a question mark (?), giving us the formula

(2)
$$(\downarrow B + ?) > (\downarrow T + ?) \rightarrow \uparrow v$$

Similarly, the dollar appreciated because capital inflows—$\downarrow (N + S)$—exceeded the trade deficit:

(3)
$$\downarrow T < \downarrow (N + S) \rightarrow \uparrow e$$

These two relationships are the mainstays of the Imperial Circle.

There are many other relationships at work, so many that it would be onerous to list them all. Some reinforce the Imperial Circle; others work against it; yet others reinforce it in the short run but cannot be sustained in the long run. The most important self-reinforcing connection is between the exchange rate and speculative capital inflows:

(4)
$$\uparrow e \rightarrow \downarrow S \rightarrow \uparrow e \rightarrow \downarrow S$$

We have already identified two connections that work against the Imperial Circle (Equation 1), and here we can mention two connections that are self-reinforcing in the short run, but unsustainable in the long run. First, while speculative capital inflows are self-reinforcing in the short run, they also generate interest and repayment obligations that are cumulative and work in the opposite direction.

(5)

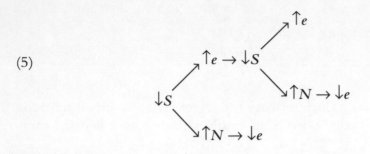

Eventually the growing debt service ($\uparrow N$) is bound to undermine the relationship on which the Imperial Circle rests and the trend of the exchange rate is going to be reversed:

(6) $(\downarrow T + \uparrow N) > \downarrow S \rightarrow \downarrow e \rightarrow (\uparrow S + \downarrow T + \uparrow N) \rightarrow \downarrow \downarrow e$

At that time, debt service and the flight of speculative capital may combine with the trade deficit to generate a catastrophic collapse of the dollar: central bank officials, Volcker foremost among them, are aware of the danger and are publicly warning against it.[2] To put matters in perspective, it should be pointed out that it would take many years for interest charges to accumulate to a point where they would reverse the balance. The likelihood is that the Imperial Circle will be reversed or at least brought to a halt long before that. Volcker and other responsible government officials are certainly working toward that end.

The crucial question confronting the world is whether the Imperial Circle can be arrested without precipitating a catastrophic collapse of the dollar. The longer it lasts, and the higher the dollar climbs, the greater the danger of a fall. The problem is that a clear-cut reversal in the trend of the dollar could, even at this stage, cause a shift not only in the ongoing flow of investment but also in the accumulated stock of speculative capital. The stock is, of course, many times larger than the ongoing flow. The problem is widely recognized, making the holders of dollar assets very nervous. That is why foreign holdings of marketable assets are aptly described as "hot money."

The second example is the budget deficit, which is stimulative in the short run but may be counterproductive in the long run because it diverts resources from more productive uses through the interest rate mechanism:

(7)

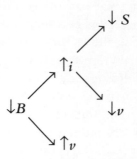

As long as high interest rates suck in capital from abroad, the problem remains latent. With the help of foreign savings, the domestic economy can consume more than it produces. Only when the capital inflow ceases to match the budget deficit does the problem become acute. Interest rates must rise in order to generate the domestic savings necessary to finance the budget deficit. The consequent decline in consumption depresses the economy, making foreigners all the less willing to hold dollar assets. This may give rise to a "disaster scenario" in which a weak economy and a large budget deficit combine to produce high interest rates and a weak dollar.

We can combine these relationships to create an integrated model of the Imperial Circle:

(8)

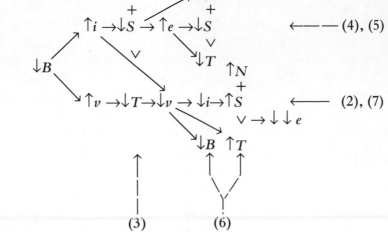

In this model, one of the mainstays of the Imperial Circle, Equation 2, is shown horizontally and the other, Equation 3, vertically. It will be seen that the model is not stable: some connections reinforce it while others undermine it. The factors best reinforced are the speculative inflows and the trade deficit; the factor most endangered is the level of economic activity. The main threats to the stability of the Imperial Circle come from the trade deficit and the budget deficit. The twin pillars of the arrangement are a strong dollar and a strong economy; but a strong dollar leads to a rising trade deficit that weakens the economy and the budget deficit keeps interest rates higher than they would be otherwise, which also weakens the economy. These are the internal inconsistencies that are likely to destroy the Imperial Circle long before the accumulation of debt service obligations would do so.

Needless to say, the model is incomplete. There are many connections that are not shown; the illustration is complicated enough as it is. Perhaps some connection that has been ignored here will come to the rescue of the Imperial Circle when the need arises. We have already witnessed such occasions. For instance, until the middle of 1984, banks were active in expanding credit at home and attracting funds from abroad. When they stopped functioning as the main conduit, for reasons that will be explained in Chapter 7, the Treasury took their place: the withholding tax was abolished, and a large portion of the government debt was sold directly to foreigners.

It would be interesting to construct a more complete model and endow the variables with numerical values. I believe it would be possible to simulate the evolution of the U.S. economy since 1982, but I am not equipped to carry out such an operation. I have to confine myself to an impressionistic presentation.

We are dealing with a system that is not stable, but constantly evolving. What will succeed the Imperial Circle? That is the question that needs to be answered. Before I attempt to do so, let me complete the picture by taking a closer look at the banking system and the corporate restructuring that is currently sweeping the country.

7

Evolution of the Banking System

It is generally recognized that the international debt crisis of 1982 constituted a dramatic point for the debtor countries. The direction of resource transfers was reversed and the magnitude of the swing was limited only by the debtor countries' capacities to pay. In our model of the Imperial Circle the swing shows up as a nonspeculative inflow ($\uparrow N$) because it is guided by considerations other than total return. The amounts involved are significant: net resource transfers to heavily indebted countries swing from $50.1 billion in 1982 to a reverse flow of $13.8 billion in 1983,[1] most of it in dollar form. Resource transfers from the heavily indebted countries have provided one of the major underpinnings for the Imperial Circle.

It is less well recognized that the crisis of 1982 did not bring a similar turning point for the banking system. The largest banks were too deeply involved to allow them to reverse direction. Had they stopped lending altogether, the heavily indebted countries would have had to default. Had they tried to set up adequate reserves, their capital position would have been impaired. It was to preserve these banks that the Collectives were established. We have dealt with the role of the Collectives in tiding over the debtor countries; now we must examine what happened to the banking system.

The Collective system of lending operates on the principle of voluntary cooperation. The regulatory authorities had to exert themselves to make it possible for the heavily involved banks to extend new loans and to induce less involved banks to cooperate. The only way they could achieve these objectives was by maintaining the fiction that the outstanding loans were unimpaired and no special reserves had to be set up against them. There was some divergence of opinion among the various supervisory agencies but the Federal Reserve, as lender of last resort, maintained the upper hand. The banking system was considered too weak to be given any strong medicine. Accounting standards were modified and special efforts were made to enable banks to meet them. The last-minute bridge loan to Argentina on March 1, 1984, stands out as the most dramatic intervention by the Federal Reserve.

European central banks took a different tack. They encouraged commercial banks to set up reserves and write down bad loans. They could afford to do so. European banks were, on the whole, less deeply involved, and their accounting system permitted the accumulation of large hidden reserves. The United Kingdom occupied a halfway position between the Continent and the United States. Some British banks were amongst those with the highest loan exposure to less developed countries, but they had a much sounder deposit base in their own branch system so that they were never as susceptible to a crisis of confidence as their American counterparts.

It may be argued that the Federal Reserve went too far in supporting the money center banks. These banks were allowed to treat as current income the rescheduling fees and exceptionally wide spreads they charged on paper but did not collect in cash. As a result, they could report substantial earnings gains, and some of them actually increased their dividends in 1983.

Ironically, the formation of the Collectives, and the permissive attitude of the regulatory authorities that accompanied it, delayed and diverted the adjustment process in the U.S. banking industry. Debtor countries had to face harsh reality, but banks were left with a large load of doubtful debt whose doubtful quality they had to hide. The only way they could collect the interest was by making additional loans. Thus the problem was not only unacknowledged but also growing. The banks responded by trying to grow even faster. The most desirable way to grow was to provide services without tying up assets. Money center banks developed a host of new services and marketed them aggressively. But they were not averse to expanding their balance sheets, either. Almost any loan was of better quality than their portfolio of loans to the less developed countries. This was the heyday of leveraged buyouts; banks were willing to grant very generous terms. Banks were also aggressive bidders for deposits abroad and used the funds to build up their domestic asset base. Thus they became the primary vehicle for attracting capital to the United States.

Unfortunately, banks were unable to use their remarkably good reported earnings to raise equity capital, because the stock market saw through the charade and bank shares were valued at substantial discounts from stated asset values. Chemical Bank managed to seize a propitious moment and sell some shares; Manufacturers Hanover also placed shares in connection with its acquisition of CIT Corp.—but these were exceptions. On the whole, banks had to rely on retained earnings, which could not keep pace with the growth in assets.

Nevertheless, there was a race to expand and diversify. Manufacturers Hanover acquired CIT Corp. at a hefty price and the artifice of the "nonbank bank" was invented in order to circumvent existing restrictions on geographical diversification. The money center banks were pressing for permission to expand across state lines, but they ran into stiff opposition from regional banks who wanted protection. The protracted battle has only recently been resolved, giving the regional banks a breathing space before the money center banks are allowed to buy up banks outside state limits.

The Federal Reserve did not wish to put any constraints on the banking system that would have a negative effect on the economy. The first priority was to prevent a collapse and to that end they wanted to engineer a strong recovery. Only when the recovery was well under way did they rein in the money supply, allowing interest rates to rise. They could have also tried to rein in the banks, but that is not what happened. Bad loans continued to accumulate and capital ratios continued to deteriorate. Confidence in the banking system remained precarious.

Eventually troubles surfaced in the domestic loan portfolios. Large segments of the economy, notably agriculture and the oil industry, did not participate in the recovery. In contrast to the international debt, it was impractical to keep the domestic borrowers afloat by lending them the money to pay the interest because there were just too many of them. Continental Illinois Bank was particularly badly hit because it had followed loose lending practices. Specifically, it had purchased a large amount of unsound energy loans from Penn Square Bank, which had gone bankrupt. Having no branches, it was in the unfortunate position of being heavily dependent on borrowed funds. Thus it became the focal point of concern.

There was also trouble brewing in the savings and loan industry. The equity of many institutions had been wiped out by the rise in interest rates prior to 1982. To prevent wholesale collapse, a large number of institutions had to be merged or otherwise salvaged during 1982. The Reagan administration was looking to the market mechanism for a solution. In one of the most remarkable episodes in financial history many of the regulatory constraints were removed just at a time when the capital of the industry was seriously impaired. The range of activities in which savings and loan companies could engage and the range of assets they could invest in were greatly extended. Since the savings and loans had gotten into trouble in a regulated environment it was assumed that the removal of constraints would help to get them out of trouble. Private enterprise did in fact devise ingenious ways to salvage bankrupt savings and loan companies. Most of the new money invested was immediately recouped as a tax loss and savvy investors gained control of institutions licensed to gather government-insured deposits with very little cash investment. Some of these institutions fell into the hands of operators who could use such deposits in support of other activities from which they profited. They had much to gain but little to lose from expanding aggressively. This was a formula for disaster. It is surprising that it was not recognized as such.

The company that exploited the opportunity presented by the regulators most aggressively was Financial Corporation of America under the dynamic leadership of its president, Charles Knapp. Having acquired First Charter Financial, an old established institution whose deposits were insured by the Federal Savings and Loan Insurance Corporation (FSLIC), it went on a borrowing spree, using brokers as well as a high-powered in-house sales force. It then invested heavily in rather risky real estate loans as well as fixed-rate mortgages. If any of the loans went sour, another developer was found who would take it over in exchange for a much larger loan on his own development. As interest rates began to rise, the company averaged up its fixed-rate mortgage portfolio at an exponential rate. Knapp figured that in this way he would have a high-yielding portfolio when interest rates finally declined and if he grew large enough he could not be allowed to go broke even if interest rates did not decline: heads he would win, tails he could not lose. The calculation was correct. The company grew from $4.9 billion in deposits in 1982 to $20.3 billion in 1984. As the financial position of the company deteriorated, Knapp was forced out (after receiving severance pay in seven figures) but the company was rescued.[2]

The crisis in Continental Illinois Corp. and Financial Corporation of America came to a head more or less concurrently in the summer of 1984. That was the true turning point for the banking and thrift industries, although this fact is still not properly appreciated. Bank examiners remembered their statutory duty and began to take a stand on bad loans. Regulators tightened capital requirements, and insisted on strengthening bad debt reserves. Banks responded by shrinking their balance sheets, selling off assets, and packaging loans for resale rather than putting them on the books. The period of unsound growth came to an end and the adjustment process finally began.

At first blush, the adjustment has been remarkably smooth. Banks became adept at packaging loans for resale, developing a variety of financial instruments ranging from floating rate notes to mortgage pass-through certificates. Whenever necessary, other institutions have taken over the banks' role. Junk bonds have replaced bank loans in financing mergermania, and Treasury bonds have taken the place of Eurodollar deposits in sucking in capital from abroad. It is no coincidence that the withholding tax on foreign-owned bonds was removed just as the turning point in bank expansion was reached.

With every passing quarter, the financial position of the banks ought to improve. Individual banks may be hurt when they have to recognize losses but the industry as a whole ought to become sounder. The stock market responded positively to the changed outlook: bank shares rose to levels where they were selling at premiums over book value.

But the period of danger is not yet over. It is after a trend has been reversed that the full effect of the preceding excesses is felt. While banks were given leeway, they could cover up their bad loans by extending additional credit. But when banks are required to set up reserves against bad or doubtful loans it does not pay them to throw good money after bad. On the contrary, they have every reason to liquidate bad loans, because by doing so they can convert non-earning assets into earning assets and they may also be able to recapture some of the reserves they have been obliged to set up. The danger is that the liquidation of bad loans uncovers other bad loans.

For instance, there were many farmers who could not service their debt but the value of their land was still high enough to provide adequate collateral: these farmers were given additional credit rather than forced into bankruptcy. But the liquidation of bankrupt farmers is depressing land prices, so that additional farmers are forced into bankruptcy. The same is happening in the oil industry, and at the time of this writing (September 1985) ominous signs are emerging in real estate. Shipping is probably next in line.

The bankruptcy of Community Savings Bank of Maryland and its subsidiary, Equity Programs, Inc. (EPIC), in 1985 serves as a paradigm of what happens when the trend is reversed. The institution in question had been acquired by real estate developers who carried on their syndicating activities as a subsidiary of the thrift institution. They specialized in financing model homes and enjoyed a good reputation. The mortgages on these homes were insured by private mortgage insurance companies and sold to investors in the form of mortgage-backed securities. Following a run on state-insured savings banks in Ohio, savings banks in Maryland were required to seek federal insurance. The Federal Savings and Loan Insurance Corporation, in its chastened mood, insisted that the real estate syndicating subsidiary should be sold before the parent was granted FSLIC cover. That caused the whole situation to unravel. The subsidiary could not syndicate any new loans, and without new syndications it could not service its outstanding mortgages. It turned out that the income from the already syndicated homes had been insufficient to cover the mortgages and the deficiency had been habitually made up from new syndications. In theory, the model homes would eventually be sold and would start to produce income, but, in practice, the subsidiary had become heavily indebted to the parent and it appears that some of the model homes did not even exist. The subsidiary had issued about $1.4 billion of mortgage-backed securities and the mortgage insurance companies were on the hook. The potential liability exceeded the assets of some of the insurance companies in question, and if they cannot meet their obligations the security of mortgage-backed securities may be endangered.*

My brief account of recent events is sufficient to show that regula-

---

*Subsequently, one of the mortgage insurance companies, Ticor Mortgage Insurance Company, went out of business, but the mortgage-backed securities market was not endangered.

tors are not exempt from bias. They are participants in a reflexive process and operate on the basis of imperfect understanding, just like those whom they regulate. On balance the regulators understand the business they supervise less well than those who engage in it. The more complex and innovative that business is, the less likely that the supervisory authority can do a competent job.

Regulation always lags behind events. By the time regulators have caught up with excesses, the corrective action they insist on tends to exacerbate the situation in the opposite direction. That is what has happened in the period under study. By the time the authorities discovered that international lending was unsound it was too late to correct the situation because the correction would have precipitated a collapse. When they finally insisted that banks recognize their losses, their insistence reinforced the collapse of collateral values in areas such as agriculture, the oil industry, and shipping.

Commercial bankers have also committed many mistakes, but at least they have an excuse: they operate within guidelines laid down by the regulators. Their job is to compete, not to worry about the soundness of the system. Their excuse is valid in the sense that, as long as there is no fraud involved, the authorities will, in fact, bail them out if they get into difficulties. This compounds the responsibility that regulators have to shoulder.

The authorities have given a good account of themselves whenever the situation has deteriorated to the crisis point. To some extent, this is due to the merit of the individuals involved. Events might have taken a different course if it had not been Volcker who was in charge of the Federal Reserve. He displayed a positive eagerness in confronting difficult situations and coming up with innovative solutions that is rare in a bureaucrat. But there is also an institutional reason. Central banks are given a mandate to act as lenders of last resort. They have incomparably more authority in an emergency than in the ordinary course of events. They are geared to crisis management and quite incompetent when it comes to problem solving. To achieve any lasting solutions, the whole machinery of the administration and Congress needs to be involved. That means that needed reforms are rarely enacted in time.

The banking crisis of 1984 has left us with an unresolved dilemma. There is a basic imbalance in deregulating deposit-taking institutions and guaranteeing depositors against loss. The guarantee enables financial institutions to attract additional deposits at will, and deregulation gives them wide latitude in putting those deposits to use. The combination of the two is an invitation to unrestrained credit expansion. The problem has been inherent in the system of Federal deposit insurance since its inception but at the time the FDIC was founded banks were strictly regulated. The imbalance between risk and reward became more pronounced as the trend toward deregulation gained momentum, and it reached a critical point in the crisis of 1984.

The Federal Reserve was forced to expand its role as lender of last resort and guarantee all depositors against loss whatever the size of their deposits. This removed the last vestige of the discipline that depositors are supposed to impose on banks. In the absence of that discipline there is nothing left but the regulatory authorities to stop financial institutions from engaging in unsound lending practices.

It may be argued that shareholders would act as a constraining influence because they remain at risk, but the constraint is not very effective since a bank can cover up its losses by lending even more. By the time the losses can no longer be hidden, much more will have been lost than the equity capital. Thus, having equity and loan capital at risk is not sufficient to ensure sound lending practices.

The regulatory authorities have, in fact, become much stricter since 1984. Yet the popular and political bias in favor of deregulation is as strong as ever. The geographic and functional restrictions imposed in the Great Depression are in the process of being dismantled. Theoretically, there need be no conflict between deregulation and stricter supervision; but in practice there is. As we have seen, regulators make mistakes; the more varied and changeable the business, the less likely that it will be adequately supervised. There is a strong prima facie case for keeping the deposit-taking business as simple as possible. On the other hand, simple, regulated businesses tend to breed stodgy, conservative managements. It boils down to a choice between stability and innovation. When one of these ingredients is missing its absence is sorely felt. As a consequence, preferences tend to swing from one extreme to another. At present we are still elated by the opportunities that have been opened up by the removal of outdated regulations; but the need for stability is increasingly pressing.

There is another simmering problem that is approaching boiling point. It concerns the treatment of insolvent financial institutions. Traditionally, the authorities prefer to arrange the acquisition of failing institutions by larger, sounder ones. Such forced mergers used to offer an easy way out when the industry was tightly regulated, failures were few and far between, and the acquiring institutions were financially strong. The failing bank had a valuable franchise that could be auctioned off to the highest bidder without endangering the structure of the industry. But as the process of credit expansion and deregulation progressed, the procedure of "merging out" insolvent units became both more frequent and less satisfactory. The franchises became less valuable and the acquiring institutions less able to withstand a dilution of their financial strength. A concentrated industry is seemingly stronger. For instance, the clearing banks of the United Kingdom have never had any difficulty in attracting deposits, although Midland Bank, for one, was in worse shape than any of the surviving banks in the United States. But increasing concentration increases the danger of catastrophic losses. What would happen to the United Kingdom if the clearing banks were unable to collect the interest on their loans to less developed countries? Closer to home, Bank of America was encouraged to acquire First of Seattle; but who is going to acquire Bank of America if the need arises?* We have already had the first instance, that of Continental Illinois Bank, where no buyer could be found. We may yet arrive at a point where several of our largest banks end up as public property. It has happened in other countries.

In no instance was the idea of merging out sick units so ill conceived as in the savings and loan industry. As we have seen, much of the industry became insolvent during the 1980–82 period of record high interest rates. The authorities devised the brilliant scheme of selling off ailing units to adventurous entrepreneurs who appreciated the privilege of being able to attract federally issued deposits. We have seen how entrepreneurs like Charles W. Knapp of the Financial Corporation of America exploited the privilege. Now that the regulators have put a stop to uncontrolled expansion, many of the excesses are beginning to surface. Only the decline in interest rates has saved us from an avalanche of insolvencies.

---

*To my great surprise, as of December 1986, First Interstate is avidly pursuing BankAmerica, Chemical Bank is buying Texas Commerce Bank, and RepublicBank is willing to take over one of the weakest banks in Texas, Interfirst, in order to prevent out-of-state competitors from gaining a foothold in the state.

8

The "Oligopolarization" of America*

Within the context of Reagan's Imperial Circle there is another important reflexive development under way: the corporate structure of the United States is being reshaped by means of mergers, acquisitions, divestitures, and leveraged buyouts. The move has the dramatic quality usually associated with reflexive processes and it has reached proportions that endow it with historical significance. Its roots go back to well before the inception of the Imperial Circle but it has gained tremendous momentum since 1982. The process of corporate restructuring is clearly interrelated with the Imperial Circle but so far the relationship is rather lopsided: prevailing economic and political conditions provide the context in which the restructuring occurs but the evolution of the Imperial Circle has not been significantly affected by corporate restructuring. The process that can be loosely described as mergermania is therefore best regarded as a sideshow rather than an essential ingredient of the Imperial Circle.

In its impact on the corporate structure of the United States, mergermania has already exceeded the conglomerate boom. Conglomerates started out as relatively small companies that became large through acquisitions; mergermania has involved the largest entities in corporate

---

*This chapter has been kept as it was originally written in June 1985, with a brief postscript added in December 1986.

133

America. There are many similarities between the two developments but the differences are more pronounced. If the conglomerate boom represents the simplest case of an initially self-reinforcing and eventually self-defeating process, mergermania is perhaps the most complex. The conglomerates provided a paradigm of boom and bust; mergermania exemplifies a reflexive process in which the self-reinforcing and self-defeating interactions are not sequential but simultaneous.

I shall not attempt a descriptive history of mergermania. I shall simply assume that the reader is more or less familiar with the discrete corporate events that have occurred in the last few years. My own familiarity with mergermania is not much greater than that of a well-informed member of the public because I did not participate in it in a professional capacity.

Corporate events have been occurring continuously ever since there have been organized stock markets. Whenever the market value of the shares is higher than the value of a company as a privately owned entity the corporate event consists of a sale of shares; whenever the market value is lower, a purchase of shares is involved. The purchaser may be the company itself, the management, an outside group, or another company that may have a special reason for putting a high value on the shares.

The conglomerate boom combined the buying and selling of shares. Conglomerates were selling their own shares at inflated prices and buying the shares of other companies. They could put a higher value on the shares of other companies than the market because the acquisitions helped to support the overvaluation of their own shares. Thus the conglomerate boom was essentially a phenomenon of overvaluation with inflated securities serving as the means of exchange.

By contrast, in the current process of corporate restructuring the primary means of exchange is cash. The cash may be borrowed in a number of ways, but the final result is the same: shares are bought for cash. There are occasional mergers that are accomplished by an exchange of shares but they are not characteristic of the trend. There are also many developments, notably the disposition of assets and operating divisions, that do not involve the purchase or sale of shares at all; yet the event that characterizes the current process and qualifies it as a reflexive one is the purchase of shares for cash. Thus mergermania is predicated on the undervaluation of shares: the company as a whole must be worth substantially more than the market capitalization of its shares.

The undervaluation started to develop after the second oil shock when a concerted effort was made to bring inflation under control through stringent monetary policy. It was greatly reinforced after Reagan became president and the Imperial Circle evolved.

We can discern three factors in the relative undervaluation of shares: economic, political, and tax related. The first two are definitely interconnected with Reagan's Imperial Circle; the third is due to the peculiarity of our tax system. I shall emphasize it because it provides that element of distortion that seems to be an essential ingredient in reflexive processes.

As long as interest expense is tax deductible, it pays to acquire companies with borrowed cash, because there is a saving on taxes. That is one of the major motivations in leveraged buyouts. There are many other, more arcane, tax benefits involved, but this is not the place to explore them.*

Shares traditionally have been valued as a multiple of earnings. When the rate of interest is high, the multiple tends to be low. But earnings are only a part of pretax cash flow, often a minor part. Yet, it is cash flow that is the primary criterion in determining the value of a business as a candidate for acquisition. Thus the traditional method of valuing shares has helped to create opportunities for acquisition, especially in periods, such as the Imperial Circle, when earnings are depressed and interest rates relatively high.

Let us take a profitable but mature company with little scope for expansion—a so-called cash cow. If it is acquired with borrowed funds, the interest can be paid out of pretax earnings. To the extent that the market discounts pretax earnings at a rate higher than the prevailing interest rate, there is a margin of earnings, in addition to the free-cash flow, that can be used to pay down the loan. Eventually, the acquirer is left with a debt-free company. As that point approaches he could, in theory, sell the shares to the public, realizing a capital gain. He could then turn around and buy back the shares from the public and start the process all over again. In practice, several of the early

*Several of them, notably the so-called General Utilities doctrine, which allows the acquiring company to write up assets and depreciate them from a higher base, have been eliminated in the Tax Reform Act of 1986. The tax deductibility of interest has not been changed, but the corporate tax rate has been lowered from 48% to 34%, thereby reducing the tax benefit of using borrowed money.

leveraged buyouts have resurfaced as new issues. I do not know of any instances where a refloated company has gone private again, but I know of cases where previous leveraged buyouts have been releveraged in private transactions.

It can be seen that the tax system has made cash cows particularly susceptible to leveraged buyouts, while the Imperial Circle has had the unintended consequence of turning companies into cash cows. The mechanism by which the effect is achieved is high real interest rates and an overvalued currency. High real interest rates render financial assets more attractive, and physical investments less attractive; thus they provide an incentive not to put cash to work in expanding the business but rather to use it as a financial asset: buying in shares or acquiring other companies. An overvalued currency tends to render industrial activity less profitable: export markets shrink and domestic markets come under price pressure from imports.

The combination of high real interest rates and an overvalued currency proved to be a potent brew. The producers of tradable goods have been put under great strain; often their survival is at stake. They have reacted by consolidating: shedding unprofitable divisions, abandoning activities where their market position is weak, and concentrating on those areas where their position is worth defending. Traditional attitudes have been shaken up; often there has been a change in management. Gone are the days when corporations pursued growth for its own sake; free cash flow and profits have assumed an importance which they had previously enjoyed only in textbooks. Managements have started to look at their businesses more like an investment fund manager looks at his portfolio. This has created a suitable atmosphere for corporate restructuring.

Every time an acquisition occurs, it tends to narrow the gap between market prices and the value to the acquirer. This brings us to the most curious feature of the process. One would expect that the acquisitions of shares for cash would reduce the extent of undervaluation to a point where acquisitions are no longer profitable and the movement comes to a stop. Why has the gap not been closed? To answer this question, we must invoke a political factor. The Reagan administration believes in the magic of the marketplace. This finds expression, first of all, in the deregulation of regulated industries, but it also permeates the government's attitude toward corporate activity in general.

There has been no formal reform of antitrust laws but there has been a radical shift in what is considered an antitrust violation. Market share is no longer viewed in a static but in a dynamic context. Competition need not be preserved within a given industry because companies can compete with each other across industry lines. Bottles compete with cans, plastic competes with glass, aluminum with steel. Technological advances can open up avenues of competition that did not exist previously. Long-distance telephone service is the best example: what had been considered a natural monopoly has become a highly competitive market. Moreover, the U.S. market is no longer viewed in isolation: international competition protects the interests of the consumer, especially when the dollar is so strong, and the national interest dictates the consolidation of U.S. producers into fewer and stronger units. Whether these considerations will remain as valid in the future as they seem at present is open to question; but, while they prevail, large-scale combinations do not face the political obstacles they would have encountered in previous administrations. I call the process the "oligopolarization" of America.

Under the Carter administration any large-scale acquisition, like the purchase of Utah International by General Electric, provoked an antitrust investigation that slowed down the transaction even if it did not abort it. It was generally believed that companies above a certain size were both immune from attack and disqualified from making significant corporate moves. They lived in a sort of suspended animation with managements safely ensconced and confined to operating their existing businesses. Since this view was rarely challenged, it was not corroborated by evidence but prevailed in the form of a bias. The bias found expression in stock valuations. Smaller companies were perceived as having greater exposure to corporate activity and in consequence tended to be more highly priced. Between 1974 and 1979 the shares of small companies outperformed large ones by a considerable margin, and investors specializing in small capitalization stocks enjoyed a field day. Corporate activity, such as leveraged buyouts, was in fact concentrated in that sector.

After 1980 there was a gradual but perceptible shift. The size of deals increased and industries once considered immune became susceptible to attack. For instance, a few years ago beleaguered companies used to acquire radio or TV stations as a way of defending themselves; now the industry is up for grabs. Both ABC and RCA (which owns NBC) were taken over in friendly deals and CBS, under attack, gained a new controlling shareholder.

The trend was not recognized at first, but as it spread from industry to industry it captured the imagination of investors and it is now fully reflected in share valuations. Since 1980, relative performance has shifted back in favor of large capitalization stocks, and mergermania has undoubtedly played a part in the move. As the process continues, a point will be reached when expectations exceed reality and the stock prices of the candidates will hamper the conclusion of deals. The spread between pre-deal prices and the prices actually paid has already narrowed but the pace of transactions has not yet slackened. Mergermania has generated a momentum of its own and undoubtedly there will be some deals concluded at unreasonable prices before the process exhausts itself.

Looking at mergermania analytically, we may classify the reflexive interaction as primarily self-defeating or self-correcting. If there is a self-reinforcing connection, it is lateral rather than vertical: it expands the number and size of companies affected rather than raising stock values to unsustainable heights. There is relatively little vertical or price action. Successful acquirers, such as GAF Corp., attain higher stock prices and, if they can successfully recapitalize themselves, they can swallow another company. If the process lasts long enough, favorites will emerge with premium valuations that will make it easier for them to fulfill expectations. Mesa Petroleum was in the process of emerging as such a premium company until Unocal stopped it in its tracks. On the other hand, Esmark has gone full circle, first acquiring and then being acquired.

The self-reinforcing connection comes at first from the elimination of a negative bias. What has been done with one company can be done with another and, encouraged by success, people attempt what had not been thought possible before. Eventually excesses are bound to develop. In order to get a better insight we must take a closer look at the players. First, there are the merger and acquisition departments that engineer the corporate transactions; then there are the lawyers who dream up new attacks and new defenses; the actual acquirers; the providers of credit; and the arbitrage traders who hold the stocks before and during deals and often become active participants; finally, there are the regulators who are supposed to supervise the process. All the participants, with the exception of the regulators, stand to earn very large profits from successful transactions.

Excessive profits often lead to other excesses, especially when credit is involved. There is not much point in listing them in a general way. Each transaction is high drama and drama is constructed out of human foibles. A narrative of specific events would recount many mistakes, exaggerations, abuses, as well as some bold maneuvers and brilliant inventions. In this respect, mergermania does not differ from other activities that generate windfall profits. There is a general predilection to pursue such activities until some failures exert a discouraging effect. When credit is used on a large scale, failures can snowball. We have already had at least one occasion when a large arbitrage trader, Ivan Boesky, was forced to liquidate his positions, forcing some others to do likewise. There has also been much concern about the debt accumulated in leveraged buyouts. Until recently most of the credit came from banks. As we have seen, they were trying to grow their way out of their difficulties after the international debt crisis, and leveraged buyouts provided a ready market. But the regulatory authorities started to discourage bank lending for leveraged buyouts even before the twin crises of the Continental Illinois Bank and the Financial Corporation of America. For a time it looked like financing would dry up, and the pace of corporate activity did slow down. That was in the second half of 1984 just after some large oil companies had been gobbled up; the elections were approaching and it was felt that additional takeovers might be politically embarrassing. Mergermania resumed with renewed vigor after the elections but the main source of financing shifted from banks to junk bonds. The shift was probably dictated by necessity—Unocal sued Security Pacific Bank for providing credit to a corporate enemy—but it turned out to be a technical improvement. Junk bonds are more flexible and more easily arranged; they also offer some wrinkles that can be exploited for tax purposes. Drexel Burnham, the dominant force in junk bond financing, can provide almost unlimited funds at short notice.

Will it all come to a bad end? That is impossible to predict. As we have seen, the main reflexive connection is a self-correcting one. The boom/bust model we have developed for conglomerates is not applicable. It is quite likely that the process will burn itself out after it has swept all the ground that is susceptible to it. But a disaster cannot be ruled out. The net effect is to introduce a great deal of debt into the restructured companies. A number of different scenarios could lead to situations where the debt is difficult to service. If the Imperial Circle is reversed and the dollar falls just as the economy slips into recession, interest rates may also rise at the same time and highly leveraged companies would confront the worst of all possible worlds. In the more immediate future, a precipitous fall in oil prices could endanger the cash flow of heavily indebted oil companies like Phillips Petroleum. One major default might unravel the magic circle of junk bond holders.

Up till now, mergermania has not had a detectable influence on the fate of the Imperial Circle. It has probably reduced physical investment activity in the United States by making managements more oriented toward the short term, but investment remained surprisingly strong until recently. Mergermania has probably contributed to credit demands and induced banks to borrow abroad in order to lend at home; but when the role of the banks diminished, the influx of capital from abroad continued. If there is a reflexive connection, it is too subtle to be readily discerned: it has to do with the general attraction the United States holds for foreign capital at the present time.

Another, more ominous, connection is beginning to surface. A great deal of credit is employed in the acquisition of companies; the credit is then repaid by disposing of the assets that served as collateral. Both activities, the nonproductive use of credit and the sale of collateral assets, aggravate the prevailing deflationary trends. Mergermania may thus hasten the unwinding of the Imperial Circle.

Assuming that the process does not end in disaster, what is its overall effect? We find a mixed bag. In contrast to the conglomerate boom where most of the activity was confined to the stock market, many changes will have occurred in the real world. On balance, the profitability of corporations will be enhanced, assets redeployed, and stodgy managements shaken up. Industries will have become more oligopolistic. As long as the Imperial Circle prevails these changes are desirable and probably necessary for the survival of many industries. If and when the competition from imports abates, the changes may turn out to be just the opposite of what is appropriate to the new conditions.* Accepting mergermania as a process of adjustment, we en-

---

*P.S., February 1987: The stock market has begun to reflect the excess profits expected from the "oligopolarization" of America after price competition from abroad has abated.

counter a problem that is inherent in a world of reflexive interactions: adjustment to what? It is like shooting at a target when the act of shooting moves the target.

Even if corporate restructuring qualified as an adjustment process, it would benefit from being slowed down. If the pace were slower, fewer deals would be made because the rate of return would become less favorable. That would be an improvement because there is a tendency to make more deals than are justified by long-term economic considerations. The tax laws are primarily responsible, but the participants playing with other people's money must also share part of the blame. England has a takeover panel that reviews the rules of the game; we could benefit from a similar arrangement.

On the level of theory, this analysis shows that the boom/bust model is not directly applicable to all reflexive processes. With this lesson in mind, we shall now address the question: what will be the eventual outcome of the Imperial Circle?

P.S., DECEMBER 1986

As it happened, mergermania outlasted the Imperial Circle. Junk bonds suffered a few nasty moments when oil dropped below $10 and LTV Corp. defaulted, but the market recovered. Both the equity and the junk bond holders of leveraged buyouts have been greatly helped by the decline in interest rates, although junk bonds have lagged behind high-quality bonds. The Tax Reform Act of 1986 has had the perverse effect of accelerating the pace of transactions prior to its taking effect on January 1, 1987.

Then came the Boesky affair and the arbitrage community was shaken to its core. The full extent of the scandal is not yet known but can be easily imagined. The investigation has already immobilized many of the major players, and it is going to change the way the game is played. By and large, the speculative excesses generated by mergermania will be removed; what will be left is the continuing restructuring of American corporations. The net inflow of cash into junk bonds will be reversed and the extent to which buyouts can be leveraged will be greatly reduced. Most important, it will become more difficult to refinance deals when they turn sour, and the junk aspect of junk bonds will become more apparent.

In short, the Boesky affair constitutes not the end of corporate restructuring but rather a well-defined and highly dramatic turning point in the reflexive aspect of mergermania. As in other similar instances, it will be some time after the turning point when the casualties surface. The EPICs of mergermania are yet to come. (EPIC was the subsidiary that pushed the Community Savings Bank of Maryland into bankruptcy.)

Part Three

THE REAL-TIME
EXPERIMENT

9

The Starting Point:
August 1985

We shall take up the history of the Imperial Circle at around the elections of 1984. Until then, the Imperial Circle had operated without a hitch with both the U.S. economy and the U.S. dollar continuing to rise. The central bankers of the world were fully aware that the situation was unsound and ultimately unsustainable, and there was an episode at the beginning of 1984 when they tried to talk down the dollar but the attempt failed and the dollar rose higher than ever. The economy continued so strong that it overcame even a modest rise in interest rates. Foreigners holding dollar-denominated financial assets were really raking it in. So were those exporting to the United States. Surprisingly, American industry hung in there in the face of severe pressure from imports, reluctant to transfer manufacturing abroad and trying to stay competitive by investing in high technology. The critical point was reached around the final quarter of 1984. The pace of the economy was beginning to slacken and interest rates started to ease but the dollar, after an initial dip, continued to rally. Prevailing opinion had linked the strength of the dollar to the strength of the economy and to the interest rate differential. When the dollar refused to weaken, the last of the trend fighters gave up and the exchange rate went through the roof. That was the straw that broke the camel's back: American industry started in earnest to switch to imports and to foreign-based manufacturing. The strong dollar finally became an American problem.

The conduct of U.S. economic policy underwent a significant change after the elections. Treasury Secretary Donald Regan and presidential adviser James Baker switched places. Until then, the Federal Reserve and the Treasury had been at loggerheads, but now an understanding was reached between them. Slowing down the Imperial Circle became the clear-cut objective. It was to be achieved by reducing the budget deficit and relaxing monetary policy. America's main trading partners were encouraged to give their policy the opposite twist, engaging in fiscal stimulation but keeping up interest rates. It was hoped that under these influences the dollar would finally decline. Treasury Secretary Baker went so far as to express willingness to discuss a reform of the exchange rate system prior to the Bonn economic summit in May 1985, but he failed to follow through. He was also unsuccessful in gaining control of the budget-cutting process in Congress; nevertheless, the administration is clearly determined to accept whatever form Congress chooses for cutting the budget.

The dollar did respond with a thump, falling by about 15% against the German mark. Then it stabilized for about three months, and recently it started declining again. The adjustment so far is unlikely to bring any significant relief to industry. The economy is now divided into two segments: the tradable goods sector is in recession with the capital goods sector particularly weak, but the service and defense sectors are still strong. Interest rates have fallen significantly and that is stimulating the economy, but as long as the dollar remains anywhere near its present level, much of the stimulation will find its way abroad through increased imports. Most important, the pressure on profits in the tradable goods sector is unlikely to relent.

What is the outlook? We can draw up two scenarios. In the first the dollar declines by, say, 20–25%, bringing relief to the tradable goods sector. Inflation may pick up a little, although the rise in import prices may be compensated for by a decline in oil prices, but the economy recovers, putting a floor under the dollar. This is the so-called soft landing scenario. Its prospects are better than at any time since the inception of the Imperial Circle because the authorities have finally recognized the need to bring the self-reinforcing process under control and are cooperating to that end. It is conceivable that the ever more violent swings in exchange rates will moderate as—unannounced and unrecognized as usual—we pass from a system of free floating to a system of managed floating.

The other possibility is that the dollar refuses to decline and, when it finally breaks, it does so precipitously. At first, foreign exporters absorb whatever small decline occurs and do not raise their selling prices in the face of a weakening market. The tradable goods sector continues under pressure, and the weakness threatens to spread to the other sectors. The Federal Reserve, determined not to allow the economy to slip into recession because of the dire consequences it would have on the banking system, continues to pump money into the economy but much of the stimulation continues to leak out in the form of imports. Eventually, a critical point is reached when foreigners become reluctant to hold dollars, long-term interest rates rise in the face of rising money supply numbers, the dollar declines precipitously, and inflation prospects deteriorate even as the economy enters into a full-fledged recession.

This may be called the disaster scenario, because a recession would expose an exceedingly fragile financial structure to a test that it is unlikely to withstand without severe damage. The heavily indebted countries have barely entered into Phase 3 of their adjustment process. A weakening in demand for their exports could push them back into Phase 2 and the setback may be more than they can bear. At home, the adjustment process is even less advanced. A recession would reduce the earnings capacity of borrowers; it would also undermine the resale value of the assets that serve as collateral. As banks try to liquidate foreclosed property they set into motion a self-reinforcing process: other borrowers are pushed over the brink. The process is already under way in the oil patch and in farming; in a recession it would spread to other sectors of the economy.

This is where we stand at present (August 1985). As a market participant, I must make some decisions based on my evaluation of the probable course of events. The theory of reflexivity, as it has been developed so far, does not yield any clear-cut predictions, but it can be helpful in formulating my views. I have used it in that capacity before and I shall attempt to do so now.

I propose an experiment. I shall record the views that guide me in my investment decisions at the present time and I shall revise them on a real-time basis while the book is in preparation. I shall terminate the experiment when the book goes to the printer and the reader will be able to judge the results. This will provide a practical test of the value, if any, of my approach. It will also provide an insight into the decision-making process of one market participant.

A few words of explanation are needed about the investment

fund I manage.★ Quantum Fund is a unique instrument: it uses leverage; it operates in many markets; and, most important, I manage it as if it were my own money—which it is to a large extent. Many funds share one of these features, but I do not know of any other that combines them all.

The best way to understand the role of leverage is to think of an ordinary investment portfolio as something flat and loose, as its name implies. Leverage adds a third dimension: credit. What was a loosely held together, flat portfolio becomes a tightly knit three-dimensional structure in which the equity base has to support the credit used.

Leveraged funds usually employ their borrowed capital in the same way as their equity base. That is not the case in Quantum Fund. We operate in many markets, and we generally invest our equity in stocks and use our leverage to speculate in commodities. Commodities in this context include stock index futures as well as bonds and currencies. Stocks are generally much less liquid than commodities. By investing less than our entire equity capital in relatively illiquid stocks, we avoid the danger of a catastrophic collapse in case of a margin call.

In managing the Fund, I distinguish between macroeconomic and microeconomic investment concepts. The former usually dictate our exposure in the various commodity markets, including the stock market, while the latter find expression in our stock selection. Thus the ownership of a specific stock has both a macro and a micro aspect in the sense that it affects the total size of the Fund's stock market exposure, and, if it is a foreign stock, it also affects the Fund's currency exposure. By contrast, a stock index or currency position has only a macro aspect. We can, of course, always neutralize the macro aspect of a stock position through stock indexes and currency futures.

As far as currencies are concerned, I believe that a system of fluctuating exchange rates presents an existential choice: one cannot avoid having one's equity invested in some currency, and not making a decision about currency exposure is also a decision—unless, of course, one were to buy a currency option, in which case one would pay a measurable price for avoiding the choice. The logical consequence of my attitude is that I feel obliged to make a decision about currencies even if I do not have a well-formulated macroeconomic investment concept.

★Written in January 1987.

The results can be disastrous. Sometimes I envy my more ignorant fund-managing colleagues who do not know that they face an existential choice; for instance, they avoided the losses I incurred in the 1981–1985 period when the dollar continued to appreciate.

It can be seen that Quantum Fund combines some of the features of a stock market fund with those of a commodity fund. Historically, Quantum Fund operated at first almost exclusively in stocks; only as macroeconomic conditions became increasingly unstable did bonds and currencies assume increased importance. In the last few years macroeconomic speculation has become paramount. The degree of leverage we employ is much more modest than in pure commodity funds, and the exposure in various markets serves to balance as well as to leverage the portfolio.

The Fund's maximum exposure in any direction is subject to self-imposed limits. If one relied on the limits imposed by margin regulations, one would be asking for trouble, because one would be forced to liquidate positions at the most inconvenient moments. One needs a safety margin over and above the margin requirements. The safety margin can be quantified by looking at the uncommitted buying power, but it is not a reliable measure because different types of investments carry widely divergent margin requirements. For instance, most U.S. stocks require a 50% margin, foreign stocks only 30–35%, and the margin on S&P futures is only 6%. Where to limit one's exposure is one of the most difficult questions in operating a leveraged fund, and there is no hard and fast answer. As a general rule, I try not to exceed 100% of the Fund's equity capital in any one market, but I tend to adjust my definition of what constitutes a market to suit my current thinking. For instance, I may add non-market-related stocks and market-related stocks together or keep them separate as the mood takes me.

Generally speaking, I am more concerned with preserving the Fund's capital than its recent profits, so that I tend to become more liberal with self-imposed limits when my investment concepts seem to be working. Where to draw the line between capital and profit is no easy task when practically the entire capital consists of accumulated profits. The historical record up to the beginning of the experiment is summarized below. It will be seen that the only year prior to 1985 when the Fund more than doubled was 1980, and that was followed by a debacle in 1981.

Quantum Fund N.V.			
Date	Net Asset Value Per "A" Share	Change from Preceding Year	Size of Fund
01/31/69	$ 41.25	—	$ —
12/31/69	53.37	+29.4%	6,187,701
12/31/70	62.71	+17.5%	9,664,069
12/31/71	75.45	+20.3%	12,547,644
12/31/72	107.26	+42.2%	20,181,332
12/31/73	116.22	+8.4%	15,290,922
12/31/74	136.57	+17.5%	18,018,835
12/31/75	174.23	+27.6%	24,156,284
12/31/76	282.07	+61.9%	43,885,267
12/31/77	369.99	+31.2%	61,652,385
12/31/78	573.94	+55.1%	103,362,566
12/31/79	912.90	+59.1%	178,503,226
12/31/80	1,849.17	+102.6%	381,257,160
12/31/81	1,426.06	−22.9%	193,323,019
12/31/82	2,236.97	+56.9%	302,854,274
12/31/83	2,795.05	+24.9%	385,532,688
12/31/84	3,057.79	+9.4%	448,998,187
8/16/85★	4,379.00	+43.2%	647,000,000

★Unaudited.

During Phase I of the experiment, the Fund's activities revolved mainly around macroeconomic issues; the microeconomic concepts did not change much, and their contribution to the fund's performance was relatively insignificant. Accordingly, in summarizing the Fund's investment posture I focused only on the macro aspect. The situation changed during the Control Period: specific investment concepts made an increasing contribution to the Fund's performance. This was in accordance with my macro conclusion that it was time to play the stock market. Since the microplays became important only during the Control Period, I refrain from discussing them, with one exception: my play in Japanese real-estate-related stocks enters into the discussion in Phase 2.

The macro posture of the Fund is summarized in a table following each diary entry, and the activities and performance of the Fund are shown graphically at the end of each phase of the experiment. The graphic presentation for the Control Period has been subdivided into two parts because it is roughly twice as long as the experimental phases. Thus, the graphs are broken down into four roughly equal time periods.

NOTE: Here is the key for the parenthetical numbers (1) through (6) that appear in the diary-entry tables throughout the real-time experiment:

(1) Includes net dollar value of futures contracts.

(2) Net purchases (+) or sales (-) since previous report.

(3) Reduced to a common denominator of 30-year government bonds. For instance, $100 million in face value of 4-year Treasury notes is equivalent to $28.5 million in market value of 30-year government bonds.

(4) U.S. Treasury bills and notes up to two years to maturity; these also have been reduced to a common denominator of 30-year bond equivalents (see note 3).

(5) These bonds have considerably less volatility than U.S. government bonds. For instance, as of June 30, 1986, $100 million in face value of Japanese government bonds had the same volatility as roughly $66.2 million in 30-year U.S. government bonds. We have not adjusted for this difference.

(6) Net currency exposure includes stocks, bonds, futures, cash, and margins and equals the total equity of the Fund. A short position in dollars indicates the amount by which exposure in the major currencies (DM-related European currencies, yen, and sterling) exceeds the capital of the Fund. Exposure in other currencies (most of which do not fluctuate as much as the major currencies) are shown separately. They are not deemed relevant in calculating the Fund's dollar exposure.

Also, the percentage changes in net asset values in these tables refer to per-share figures. The figures for Quantum Fund's aggregate equity are affected, albeit modestly, by subscriptions and redemptions.

10

Phase 1: August 1985– December 1985

BEGINNING OF THE EXPERIMENT: SUNDAY, AUGUST 18, 1985*

The stock market has recently adopted the thesis that the rapid rise in money supply is presaging a stronger economy. Cyclical stocks started to improve, while interest-rate-sensitive and defensive stocks suffered a setback. I had to decide what posture to adopt. I was inclined to doubt the thesis, but I did not have enough conviction to fight it. Accordingly, I did nothing. My stock portfolio consists primarily of companies that stand to benefit from corporate restructuring and of property insurance shares that follow a cycle of their own.

As regards currencies, I have been leaning toward a soft-landing scenario. In fact, I could envision the possibility that a stronger economy would tend to strengthen the dollar. With so many speculators short, this could lead to a sharp, if temporary, rebound. Thus, being short the dollar was not without risk. Accordingly, I had significantly reduced my currency positions. For reasons I shall outline below, I rebuilt them in the last few days.

I have been inclined to be optimistic on the prospects of a soft

---

*Charts showing the posture and performance of Quantum Fund in Phase 1 follow p. 190. The key to the parenthetical note references (1) through (6) in the diary-entry tables can be found on p. 151.

Aug. 16, 1985					
	Closing *8/16/85*			*Closing* *8/16/85*	
DM	2.7575		S&P 500	186.12	
¥	236.75		U.S. T-Bonds	76²⁴/₃₂	
£	1.4010		Eurodollar	91.91	
Gold	337.90		Crude Oil	28.03	
			Japanese Bonds	—	

QUANTUM FUND EQUITY $647,000,000
Net Asset Value Per Share $4,379
Change from 12/31/84 +43.2%

Portfolio Structure (in millions of dollars)

Investment Positions (1)	Long	Short	Net Currency Exposure (6)	Long	Short
Stocks			DM–related	467	
US Stocks	666	(62)	Japanese Yen	244	
Foreign			Pound Sterling	9	
Stocks	183		US Dollar		(73)
Bonds (3)			Other		
US Gvt.			Currencies	50	
Short					
Term (4)		(67)			
Long					
Term		(46)			
Commodities					
Oil		(121)			
Gold					

landing because the decline of the dollar was induced by the authorities; a spontaneous fall would have been much more dangerous. Since the reelection of Reagan, the authorities have been moving in the right direction and there seems to be a greater degree of cooperation among them. Practically all the excesses of the Imperial Circle are in the process of being corrected: banks are returning to sounder practices, the budget deficit is being cut, and interest rates are being reduced.

My optimism is tempered by the insight that the time when past excesses are corrected is the period of greatest risk. The excesses were meeting a certain need; otherwise they would not have developed in the first place. Can the system function without them? Moreover, the process of correction can develop its own momentum, setting off a self-reinforcing trend in the opposite direction.

Everything hinges on the outlook of the economy. If the economy strengthened in the second half of 1985, all would be well. Even if there were renewed weakness in 1986, the financial structure would already be in a stronger position to withstand the consequences. In any case, that eventuality is too far removed to have any relevance to current investment decisions.

I consider myself ill-qualified to match wits with professionals who have much more information at their disposal in predicting the actual course of the economy. That is why I have chosen to stay on the sidelines in cyclical stocks.

The single most important variable is consumer spending. Some experts claim that consumers are overextended; others argue that if you make money available, the American consumer can be counted on to spend it. Who am I to judge? The only competitive edge I have is the theory of reflexivity. It leads me to diverge from the consensus opinion on the negative side. I believe we are in a period of credit contraction where collateral values are eroding. It would be appropriate if consumers failed to respond to stimulation. This is a typical Keynesian situation where the horse is taken to the water: will it drink? I need more evidence before I can develop any conviction on the negative side.

Recently, I have perceived such signals. Perhaps the most convincing was the market action itself. The stock market was acting suspiciously badly. It may be surprising that I should accept the stock market as a valid indicator after I had enunciated the principle that markets are always biased. But I have also claimed that the market has a way of making predictions come true.

Various economic reports also indicated continued weakness. For instance, auto sales were down. I did not attribute any great importance to these reports, because the current weakness is well recognized. What happens when General Motors starts its low interest-rate promotion will be more significant. I was much more impressed with the report that this year's crops are going to set records. This meant that either the distress in the farming sector would increase or much more money would have to be spent on farm price support.

The currencies were pushing against the upper limits of their trading range. The Bundesbank was expected to lower the discount rate, but the mark refused to give ground. On Wednesday, August 14, I decided to establish a half position in the German mark; after the German discount rate was in fact lowered and the mark remained firm, I bought the rest of my position. On Thursday afternoon, the Federal Reserve announced a large increase in M1; the increase in M3 was more moderate. Bonds fell and I recognized that my thesis on currencies was going to be tested. If the conventional wisdom prevailed, currencies ought to fall in the expectation of a stronger economy and higher interest rates. But if the tide has turned, holders of dollar assets ought to respond to a rise in money supply by converting part of that supply into foreign currencies. As it happened, the currencies did not yield, and my thesis was reinforced.

Then came further evidence. On Friday, both housing starts and new permits were weak, especially for multifamily dwellings. This confirmed my suspicion that the housing industry is in trouble. In that case, commercial real estate must be in even worse shape. Bonds rallied, but the stock market continued under pressure.

I am now willing to bet that the slowdown in the economy is going to deteriorate into a recession: the contraction in credit is going to outweigh the increase in money supply. I suspect that the divergence between M1 and M3 is an indication that the horse is not drinking. I am ready to take on a maximum position in currencies, both on a long-term and on a short-term basis and to short bonds on the rally. If the currencies do not respond vigorously, I may have to become more cautious and take a loss on the short-term portion of my currency positions.

It may be asked why I should short bonds if I expect a recession. The answer is that I expect a recession because long-term interest rates will rise on account of a weakening dollar. This is the Imperial Circle moving into reverse gear. I realize that my sale may be premature; consequently I will take only a small starting position. I am also contemplating selling the stock market short but only if it rallies in response to a declining dollar. Both my currency and my bond positions ought to work before I take on the additional exposure.

The majority of my currency positions are in German marks. I also have a significant position in yen but I expect the yen to move slower and later. I should explain why. Japan has a very high savings rate and domestic investment has tapered off. By investing its savings abroad, Japan is able to maintain a level of production well in excess of domestic consumption. This is the way Japan can become a leading economic power in the world: a high savings rate, a persistent export surplus, and an accumulation of foreign assets go hand in hand to enhance Japan's power and influence in the world. Japan is very happy with the Imperial Circle and wants to prolong it as long as possible. The policy is articulated by Japanese officials as follows: "We want the United States to prosper as the leading economic power in the world, because it allows us to prosper as number two." In actual fact, Japan uses the United States as a cyclist uses a car in front of him: to cut the wind resistance. Japan wants to stay behind the United States as long as possible, and it is willing to finance the U.S. budget deficit to this end. Long-term capital outflows from Japan rose from $17.7 billion in 1983 to $49.7 billion in 1984 and the trend is still rising. This has been the single most important factor in keeping the yen down. Now that the trend of the dollar has been reversed, the yen may appreciate against the dollar, but it is likely to fall against the European currencies.

I have had considerable difficulty in arriving at this conclusion. In the 1970s, Japan followed a policy of keeping the value of the yen high, creating a high hurdle that exporters had to pass in order to export profitably. The policy was very successful in favoring the industries in which Japan had the greatest competitive advantage and in discouraging the older, less profitable exports. I would have expected that in an environment where the rest of the world was increasingly unwilling to tolerate a Japanese export surplus, Japan would once again use the price mechanism to ration its exports rather than to expose itself to quantitative restrictions. This would have meant a high exchange rate policy.

I failed to recognize the fundamental dissimilarity between the two sets of circumstances. In the 1970s domestic investment was still very high and available savings needed to be rationed; a high exchange rate served as an efficient method of allocating resources. Now there is an excess of savings for which outlets have to be found. Exporting capital is the best answer. The resistance to Japanese exports remains a stumbling block, but the Japanese hope to overcome it by providing generous credit terms. Hence the willingness to finance the U.S. budget deficit.

The American response is ambivalent. Some elements within the administration are pushing for a higher yen; others are pushing for the sale of U.S. government securities to the Japanese. Ironically, it was American pressure for the liberalization of capital markets that led to the current massive Japanese purchases of U.S. treasury bonds. The interest rate differential in favor of the U.S. was very great, running as high as 6% at times. Once the floodgates were released, Japanese institutions piled in. Since the dollar has started to decline, the total return has become less favorable, but it has not discouraged Japanese investors. On the contrary, they seem to feel that the currency risk is less now that the dollar has declined. Japanese investors are even more herdlike than their American counterparts. Should their bias shift, there could be a stampede in the opposite direction. But that is highly unlikely: the authorities act as shepherds, and they will do whatever is necessary to prevent a stampede. If my analysis is correct, they are likely to keep the appreciation of the yen moderate enough to preserve the prevailing bias in favor of U.S. government bonds.

I should also explain my views on oil prices. A decline is more or less inevitable. Production capacity far exceeds demand and the cartel is in the process of disintegration. Almost every member of OPEC with the exception of Saudi Arabia and Kuwait cheats on prices. As a consequence, Saudi production has fallen to unsustainably low levels. Saudi influence within OPEC has declined in step with output. The only way Saudi Arabia could reassert control is by engaging in an all-out price war that would demonstrate the strength of its market position as low-cost producer. But its market strength is matched by its political weakness. The result is a stalemate that leaves Saudi Arabia immobilized. Market participants are bracing themselves for the impending storm, but in the meantime calm prevails. Spot prices are quite firm, because nobody wants to carry any inventory. The longer the pressures build, the more violent the storm is likely to be when it finally occurs. The supply curve is inverted. Most producers need to generate a certain amount of dollars; as the price falls, they will try to increase the amount sold until the price falls below the point at which high cost producers can break even. Many of them will be unable to service their debt. The U.S. will be forced to introduce a protective tariff to save the domestic producers, and the protection is likely to be extended to Mexico, provided it continues to toe the line on the debt issue.

I have been carrying a short position in oil for quite a while and it has cost me a lot of money. Futures sell at a large discount from cash: carrying the position forward can cost as much as 2% a month. I am now inclined to close out the positions I hold in nearby months and establish a short position for next spring. The price would be lower, but the discount per month would also be lower. If my analysis is correct, the later the break comes the bigger it will be.

The views I have outlined here are sufficient to serve as a basis for what I call macroeconomic investment decisions. But they do not answer the question: what is going to happen to the Imperial Circle? On that issue, my crystal ball is cloudy.

Other things being equal, the recession, if any, ought to be a mild one. Monetary policy has been eased even before we entered a recession; inventories are tightly controlled, and a declining dollar should bring relief to the tradable goods sector, although the benefit may be felt only with a delay of 6 to 18 months. But other things are not equal. The financial structure is already under strain and it may not be able to withstand a recession: defaults could be self-reinforcing, both domestically and internationally. The financial authorities are fully aware of the danger and are determined to do everything in their power to prevent it. If it comes to a choice between recession and inflation, the odds favor inflation. This is not a forecast, but a reading of current monetary policy.

Inflation would not be all bad: it would make the burden of debt more bearable both by reducing real interest rates and by boosting commodity prices. The question is whether a policy of inflation could succeed. It is likely to elicit an allergic reaction from the financial markets, inducing a flight from the dollar and a rise in nominal interest rates. If foreigners become unwilling to finance our budget deficit, there must be a reduction in our GNP one way or another. But then, the Japanese may be willing to continue lending to us even if it provides them with a negative total return.

MONDAY, SEPTEMBER 9, 1985

The experiment is off to a bad start. Currencies peaked shortly after I had taken my full position and plunged precipitously in the last three days. Bonds also peaked and fell. The rise in bonds was sufficient to

	Closing 9/6/85	% Change from 8/16		Closing 9/6/85	% Change from 8/16
			Sept. 6, 1985		
DM	2.9235	−6.0	S&P 500	188.24	−1.1
¥	242.10	−2.3	U.S. T-Bonds	75^{16}/$_{32}$	−1.6
£	1.3275	−5.2	Eurodollar	91.66	−.3
Gold	320.70	−5.1	Crude Oil	27.75	−1.0
			Japanese Bonds	—	

QUANTUM FUND EQUITY $627,000,000
Net Asset Value Per Share $4,238
Change from 8/16/85 -3.2%

Portfolio Structure (in millions of dollars)

Investment Positions (1)	Long	Short	Net Change (2) from 8/16	Net Currency Exposure (6)	Long	Short	Net Change (2) from 8/16
Stocks				DM-related	491		+24
US Stocks	653	(65)	+16	Japanese Yen	308		+64
Foreign				Pound Sterling	10		+1
Stocks	163		−20	US Dollar		(182)	−109
Bonds (3)				Other			
US Gvt.				Currencies	45		−5
Short							
Term (4)			+67				
Long							
Term			+46				
Commodities							
Oil		(145)	−24				
Gold							

scare me out of my small short position with a loss, but I held on to my currency long positions on which I now also show a loss. The only thing that has worked in my favor is oil, where I used a strong market to extend my short positions to next spring. On balance, my trading has been poor, and I am losing heavily since the start of the experiment. Fortunately, the profits I made earlier this year leave me in a still comfortable position.

The cause of the reverse is a spate of statistics that indicate an economic pickup. Money supply soared, the trade deficit declined, employment figures improved, as did retail sales. Auto sales in particular exploded during the first ten days in which the auto companies offered concessionary credit terms. The evidence implies that the horse is drinking, after all.

I am inclined to fight the evidence and if I look hard enough I can find enough quirks to explain most of the figures. One fact remains: the surge in auto sales is sufficient to justify the rather aggressive production schedule auto companies have been working on. Closer inspection shows that almost all the employment gains were auto related. The crucial question is: what is happening to consumer spending as a whole? Are auto sales symptomatic of consumer behavior, or will they be offset by reduced expenditures in other areas? We shall only know the answer when it is too late.

For the time being, I am clinging to the view that the economy is quite weak. The decline in the dollar has not been large enough to bring any relief to manufacturing. Agriculture is in worse shape than ever. Homebuilding could give the economy another boost—housing is primarily dependent on interest rates and employment—but I believe that the fallout from the contraction of credit and erosion of collateral values as exemplified by the collapse of EPIC, the Equity Planning subsidiary of the Community Savings & Loan Association of Maryland, is going to depress the construction industry. Consumer debt is heavy, and strong auto sales now will reduce sales in the future. When 1986 models go on sale next month, the economy ought to slip back to the same position it was in before the auto companies started to force-feed it with promotional credit terms.

The Federal Reserve is reluctant to tighten credit because of the many weaknesses in the financial structure. If dollars are being created faster than foreigners are willing to absorb them, the exchange rate ought to resume its decline—unless the economy is strong enough to induce the Federal Reserve to tighten. It always comes back to the same question: the strength of the economy.

Since I cannot resolve it, I shall be guided by the market. The German mark seems to have established a pattern that consists of a sharp rise, an equally sharp break, and a halfway retracing of the decline followed by a period of consolidation. If the pattern holds, we ought to be at the bottom end of the second break. That would fit in well with my economic scenario. If the pattern is broken, I shall have to cut my exposure in half

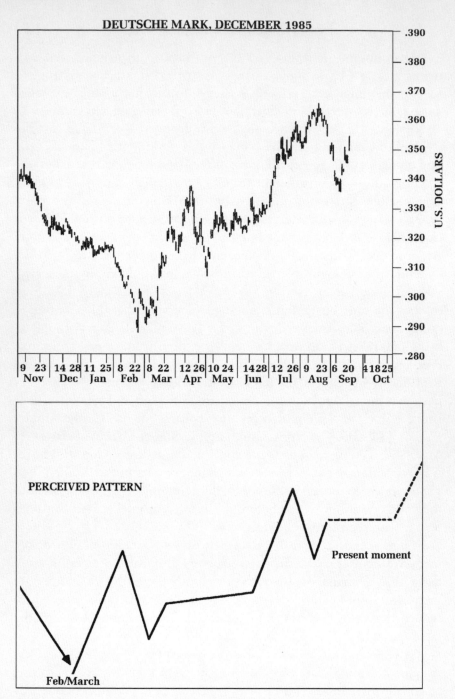

DEUTSCHE MARK, DECEMBER 1985

PERCEIVED PATTERN

Present moment

Feb/March

Chart reprinted by permission from the weekly CRB Futures Chart Service. The FCS is a publication of Commodity Research Bureau, a Knight-Ridder Business Information Service. Editorial offices of CRB are located at 100 Church St., Suite 1850, New York, NY 10007. All material is protected by copyright and may not be reproduced without permission.

162

until I can reassess the economic scenario. This will inevitably result in a loss because, if my expectations are correct, I shall not be able to reestablish my position without paying up, and, if I am wrong, I will have an additional loss on the half position that I kept. That is the penalty I must pay for having taken too large a position at the wrong time.

If my currency positions looked safer, I would consider buying some government bonds in the next refunding because real interest rates are once again reaching unsustainable levels, especially if Saudi Arabia is really going to step up oil production.

My views on the longer term outlook are once again beginning to veer toward the pessimistic side. The financial structure has sustained additional damage. I have already mentioned the EPIC story; the Farm Credit System has gone public with its problems; and the liquidity crisis in South Africa is establishing a new precedent that may encourage banks to act even faster the next time a similar situation arises. Although the U.S. economy is showing signs of strength, the position of our financial institutions is weaker than it seemed a few weeks ago.

SATURDAY, SEPTEMBER 28, 1985

We live in exciting times. The emergency meeting of the Group of Five finance ministers and heads of central banks at the Plaza Hotel last Sunday constitutes a historic event. It marks the official transition from a system of free floating to a system of managed floating. Readers of my chapter on reflexivity in currency markets will realize that I regard the change as overdue.

I managed to hang on to my currency positions by the skin of my teeth and after the meeting of the Group of Five last Sunday, I made the killing of a lifetime. I plunged in, buying additional yen on Sunday night (Monday morning in Hong Kong) and hung on to them through a rising market. The profits of the last week more than made up for the accumulated losses on currency trading in the last four years, and overall I am now well ahead.

What gave me the courage to hold on to my currency positions was the pronounced weakness of the stock market. The strength of the dollar depends on the strength of the economy. A decline in stock prices can have considerable influence on the spending decisions of consumers and the investment decisions of those in business. Moreover, if there is going to

	Closing 9/27/85	% Change from 9/6		Closing 9/27/85	% Change from 9/6
DM	2.6820	+8.3	S&P 500	181.30	−3.7
¥	217.24	+10.3	U.S. T-Bonds	$75^{18}/_{32}$	+.1
£	1.4190	+6.9	Eurodollar	91.71	+.1
Gold	328.40	+2.4	Crude Oil	28.93	+4.3
			Japanese Bonds	—	

Sept. 27, 1985

QUANTUM FUND EQUITY $675,000,000
Net Asset Value Per Share $4,561
Change from 9/6/85   +7.6%
Change from 8/16/85   +4.2%

Portfolio Structure (in millions of dollars)

Investment Positions (1)	Long	Short	Net Change (2) from 9/6	Net Currency Exposure (6)	Long	Short	Net Change (2) from 9/6
Stocks				DM–related	550		+59
US Stocks	530	(85)	−143	Japanese Yen	458		+150
Foreign				Pound Sterling		(44)	−54
Stocks	142		−21	US Dollar		(289)	−107
Bonds (3)				Other			
US Gvt.				Currencies	16		−29
Short							
Term (4)							
Long							
Term		(77)	−77				
Commodities							
Oil		(176)	−31				
Gold							

be a recession, it will be brought on by the decline in collateral values, and the stock market is one of the most important repositories of collateral.

The deutsche mark barely held within the perceived pattern and my nerves were sorely tested, but by the time the Group of Five met, the mark had rallied in conformity with the perceived pattern. I am glad to report that the market reaction to the meeting broke the per-

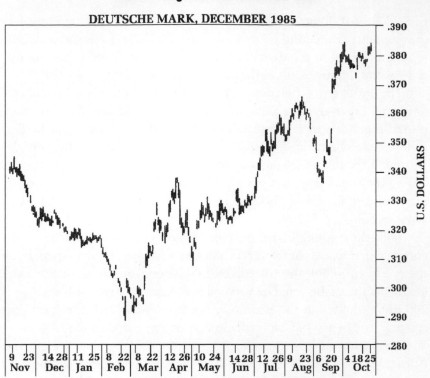

DEUTSCHE MARK, DECEMBER 1985

U.S. DOLLARS

Chart reprinted by permission from the weekly CRB Futures Chart Service. The FCS is a publication of Commodity Research Bureau, a Knight-Ridder Business Information Service. Editorial offices of CRB are located at 100 Church St., Suite 1850, New York, NY 10007. All material is protected by copyright and may not be reproduced without permission.

ceived pattern. Patterns are there to be broken by historic events and the meeting truly qualifies as one.

The meeting was organized at the initiative of the Treasury. The Federal Reserve was brought in relatively late. Its main purpose was to relieve the intensity of protectionist pressure. It was held on an emergency basis and no comprehensive policy was developed in advance. Still, a commitment was made and the policies will follow. How the currencies are going to be managed remains to be seen. Market intervention can be effective only in the short run: it needs to be backed up by other measures. In my opinion, most of the running will have to be done by the Japanese. In Japan, the central bank still has sufficient prestige and influence that it can move up the yen more or less at will; but, to keep it up, the authorities will have to stem the outflow of capital and find additional domestic uses for savings by cutting taxes or increasing governmental expenditures or both. In addition, significant steps will have to be taken to remove nontariff barriers to imports. If not enough is done, the improvement in the yen will be difficult to maintain.

The problem of the European currencies is different. Speculative flows are larger and the influence of central banks weaker. The mark moved much less than the yen, indicating that speculators and holders of liquid assets remain doubtful about the significance of the new departure. If the mark continues to appreciate, the difficulty will be in arresting the trend. It would not surprise me if Volcker spent most of his time Sunday discussing not how to bring down the dollar, but how to arrest its fall.

Since the meeting I have concentrated on the yen because that is the currency that matters as far as protectionist sentiment is concerned, but if the policy of intervention is successful, I intend to stay with the mark longer than with the yen. The yen will appreciate to a reasonable level, say 200 to the dollar, but the mark may become overvalued. Eventually, the real play may be in gold, especially in case of a recession in the U.S.

The action in stock prices has been much worse than I expected. In fact, I bought the S&P Futures after the Group of Five meeting for a trade and I had to liquidate the position with a loss. Altogether, the market action is quite ominous. The erosion of collateral values seems to be much worse than I anticipated a few months ago. I now believe that the economy will slip into a recession before the measures now undertaken will have had time to bring relief. I also believe that additional measures will be forthcoming. Just as protectionist pressures brought a change in the exchange rate regime, the pressure of high real interest rates may well bring a far-reaching arms agreement and détente at the November summit. I am worried about the next six months, but I see better prospects for positive policy initiatives than at any time since the Imperial Circle came into existence. On balance, I do not see much scope in taking a bearish posture in stocks, although I see a lot of merit in liquidity and I wish I had more of it.

My short positions in oil have been going against me. The Soviet Union cut back on deliveries and Kargh Island has been effectively put out of action. I decided to cover my short position for March and April by going long for January. The discount is the largest between now and January. Keeping a short position open has become very expensive. By buying for January, I have effectively stopped the clock; I intend to reestablish my short position later.

SUNDAY, OCTOBER 20, 1985

The currency market has been rife with rumors of impending action during the weekend or during Japanese Prime Minister Yasuhiro Nakasone's visit to the United States. I am inclined to discount the rumors. In fact, I am using the current strength to somewhat reduce my short positions in the dollar. I intend to increase them further during the refunding period for U.S. government bonds.

Since the Group of Five meeting, there has been a lot of controversy between the Treasury and the White House, on the one hand, and the Federal Reserve on the other, some of which has seeped into the press. The politicians seem to advocate "dirty intervention" in currency markets, while the Federal Reserve has religiously sterilized all the dollars it sold by selling an equivalent amount of Treasury bills. The politicians argue that sterilized intervention never works in the long run, but if the sale of dollars is allowed to increase the money supply the exchange rate is bound to fall. Volcker's reply is that there is no need to be so aggressive because the dollar is going to decline anyhow. If the markets are flooded with dollars, the dollar may go in to a free fall that may be difficult to arrest. Volcker seems to be more concerned with preventing a collapse than with inducing a decline, and I sympathize with what I believe to be his position.

If I were in his place I would keep interest rates stable until the refunding is completed, selling foreigners all the dollars they want for the purchase of government securities, and I would lower interest rates after the auctions. This would ensure that the auctions are successful and it would provide me with a large war chest to arrest the decline of the dollar when it has gone far enough. The economy is very weak and both interest rates and the dollar need to be brought down. By waiting with an interest rate reduction until after the auctions I could make a large-scale, sterilized sale of dollars at a level that would look very good later.

It is this line of argument that prompts me to buy some dollars now. The market may be disappointed if there is no immediate action on interest rates, allowing the Federal Reserve to sell dollars at higher prices. That is when I want to increase my short position even further. I am also interested in buying bonds in the refunding unless they go up too much in the meantime. I have not made any major moves in the stock market but I have whittled down my long positions and enlarged my short positions to a point where I seem to have a slight negative market exposure, although my long positions far outweigh my shorts in actual dollar amounts. I am increasing my short positions in Texas and California banks.

Oct. 18, 1985

	Closing 10/18/85	% Change from 9/27		Closing 10/18/85	% Change from 9/27
DM	2.6265	+2.1	S&P 500	187.04	+3.2
¥	214.75	+1.1	U.S. T-Bonds	76²²/₃₂	+1.5
£	1.4290	+.7	Eurodollar	91.80	+.1
Gold	362.80	+10.5	Crude Oil	29.52	+2.0
			Japanese Bonds	—	

QUANTUM FUND EQUITY	$721,000,000
Net Asset Value Per Share	$4,868
Change from 9/27/85	+6.7%
Change from 8/16/85	+11.2%

Portfolio Structure (in millions of dollars)

Investment Positions (1)	Long	Short	Net Change (2) from 9/27	Net Currency Exposure (6)	Long	Short	Net Change (2) from 9/27
Stocks				DM-related	680		+130
US Stocks	522	(148)	−71	Japanese Yen	546		+88
US Index				Pound Sterling		(72)	−28
Futures		(121)	−121	US Dollar		(433)	−144
Foreign				Other			
Stocks	152		+10	Currencies	34		+18
Bonds (3)							
US Gvt.							
Short							
Term (4)							
Long							
Term			+77				
Commodities							
Oil		(37)	+139				
Gold							

SATURDAY, NOVEMBER 2, 1985

I got my timing wrong. My dollar sales looked good until the Japanese central bank surprised me and the rest of the market by raising short-term interest rates. I took this as the beginning of a new phase in the Group of Five plan in which exchange rates are influenced not

Nov. 1, 1985					
	Closing 11/1/85	*% Change from 10/18*		*Closing 11/1/85*	*% Change from 10/18*
DM	2.5910	+1.4	S&P 500	191.48	+2.4
¥	208.45	+2.9	U.S. T-Bonds	$78^{23}/_{32}$	+2.6
£	1.4415	+.9	Eurodollar	92.07	+.3
Gold	326.10	−10.1	Crude Oil	30.39	+2.9
			Japanese Bonds	92.75	

QUANTUM FUND EQUITY $759,000,000
Net Asset Value Per Share $5,115
Change from 10/18/85   +5.1%
Change from 8/16/85   +16.8%

Portfolio Structure (in millions of dollars)

Investment Positions (1)	Long	Short	Net Change (2) from 10/18	Net Currency Exposure (6)	Long	Short	Net Change (2) from 10/18
Stocks				DM-related	630		−50
US Stocks	546	(148)	+24	Japanese Yen	813		+267
US Index				Pound Sterling		(88)	−16
Futures		(46)	+75	US Dollar		(596)	−163
Foreign				Other			
Stocks	209		+57	Currencies	34		0
Bonds (3)							
US Gvt.							
Short							
Term (4)	28		+28				
Long							
Term	456		+456				
Commodities							
Oil		(186)	−149				
Gold							

only by direct intervention but also by adjusting interest rates. Accordingly, I piled into the yen. When the yen moved, I also bought back the marks I had sold. I lost money on the trade but ended up with the increased position I wanted. At today's prices I have a profit on the maneuver.

There is something unsound about increasing one's exposure in the course of a trend because it makes one vulnerable to a temporary reversal. It will be recalled that a reversal came close to making me disgorge my currencies at the wrong time earlier in this experiment. The reason I am nevertheless willing to increase my exposure is that I believe that the scope for a reversal has diminished. One of the generalizations I established about freely floating exchange rates is that short-term volatility is greatest at turning points and diminishes as a trend becomes established. That is the case now. The fact that we are no longer in a system of freely floating exchange rates should diminish the risk of a reversal even further. Market participants have not yet recognized the new rules; the amount of exposure they are willing to carry is influenced by the volatility they have experienced in the past. The same is true of me, or I would have reached my present level of exposure much earlier, and I would have made even more money on the move. By the time all the participants have adjusted, the rules of the game will change again. If the authorities handle the situation well, the rewards for speculating in currencies will become commensurate with the risks. Eventually, speculation will be discouraged by the lack of rewards, the authorities will have attained their goal, and it will be time for me to stop speculating.

I have also missed the beginning of a move in bonds. When interest rates rose in Japan and to a lesser extent in Germany, the market recognized that interest rates must fall in the United States and bond prices rose in anticipation. My well-laid plan of buying in the auction was preempted. I had to run after a moving vehicle and climb aboard the best I could. So far, I have established a half position at not very good prices. I intend to double up in the next auction series in November. I must also consider increasing my stock market exposure for reasons that I shall explain.

This is a good time to reassess the entire outlook. The controversy surrounding the Gramm-Rudman amendment has clearly demonstrated that public opinion is in favor of cutting the budget deficit. The Gramm-Rudman amendment was a brilliant device to enable the president to cut programs that would be otherwise untouchable. The cuts would start to take effect after the 1986 elections. The House of Representatives has gone one better by insisting that the cuts should start in the current fiscal year and fall more heavily on defense. The Senate version would have favored the Republicans in the 1986 election, but the House Democrats turned the table by exempting many social programs and bringing forward the effective date. The White House is in a quandary: it must do something about the budget deficit in order to pave the way to lower interest rates, but to raise taxes before the 1986 elections would be suicidal. There is a way out: to reach some accommodation with the Soviet Union at the summit meeting and reduce defense spending. The budget issue would be resolved and the Republicans could run in the 1986 election as the party of peace. It remains to be seen whether Reagan is interested in this solution.

If it came to pass, we would enter a phase of great prosperity with lower interest rates, a lower dollar, and a stock market boom. The enthusiasm generated by these moves would help to get the economy going again and the Baker Plan announced at the recent annual meeting of the World Bank in Seoul would help to keep the heavily indebted countries from collapsing. Mergermania would receive one last push from lower interest rates but it would eventually run out of steam because rising stock prices would make new deals uneconomic. With the benefits of corporate restructuring, profits would soar in a more benign environment and, with the shrinkage of equity capital that has occurred, stock prices could go through the roof. Eventually, the boom would be followed by a bust in which the uneconomic deals come apart and the international debt problem also comes back to haunt us, but stock prices would have to rise before they can collapse. That is why I am contemplating raising my stock market exposure.

We are approaching the moment of truth. If Reagan flubs his opportunity, the consequences could be serious. We are hovering on the edge of a recession and we need both lower interest rates and a lower dollar to prevent an unraveling of credit. Even then, quite a lot of monetary stimulation may be needed to get the economy going again. It takes time for the decline in the value of the dollar to bring relief from import competition. In the first instance, the expectation of higher prices may divert domestic demand to imported goods. Only a significant drop in short-term interest rates, accompanied by better bond and stock prices, could reverse sentiment in time to prevent a recession. Without an agreement on Gramm-Rudman, the bond market could be disappointed, the Federal Reserve would be reluctant to lower interest rates aggressively, and the erosion in collateral values would continue.

The collapse of the International Tin Council provides a perfect illustration of the erosion of collateral values. The collapse of OPEC is only a matter of time now. I am increasing my short positions in oil for January to March delivery. By the same token I am buying oil-refining stocks, because the increased flow should help their margins. As for the big picture, the next couple of weeks will tell the tale. The summit meeting is on November 19 and the budget debate has to be resolved before the next auction can take place. That is why I have decided to wait until the auction before taking a full position in bonds.

SATURDAY, NOVEMBER 9, 1985

My views on currencies are being tested. After a sharp rise in the yen, there was a sharp reversal last Thursday. I was told that the Bundesbank had bought dollars below DM 2.60 but it sold them again at DM 2.645 on Friday. In accordance with my contention that there is less risk in the market I refused to be panicked.

The bond market is poised for a breakout on the upside. There are large option positions in Treasury bond futures that expire next Friday. If the futures price moves above 80 before then, I intend to sell all or part of my position, because I believe the market is vulnerable. The White House cannot compromise on the budget before the summit on November 19 and the Democrats will continue to press their advantage. This means a stalemate for the next week or so, followed by an auction as soon as it is resolved. I would be happy to withdraw from the market with a profit, putting me in a strong position to buy at the time of the auction.

The stock market has also been strong. Divergences have persisted but the market broadened out on Friday. A breakout in bonds could coincide with a temporary top in the stock market, to be followed by a correction. I want to use that opportunity to cover my shorts and prepare to take a long position. If the correction does not occur, I shall cover my shorts with a loss and if the summit is successful go long at higher prices.

	Nov. 8, 1985				
	Closing *11/8/85*	*% Change* *from 11/1*		*Closing* *11/8/85*	*% Change* *from 11/1*
DM	2.6220	−1.2	S&P 500	193.72	+1.2
¥	205.50	+1.4	U.S. T-Bonds	79$^{21}/_{32}$	+1.2
£	1.4170	−1.7	Eurodollar	92.14	+.1
Gold	324.20	−0.6	Crude Oil	30.45	+.2
			Japanese Bonds	93.70	+1.0

QUANTUM FUND EQUITY $782,000,000
Net Asset Value Per Share $5,267
Change from 11/1/85   +3.0%
Change from 8/16/85   +20.3%

Portfolio Structure (in millions of dollars)

Investment Positions (1)	Long	Short	*Net Change (2) from 11/1*	*Net Currency Exposure (6)*	Long	Short	*Net Change (2) from 11/1*
Stocks				DM-related	654		+24
US Stocks	569	(127)	+44	Japanese Yen	806		−7
US Index				Pound Sterling		(86)	+2
Futures			+46	US Dollar		(592)	+4
Foreign				Other			
Stocks	206		−3	Currencies	42		+8
Bonds (3)							
US Gvt.							
Short							
Term (4)	82		+54				
Long							
Term	498		+42				
Commodities							
Oil		(187)	−1				
Gold							

SATURDAY, NOVEMBER 23, 1985

The markets continue to preempt me. Both stocks and bonds rose strongly in advance of the summit meeting and the buying opportunity I was waiting for in connection with the government bond auction did not materialize. Instead of selling my bonds, I increased my position and I also bought some stock index futures because I did not want to miss a strategic opportunity on account of a tactical error.

I also took a significant position in Japanese bond futures. This is a new market in which I have no previous experience, but the market participants I compete with must have even less experience. The Japanese bond futures market collapsed (from 102 to 92) when the Japanese government raised short-term interest rates. Experience has taught me that the best buying opportunities in long-term bonds present themselves when the yield curve is inverted—which is the case in Japan today. The rise in Japanese interest rates is bound to be temporary: the Group of Five wants to stimulate worldwide economic activity, not to dampen it. A reduction in U.S. interest rates would be matched by the other major industrial countries and, if the impact on exchange rates can be neutralized, the reduction may go further than currently envisioned. I am making the same bet in Japan as in the U.S. and the odds seem even better.

I am now fully invested in all directions: stocks, bonds, and currencies. I would have obtained better prices if I had not tried to finesse it, or if the finesse had worked—but the main thing is that I reached the posture I wanted. I am looking for an opportunity to shift from bonds to stocks but I consider it prudent not to increase my overall exposure any further.

Events have unfolded more or less as I expected. The only hitch was in the Gramm-Rudman amendment. Congress passed a one-month extension of the debt ceiling, enabling the auction to go forward while the fate of Gramm-Rudman remains unresolved.

The summit meeting lived up to my expectations. I believe a radical shift in U.S.-Soviet relations is in the making. Both sides need to reduce their military spending and both sides have much to gain from closer cooperation. The opportunity was there and President Reagan seized it. By not making any concessions on Star Wars, Reagan has put himself in a position to usher in another period of détente without exposing himself to criticism for selling out to the Russians. In this context, the Gramm-Rudman amendment may come in positively useful as a mechanism for cutting the military budget without appearing to want to. The most eminently cuttable part of the military budget is retirement benefits—

Nov. 22, 1985					
	Closing 11/22/85	*% Change from 11/8*		*Closing 11/22/85*	*% Change from 11/8*
DM	2.5665	+2.1	S&P 500	201.52	+4.0
¥	201.00	+2.2	U.S. T-Bonds	80$^{27}/_{32}$	+1.5
£	1.4640	+3.3	Eurodollar	92.02	−.1
Gold	326.90	+.8	Crude Oil	30.91	+1.5
			Japanese Bonds	94.80	+1.2

QUANTUM FUND EQUITY $841,000,000
Net Asset Value Per Share $5,669
Change from 11/8/85   +7.6%
Change from 8/16/85   +29.5%

Portfolio Structure (in millions of dollars)

Investment Positions (1)	Long	Short	Net Change (2) from 11/8	Net Currency Exposure (6)	Long	Short	Net Change (2) from 11/8
Stocks				DM-related	668		+14
US Stocks	664	(83)	+139	Japanese Yen	827		+21
US Index				Pound Sterling		(87)	−1
Futures	126		+126	US Dollar		(567)	+25
Foreign				Other			
Stocks	251		+45	Currencies	40		−2
Bonds (3)							
US Gvt.							
Short							
Term (4)	105		+23				
Long							
Term	969		+471				
Japanese							
(5)	354		+354				
Commodities							
Oil		(214)	−27				
Gold							

Stockman made an impassioned plea on the subject before quitting—and Gramm-Rudman may provide the perfect excuse. I expect a fairly stiff version of Gramm-Rudman to be enacted—one that is closer to the House version than to the Senate. In the present setting, that would no longer be as detrimental to the Republicans' election chances in 1986 as it seemed a few weeks ago.

Gramm-Rudman would be followed by a discount rate cut in short order. That is what makes me take on the maximum exposure in bonds at the present time. I realize there may be some indigestion in the market after the auctions, but if my analysis is correct there is still something left to go for.

After a discount rate cut I intend to cut my bond exposure and increase my stock positions. Stocks are more open-ended on the upside than bonds. If and when the economy rebounds, stocks will do better than bonds. If the economy continues to languish, the reduction in short-term interest rates may go much further than currently expected, but the dollar would also come under pressure so that the yield curve is likely to steepen. It should be remembered that détente is bearish for the dollar vis-à-vis European currencies. If one wants to stay in bonds, the place to be is the short end.

We may be on the verge of a great stock market boom. Industrial companies have suffered from a combination of inadequate prices and inadequate demand. These adverse conditions have resulted in the wholesale restructuring of corporate America. Many companies have been swallowed up by takeovers and leveraged buyouts. Those which have survived have tightened their belts, disposing of losing divisions and cutting corporate overhead. Productive capacity has been cut rather than increased, and market share has been concentrated in fewer hands. The lower dollar is now in the process of relaxing pricing pressures; if there is any pickup in demand, it goes straight to the bottom line. Lower interest rates and the lower inflation rate combine to make a given level of earnings more valuable. After a period when industrial shares were selling at a discount from their breakup value we may enter a period when they once again sell at a premium. But before we get there, we are likely to experience another wave of takeovers, induced by the decline in interest rates.

END OF PHASE 1: SUNDAY, DECEMBER 8, 1985

This may be a good point to terminate the real-time experiment. I have assumed maximum market exposure in all directions and I have also

Dec. 6, 1985

	Closing 12/6/85	% Change from 11/22		Closing 12/6/85	% Change from 11/22
DM	2.5115	+2.1	S&P 500	212.02	+5.2
¥	202.10	−.5	U.S. T-Bonds	$83^{28}/_{32}$	+3.7
£	1.4425	−1.5	Eurodollar	92.33	+.3
Gold	322.30	−1.4	Crude Oil	28.74	−7.0
			Japanese Bonds	99.21	+4.7

QUANTUM FUND EQUITY $867,000,000
Net Asset Value Per Share $5,841
Change from 11/22/85   +3.0%
Change from 8/16/85   +33.4%

Portfolio Structure (in millions of dollars)

Investment Positions (1)	Long	Short	Net Change (2) from 11/22	Net Currency Exposure (6)	Long	Short	Net Change (2) from 11/22
Stocks				DM-related	729		+61
US Stocks	724	(72)	+71	Japanese Yen	826		−1
US Index				Pound Sterling		(119)	−32
Futures	368		+242	US Dollar		(569)	−2
Foreign				Other			
Stocks	271		+20	Currencies	33		−7
Bonds (3)							
US Gvt.							
Short							
Term (4)	90		−15				
Long							
Term	661		−308				
Japanese							
(5)	300		−54				
Commodities							
Oil		(150)	+64				
Gold							

announced my intention to shift gradually from bonds to stocks within the constraints of prudence. At present a large part of my stock market exposure is in the form of index futures. With the passage of time I shall try to develop specific stock investment concepts, and my performance will be increasingly influenced by the validity of those concepts. To keep a detailed account of my investment activities beyond this point would take us too far afield from the subject of the experiment, namely, predicting the future of the Imperial Circle. I shall continue my periodic diary but it will serve the purpose of control and not of formulating a prediction. In other words, I wish to "freeze" my expectations about the future of the Imperial Circle at the present time and submit it to the test of events. Needless to say, I shall continue changing my portfolio as I see fit.

I have about as firm a conviction about the shape of things to come as I shall ever have, as witnessed by the level of market exposure I am willing to assume. At the beginning of the experiment I said that my crystal ball about the longer term outlook was rather cloudy. The experiment has brought about a remarkable transformation: I now have a relatively clear vision of the future and that vision differs significantly from the admittedly tentative views I started with. I regarded the Imperial Circle as a temporary expedient whose internal contradictions were bound to render it unsustainable, and my presumption was that the problems that the Imperial Circle had managed to keep at bay would resurface with renewed vigor after its disintegration. Specifically, the Imperial Circle constituted an artificial extension of the period of credit expansion with the U.S. government acting as "borrower of last resort." When the Imperial Circle ceased to attract capital from abroad in ever-increasing quantities, the last engine of economic stimulation would be extinguished, and the contraction of credit would create an untenable situation. Without a significant expansion of money supply the burden of debt would become unbearable; with a significant expansion, the dollar would go into a free fall.

I am now beginning to discern the outlines of another temporary solution that may succeed in unwinding the excesses of the Imperial Circle without plunging us into a vicious circle. The solution consists of switching from fiscal to monetary stimulation in the United States and controlling the descent of the dollar through international cooperation. The new constellation is almost the exact opposite of the Imperial Circle: a weaker dollar and a subdued economy are accompanied by lower budget and trade deficits and, most important, by lower interest rates. With the help of a weaker dollar, prices are going to rise somewhat faster than previously, rendering the change in real interest rates all the more pronounced. Declining real interest rates, together with a possible pickup in exports, will replace the budget deficit as the main driving force in the economy. Rising prices will help to counteract the erosion of collateral values and prevent a self-reinforcing, deflationary process from taking hold. At the same time, the coordination of economic policies will keep the decline of the dollar within bounds, thereby eliminating the possibility of a self-reinforcing inflationary process. The outcome would be a greater degree of stability than we have experienced since the breakdown of Bretton Woods.

Using the notation adopted earlier, we can depict the key relationship in the newly emerging state of affairs as follows:

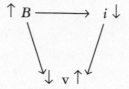

The picture is much simpler than that of the Imperial Circle because exchange rates are stabilized. The extent to which interest rates will decline depends on the amount of stimulation that will be necessary to keep the economy from sliding into a recession.

Although the new constellation is almost the exact opposite of the Imperial Circle, there is one essential difference between them. The new constellation is the deliberate outcome of a concerted economic policy, whereas the Imperial Circle was the unintended consequence of conflicting economic policies. The Imperial Circle was self-reinforcing until it became excessive and ripe for a reversal; the reversal would also become self-reinforcing unless it were deliberately controlled. The mechanism of control is the management of exchange rates in the first instance and the coordination of monetary and fiscal policies in the second.

It is the emergence of a concerted economic policy that has caused me to change my expectations in the course of the experiment. I was aware of the possibility of such a policy emerging and I stressed the difference between the first and the second Reagan administrations. During the three months of the experiment, there occurred several historic events that converted a mere possibility into a historical reality: the Group of Five meeting, the Baker speech in Seoul, the Gramm Rudman amendment and the summit meeting in Geneva.

What makes the emergence of the new economic direction so fascinating is that the actual policy measures of which it will be made up have not even been formulated. The Group of Five meeting was merely a commitment to follow a coordinated exchange rate policy, not an agreement on what that policy is; the Baker Plan for international debt is certainly not a plan but merely the announcement of a need for a plan; the summit meeting may mark a new departure in relations between the superpowers, but it produced no concrete results; and the fate of the Gramm-Rudman amendment is still uncertain at the time of writing.

The actual policies are yet to be formulated. How far they will reach will depend partly on the farsightedness of the policymakers but mainly on the pressure of necessity. Necessity may be defined in this context as the need to preserve the integrity of the financial and trading systems, or, in other words, to forestall a collapse in credit and to keep protectionism at bay. The definition is rather cavalier: it does not rule out individual defaults or particular instances of trade restraint; the crucial issue is that neither defaults nor protectionism should reach the point where they become self-reinforcing.

Success is far from assured. Past experience is not encouraging. A somewhat similar set of circumstances led to the collapse of both credit and international trade in the 1930s. But exactly because the memory of the 1930s is still so vivid, the prospect that we shall avoid similar mistakes is rather favorable. There is general agreement on some policy objectives: a controlled descent of the dollar and a concerted reduction in interest rates. There is less agreement on other points: how to reduce the U.S. budget deficit and how to stimulate the economies of the debtor countries. It is difficult to obtain concerted action even on the generally agreed objectives. For instance, Japan was obliged to raise interest rates because the United States was unable to resolve the issue of the budget deficit in time. How can one have any confidence that appropriate action will be taken in those areas where even the agreement on objectives is missing?

Clearly, the situation is far from riskless, and, as we shall see, the risks are the greatest in the short term. It is exactly because the risks are so great, and their severity is recognized, that one can have a fair degree of confidence that the necessary measures will be forthcoming. I am not the only one to think so: the financial markets have endorsed the new policy departure in no uncertain fashion. The rise in bond and stock prices is helpful in two ways: it encourages the authorities to pursue the course on which they have embarked, and it enhances the chances of success. For instance, the strength of the bond market enlarges the Federal Reserve's freedom of action in lowering interest rates. We are dealing with a reflexive process where the direction of economic policy and the direction of the financial markets mutually reinforce each other.

It is the response of the financial markets that has given me the courage to take on such a large market exposure. It will be recalled that in the case of currencies when the change in trend was still uncertain I was much more tentative and when the market moved against me I was a hair's breadth away from cutting back my position. In fact, the real-time experiment was instrumental in helping me to hang in there because seeing my ideas clearly formulated strengthened my convictions. My success in the marketplace has reinforced my confidence in my ability to predict the course of events even further. 1985 is shaping up as a record-breaking year for Quantum Fund: a more than 100% appreciation within a year is heady stuff. I have to be careful. Using the concept of reflexivity to predict the future course of events is itself a reflexive process, and a high degree of success is often the precursor to a severe setback. It is clear from the experiment that my perceptions are partial and subject to correction by events. If I begin to lay store on my longer term expectations—and what is worse, go public with them—I may be setting myself up for a great fall. It is a danger I intend to guard against. It will be interesting to see, when we control the experiment, what will have remained of my current game plan.

Actually, it is less dangerous to carry a large market exposure at the present juncture than to predict the eventual outcome of the policies that are now being formulated. The mere fact that there is an attempt to take charge of the world economy is sufficient to give the financial markets a boost and, even if the hopes are going to be disappointed, it will take time for the failure to become evident; thus the attempt at a concerted policy should be sufficient to sustain the present rally for a while. The eventual outcome is quite another matter. There can be no assurance that the market's expectations will be fulfilled. I must beware not to allow my confidence in a bull market to affect my judgment about the real world. I have become so involved in the market that I find it difficult to maintain perspective.

I shall try to assess the future of the Imperial Circle in two different ways: one is to identify the "thesis" that the current market rally incorporates and evaluate its chances of success; the other is to locate the present moment within the theoretical framework of credit expansion and contraction that I have been trying to formulate. Both approaches employ the concept of reflexivity, but the first one sticks closely to the reflexivity inherent in financial markets while the second seeks to explore the reflexive connection between credit and collateral values. Needless to say, I am on much surer grounds with the first approach.

I believe the market has come around to the view that the economy is fundamentally weak and inflation nonexistent. A brief rally in cyclical stocks in early summer has petered out and the highs reached then have still not been surpassed. That rally has been based on the mistaken expectation of an imminent pickup in the economy, and it was very narrow: other segments of the stock market were declining while the cyclicals rose. It was followed by a general market decline that was cushioned by takeover and stock buy-back activity. Commodities also made new lows and have been lagging in the current recovery. Metals, in particular, have acted very poorly in relation to currencies.

The recent stock market rally is much more broadly based than the earlier flurry in cyclicals; it follows on the heels of a bond market rally and it was preceded by a decline in the dollar. Obviously the markets are discounting a decline in the economy. Whether it will deteriorate further is an open question. Economists are almost unanimous in ruling out a recession, but the stock and bond markets are acting as though it were an accomplished fact: stock prices are rising because investors are "looking across the valley." It is possible that the slowdown of the past year served as the equivalent of a recession; alternatively, there is some further weakness to come. Either way, the sequence of events is highly unusual and investors have been taken by surprise: none of the technical indicators that normally signal a significant upturn in the stock market has been present. The November 27 lead article in the *Wall Street Journal* entitled "Strange Rally" has highlighted this fact.

Every recession since the end of the Second World War has been preceded by the Federal Reserve tightening the money supply, causing an inverted yield curve to appear at some point along the line. An inverted yield curve preceded the rally in the summer of 1982, but we have not seen an inverted yield curve since. The explanation for the current sequence of events has to be sought elsewhere. That is where the second approach using my hypothesis about the credit cycle comes in handy.

It will be recalled that I envision a reflexive relationship between the act of lending and the value of the collateral that serves as security for the loans. Net new lending acts as a stimulant that enhances the borrowers' ability to service their debt. As the amount of debt outstanding grows, an increasing portion of new lending goes to service outstanding debt and credit has to grow exponentially to maintain its stimulating effect. Eventually the growth of credit has to slow down with a negative effect on collateral values. If the collateral has been fully utilized, the decline in collateral values precipitates further liquidation of credit, giving rise to a typical boom/bust sequence.

Using this model, I contend that the postwar period of credit expansion has run its course and we are now in a period of credit contraction as far as the real economy is concerned. All previous postwar recessions occurred during the expansionary phase: that is why they had to be induced by tight money. We are now in the contractionary phase where a slowdown need not be induced: in the absence of new stimulants, such as a growing budget deficit, the erosion of collateral values will do the job.

The trouble is that real life is not as simple as the model I have been working with. In particular, the transition from credit expansion to credit contraction does not occur at a single point of time because it would precipitate an implosion that the authorities are determined to prevent. Official intervention complicates matters. The turning point does not occur at a single moment of time, but different segments of the credit structure follow different timetables. To locate our position in the credit cycle, it is necessary to disaggregate the process and consider the main elements of credit separately.

This approach yields 1982 as the turning point for the heavily indebted countries, 1984 as the turning point for U.S. financial institutions, and 1986 as the turning point for the U.S. budget deficit. The contraction of credit in less developed countries has probably reached its peak in 1984; the adjustment process is largely responsible for the oversupply of basic commodities. The adjustment process by U.S. banks and savings and loan institutions has only recently begun to make its effect felt on collateral values in real estate, land, shipping, and the oil industry. The reduction in the budget deficit has not yet taken effect and it is to be expected that it will be fully compensated for by a reduction in interest rates. Two more important pieces need to be fitted into the jigsaw puzzle: mergermania and consumer spending.

Leveraged buyouts and other manifestations of mergermania are great users of credit but they tend to produce a corresponding amount of liquid assets. Superficially, they seem to be expansionary but in fact they fit into the declining phase of the credit cycle: they increase the total amount of debt without stimulating the economy. Cash flow is used to service debt rather than to purchase physical assets; the disposal of assets adds to the downward pressure on collateral values; and the sale of junk bonds tends to steepen the yield curve: the net effect on the economy is depressing rather than stimulating.

Consumer spending is the great unknown. Consumer indebtedness has been rising steadily over the years, and repayment terms have been extended to a point where it is hard to see how they can be extended any further. Until recently, houses could be bought with a 5% down payment and auto loans could be repaid over five years. Delinquencies in consumer loans have risen ominously in the course of 1985, but the simultaneous decline in interest rates and the dollar should alleviate the situation. Will these developments merely serve to contain the delinquency problem, or will they stimulate new demand? That is the crucial question on which the near-term outlook hinges.

If consumer spending remains sluggish, the bull market in bonds and stocks may have considerable staying power; in fact, we could have one of the great bull markets of all times. A pickup in the domestic savings rate would offset the reduction in the inflow of foreign capital allowing interest rates to decline in spite of the decline in the dollar. The stock market would benefit from both developments. Lower interest rates would enhance the value of a given level of earnings, and the lower dollar would enhance the level of earnings by mitigating pricing pressures from imports. In a sluggish economy the cost of labor would remain depressed. Threatened by adverse economic conditions and corporate takeovers, managements have redeployed assets and reduced overhead expenses; as conditions improve, the benefits flow directly down to the bottom line. As interest rates decline, there would be one last rush of corporate takeovers and leveraged buyouts, in the course of which exaggerated prices may be paid; but recent events make past acquisitions more viable and deals that may have been unsound when consummated are now looking healthier. Eventually the rise in stock prices should render leveraged buyouts uneconomic, and merger activity should peter out. That would be a very positive development for the real economy because it would enhance the attraction of investing in physical assets stimulating not only demand but also supply. Should we reach that point, our economy would be healthier than it has been for some time. The boom may eventually get out of hand and set us up for a great crash, but share prices would have to rise a great deal before we reach that point. It is an argument for buying stocks now.

On the other hand, if consumer spending does pick up under the impetus of lower interest rates, the boom in financial markets will be short-lived and the real economy is likely to follow the stop-go pattern familiar from the British example. With inadequate domestic savings and domestic investment, the excess of both credit and consumption would have to be met from abroad and we would be back in the situation that prevailed at the end of the Imperial Circle. Either we raise interest rates, restarting the Imperial Circle and choking off the domestic economy, or we print money, setting in motion a vicious circle in the opposite direction.

Reality is likely to fall between these extremes, but that is not saying much because the extremes open up an almost infinite range of possibilities. I am no better qualified to predict consumer behavior than I was at the beginning of the experiment. All I can do is evaluate the consequences of the various alternatives.

It can be seen that a period of subdued consumer spending could do much to correct the last two major areas of excess credit. Merger-mania would run out of steam as the stock market rises and the overindebtedness of consumers would be corrected as the savings rate rises and lenders tighten their criteria. After a while, conditions would be ripe for more balanced growth.

When past excesses are being corrected it is always a period of maximum risk. That is the case now. There have already been a number of minor catastrophes: the EPIC debacle has been followed by others in the real estate lending arena; the Federal Savings and Loan Insurance Corporation and the Farm Credit System have gone public with their woes; the International Tin Council has been unable to meet its obligations, tin trading on the London Metal Exchange has been suspended, and many metal traders are going out of business; the largest Japanese shipping company has gone broke; just now the Singapore Stock Exchange has had to close for a few days; and there are obviously other events yet to come. We are facing at least two shocks that exceed in magnitude anything we have experienced to date. One relates to oil, the other to international debt.

The collapse of oil prices is only a matter of time. Once it begins it will not stop of its own volition. Most countries operate with a perverse supply curve: the lower the price of oil, the more they need to sell in order to meet their needs. Left to itself, the price of oil could temporarily fall to a single digit, but it will not be left to itself. Domestic industry will have to be protected below $22, otherwise the losses would exceed the capacity of the banks to absorb them. I would expect to see some kind of protection that would also extend to Mexico and Canada. I wonder how the North Sea producers will be protected. The problem will be a difficult one for the European Economic Community to resolve. How it is dealt with may determine the future of the Common Market.

The problem of international debt has not gone away. Indeed, the debt of the less developed countries has continued to grow, although some countries have been able to improve their debt ratios. Negative resource transfers probably reached their peak in 1984 and, as debtor countries insist on reflating their economies, negative resources transfers are beginning to decline. The cohesion of the lenders' collective has eroded. The run on South Africa, in particular, has driven a wedge between American and European banks. In the United States, the interests of money center banks and regional banks diverge. The Baker Plan demonstrates an awareness of the problem but it falls far short of a solution. Until a solution is developed, the system remains accident prone, although it is not clear where the next accident is likely to occur. The banking system is now strong enough to withstand a single shock; the danger is that several shocks may coincide.

There is yet a third danger that will develop as the stock market boom gathers momentum: the danger of a crash in the stock market. At present, market participants are still very conscious of the problems and as a consequence are quite liquid. But it is in the nature of a boom that it attracts ever-increasing amounts of credit. If a financial shock occurs when many stock market participants are overextended, margin liquidation could cause an implosion of stock prices. We are a long way from that stage: at present, a sudden financial shock, like the failure of yet another bank, could cause a short, sharp break in prices, but the market would recover. The bull market is likely to be punctuated with such breaks until participants will cease to fear them. That is when we shall be set up for a crash.

The financial system has been severely tested and the testing is not yet over. The fact is that the system survived and the recent changes in economic management improve the chances that it will continue to survive. The process of credit contraction has been accomplished without a bust so far and one can now see a way in which it could be completed without a bust, albeit at the cost of a prolonged period of substandard growth.

Substandard growth is less than desirable almost by definition, but it may meet the policy objectives of the present administration perfectly. It has been long recognized that conditions in which goods and services are freely available are more rewarding to the owners of capital than conditions in which resources are fully employed. Not only does a larger share of the national product accrue to the owners of capital but entrepreneurs enjoy much greater freedom of action. That is certainly the case today. The reins of government are in the hands of people who believe in free enterprise and encourage it to the greatest possible extent or even beyond.

Incidentally, Japan has also found it advantageous, for different reasons, to expand its economy at a rate that is decidedly below its potential. Japan wants to become a great power in the world and the way to achieve that status is not by encouraging domestic consumption but by maintaining a high domestic savings rate that is used first to build up productive capacity at home and then to acquire assets abroad. Japan has yielded to American pressure by raising the value of its currency but it will change its domestic economic policy only to the extent that is necessary to support the yen.

One of the most potent reasons for expecting economic growth to remain sluggish is that it suits the policy objectives of the two leading countries. The constellation that seems to be emerging as a sequence to the Imperial Circle deserves to be described as the Golden Age of Capitalism.

It is hard to believe that the golden days of capitalism could come back again. After all, untrammeled free enterprise has produced horrendous results in the past. Are we to repeat the same experience again? Hopefully not. Perhaps we have learned something from past mistakes.

The fatal flaw of a free market system is its inherent instability. The belief that financial markets are self-regulating is simply false. Fortunately, Secretary Baker is aware of this fact and the administration has begun to exert active economic leadership since he moved to the Treasury. Certainly it is not laissez-faire that has brought us to the threshold of a new golden age of capitalism but a concerted economic policy designed to counteract the excesses of a free market system. It remains to be seen how well we have learned our lessons.

In any case, the benefits of the new golden age are very unevenly spread. It is in the nature of capitalism that the gap between winners and losers is rather wide. Large segments of the population, especially in the financial, technology, service, and defense sectors, are flourishing. Others, especially in the older industries, agriculture, and the welfare sector, are suffering. Fortunes are made in financial deals and shareholders wield more power than at any time in the last fifty years; at the same time, bankruptcies are also at a fifty-year high, in both size and numbers. Debtor countries are wallowing in depression and a whole continent, Africa, is starving; at the same time China is converting to a free market system with all possible speed and the Soviet Union is on the verge of moving in the same direction, albeit much more cautiously.

Why the Reagan administration has been so successful in achieving its objectives is a fascinating question. To all intents and purposes the Democrats have been reduced to the party of losers, as manifested by the fact that it is the Democrats who push for protectionism in Congress, while President Reagan has an unquestionable gift for making Americans feel like winners. But the improvement in sentiment has been achieved at the cost of considerable deterioration in the underlying reality, as manifested in our national indebtedness.

Frankly, I have been surprised by the vitality of resurgent capitalism. I considered the Imperial Circle as a temporary expedient that was bound to break down. Seeing it replaced by a new arrangement that can be described as the Golden Age of Capitalism, I must acknowledge the adaptability of the system and its ability to survive. It remains to be seen whether policymakers succeed in containing its weaknesses: the inherent instability of financial markets and the iniquities caused by instability.

P.S., MONDAY EVENING, DECEMBER 9, 1985

I have decided to move forward the date of switching from bonds to stocks. I am influenced partly by the prospect for "the bull market of a lifetime" that I have just articulated and partly by more practical

Dec. 9, 1985

	Closing 12/9/85	% Change from 12/6		Closing 12/9/65	% Change from 12/6
DM	2.5345	−.9	S&P 500	204.25	−3.7
¥	203.55	−.7	U.S. T-Bonds	$82^{16}/_{32}$	−1.6
£	1.4575	+1.0	Eurodollar	91.87	−.5
Gold	316.20	−1.9	Crude Oil	27.51	−4.3
			Japanese Bonds	97.00	−2.2

QUANTUM FUND EQUITY $890,000,000
Net Asset Value Per Share $5,998
Change from 12/6/85   +2.7%
Change from 8/6/85   +37.0%

Portfolio Structure (in millions of dollars)

Investment Positions (1)	Long	Short	Net Change (2) from 12/6	Net Currency Exposure (6)	Long	Short	Net Change (2) from 12/6
Stocks				DM-related	693		−36
US Stocks	739	(66)	+21	Japanese Yen	828		+2
US Index				Pound Sterling		(115)	+4
Futures	277		−91	US Dollar		(516)	+53
Foreign				Other			
Stocks	270		−1	Currencies	45		+12
Bonds (3)							
US Gvt.							
Short							
Term (4)	90						
Long							
Term	717		+56				
Japanese							
(5)	253		−47				
Commodities							
Oil		(157)	−7				
Gold							

considerations. A cut in the discount rate may not follow immediately upon agreement on Gramm–Rudman. Markets are firm and the Federal Reserve is cautious. The statistics for December may look quite good, partly because the Christmas shopping season is crowded into fewer days and partly because investment orders may be placed before the end of the year to beat the changes in taxation. The next advance indicators may also look good because they include stock prices and money supply. In these circumstances, bonds may be vulnerable and stocks may offer better prospects on the upside. The thesis I have just formulated is beginning to enter investors' consciousnesses, yet caution is still prevalent. The year's end is seasonally a strong period: we could have some fireworks in the next four to five weeks.

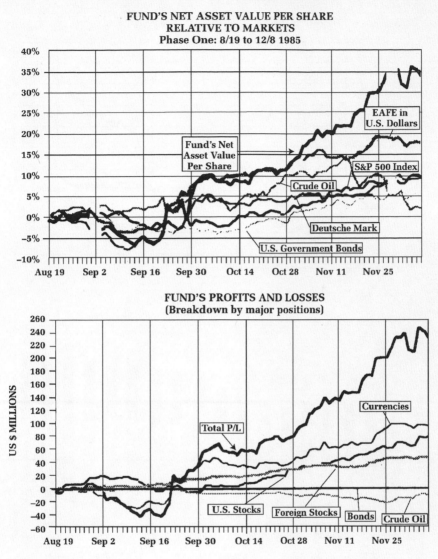

**FUND'S NET ASSET VALUE PER SHARE
RELATIVE TO MARKETS
Phase One: 8/19 to 12/8 1985**

**FUND'S PROFITS AND LOSSES
(Breakdown by major positions)**

Notes:

(1) All prices are calculated as percent change over the first day shown.

(2) EAFE is Morgan Stanley's Capital International Index in U.S. dollars for European, Australian, and Far Eastern stock markets.

(3) The Oil and the Government Bond prices are the closing prices of the nearest futures contracts.

(4) Currency profits and losses include only forward and futures contracts. P&L on foreign stocks includes the currency gain or loss on the positions.

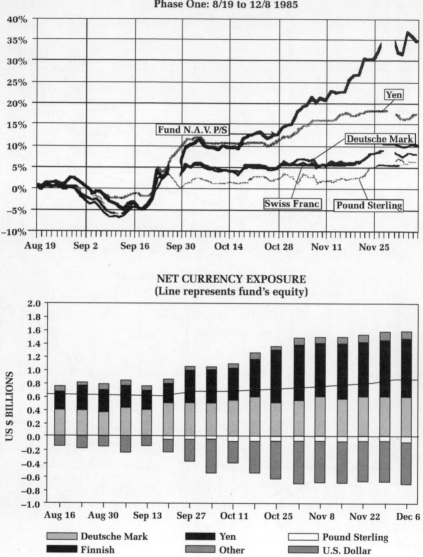

CURRENCY PRICES
Phase One: 8/19 to 12/8 1985

NET CURRENCY EXPOSURE
(Line represents fund's equity)

Notes:

(1) Prices in U.S. dollars shown as percent change over the first day shown. New York closing prices are used.

(2) Net currency exposure includes stock, bonds, futures, forwards, cash, and margins, and equals the total equity of the fund. A short position in U.S. dollars indicates the amount by which the currency exposure exceeds the equity of the fund.

(3) Currency exposure shown as of end of week.

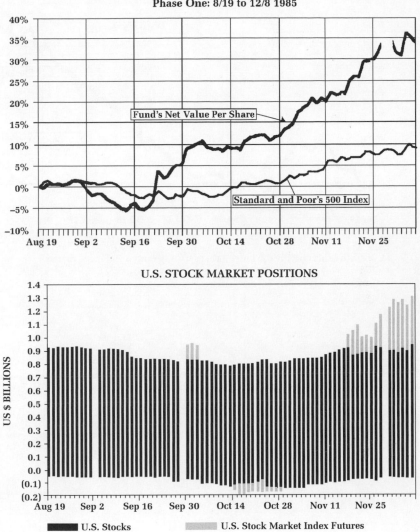

U.S. STOCK MARKET
Phase One: 8/19 to 12/8 1985

U.S. STOCK MARKET POSITIONS

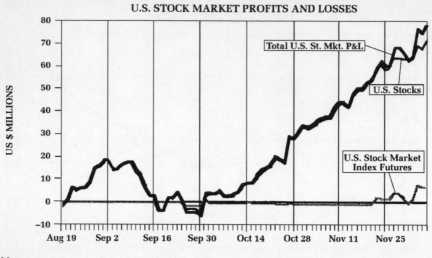

Note:

(1) Total U.S. stock market profits and losses include stock positions and index futures.

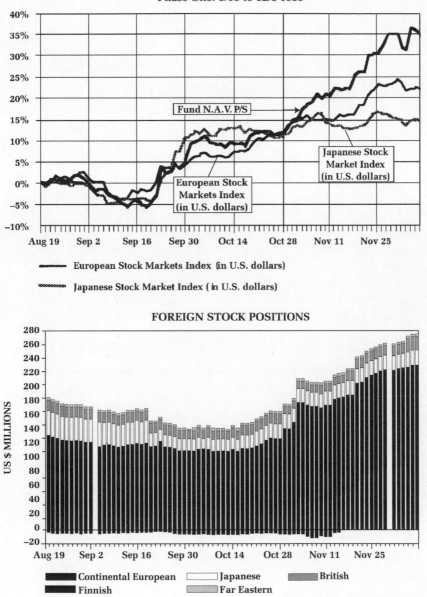

FOREIGN STOCK MARKET
Phase One: 8/19 to 12/8 1985

European Stock Markets Index (in U.S. dollars)

Japanese Stock Market Index (in U.S. dollars)

FOREIGN STOCK POSITIONS

US $ MILLIONS

Continental European   Japanese   British

Finnish   Far Eastern

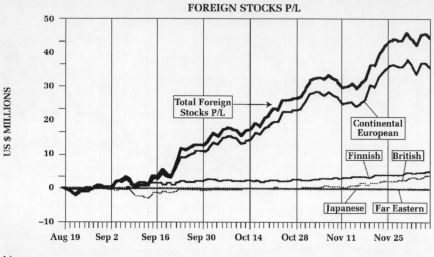

Notes:

(1) Total foreign stock market profits and losses include foreign exchange gains or losses on foreign stock positions.

(2) Far Eastern positions include Hong Kong, Korea, Taiwan, Australia, and Thailand.

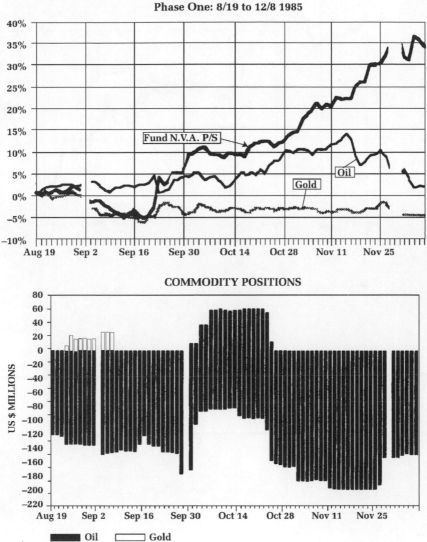

COMMODITY PRICES
Phase One: 8/19 to 12/8 1985

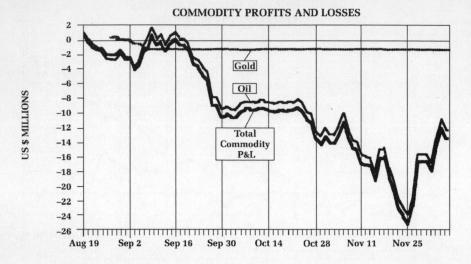

FIXED INCOME SECURITIES
Phase One: 8/19 to 12/8 1985

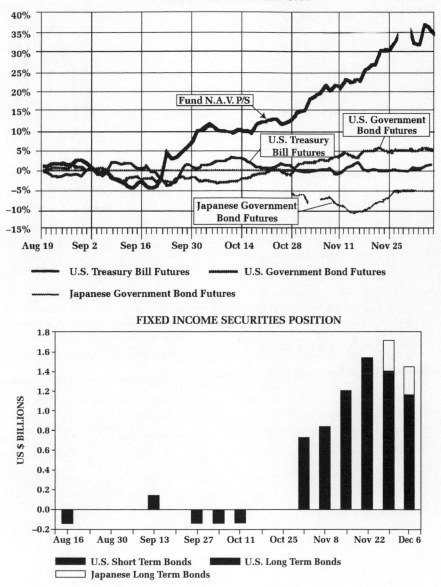

U.S. Treasury Bill Futures   U.S. Government Bond Futures

Japanese Government Bond Futures

FIXED INCOME SECURITIES POSITION

U.S. Short Term Bonds   U.S. Long Term Bonds
Japanese Long Term Bonds

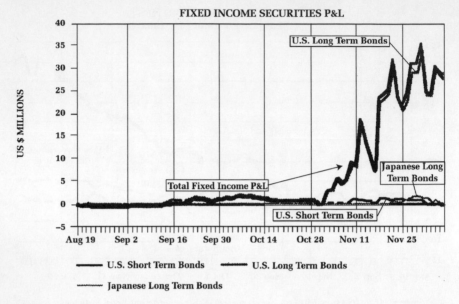

FIXED INCOME SECURITIES P&L

Notes:

(1) U.S. Short Term Bond positions and P&L include Treasury Bills. Treasury Bill and Eurodollar Futures, and Treasury Notes up to two years to maturity.

(2) All U.S. Government Bonds are reduced to a common denominator of 30-year Government Bonds. The basis of the conversion is the effect on price of a given change in yield. For instance, $100 million in face value of 4-year Treasury Notes are equivalent to $28.5 million in market value of 30-year Government Bonds.

(3) Japanese Government Bond Futures have considerably less volatility than U.S. Government Bonds. For instance, as of June 30, 1986, $100 million in face value of Japanese Government Bonds had the same volatility as roughly $66.2 million in 30-year U.S. Government Bonds. We have *not* adjusted for this difference.

(4) Positions shown as of end of week.

11

Control Period: January 1986–July 1986*

SATURDAY, JANUARY 11, 1986†

The stock and bond markets suffered a nasty break and I have been caught badly. I had taken on my maximum exposure in the stock market at the time of the December futures expiration—which corresponded with a temporary market peak—and did not dispose of my bond positions. As a consequence, I was fully exposed in both bonds and stocks at the time of the break. I was toying with the idea of cutting my bond position in half and in fact sold about $100 million when the market dropped and I did not feel inclined to follow it down. Subsequently, I bought back prematurely the bonds I had sold. Only in currencies and in European stocks did I trade correctly. I eliminated my excess currencies at a moment of temporary strength so that I now have only my equity invested in foreign currencies—with a short position in sterling against the DM—but no leverage. I also sold into strength in foreign stock markets so that my overall exposure remained stable despite the rise in prices.

---

*This chapter is included mainly for its documentary value. It becomes quite repetitive. Readers not particularly interested in my macro-manipulations are advised to turn to p. 241.
†Charts showing the posture and performance of Quantum Fund from Dec. 9, 1985, to April 3, 1986, follow p. 212. The key for the parenthetical note references (1) through (6) in the diary entry tables can be found on p. 151.

Jan. 10, 1986

	Closing 1/10/86	% Change from 12/9		Closing 1/10/86	% Change from 12/9
DM	2.4675	+2.6	S&P 500	205.96	+.8
¥	202.45	+.5	U.S. T-Bonds	$83^{04}/_{32}$	+.8
£	1.4880	+2.1	Eurodollar	91.85	0
Gold	341.70	+8.1	Crude Oil	25.79	−6.3
			Japanese Bonds	98.55	+1.6

QUANTUM FUND EQUITY	$942,000,000
Net Asset Value Per Share	$6,350
Change from 12/9/85	+5.9%
Change from 8/16/85	+45.0%

Portfolio Structure (in millions of dollars)

Investment Positions (1)	Long	Short	Net Change (2) from 12/9	Net Currency Exposure (6)	Long	Short	Net Change (2) from 12/9
Stocks				DM–related	609		−84
US Stocks	1,011	(65)	+273	Japanese Yen	612		−216
US Index				Pound Sterling		(278)	−163
Futures	717		+440	US Dollar		(1)	+515
Foreign				Other			
Stocks	318		+48	Currencies	21		−24
Bonds (3)							
US Gvt.							
Short							
Term (4)			−90				
Long							
Term	958		+241				
Japanese							
(5)	259		+6				
Commodities							
Oil		(224)	−67				
Gold							

As usual, the break was caused by a combination of factors. The most important was a strong employment report that convinced the market that no discount rate cut is to be expected. The measures taken against Libya also had an unsettling effect—there were various unconfirmed rumors about Arab selling of stocks, bonds, and dollars. I used one of these rumors to unload my currencies. The stock market may also have been affected by the imposition of margin requirements on junk bonds. On Friday afternoon, two days after the initial break, the bond market broke through an important resistance point, $9\frac{1}{2}\%$ yield on 30-year bonds, amid concern about the constitutionality of Gramm-Rudman.

What made the market vulnerable to these developments was the euphoria that prevailed at the time they occurred. Unfortunately, I was also caught up in it. That is why the break found me fully exposed. I regard the current episode as a typical correction in a bull market. Its violence—a 5% drop in index futures in a couple of hours—foreshadows what is yet to come if and when the bull market becomes more extended.

Typically, stock market booms survive a number of tests so that the market comes to be considered invulnerable and only then is it ripe for the bust. We are very far from that point yet. Sentiment is still quite cautious. All that has happened is that the market has been disappointed in its expectation of any imminent discount rate cut. The short end of the bond market has already corrected—Eurodollar futures dropped by almost half a point; the long end may overreact, but, if so, I expect it to swing back again soon. As before, my position is predicated on the belief that the economy has no real momentum. The Federal Reserve may not lower the discount rate, but it has no reason to allow the federal funds rate to trade up from the present level either. Equally, I consider the constitutional challenge to Gramm-Rudman immaterial—the process will be working by the time the issue is decided. If this view is wrong, I shall have to revise my position at a considerable loss. Until then, I intend to hang in there. I expect the maximum pressure in the bond market to be felt tomorrow: it remains to be seen how much damage will be done. The stock market ought to do better than the bond market from here on.

The trouble is that not having sold I cannot buy now. All I can do is sit out this round and hope that the situation does not get out of hand. My cash reserves ought to be sufficient to see me through, but one can never be sure. The decline depletes my cash reserves and leaves me more exposed than I was before the break. Since I expect the break to be temporary there is no point in raising cash now. By the same token, it would be totally unsound to reduce my cash reserve any further.

P.S., WEDNESDAY, JANUARY 15, 1986

The Group of Five are meeting this weekend. I know what I would do in their place: I would lower interest rates on a multilateral basis. This would show that the authorities are cooperating and are in command of the situation. It would help maintain stability in the foreign exchange market; without it, it may be difficult to prevent a temporary rise in the dollar. The ground has been thoroughly prepared: the Gramm-Rudman process is in operation and the use of junk bonds has been curbed. Japan is waiting for the United States to take the lead in lowering interest rates. It is true that M1 has exceeded the target range and the economy has probably grown about $3\frac{1}{2}\%$ in the fourth quarter of 1985. If it is business as usual, there is no need to move; but if the authorities feel the need to maintain the initiative, this is the time to do it. Lowering the discount rate would mean publicly abandoning monetarism; but the bond market would accept the move because it is done in concert with other nations, exchange rates are stable, and Volcker's reputation as a sound money man is unscathed. The question is, does he want to do it?

I am reluctant to believe that the authorities will do what I would like them to. Nevertheless, I am willing to bet on it at this time, subject to the constraints of my already exposed position. That means that I will buy some Eurodollar futures that are relatively riskless. The only risk is that I become even more exposed and must cut my exposure at the wrong time. I am willing to take the risk because, if the bet fails, I intend to cut back my exposure anyhow. After all, my thesis is that the authorities have taken the initiative; if they do not maintain it, what reason do I have to maintain a leveraged position other than a reluctance to take a loss? There is a French military expression, *reculer pour mieux sauter*. I shall do the opposite: I shall advance in order to regroup. I shall relieve my present exposure, which I find unsustainable in the long run, by increasing it in the short run.

TUESDAY MORNING, JANUARY 21, 1986

The Group of Five meeting did not produce any clear-cut results. One could hardly expect any dramatic announcements after all the ballyhoo and leaks that preceded the meeting; nevertheless, the terse statement was less than enlightening. I am left to my own devices in conjecturing about what actually happened.

Jan. 20, 1986

	Closing 1/20/85	% Change from 1/10		Closing 1/20/85	% Change from 1/10
DM	2.4580	+.4	S&P 500	207.53	+.8
¥	202.45	0	U.S. T-Bonds	83^{17}/$_{32}$	+.5
£	1.4125	−5.1	Eurodollar	91.91	+.1
Gold	354.10	+3.6	Crude Oil	21.27	−17.5
			Japanese Bonds	98.00	−.6

QUANTUM FUND EQUITY $1,006,000,000
Net Asset Value Per Share $6,775
Change from 1/10/86   +6.7%
Change from 8/16/85   +54.7%

Portfolio Structure (in millions of dollars)

Investment Positions (1)	Long	Short	Net Change (2) from 1/10	Net Currency Exposure (6)	Long	Short	Net Change (2) from 1/10
Stocks				DM-related	559		−50
US Stocks	1,014	(73)	−5	Japanese Yen	612		0
US Index				Pound Sterling		(270)	+8
Futures	584		−133	US Dollar	105		+106
Foreign				Other			
Stocks	314		−4	Currencies	31		+10
Bonds (3)							
US Gvt.							
Short							
Term (4)	88		+88				
Long							
Term	1,026		+68				
Japanese							
(5)	261		+2				
Commodities							
Oil		(159)	+65				
Gold							

I believe that the goal of reducing interest rates on a worldwide basis was recognized, but the two truly independent central banks, those of Germany and the United States, refused to make a commitment to concerted action. I suspect that the Federal Reserve has subtly moved to ease monetary policy even before the meeting—next Thursday's figures should provide more conclusive evidence—but it wants the market response to determine when the discount rate should be cut and not a consortium of governments. Allowing the Group of Five to dictate U.S. monetary policy would constitute far too dangerous a precedent to be acceptable to a central bank that wants to preserve its independence.

What is disturbing about the outcome is the implication of a possible rift between Baker and Volcker. In retrospect, the dissent between Volcker and the administration on the issue of imposing margin requirements on junk bonds assumes greater significance. Volcker seems to be worried that lowering interest rates too aggressively would merely fuel a stock market boom that could end in a crash—and I would be the last person to contradict him. The fact that he is worried about it makes the boom less likely to develop. In any case, the Group of Five has lost some momentum and that is a dangerous development.

I felt it incumbent on me to reduce the extra exposure I assumed prior to the meeting, but I decided to wait before executing my plan of deleveraging until the next set of Federal Reserve figures become available. Instead of selling the Eurodollar futures I bought, I sold some S&P 500 index futures because I considered the stock market more vulnerable.

In the course of the day, the decline in energy prices accelerated until it turned into a veritable rout. By the end of the day, stocks, bonds, and currencies have all recouped the day's losses. This constitutes a major event. The long-awaited collapse of oil prices is finally happening.

There is nothing to stop a free fall from developing except government intervention; but governments intervene only in emergencies. The suspicion of a disagreement between Volcker and Baker further weakens the chances of timely action. We are therefore headed for a period of maximum risk for the banking system. What is going to happen to all the energy loans and the energy-dependent debtor nations?

I am convinced that the situation is not going to be allowed to get out of hand because a remedy is readily available: an import tax on oil with special provisions for Mexico. But in order to impose a tax, President Reagan would have to reverse himself; only an emergency would provide him with an excuse: therefore the situation will have to deteriorate before the remedy is applied. It behooves me to deleverage as far as possible. The fall in oil prices has many positive implications for both stocks and bonds, but it would be inappropriate to speculate on them on a leveraged basis, especially as the initial response of the market is likely to be the same as my own.

SATURDAY, FEBRUARY 22, 1986

I deleveraged too soon: I failed to take full advantage of a powerful up-surge in both the stock and bond markets. I even got myself short bond futures temporarily when I heard that the lower court was going to rule against the constitutionality of Gramm-Rudman, but the decision was de-layed a week and the collapse in oil prices outweighed everything else in importance so that I was forced to cover with a loss. In short, my trading was poor. Nevertheless, the fund did well, helped by our short positions in oil and the dollar. Our stock selection has also been working for us.

The fact is, I would feel uncomfortable to be too heavily exposed at the present time—that is probably why I traded poorly when I did have a leveraged position. I look at the decline in oil prices as a combi-nation of two influences: an economic stimulus and a financial shock. The markets are reacting to the first influence, while I am extremely sensitive to the second.

We are approaching the moment of truth on the international debt issue. With oil below $15, Mexico has a prospective debt service defi-ciency on the order of $10 billion. To make it up, a number of things have to happen. Mexico must tighten its belt further; the banks will have to take a hit; and the United States will have to fork out some money, in the form of either grants or price protection on Mexican oil. It can be done, but it will be a complex and delicate operation. The concessions made by the banks will have to be extended to other debtor countries. Money center banks as a group are now in a position to absorb a significant cut in interest rates on loans to the less devel-oped countries, but Bank of America, for one, is likely to be pushed over the brink. It will be bailed out, along the lines of Continental Illi-nois Bank, and depositors will be protected. Depositors may not even panic, but the stock market may. The strength of the market, combined with the amount of credit involved in futures and options trading, makes the market extremely vulnerable to a sudden reverse. It was 5% in two hours in January; it may be 10% or 15% next time. I believe that

Feb. 21, 1986

	Closing 2/21/86	% Change from 1/20		Closing 2/21/86	% Change from 1/20
DM	2.2960	+6.6	S&P 500	224.62	+8.2
¥	182.20	+10.0	U.S. T-Bonds	$90^{06}/_{32}$	+8.0
£	1.4545	+3.0	Eurodollar	92.10	+.2
Gold	341.00	−3.7	Crude Oil	13.53	−36.4
			Japanese Bonds	101.60	+3.7

QUANTUM FUND EQUITY $1,205,000,000
Net Asset Value Per Share $8,122
Change from 1/20/86   +19.9%
Change from 8/16/85   +85.5%

Portfolio Structure (in millions of dollars)

Investment Positions (1)	Long	Short	Net Change (2) from 1/20	Net Currency Exposure (6)	Long	Short	Net Change (2) from 1/20
Stocks				DM–related	783		+224
US Stocks	1,064	(185)	−62	Japanese Yen	726		+114
US Index				Pound Sterling		(343)	−73
Futures		(92)	−676	US Dollar	39		−66
Foreign				Other			
Stocks	426		112	Currencies	81		+50
Bonds (3)							
US Gvt.							
Short							
Term (4)			−88				
Long							
Term	215		−811				
Japanese							
(5)			−261				
Commodities							
Oil		(55)	+104				
Gold							

the risk of a collapse has shifted from the banking system to the financial markets and I would feel very foolish if I got caught. My caution may cost me dearly, but it will also ensure my survival.

When I heard that President de la Madrid of Mexico is going to make a speech tonight, I sold some S&P futures and some dollars short as an insurance policy over the weekend.

THURSDAY, MARCH 27, 1986

I have made very few macro moves since I reduced my leverage at the end of January. In retrospect, I moved too soon because I missed the best part of the bond market rally. Obviously I underestimated the bullish implications of the decline in oil prices. Frankly, I did not think that oil would be allowed to fall so far without government intervention. There is nothing to stop oil from falling except government intervention, because the supply curve is inverted: the lower the price goes, the more oil has to be sold in order to meet the producing countries' requirements. Eventually, domestic producers will have to be protected. That was the reason I switched my short position from West-Texas to Brent contracts—a move that turned out to be expensive because I got caught in a short squeeze.

I can justify my decision to reduce leverage only on subjective grounds. Operating on leverage involves considerable strain and I have made enough money recently not to want to live with it. But missing an opportunity is also painful. Fortunately I did not miss the market: I merely failed to take maximum advantage of it.

I remained largely inactive in currencies. The only thing I did was to build up the DM/£ cross position further. I recognized that the nature of the currency markets was, once again, changing: the spirit of cooperation that emerged from the first Group of Five meeting was weakened in the second and the authorities were losing control over the market. The dollar was moving faster and lower than the authorities desired. Both the Japanese and the Germans were getting worried. The American authorities were divided: Volcker shared their concern while the rest of the administration felt that the Japanese squirming was a welcome sign that the lower dollar was beginning to bite. The dollar was falling of its own momentum and it was not clear what caused the decline: the fall in oil prices must have had something to do with it. Part of the impact was nonrecurring—fewer dollars were needed to finance oil transactions—but the trend was pronounced enough to attract speculative positions.

	Closing 3/26/86	% Change from 2/21		Closing 3/26/86	% Change from 2/21
			Mar. 26, 1986		
DM	2.3305	−1.5	S&P 500	237.3	+5.6
¥	179.65	+1.4	U.S. T-Bonds	98¹⁵⁄₃₂	+9.2
£	1.475	+1.4	Eurodollar	92.83	+.8
Gold	344.40	+1.0	Crude Oil	12.02	−11.2
			Japanese Bonds	105.50	+3.8

QUANTUM FUND EQUITY $1,292,000,000
Net Asset Value Per Share $8,703
Change from 2/21/86   +7.2%
Change from 8/16/85   +98.7%

Portfolio Structure (in millions of dollars)

Investment Positions (1)	Long	Short	Net Change (2) from 2/21	Net Currency Exposure (6)	Long	Short	Net Change (2) from 2/21
Stocks				DM-related	1,108		+325
US Stocks	1,272	(170)	+223	Japanese Yen	492		−234
US Index				Pound Sterling		(389)	−46
Futures	124		+216	US Dollar	81		+42
Foreign				Other			
Stocks	536		+110	Currencies	63		−18
Bonds (3)							
US Gvt.							
Short							
Term (4)							
Long							
Term	326		+111				
Japanese (5)							
Commodities							
Oil		(28)	+27				
Gold							

I kept my short position in the dollar intact not because I had any great convictions but because I had no firm views and I felt that my chances of making money by trading currencies did not justify the trouble and aggravation. Holding the position was more comfortable than changing it and my lack of convictions put me in a good position to reassess the situation when necessary.

Then came Preston Martin's resignation and the behind-the-scenes struggle over interest rates came out into the open. The market responded with a sharp rally in the dollar. Sterling also rallied against the DM and I was facing a big loss in currencies—the first since the inception of dirty floating. It forced me to reassess the macroeconomic situation.

What I find is continued economic stagnation. Elements of strength and weakness are well balanced. The strength comes mainly from lower interest rates and the optimism generated by improving profit margins; housing, restocking, new business formation, increased employment in the service sector are also positive influences. The major source of weakness is in the oil industry. Oil is a major component in capital spending and probably equals in importance the automobile industry. Other forms of capital spending are also weak, although they can be expected to improve with the passage of time. Another source of weakness, the reduced budget deficit, has not yet had time to make its impact felt. The savings rate seems to be improving, keeping consumer spending in check. Investors are responding to lower interest rates by moving into stocks and long-term bonds. All this is very bullish, both for bonds and stocks.

In view of the soft economy, I see no reason to cut my short position in the dollar. Rather, I take the current strength of the dollar as a reason to expect interest rates to fall further. Accordingly, I have decided to reestablish my long position in bonds. To buy bonds on a $7\frac{1}{2}\%$ yield basis when I sold them with a 9 to $9\frac{1}{4}\%$ yield is not an easy decision to make; but the logic of the situation forces me into it. It is inconsistent to be short dollars without being long bonds—and I think it would be wrong to buy dollars now. What about the leverage involved? After all, it was the reluctance to carry leverage that induced me to reduce my exposure in the first place. Undoubtedly, it increases the tension, but by the same token it relieves the tension that was inherent in being short dollars without being long bonds. I shall have to cope by being more alert.

What are the prospects for a significant setback in both stocks and bonds? When I look at the internal dynamism of the market, I find that the boom is far too young and vigorous to collapse of its own weight.

Investors are still very cautious, including myself. Stocks are just on the verge of becoming too expensive for leveraged buyouts, and the real rate of interest is still too high, given the collapse in oil prices. Either the dollar or interest rates have to decline, or both. Since the dollar has stabilized, it is interest rates that have to move further.

On internal grounds alone, the boom has a long way to go: stock prices could double or more before they become vulnerable. Some of the smaller stock markets are far more exposed. Italy is a case in point. If and when we have a crash it ought to affect Italy before it affects the United States.

At present, the only danger is an external shock. Its potential origin is clearly visible: oil prices are set on a collision course. Oil will continue falling until it sets off some catastrophic event that will arrest or reverse the trend. We may distinguish between the two kinds of cathartic events: military and financial.

Military/political developments are notoriously difficult to anticipate. Tensions in the Middle East are rising. We have had a near-revolution in Egypt; the Iran-Iraq war shows signs of escalating; the incursion of the American fleet into the Bay of Sidra passed off without serious repercussions, but we can expect other incidents. Since they cannot be anticipated, all I can do is stay alert. A mild degree of leverage serves to heighten awareness.

The financial repercussions of lower oil prices are much more obvious. Mexico, in particular, is an event waiting to happen. Will it be an orderly bailout or a confrontation? Mexico has backed down from asking for interest rate concessions. The likelihood is that some kind of oil-denominated security will be offered to disguise the concession that Mexico needs and to prevent it from spreading to other debtor countries.

What is more difficult to fathom is the reaction of the markets. An orderly settlement would reinforce the bullish trend, but doubts about an orderly settlement would test the market. At present, the odds are that the market will pass the test, but it would be best not to be exposed while the issue is decided.

SUNDAY, APRIL 6, 1986*

Last Tuesday, I shorted the S&P futures in an amount equal to my long position in bonds. This has effectively eliminated my leveraged exposure

*Charts showing the posture and performance of Quantum Fund from Mar. 31, 1986, to July 20, 1986, follow p. 230. The key to the parenthetical note references (1) through (6) in the diary-entry tables can be found on p. 151.

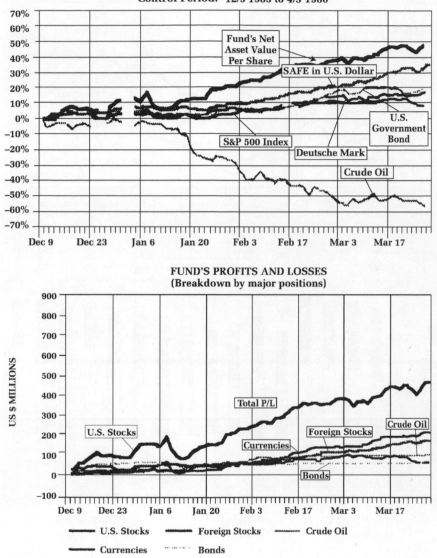

FUND'S NET ASSET VALUE PER SHARE
RELATIVE TO MARKET
Control Period: 12/9 1985 to 4/3 1986

FUND'S PROFITS AND LOSSES
(Breakdown by major positions)

Notes:

(1) All prices are calculated as percent change over the first day shown.

(2) EAFE is Morgan Stanley's Capital International Index in U.S. dollars for European, Australian, and Far Eastern stock markets.

(3) The Oil and the Government Bond prices are the closing prices of the nearest futures contracts.

(4) Currency profits and losses include only forward and futures contracts. P&L on foreign stocks includes the currency gain or loss on the positions.

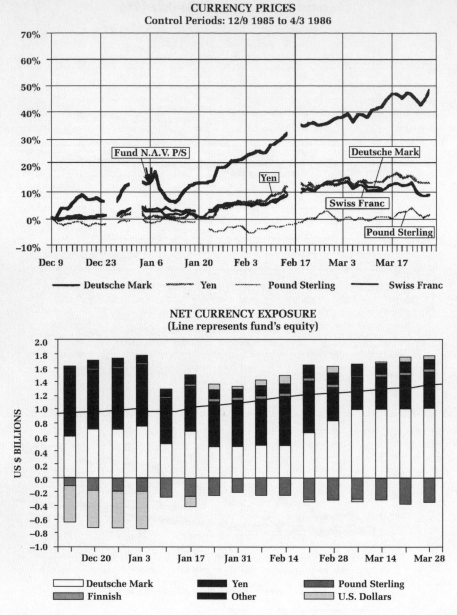

CURRENCY PRICES
Control Periods: 12/9 1985 to 4/3 1986

Fund N.A.V. P/S

Deutsche Mark

Yen

Swiss Franc

Pound Sterling

Dec 9   Dec 23   Jan 6   Jan 20   Feb 3   Feb 17   Mar 3   Mar 17

—— Deutsche Mark   ~~~~ Yen   ······ Pound Sterling   —— Swiss Franc

NET CURRENCY EXPOSURE
(Line represents fund's equity)

US $ BILLIONS

Dec 20   Jan 3   Jan 17   Jan 31   Feb 14   Feb 28   Mar 14   Mar 28

☐ Deutsche Mark   ■ Yen   ▨ Pound Sterling
▨ Finnish   ■ Other   ☐ U.S. Dollars

Notes:

(1) Prices in U.S. dollars shown as percent change over the first day shown. New York closing prices are used.

(2) Net currency exposure includes stock, bonds, futures, forwards, cash, and margins, and equals the total equity of the fund. A short position in U.S. dollars indicates the amount by which the currency exposure exceeds the equity of the fund.

(3) Currency exposure shown as of end of week.

U.S. STOCK MARKET
Control Period: 12/9 1985 to 4/3 1986

Fund's Net Asset
Value Per Share

Standard and Poor's
500 Index

U.S. STOCK MARKET POSITIONS

US $ BILLIONS

█ U.S. Stocks   ▒ U.S. Stock Market Index Futures

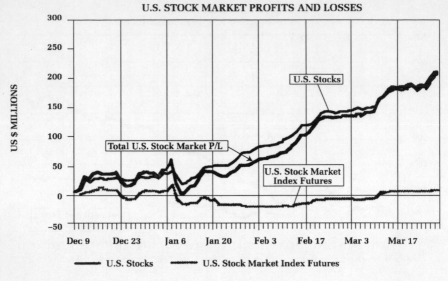

Note:

(1) Total U.S. stock market profits and losses include stock positions and index futures.

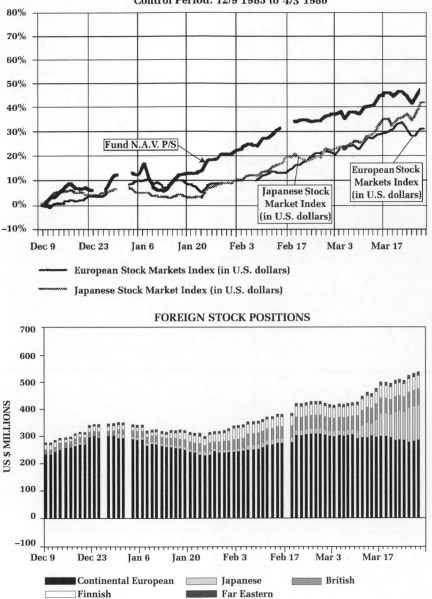

FOREIGN STOCK MARKET PRICES
Control Period: 12/9 1985 to 4/3 1986

Fund N.A.V. P/S

European Stock Markets Index (in U.S. dollars)

Japanese Stock Market Index (in U.S. dollars)

European Stock Markets Index (in U.S. dollars)

Japanese Stock Market Index (in U.S. dollars)

FOREIGN STOCK POSITIONS

US $ MILLIONS

Continental European   Japanese   British
Finnish   Far Eastern

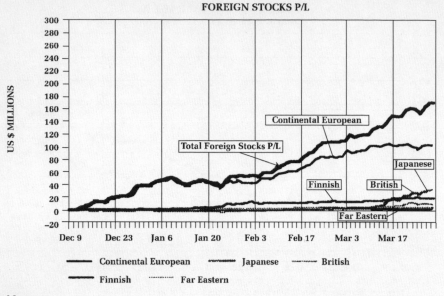

FOREIGN STOCKS P/L

Notes:

(1) Total foreign stock market profits and losses include foreign exchange gains or losses on foreign stock positions.

(2) Far Eastern positions include Hong Kong, Korea, Taiwan, Australia, and Thailand

COMMODITY PRICES
Control Period: 12/9 1985 to 4/3 1986

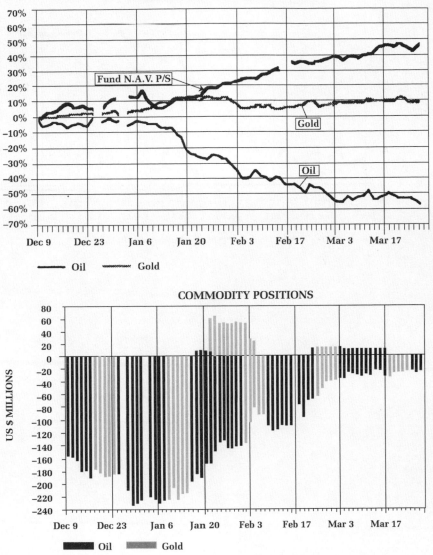

COMMODITY POSITIONS

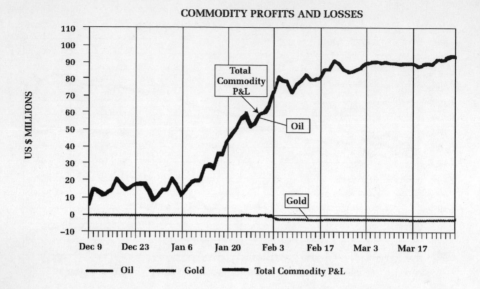

COMMODITY PROFITS AND LOSSES

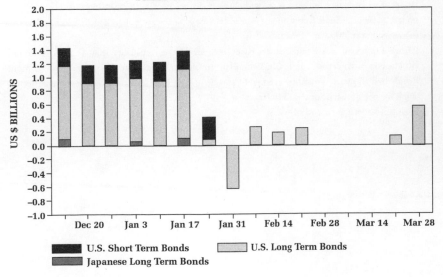

FIXED INCOME SECURITIES
Control Period: 12/9 1985 to 4/3 1986

Fund N.A.V. P/S

Japanese Government Bond Futures

U.S. Government Bond Futures

U.S. Treasury Bill Futures

━━━━ U.S. Treasury Bill Futures　　〰〰〰 U.S. Government Bond Futures

··········· Japanese Government Bond Futures

FIXED INCOME SECURITIES POSITION

US $ BILLIONS

■ U.S. Short Term Bonds　　▢ U.S. Long Term Bonds
■ Japanese Long Term Bonds

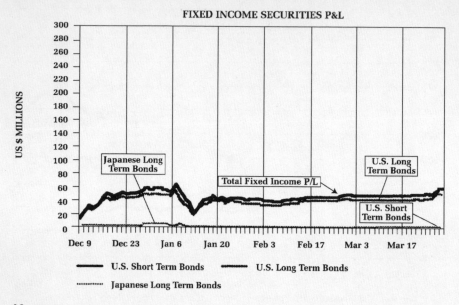

FIXED INCOME SECURITIES P&L

Notes:

(1) U.S. Short Term Bond positions and P&L include Treasury Bills, Treasury Bill and Eurodollar Futures, and Treasury Notes up to two years to maturity.

(2) All U.S. Government Bonds are reduced to a common denominator of 30-year Government Bonds. The basis of the conversion is the effect on price of a given change in yield. For instance, $100 million in face value of 4-year Treasury Notes are equivalent to $28.5 million in market value of 30-year Government Bonds.

(3) Japanese Government Bond Futures have considerably less volatility than U.S. Government Bonds. For instance, as of June 30, 1986, $100 million in face value of Japanese Government Bonds had the same volatility as roughly $66.2 million in 30-year U.S. Government Bonds. We have *not* adjusted for this difference.

(4) Positions shown as of end of week.

Apr. 4, 1986

	Closing 4/4/86	% Change from 3/26		Closing 4/4/86	% Change from 3/26
DM	2.3955	−2.8	S&P 500	228.69	−3.6
¥	180.42	−.4	U.S. T-Bonds	$100^{11}/_{32}$	+1.9
£	1.4500	−1.7	Eurodollar	93.13	+.3
Gold	335.40	−2.6	Crude Oil	12.74	+6.0
			Japanese Bonds	104.15	−1.3

QUANTUM FUND EQUITY $1,251,000,000
Net Asset Value Per Share $8,421
Change from 3/26/86 −32%
Change from 8/16/85 +92.3%

Portfolio Structure (in millions of dollars)

Investment Positions (1)	Long	Short	Net Change (2) from 3/26	Net Currency Exposure (6)	Long	Short	Net Change (2) from 3/26
Stocks				DM-related	1,094		−14
US Stocks	1,171	(167)	−98	Japanese Yen	474		−18
US Index				Pound Sterling		(380)	+9
Futures		(572)	−696	US Dollar	63		−18
Foreign				Other			
Stocks	499		−37	Currencies	50		−13
Bonds (3)							
US Gvt.							
Short							
Term (4)							
Long							
Term	652		+326				
Japanese (5)							
Commodities							
Oil		(29)	−1				
Gold							

on the long side. I am now looking for the right entry point for increasing my short position, so as to reduce my net exposure even further.

Vice-President Bush has announced his intention to discuss oil prices on his visit to Saudi Arabia. This has elicited a negative reaction from the administration, engineered no doubt by his old enemy Donald Regan. The net effect is to reduce the chances of an import tax on oil. There is always the possibility that OPEC will get together and reduce output but I rate the chances rather low. Now that the structure has fallen apart, it will need a cathartic event to put a new structure in place. Having taken the plunge, why should Saudi Arabia take the risk of a makeshift solution? The United States is the high-cost producer; by staying the course, U.S. production can be permanently reduced. It was to be expected that U.S. production would be protected, but recent events reduced that possibility. I expect the pressure on oil prices to continue.

Declining oil prices are bullish until they turn bearish. Strange as it may seem, most forecasts have failed to take into account the reduction in U.S. oil production. Instead of stimulating the economy, the initial impact is negative. Altogether, the economy seems weaker than prevailing expectations. That is why I am unwilling to reduce my short position in the dollar. In fact, I intend to increase it by covering my short position in sterling. I seem to have overstayed my welcome. The interest rate differential is attracting funds to sterling and I do not have a strong enough case to fight the trend.

I am happy with the cross position I have established, long bonds/short S&P futures, but I am less happy with my net long position in stocks. I am looking for an opportunity to reduce the exposure. I do not expect a collapse, but a correction of undetermined magnitude. The right entry point will be when oil prices start declining again. The initial response ought to be positive, for both bonds and stocks. It may come only after the April 15 meeting of OPEC.

WEDNESDAY, APRIL 9, 1986

The market flip-flopped in the last two days and so did I. On Monday, oil rallied sharply, and bonds, stocks, and currencies sold off; on Tuesday, all these markets reversed themselves. The move on Monday hurt me on all fronts. I discovered how sensitive my portfolio was to oil prices; I also discovered that there was more leverage in it than I thought. I had neglected

Apr. 8, 1986

	Closing 4/8/86	% Change from 4/4		Closing 4/8/86	% Change from 4/4
DM	2.3325	+2.6	S&P 500	242.38	+6.0
¥	179.80	+.3	U.S. T–Bonds	$101^{31}/_{32}$	+1.6
£	1.4650	+1.0	Eurodollar	93.30	+.2
Gold	340.00	+1.4	Crude Oil	12.47	−2.1
			Japanese Bonds	103.58	−.5

QUANTUM FUND EQUITY $1,290,000,000
Net Asset Value Per Share $8,684
Change from 4/4/86   +3.1%
Change from 8/16/85   +98.3%

Portfolio Structure (in millions of dollars)

Investment Positions (1)	Long	Short	Net Change (2) from 4/4	Net Currency Exposure (6)	Long	Short	Net Change (2) from 4/4
Stocks				DM–related	810		−284
US Stocks	1,231	(169)	+58	Japanese Yen	504		+30
US index				Pound Sterling		(177)	+203
Futures			+572	US Dollar	153		+90
Foreign				Other			
Stocks	578		+79	Currencies	57		+7
Bonds (3)							
US Gvt.							
Short							
Term (4)							
Long							
Term	656		+4				
Japanese (5)							
Commodities							
Oil		(12)	+17				
Gold							

my DM/£ cross position, which turned against me with a vengeance. To quantify it, I dropped a cool $100 million from the onset of the correction, despite my S&P futures hedge, which saved me some $20 million.

On Monday, I cut both my DM/£ exposure and my short position in oil in half and covered 40% of my S&P short; on Tuesday, I covered the rest of my S&P short and did some bargain hunting in stocks. The net effect is that I increased my exposure in stocks and bonds while I reduced it in currencies and oil.

Based on information received Monday morning, I modified my short-term outlook on oil. Two positives came to my attention: the likelihood that motorists would use more gasoline this summer, especially with the impact that terrorism is making on foreign air travel, and the probability that oil companies will shut down their North Sea oil production for extended maintenance because they can make almost as much money on their net-back agreements with Saudi Arabia. There is therefore room for a trading rally prior to the OPEC meeting next week. By buying Brent, I am setting up a cross position of Brent vs. WTI (domestic oil). With the prospect of import duties receding, this makes sense to me.

I have no particular views on sterling. It is now reacting to the favorable interest rate differential, rather than to the price of oil. As it strengthens, the interest rate differential will be reduced because the government cannot allow sterling to appreciate. This limits the upside potential for sterling, but that is not a good reason for staying short. The plain fact is, I neglected the position and failed to take my profit; now I must disengage myself without a profit. I liquidated half my position immediately and hoped to do the rest at more favorable prices. The U.K. lending rate was in fact cut by ½% on Tuesday, touching off the rally in U.S. stocks and bonds.

The stock and bond markets reacted negatively to the rise in oil prices, but it has made me more bullish. The real danger, in my view, is a further fall. I regard the decline as a healthy correction in a bull market and a buying opportunity that I decided to exploit within the limits of prudence. I am now fully extended.

The ploy seems to be working. The underlying weakness in the economy is now gaining recognition and there is a meeting of the minds on further coordinated interest rate reductions. The expectation is strong enough to overshadow concern about Libya although U.S. retaliation is almost inevitable.

After a period of increased activity I hope to sit back again. I want to reduce the leverage, but not too soon. I should like to let the profits run for a while.

WEDNESDAY, MAY 21, 1986

I remained rather inactive in April and what little I did served to reduce my exposure. I sold a small amount of stocks, a larger amount of
currencies, and almost my entire bond position. At the beginning of
May, I became more active. I made a foray into bonds at the time of the

May 20, 1986							
	Closing *5/20/86*	*% Change* *from 4/8*			*Closing* *5/20/86*	*% Change* *from 4/8*	
DM	2.3100	+1.0	S&P 500		236.11	−2.6	
¥	168.18	+6.5	U.S. T-Bonds		$96^{05}/_{32}$	−5.7	
£	1.5215	+3.9	Eurodollar		92.96	−.4	
Gold	339.00	−.3	Crude Oil		16.04	+28.6	
			Japanese Bonds		102.42	−1.1	

QUANTUM FUND EQUITY $1,367,000,000
Net Asset Value Per Share $9,202
Change from 4/8/86   +6.0%
Change from 8/16/85   +110.2%

Portfolio Structure (in millions of dollars)

Investment Positions (1)	Long	Short	Net Change (2) from 4/8	Net Currency Exposure (6)	Long	Short	Net Change (2) from 4/8
Stocks				DM–related	485		−325
US Stocks	1,208	(58)	88	Japanese Yen	159		−345
US Index				Pound Sterling		(21)	+156
Futures		(770)	−770	US Dollar	744		+591
Foreign				Other			
Stocks	573		−5	Currencies	148		+91
Bonds (3)							
US Gvt.							
Short							
Term (4)							
Long							
Term	313		−343				
Japanese							
(5)							
Commodities							
Oil		(75)	−63				
Gold		(29)	−29				

quarterly refunding, which looked promising at first but turned very sour afterward. I took my loss early, but as the bonds continued to fall, I began to accumulate a position again. On the other hand, I took a significant short position in S&P futures, so that I now have a slight negative exposure in stocks that more or less balances my positive exposure in bonds. I have also built up a short position in oil in a rising market, which is currently showing a loss. Furthermore, I am in the process of building up a short position in gold. All told, my trading activity cost me some money but it has put me in a position in which I feel comfortable. My aim is to limit my losses rather than to make a lot of money.

The outlook for the dollar is quite uncertain; a half-and-half position seems safest. The decline of the dollar has gone further than the authorities intended; there is also a greater degree of dissent among the major powers than I like to see. Moreover, the Federal Reserve, which is still laboring under the influence of monetarism, expects the economy to pick up in the second half. All this is serving to reduce the likelihood of further interest rate reductions.

MONDAY, JULY 21, 1986: END OF THE CONTROL PERIOD

I have made my first major strategic change since the end of the real-time experiment. Without abandoning the thesis that we are in "the bull market of a lifetime," I have adopted a new thesis, namely, that the bull market may be cut short by a deflationary spiral engendered by the collapse of oil prices. The second hypothesis will be tested in the next few months; if we survive the test, the case for "the bull market of a lifetime" will remain intact—indeed, its lifespan will be extended. Thus, for the near future I shall operate with two contradictory theses. This is a suitable subject for another real-time experiment; therefore, I shall wind up the control period at this point.

I have done very little outside my equity portfolio since the last report. My major move was in currencies and it was a costly one. First, I covered my entire short position in the dollar and then I reestablished a fully hedged position at lower levels. My first move was triggered by some signs that the U.S. economy may be strengthening: the advance indicators and the purchasing agents' report for May were deceptively strong. I had no firm views on the currencies, and I did not feel like losing my accumulated profits. I figured that, with a dollar-denominated fund, being in

July 21, 1986						
	Closing 7/21/86	*% Change from 5/20*			*Closing 7/21/86*	*% Change from 5/20*
DM	2.1195	+8.2	S&P 500		236.22	0
¥	179.65	−6.8	U.S. T-Bonds		99³¹/₃₂	+4.0
£	1.4995	−1.4	Eurodollar		93.64	+.7
Gold	355.00	+4.7	Crude Oil		13.09	−18.4
			Japanese Bonds		103.32	+.9

QUANTUM FUND EQUITY $1,478,000,000
Net Asset Value Per Share $9,885
Change from 5/20/86   +7.4%
Change from 8/16/85   +125.7%

Portfolio Structure (in millions of dollars)

Investment Positions (1)	Long	Short	Net Change (2) from 5/20	Net Currency Exposure (6)	Long	Short	Net Change (2) from 5/20
Stocks				DM–related	795		+310
US Stocks	1,089	(86)	−147	Japanese Yen	549		+390
US Index				Pound Sterling		(25)	−4
Futures		(950)	−180	US Dollar	159		−585
Foreign				Other			
Stocks	604		+31	Currencies	202		+54
Bonds (3)							
US Gvt.							
Short							
Term (4)	29		+29				
Long							
Term		(570)	−883				
Japanese							
(5)	1,334		+1,334				
Commodities							
Oil		(43)	+32				
Gold		(34)	−5				

dollars can just as easily be called neutral as being half in and half out. Needless to say, I covered close to the top of the trading range.

The fact is that it is very difficult to maintain a "neutral" position in a fluctuating currency market. Market participants have an existential choice to make and if they have no clear views they are bound to make the wrong choice. One can, of course, neutralize one's position by buying currency options, but, in that case, one has to pay a measurable cost for neutrality. In the last few months of the control period I was not as much in touch with the markets as during the period of the experiment itself. I was working on the more theoretical sections of this book and spent May and June in Europe. The macro moves I made during the control period have reflected this: they added very little to the overall results; if I take the currency trading into account, the net contribution was negative. As the following table indicates, the bulk of the profits came from the equity side.

To discuss the composition of the equity portfolio in detail would take us too far afield, but it is worth pointing out that at least two major investment themes, one relating to Finnish shares and the other to Japanese railroad and real estate shares, are closely related to the concept of "the bull market of a lifetime." The real estate concept also extends to Hong Kong. Taken together, these investments account for more than two-thirds of my equity positions outside the U.S., and 40% of my entire equity positions.

Whether "the bull market of a lifetime" will survive the next few months will be the subject of a new experiment; whatever the outcome, the thesis has stood me in good stead in managing my investment fund up to this point. I hope that reopening the experiment will help to focus my mind in the same way as it did last time.

Quantum Fund Profits & Losses First Half of 1986 (in millions of dollars)	
Stocks	+341.2
Bonds	+22.3
Currencies	+53.3
Oil	+82.0
Gold	−2.2
Miscellaneous	−16.8
Total	+479.8

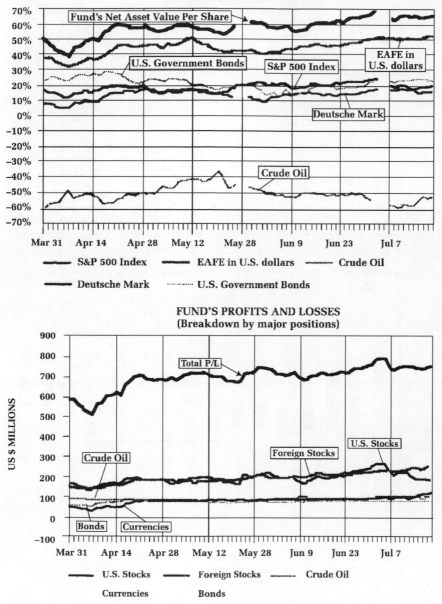

FUND'S NET ASSET VALUE PER SHARE
RELATIVE TO MARKETS
Control Period: 3/31 to 7/20 1986

Fund's Net Asset Value Per Share

U.S. Government Bonds

S&P 500 Index

EAFE in U.S. dollars

Deutsche Mark

Crude Oil

Mar 31   Apr 14   Apr 28   May 12   May 28   Jun 9   Jun 23   Jul 7

——— S&P 500 Index   ——— EAFE in U.S. dollars   ——— Crude Oil

——— Deutsche Mark   ········ U.S. Government Bonds

FUND'S PROFITS AND LOSSES
(Breakdown by major positions)

US $ MILLIONS

Total P/L

Crude Oil

Foreign Stocks

U.S. Stocks

Bonds   Currencies

Mar 31   Apr 14   Apr 28   May 12   May 28   Jun 9   Jun 23   Jul 7

——— U.S. Stocks   ——— Foreign Stocks   ——— Crude Oil

Currencies   Bonds

Notes:

(1) All prices are calculated as percent change over the first day shown.

(2) EAFE is Morgan Stanley's Capital International Index in U.S. dollars for European, Australian, and Far Eastern stock markets.

(3) The Oil and the Government Bond prices are the closing prices of the nearest futures contracts.

(4) Currency profits and losses include only forward and futures contracts. P&L on foreign stocks includes the currency gain or loss on the positions.

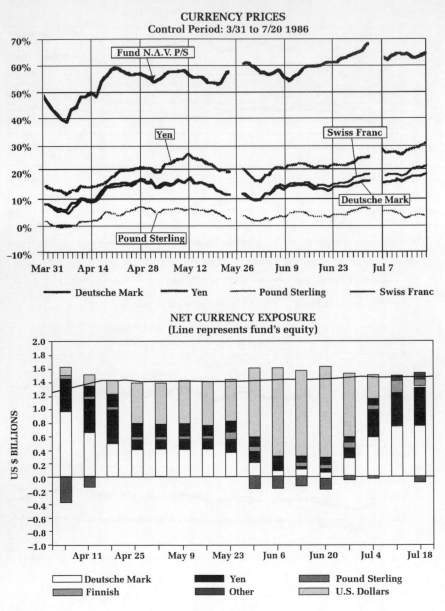

CURRENCY PRICES
Control Period: 3/31 to 7/20 1986

Legend: ──── Deutsche Mark   ▪▪▪▪ Yen   ──── Pound Sterling   ──── Swiss Franc

NET CURRENCY EXPOSURE
(Line represents fund's equity)

Legend: ☐ Deutsche Mark   ■ Yen   ▩ Pound Sterling   ▨ Finnish   ■ Other   ▨ U.S. Dollars

Notes:

(1) Prices in U.S. dollars shown as percent change over the first day shown. New York closing prices are used.

(2) Net currency exposure includes stock, bonds, futures, forwards, cash, and margins, and equals the total equity of the fund. A short position in U.S. dollars indicates the amount by which the currency exposure exceeds the equity of the fund.

(3) Currency exposure shown as of end of week.

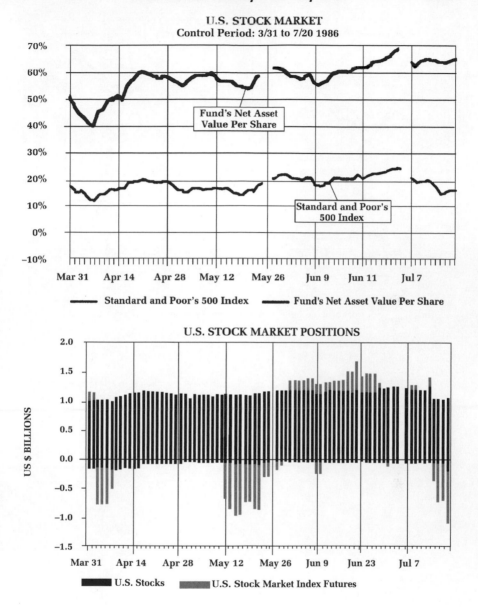

U.S. STOCK MARKET
Control Period: 3/31 to 7/20 1986

Fund's Net Asset Value Per Share

Standard and Poor's 500 Index

Standard and Poor's 500 Index   Fund's Net Asset Value Per Share

U.S. STOCK MARKET POSITIONS

US $ BILLIONS

U.S. Stocks   U.S. Stock Market Index Futures

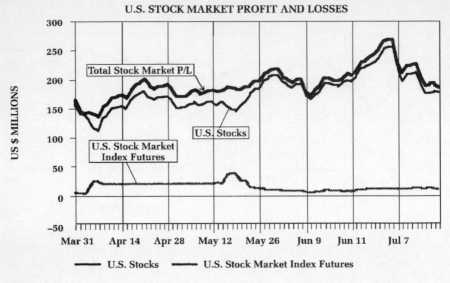

U.S. STOCK MARKET PROFIT AND LOSSES

Note:
(1) Total U.S. stock market profits and losses include stock positions and index futures.

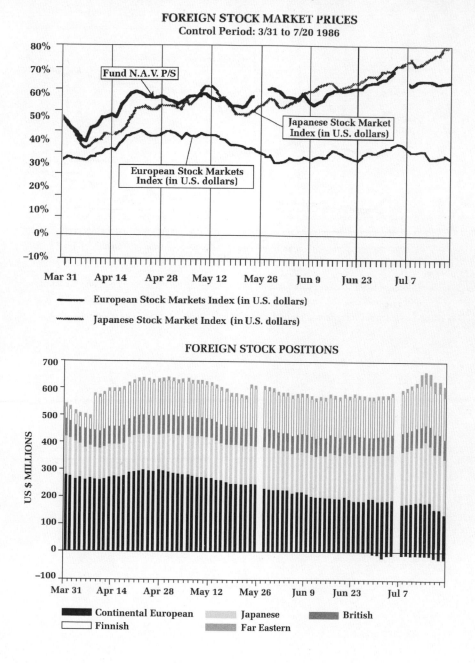

FOREIGN STOCK MARKET PRICES
Control Period: 3/31 to 7/20 1986

Fund N.A.V. P/S

Japanese Stock Market Index (in U.S. dollars)

European Stock Markets Index (in U.S. dollars)

European Stock Markets Index (in U.S. dollars)

Japanese Stock Market Index (in U.S. dollars)

FOREIGN STOCK POSITIONS

US $ MILLIONS

Continental European Japanese British
Finnish Far Eastern

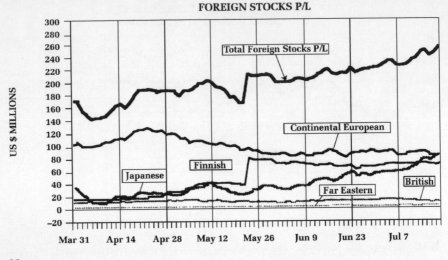

Notes:

(1) Total foreign stock market profits and losses include foreign exchange gains or losses on foreign stock positions.

(2) Far Eastern positions include Hong Kong, Korea, Taiwan, Australia, and Thailand.

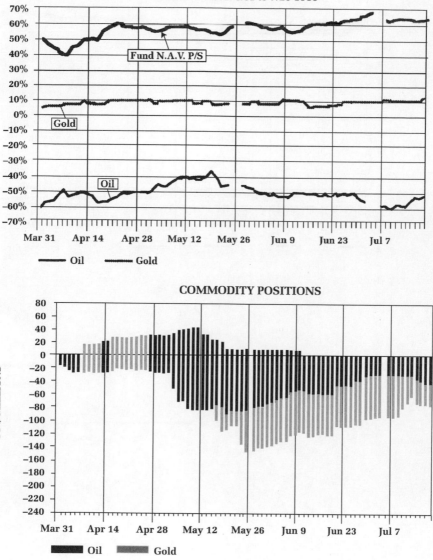

COMMODITY PRICES
Control Period: 3/31 to 7/20 1986

Fund N.A.V. P/S

Gold

Oil

— Oil   ······· Gold

COMMODITY POSITIONS

US $ MILLIONS

▇ Oil   ▇ Gold

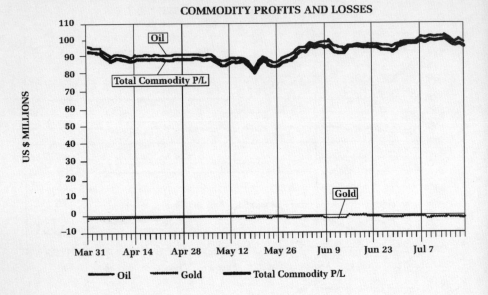

COMMODITY PROFITS AND LOSSES

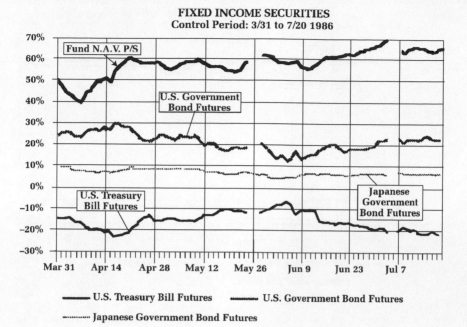

FIXED INCOME SECURITIES
Control Period: 3/31 to 7/20 1986

Fund N.A.V. P/S

U.S. Government Bond Futures

U.S. Treasury Bill Futures

Japanese Government Bond Futures

——— U.S. Treasury Bill Futures   ▬▬▬ U.S. Government Bond Futures

┈┈┈ Japanese Government Bond Futures

FIXED INCOME SECURITIES POSITION

US $ BILLIONS

■ U.S. Short Term Bonds   ☐ U.S. Long Term Bonds

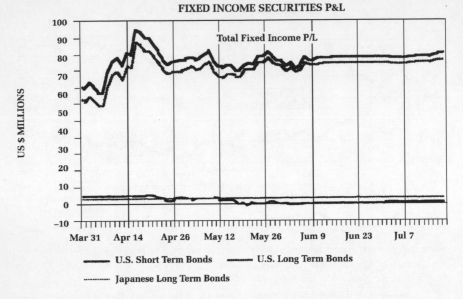

FIXED INCOME SECURITIES P&L

Notes:

(1) U.S. Short Term Bond positions and P&L include Treasury Bills, Treasury Bill and Eurodollar Futures, and Treasury Notes up to two years to maturity.

(2) All U.S. Government Bonds are reduced to a common denominator of 30-year Government Bonds. The basis of the conversion is the effect on price of a given change in yield. For instance, $100 million in face value of 4-year Treasury Notes are equivalent to $28.5 million in market value of 30-year Government Bonds.

(3) Japanese Government Bond Futures have considerably less volatility than U.S. Government Bonds. For instance, as of June 30, 1986, $100 million in face value of Japanese Government Bonds had the same volatility as roughly $66.2 million in 30-year U.S. Government Bonds. We have *not* adjusted for this difference.

(4) Positions shown as of end of week.

12

Phase 2: July 1986– November 1986

MONDAY, JULY 21, 1986*

The possibility of a deflationary spiral has never been far from my thoughts. Indeed, it was the thesis that was uppermost in my mind when I started the real-time experiment. Eventually I discarded it in favor of a bull market thesis, but I kept on considering it and occasionally acted on it during the control period.

The thesis, as I see it at present, rests on the collapse in oil prices. In the long run, lower oil prices ought to stimulate the economy because they reduce production costs and enhance disposable income. The effect is similar to a tax cut, with the additional advantage that it comes at the expense of OPEC and not of the U.S. Treasury. But in the short run, the impact is negative.

First, there is a direct hit against oil production and exploration expenditure. Even more important, when producers' prices are falling, there is a powerful inducement to delay purchases. With nominal interest around 7% in the U.S. and 4% in Japan, while producers' prices are dropping at an $8^{1}/_{2}\%$ rate in the U.S. and even faster in Japan, what can be better than building up cash balances, preferably in Japanese yen? The

---

*Charts showing the posture and performance of Quantum Fund in Phase 2, follow p. 283. The key to the parenthetical note references (1) through (6) in the diary entry tables can be found on p. 151.

241

deflationary effect is supposed to be temporary, because purchases cannot be delayed forever, especially if consumer demand, stimulated by lower interest rates and lower prices, picks up. But while it lasts, there is a danger that the burden of accumulated debt will come crashing down, obliterating the prospect of an eventual pickup in demand.

The announcement last week that LTV Corp. went into voluntary reorganization provides the paradigm. Operating under the protection of the courts, LTV Corp. can lower its costs structure and compete more effectively until Bethlehem Steel is also pushed into bankruptcy and eventually the whole industry goes broke. While the drama is acted out, customers are likely to order from hand to mouth. The scenario is a dramatization of what goes on, in one form or another, in many sectors of the economy. Texas and other oil-producing regions are rapidly turning into disaster areas. The tax reform bill threatens to destroy the market for commercial real estate; it also weakens an already weak capital goods sector. Agriculture is in the depth of a depression, and defense spending, which has been one of the driving forces in the economy, is on the decline. Consumer spending remains the last major source of strength. If consumer confidence is shaken, final demand may never pick up as it is supposed to. As Keynes said, in the long run we are all dead.

The situation is exacerbated by instability in the currency markets. The decline in the dollar greatly reduces the scope for monetary stimulation. The prospect for a vicious circle developing in which a weak economy and a weak dollar become mutually self-reinforcing is greater now than at any time since the inception of the real-time experiment.

The combination of a near-term negative and a long-term positive impact is called a J curve. The term is usually used in connection with currencies, but it can also be applied to oil prices. It depicts the effects of a one-time fall in value. If the depreciation is continuous, the downward slope of the J curve is extended until it becomes more appropriate to speak of a slippery slope than a J curve.

I have been aware of the dangers inherent in the collapse of oil prices long before the markets began to recognize them and I have been lulled into a false sense of security by the fact that the markets continued to ignore them. Indeed, I was more preoccupied with possible signs of a pickup until recent market action gave me a rude reminder. When the stock market went into a tailspin on July 7, my first reaction was to treat it as a typical technical correction in a bull market which in this case seems to occur at the beginning of each quarter. I realized that we are in a situation where any break in the stock market could be self-validating; still, I found it difficult to believe that the break would come exactly when the market was due for a technical correction. Moreover, it would be most unusual for the turn to be called correctly by a majority of technical analysts. Only a week later, when the decline exceeded the bounds of a technical correction, did I take it seriously.

I accept the bearish thesis not as a valid prediction of what is in store for us but as a potent influence in financial markets. At the same time, I see no reason to abandon the bullish thesis. On the contrary, if it survives the severe test it is currently subjected to it will be reinforced and its life span extended. Thus I find myself in the awkward position of having to operate with two contradictory theses, at least in the short run. The bearish thesis is the more potent right now, but I cannot claim to have acted upon it either in anticipation or at inception. Thus, there is a danger that I act upon it just as its influence in the market becomes fully felt—in other words, I sell at the bottom.

I have found myself in similar situations often before and I have developed certain techniques for dealing with them. Indeed, it is more usual for me to operate with two at least partially contradictory theses than to stake everything on one thesis as I did at the end of Phase 1.

As a general principle, I do not dismantle positions that are built on a thesis that remains valid; rather, I take additional positions in the opposite direction on the basis of the new thesis. The result is a delicate balance that needs to be adjusted from moment to moment. If the balancing act fails to protect the portfolio, I have to cut back all around in order to assure survival. If the balancing act is successful, I gain liquidity without having to sacrifice desirable positions. To illustrate: if I start with a fully invested position and then sell short an equal amount, a 20% decline, even if it affects the longs and the shorts equally, leaves me only 80% invested on the long side. If I cover my shorts at the right time, I come out way ahead, but even if I cover my shorts with a loss I am better off than if I had sold my longs at the wrong time. In practice, the operation is much more complex because the balancing act is not confined to the stock market.

Take the present case.* I reacted rather late. The break was already a week old, and the market was 5% off its peak when I started to move.

---

*Again, readers not particularly interested in my market maneuvers are advised to skip the rest of this chapter, with the exception of the entry for Oct. 22, 1986, which analyzes an interesting boom/bust sequence in the Japanese stock market.

On Monday, July 14, I actually bought some S&P futures on the argument that, if we are dealing with a technical reaction, the market ought to close higher. The Dow had dropped 63 points the previous Monday, July 7, and the bears would expect another sharp drop on the subsequent Monday to establish a cascade-like bear market. When the market did in fact close lower, I reversed myself on the following day and by the end of the week I built up a short position that probably outweighs my long positions. I also shorted some long bonds and went long some T-bill futures. Then I piled into the Japanese bond future market, and doubled up on my short position in U.S. government bonds. The idea behind these maneuvers is that eventually I expect concerted action to reduce interest rates but, with the dollar declining, U.S. bonds may react negatively while Japanese bonds would move up. The day-by-day evolution of the portfolio structure is shown in the tables following p. 255.

I am now in the position I wish to be in, but my posture is liable to change from minute to minute. I shall have to be much more active and nimble than I had been hitherto until the battle between the two conflicting theses is resolved. For instance, I covered 500 S&P futures contracts today (Monday, July 21) in order to be able to sell more at higher prices if and when the disappointment that the "cascade" did not continue precipitated a short-covering rally.

Which way I shall move next will be dictated by the outcome of the OPEC meeting starting next Monday. If it breaks down, I shall prepare for the worst; if, against all prevailing expectations, it manages to reach an agreement, I shall have to reassess the situation.

MONDAY EVENING, JULY 28, 1986

It is difficult to give a blow-by-blow account of my maneuvering. To summarize my activities last week: I reduced my short position in S&P futures to 5000 contracts ($587 million) at a modest loss; I covered part of my short position in U.S. government bond futures at a modest profit; and I also took a profit on a portion of my most recently acquired dollar short positions. The net effect is to reduce my risk marginally all around and to put me in what I believe to be a fully hedged position.

Today, Monday, I took my profit on the balance of my short position in U.S. government bond futures. Then the dollar fell to new lows for some unexplained reason and I felt obliged to jump off the fence on

	July 28, 1986					
	Closing 7/28/86	*% Change from 7/21*			*Closing 7/28/86*	*% Change from 7/21*
DM	2.1515	−1.5	S&P 500		240.23	+1.7
¥	158.30	+11.9	U.S. T-Bonds		97	−3.0
£	1.4795	−1.3	Eurodollar		93.43	−.2
Gold	347.9	−2.0	Crude Oil		10.90	−16.7
			Japanese Bonds		103.31	0

QUANTUM FUND EQUITY　　　　　$1,514,000,000
Net Asset Value Per Share　　　　　$10,126
Change from 7/21/86　　　　　　　2.4%
Change from 8/16/85　　　　　　　131.2%

Portfolio Structure (in millions of dollars)

Investment Positions (1)	Long	Short	Net Change (2) from 7/21	Net Currency Exposure (6)	Long	Short	Net Change (2) from 7/21
Stocks				DM-related	678		−117
US Stocks	1,020	(99)	−82	Japanese Yen	434		−115
US Index				Pound Sterling		(25)	0
Futures		(1,053)	−103	US Dollar	427		+268
Foreign				Other			
Stocks	581		−23	Currencies	341		+139
Bonds (3)							
US Gvt.							
Short							
Term (4)	59		+30				
Long							
Term		(572)	−2				
Japanese							
(5)	1,663		+329				
Commodities							
Oil		(37)	+6				
Gold			+34				

the bearish side. I was part of the crowd dumping bonds and stock index futures. I sold out the S&P index futures I had bought back at higher prices the week before, as well as the bond futures I had covered at higher prices earlier this morning. It was not clear to me whether the markets were anticipating a positive or a negative conclusion to the OPEC meeting; all I could see was that the dollar was falling for whatever reason and that was bearish for bonds and stocks. A market move that has no clear explanation can be all the more scary. I decided to act first and to look for an explanation later. I shall reexamine the situation tomorrow and, if necessary, reverse today's moves.

THURSDAY EVENING, JULY 31, 1986

On Tuesday, I took a modest profit on the S&P futures I had sold on Monday and I also covered my bond futures only to sell part of them out again at higher prices.

On Wednesday, the stock market made a modest new low. I tried to cover more S&P futures but the futures market rallied and I got only 1100 contracts done. I also continued to short into a rising oil market.

This morning, the dollar made new lows and I intend to get back into a more bearish position in stock index futures. It seems that the OPEC meeting has not succeeded in more than papering over the differences. The next move in oil should be down. This was the signal I was waiting for in deciding which way to get off the fence.

The case for a recession also seems to be getting stronger. Beyond the short-term case based on a deflationary spiral there is also a long-term case based on a decline in capital spending. The instability of financial markets provides a powerful disincentive to fixed capital formation all over the world. In the U.S., tax reform adds to the uncertainties; in Europe and Japan, the decline of the dollar puts downward pressure on profit margins. The trouble is that the governments have much less leeway than usual to embark on countercyclical policies. This is particularly true of the U.S., which is hemmed in by the need to maintain the confidence of foreign investors. Japan and Europe could do more, but they are moving slowly. In the meantime, the weight of accumulated debt is pressing: Bethlehem Steel suspended dividend payments on its preferred stock.

The downside seems open-ended, the upside limited. After yesterday's rally, the stock market is still in a mold that would fit a normal technical correction; today may be the day to break the mold. If this is true, my actions will undoubtedly contribute to it.

July 31, 1986

	Closing 7/31/86	% Change from 7/28		Closing 7/31/86	% Change from 7/28
DM	2.1040	+2.2	S&P 500	236.59	−1.5
¥	155.30	+1.9	U.S. T-Bonds	97	0
£	1.4928	+.9	Eurodollar	93.46	0
Gold	352.00	+1.2	Crude Oil	11.73	+7.6
			Japanese Bonds	103.64	+.3

QUANTUM FUND EQUITY $1,503,000,000
Net Asset Value Per Share $10,050
Change from 7/28/86   −.8%
Change from 8/16/85   +129.5%

Portfolio Structure (in millions of dollars)

Investment Positions (1)	Long	Short	Net Change (2) from 7/28	Net Currency Exposure (6)	Long	Short	Net Change (2) from 7/28
Stocks				DM–related	679		+1
US Stocks	983	(106)	−44	Japanese Yen	431		−3
US Index				Pound Sterling		(15)	+10
Futures		(973)	+80	US Dollar	408		−19
Foreign				Other			
Stocks	582	(44)	−43	Currencies	171		−170
Bonds (3)							
US Gvt.							
Short							
Term (4)	124		+65				
Long							
Term		(442)	+130				
Japanese							
(5)	1,686		+23				
Commodities							
Oil		(73)	−36				
Gold							

MONDAY EVENING, AUGUST 4, 1986

The short position I took on last Thursday seemed to be working: the index futures closed at a new low on Friday, setting up for another black Monday. Today, the stock market opened lower, but oil was higher from the start. I was concerned that OPEC may come to some kind of

Aug. 4, 1986							
	Closing 8/4/86	*% Change from 7/31*			*Closing 8/4/86*	*% Change from 7/31*	
DM	2.0865	+.8		S&P 500	236.00	−.2	
¥	154.30	+.6		U.S. T-Bonds	97^{25}/$_{32}$	+.8	
£	1.4695	−1.6		Eurodollar	93.57	+.1	
Gold	360.30	+2.4		Crude Oil	13.29	+13.3	
				Japanese Bonds	104.11	+.5	

QUANTUM FUND EQUITY $1,504,000,000
Net Asset Value Per Share $9,834
Change from 7/31/86   −2.1%
Change from 8/16/85   +124.6%

Portfolio Structure (in millions of dollars)

Investment Positions (1)	Long	Short	Net Change (2) from 7/31	Net Currency Exposure (6)	Long	Short	Net Change (2) from 7/31
Stocks				DM-related	601		−78
US Stocks	1,015	(96)	+42	Japanese Yen	421		−10
US Index				Pound Sterling		(15)	0
Futures		(703)	+270	US Dollar	497		+89
Foreign				Other			
Stocks	562	(44)	−20	Currencies	197		+26
Bonds (3)							
US Gvt.							
Short							
Term (4)	122		−2				
Long							
Term		(383)	+59				
Japanese							
(5)	2,388		+702				
Commodities							
Oil		(85)	−12				
Gold							

agreement and I tried to cover half my short position. Then the details of a deal began to filter through and the stock market rallied. I managed to cover only a quarter of my short position. I realized a modest profit on the completed transaction but I have an unrealized loss on the part I failed to cover. My present inclination is to take the loss, because the bearish case has been undermined by today's deal on oil quotas. The fact that Iran and Saudi Arabia came to terms is highly significant: it indicates that it is not in Saudi Arabia's political and military interest to see the price of oil go any lower. The deal may come apart, but that can happen only later. In the meantime, it does not make sense to be short in either oil or stocks. Unfortunately, I am short in both. I want to disengage myself, but I may have to be patient: there are many others in my position and after the first rally there may be room for second thoughts. One way or another, I have to be prepared to take a loss.

SATURDAY, AUGUST 9, 1986

I have reduced my exposure all around in the course of the week.

On Tuesday, I covered my short positions in index futures and oil and bank stocks; I also sold some of my currencies and short-term bonds. On Wednesday, after the first wave of short covering receded, I started covering my short positions in oil. On Thursday, I covered my short position in bond futures. Today, I sold the bulk of my currencies.

The only major positions I am left with are in stocks and in Japanese bond futures. The only new exposure I took on is a short position in U.S. government bond futures. This was a tactical move I made today after a sharp short-covering rally and it is hedged in a way by my Japanese bond futures.

The asset value of the Fund suffered its first setback since the beginning of January: the value of the shares dropped by 4.2% in the course of the week. The losses came primarily from the oil gamble and from some of my stock positions. The change in the market environment has finally caught up with us: several of our stock investment concepts were punctured and, without a successful hedging operation, our asset value suffered. We have probably not yet experienced the negative impact to the full extent: usually everything that can go wrong does so at the same time. That is why I prefer to retrench all around when things begin to go wrong. Two weeks of hectic activity produced no tangible results: it is time to become more quiescent. I am still too much involved in the

Aug. 8, 1986

	Closing 8/8/86	% Change from 8/4		Closing 8/8/86	% Change from 8/4
DM	2.0660	+1.0	S&P 500	236.88	+.4
¥	153.75	+.4	U.S. T-Bonds	$99^{03}/_{32}$	+1.3
£	1.4765	+.5	Eurodollar	93.61	0
Gold	375.60	+4.2	Crude Oil	14.83	+11.6
			Japanese Bonds	104.01	−.1

QUANTUM FUND EQUITY $1,472,000,000
Net Asset Value Per Share $9,628
Change from 8/4/86   −2.1%
Change from 8/16/85   +119.9%

Portfolio Structure (in millions of dollars)

Investment Positions (1)	Long	Short	Net Change (2) from 8/4	Net Currency Exposure (6)	Long	Short	Net Change (2) from 8/4
Stocks				DM-related	164		−437
US Stocks	1,002	(47)	+36	Japanese Yen	141		−280
US Index				Pound Sterling		(25)	−10
Futures			+703	US Dollar	1,192		+695
Foreign				Other			
Stocks	593	(30)	+45	Currencies	177		−20
Bonds (3)							
US Gvt.							
Short							
Term (4)	49		−73				
Long							
Term		(552)	−169				
Japanese							
(5)	2,385		−3				
Commodities							
Oil			+85				
Gold		(15)	−15				

day-to-day movements of the market, but I shall try to regain my perspective. With reduced exposure, I can reassess and regroup more easily.

I accept the OPEC agreement as a major event. The oil-producing countries went to the edge of the abyss and recoiled: they are likely to stay away from the abyss for some time. The inverse supply curve for oil works in both directions: once the price of oil rises, the pressure to pump oil at any price is diminished. In short, the oil cartel gained a new lease on life. Its duration is uncertain, but it is bound to be long enough to base my investment decisions on it. I expect oil prices not below $15 and more likely $18 by the end of the year.

Where does that leave me? My negative scenario was predicated on the collapse of oil; should I abandon it and turn unreservedly bullish again? That was my first reaction but I am held back because I am aware of too many negatives. Having passed one hurdle, namely, oil, there are others behind it. The most important is the weakness of the dollar. I prefer to remain cautious until the dollar is stabilized.

In casting around for a negative case I find myself returning to the argument I started with at the beginning of the real-time experiment. At that time, the Imperial Circle was unwinding and there was a danger it would start spinning in the opposite direction: a weak economy would produce a weak dollar and prevent a decline in interest rates. Both the economy and the dollar are weak enough to render this scenario realistic. What is there to prevent it? I believe only the realization of the danger will save us. The stock market is telling us that we are heading into a recession; the weight of bad debt is accumulating; and protectionist pressures have reached such a point that Congress fell only a few votes short of overriding a presidential veto on the subject. The authorities must realize that something has to be done. They had managed to forge a consensus once before, at the Plaza Group of Five meeting. Under the pressure of circumstances it would not be so difficult to do it again. Japan and Germany could lower their interest rates, and the United States could cooperate in supporting the dollar. Volcker flew off to Emminger's funeral in Germany over the weekend and I have no doubt the subject will be discussed. That is why I sold my currencies yesterday. Shorting U.S. bond futures makes less sense, except as a hedge. If the dollar continues to make new lows, I intend to build up the position as a replacement for my short position in the dollar; if the dollar stabilizes I can go long in stock index futures against it. In any case, I can offset my short position in U.S. bonds against my long position in Japanese bond futures.

In sum, I continue to operate with two alternative scenarios, but, instead of oil, the dollar has become the critical variable. If the authorities succeed in stabilizing the dollar, I shall back the bullish scenario more confidently; if they fail, the vicious circle looms. At present, I am willing to bet on a positive resolution, but only cautiously. Having surmounted one hurdle, we ought to be able to pass the next one. But if covering my dollar positions turns out to be a mistake I shall have to either engage in some fancy footwork or take it on the chin. Given the futility of my hedging exercise to date, I shall probably opt for the latter. After all, I have no leverage left in the portfolio to worry about.

MONDAY EVENING, AUGUST 18, 1986

The stock market has turned in a very strong performance, the bond market has also remained firm, and the currencies seem to have stabilized. The asset value of the fund reached a new high. I am now ready to opt for the bullish scenario with greater confidence.

We have been to the brink and we are in the process of pulling back from it. The groundwork has been laid for a coordinated reduction in interest rates. With oil prices rising we are heading for a period of inventory accumulation. With currencies stabilizing, the beneficial effects of the decline in the value of the dollar will begin to be felt. These short-term positives should outweigh the long-term negatives such as the downturn in construction and the weakness in capital spending. The net result should be a continuation of the substandard growth we have been experiencing. Against this background, the stock markets of the world may continue to reach new heights. The tax reform bill may exercise a dampening influence for the rest of this year because both long-term capital gains and short-term losses will have more favorable tax treatment this year than next; but this consideration may be already reflected in the market. Professional investors have raised a lot of cash and done a lot of hedging. If there is going to be a surprise it will be on the upside. This is quite a turnabout from a few weeks ago when I felt that the upside was limited and the downside open-ended.

I am now ready to conclude Phase 2 of the experiment. Instead of a turning point, it turned out to be an interlude in what I still consider a bull market. I shall revert to a more leisurely style of management and less frequent reviews. The Fund is well positioned, although I would be

Aug. 18, 1986

	Closing 8/18/86	% Change from 8/8		Closing 8/18/86	% Change from 8/8
DM	2.0170	+2.4	S&P 500	247.38	+4.4
¥	154.32	−.4	U.S. T-Bonds	$101^{04}/_{32}$	+2.0
£	1.4900	+.9	Eurodollar	93.81	+.2
Gold	376.40	+.2	Crude Oil	15.61	+5.3
			Japanese Bonds	105.08	+1.0

QUANTUM FUND EQUITY $1,594,000,000
Net Asset Value Per Share $10,423
Change from 8/8/86   +8.3%
Change from 8/16/85   +138.0%

Portfolio Structure (in millions of dollars)

Investment Positions (1)	Long	Short	Net Change (2) from 8/8	Net Currency Exposure (6)	Long	Short	Net Change (2) from 8/8
Stocks				DM-related	169		+5
US Stocks	1,088	(40)	+93	Japanese Yen	199		+58
US Index				Pound Sterling		(19)	+6
Futures	347		+347	US Dollar	1,245		+53
Foreign				Other			
Stocks	677	(19)	+95	Currencies	223		+46
Bonds (3)							
US Gvt.							
Short							
Term (4)	43		−6				
Long							
Term		(465)	+87				
Japanese							
(5)	2,427		+42				
Commodities							
Oil	28		+28				
Gold	11		+26				

happier with a somewhat larger long position in stocks and, to be adventurous, with a long position in oil.

The rather hectic activity of the last month is summarized graphically in the tables that follow p. 255.

MONDAY, SEPTEMBER 8, 1986

Last Monday, gold, influenced by a booming platinum market, broke the $400 barrier, and bonds and stocks sold off rather sharply. I ignored the sell-off and by Thursday I seemed to be justified: the Dow Jones made a new high. But the other indexes did not follow, and the whole market weakened on Friday. There has been a change in leadership: cyclical and oil stocks have come to the fore, but the old leadership, where investors have large profits, is acting poorly. I believe the tax bill is responsible: the tax rate on long-term capital gains is going to be higher next year.

	Sept. 5, 1986					
	Closing *9/5/86*	*% Change* *from 8/18*			*Closing* *9/5/86*	*% Change* *from 8/18*
DM	2.0487	−1.6	S&P 500		250.48	+1.3
¥	155.40	−.7	U.S. T-Bonds		$97^{12}/_{32}$	−3.7
£	1.4940	+.3	Eurodollar		94.09	+.3
Gold	422.80	+12.3	Crude Oil		16.37	+4.9
			Japanese Bonds		105.15	+.1

QUANTUM FUND EQUITY $1,638,000,000
Net Asset Value Per Share $10,606
Change from 8/18/86   +1.8%
Change from 8/16/85   +142.2%

Portfolio Structure (in millions of dollars)

Investment Positions (1)	Long	Short	Net Change (2) from 8/18	Net Currency Exposure (6)	Long	Short	Net Change (2) from 8/18
Stocks				DM-related	153		−16
US Stocks	1,214	(33)	+133	Japanese Yen	162		−37
US Index				Pound Sterling	5		+24
Futures	499		+152	US Dollar	1,318		+73
Foreign				Other			
Stocks	654		−4	Currencies	247		+24
Bonds (3)							
US Gvt.							
Short							
Term (4)	11		−32				
Long							
Term			+465				
Japanese	2,385		−42				
(5)							
Commodities							
Oil	76		+48				
Gold			−11				

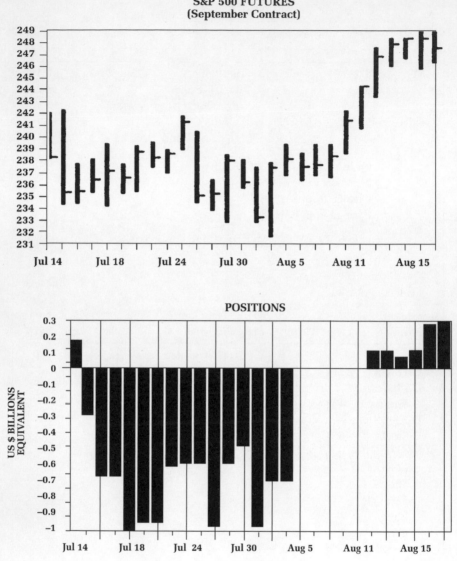

S&P 500 FUTURES
(September Contract)

POSITIONS

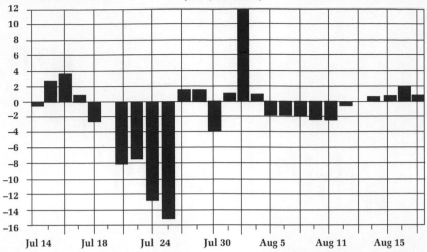

PROFITS AND LOSSES ON S&P INDEX FUTURES
(US $ Millions)

Summary of S&P Index Transactions

Date	Close Price	Outst. Position $ Mill.	Bought Amount $ Mill.	Bought Price	Sold Amount $ Mill.	Sold Price	Cum. Real. P&L $ Mill.	Unreal. P&L $ Mill.
Jul 14	238.3	153	153	238.98				(0.435)
Jul 15	235.05	(301)			(456)	237.44	(0.986)	3.059
Jul 16	235.1	(647)			(347)	236.04	(0.986)	4.377
Jul 17	236.15	(655)			(6)	237.50	(0.986)	1.523
Jul 18	236.85	(982)			(324)	236.12	(0.986)	(1.421)
Jul 21	236.35	(921)	59	236.10			(0.884)	0.613
Jul 22	238.4	(929)	35	235.45	(36)	237.50	(0.576)	(7.376)
Jul 23	237.95	(602)	334	238.75			(3.709)	(3.607)
Jul 24	238.4	(595)					(3.709)	(4.732)
Jul 25	240.9	(602)					(3.709)	(10.982)
Jul 28	234.85	(939)			(353)	235.20	(3.709)	4.668
Jul 29	235.1	(588)	374	234.58	(22)	235.20	(1.417)	2.215
Jul 30	237.7	(484)	156	234.79	(47)	235.61	(0.623)	(3.565)
Jul 31	235.95	(952)			(473)	236.68	(0.623)	1.458
Aug 1	233.15	(671)	360	233.76	(35)	234.93	2.713	8.893
Aug 4	237.05	(682)					2.713	(2.334)
Aug 5	237.75	0	685	237.80			(1.779)	
Aug 6	237.3	0					(1.779)	
Aug 7	237.45	0					(1.779)	
Aug 8	238.1	0					(1.779)	
Aug 11	241.3	0					(1.779)	
Aug 12	244.2	61	103	241.18	(43)	243.45	(1.382)	0.755
Aug 13	246.45	55			(6)	246.62	(1.246)	1.186
Aug 14	247.55	37			(19)	247.50	(0.772)	0.955
Aug 15	248.05	70	32	247.97			(0.772)	1.041
Aug 18	248.25	256	185	247.11			(0.772)	1.951
Aug 19	247.4	292	37	246.44			(0.772)	1.220

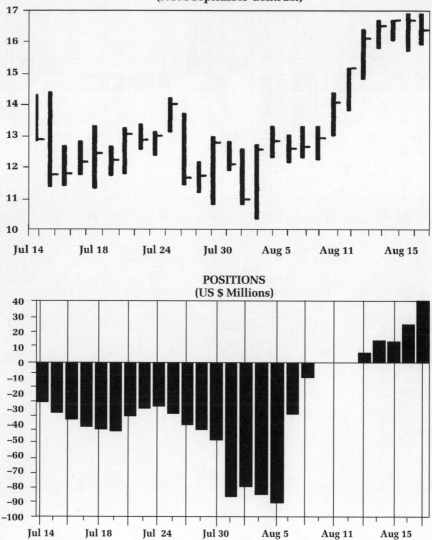

CRUDE OIL
(NYM September Contract)

POSITIONS
(US $ Millions)

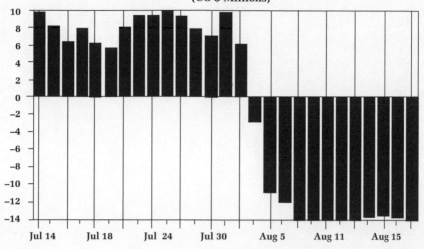

CRUDE OIL PROFITS AND LOSSES
(US $ Millions)

Summary of Transactions in Oil-Related Contracts[1]

From	To	Transaction Mode	Transaction Amount US $ Mill.	Avg. Price US $/ Barr.	Total Outstand. US $ Mill.	Real P&L In Period US $ Mill.	Total P&L US $ Mill.
	Jul 14	Outstanding short position		15.478	(25.534)		7.750
Jul 15	Jul 17	Increased short position	(14.029)	13.038	(41.924)	0.000	7.466
Jul 21	Jul 24	Bought back	13.737	12.455	(26.535)	3.090	9.032
Jul 25	Jul 31	Increased short position	(49.679)	11.449	(87.654)	0.877	9.395
Aug 1	Aug 8	Covered short position	99.156	15.271	0.000	(19.824)	(13.186)
Aug 12	Aug 19	Built new long position	29.44	15.405	28.837	0.000	(13.789)

[1]Figures include positions in NYM-Crude and NYM-Heating Oil contracts for various months.

Prices shown are weighted averages for all outstanding contracts expressed in US $ per barrel.

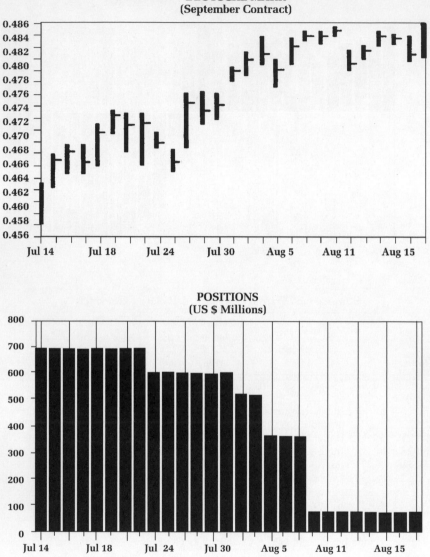

DEUTSCHE MARK PROFITS AND LOSSES
(US $ Millions)

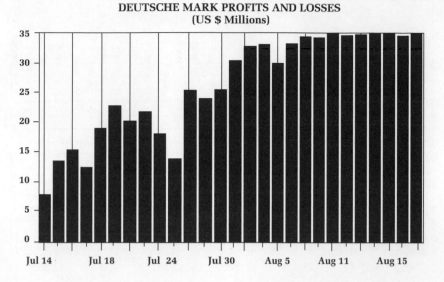

Summary of Transactions in Deutsche Mark Future and Forward Contracts[1]

Date	Transaction Mode	Transaction Amount US $ Mill.	Avg. Price US $/ 1 DM	Total Outstand. US $ Mill.	P&L on Transac. US $ Mill.	Total P&L US $ Mill.
Jul 14	Outstanding long position		0.4580	712.067		7.855
Jul 24	Decreased long position	125.182	0.4692	598.683	2.990	17.108
Aug 1	Decreased long position	81.000	0.4809	530.133	3.857	32.103
Aug 5	Decreased long position	150.380	0.4784	377.627	6.418	29.977
Aug 8	Decreased long position	297.205	0.4843	84.431	16.131	33.986

[1]Figures include positions in D. Mark Sep. futures and forward contracts due 9/17.
Price of forward contracts is assumed equal to price of futures.

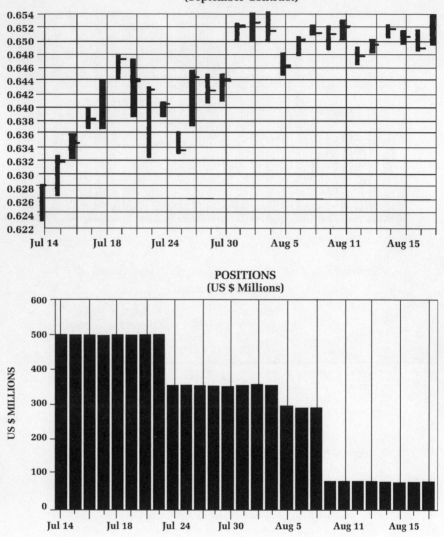

YEN
(September Contract)

POSITIONS
(US $ Millions)

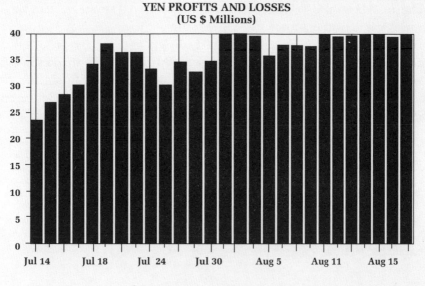

YEN PROFITS AND LOSSES
(US $ Millions)

Summary of Transactions in Japanese Yen Future and Forward Contracts[1]

Date	Transaction Mode	Transaction Amount US $ Mill.	Avg. Price US $/ 100 Yen	Total Outstand. US $ Mill.	P&L on Transac. US $ Mill.	Total P&L US $ Mill.
Jul 14	Outstanding long position		0.6122	486.666	16.742	23.634
Jul 24	Decreased long position	(132.040)	0.6408	364.170	5.215	33.178
Aug 5	Decreased long position	(96.870)	0.6458	269.812	3.140	35.747
Aug 8	Decreased long position	(188.307)	0.6507	83.977	8.382	38.161

[1]Figures include positions in Yen Sep. futures and forward contracts due 9/17.

Price of forward contracts is assumed equal to price of futures.

The market is also concerned about inflation. My strategic view has not changed: if the authorities can coordinate their policies, we ought to have continued subdued growth. I am encouraged by the relative stability of the dollar. Nevertheless, it seems that the stock market needs to test the downside. At present, I don't expect much more than, say, 40 points on the Dow Jones. Nevertheless, I decided to cut my position in S&P futures in half, in order to retain the initiative.

				Sept. 8, 1986			
	Closing 9/8/86	*% Change from 9/5*			*Closing 9/8/86*	*% Change from 9/5*	
DM	2.0750	−1.3		S&P 500	248.14	−.9	
¥	156.00	−.4		U.S. T-Bonds	$96^{24}/_{32}$	−.6	
£	1.4835	−.7		Eurodollar	94.04	−.1	
Gold	411.00	−2.8		Crude Oil	15.62	−4.6	
				Japanese Bonds	104.30	−.8	

QUANTUM FUND EQUITY $1,592,000,000
Net Asset Value Per Share $10,304
Change from 9/5/86 -2.8%
Change from 8/16/85 +135.3%

Portfolio Structure (in millions of dollars)

Investment Positions(1)	Long	Short	Net Change (2) from 9/5	Net Currency Exposure(6)	Long	Short	Net Change (2) from 9/5
Stocks				DM-related	151		−2
US Stocks	1,189	(32)	−24	Japanese Yen	137		−25
US Index				Pound Sterling	6		+1
Futures	261		−238	US Dollar	1,298		−20
Foreign				Other			
Stocks	647		−7	Currencies	223		−24
Bonds (3)							
US Gvt.							
Short							
Term (4)	8		−3				
Long							
Term							
Japanese							
(5)	2,360		−25				
Commodities							
Oil	72		−4				
Gold							

A setback in Japanese stocks and bonds is hurting, but there is nothing to be done about it.

THURSDAY MORNING, SEPTEMBER 11, 1986

I have decided to move into a more neutral position. That means selling out the rest of my S&P futures, and perhaps even going short against my stock positions, or building up my small short position in government bonds. I have also decided to short the dollar, mainly against the DM.

I expect the U.S. economy to show strength in the third quarter, and my information is that the German economy showed a strong pickup in the second quarter. The groundwork has been laid between the U.S. and Japan for a concerted reduction in interest rates in exchange for a concerted move to stabilize the dollar, and I believe that Germany would join, albeit reluctantly. Given the momentary strength, I believe the button will not be pushed until and unless a renewed attack on the dollar would force the hand of the authorities. It is to hedge against that possibility that I am buying DM. I could, of course, lose both on the DM and on Japanese bonds, if the dollar continues to strengthen; but I consider the risk modest.

The stock market is increasingly dominated by tax considerations. These are difficult to read but I believe that on balance the pressure will be on the downside for the next few months, setting up for a strong year-end rally. Where I have no strong convictions, I want to reduce my exposure.

SATURDAY, SEPTEMBER 13, 1986

The last two days' sharp sell-off found me unprepared. I completed the program I set for myself before the opening on Thursday, but obviously that was not enough to protect the portfolio: we are suffering a major setback. I am reluctant to make any further moves because they could easily compound the damage. Our exposure is not excessive: I do not need to retrench immediately. On the other hand, I have very little ammunition for further engagement. I intend to do as little as possible. This is in sharp contrast with the July/August break, which I managed to dodge successfully. In a sense, I was faked out by that break. Hedging against it left me emotionally exhausted, and when the more severe break came I was asleep at the switch.

Sept. 10, 1986

	Closing 9/10/86	% Change from 9/8		Closing 9/10/86	% Change from 9/8
DM	2.0630	+.6	S&P 500	247.06	−.4
¥	154.60	+.9	U.S. T-Bonds	$97^{21}/_{32}$	+.9
£	1.4812	−.2	Eurodollar	94.05	0
Gold	404.70	−1.5	Crude Oil	14.88	−4.7
			Japanese Bonds	104.01	−.3

QUANTUM FUND EQUITY $1,586,000,000
Net Asset Value Per Share $10,269
Change from 9/8/86   −.3%
Change from 8/16/85   +134.5%

Portfolio Structure (in millions of dollars)

Investment Positions(1)	Long	Short	Net Change (2) from 9/8	Net Currency Exposure (6)	Long	Short	Net Change (2) from 9/8
Stocks				DM–related	153		+2
US Stocks	1,098	(30)	−89	Japanese Yen	135		−2
US Index				Pound Sterling	5		−1
Futures	259		−2	US Dollar	1,293		−5
Foreign				Other			
Stocks	673		+26	Currencies	277		+54
Bonds (3)							
US Gvt.							
Short							
Term (4)	1		−7				
Long							
Term		(96)	−96				
Japanese							
(5)	2,377		+17				
Commodities							
Oil	96		+24				
Gold							

In retrospect I should have realized that the tax reform bill could dislocate the market, coming at a time when the market was consolidating anyhow. The inducement to sell first and buy back later was just about irresistible. The question now is: How far and how fast will the market de-

Sept. 12, 1986

	Closing 9/12/86	% Change from 9/10		Closing 9/12/86	% Change from 9/10
DM	2.0597	+.2	S&P 500	230.68	−6.6
¥	155.30	−.5	U.S. T-Bonds	94²²/₃₂	−3.0
£	1.4772	−.3	Eurodollar	93.96	−.1
Gold	416.50	+2.9	Crude Oil	15.06	+1.2
			Japanese Bonds	103.05	−.9

QUANTUM FUND EQUITY $1,484,000,000
Net Asset Value Per Share $9,610
Change from 9/10/86   -6.4%
Change from 8/16/85   +119.5%

Portfolio Structure (in millions of dollars)

Investment Positions (1)	Long	Short	Net Change (2) from 9/10	Net Currency Exposure (6)	Long	Short	Net Change (2) from 9/10
Stocks				DM–related	905		+752
US Stocks	1,109	(42)	−1	Japanese Yen	355		+220
US Index				Pound Sterling	3		−2
Futures	55		−204	US Dollar	221		−1,072
Foreign				Other			
Stocks	629		−44	Currencies	249		−28
Bonds (3)							
US Gvt.							
Short							
Term (4)			−1				
Long							
Term			+96				
Japanese							
(5)	2,348		−29				
Commodities							
Oil	97		+1				
Gold							

cline? The figure to watch is mutual fund redemptions. Interestingly, I do not feel that the downside is as open-ended as it was in July: whatever lows we reach in the next three months will set the stage for a strong year-end rally, which I believe will carry prices above today's levels.

SUNDAY, SEPTEMBER 28, 1986

Now that the markets have regained some measure of stability, I can collect my thoughts and establish a longer-term strategy. The main question confronting me is whether the configuration I have called the Golden Age of Capitalism is still operative or are we in transition to another phase; in the latter case, what is going to be the next configura-

Sept. 26, 1986					
	Closing 9/26/86	*% Change from 9/12*		*Closing 9/26/86*	*% Change from 9/12*
DM	2.0530	+.3	S&P 500	232.23	+.7
¥	154.60	+.5	U.S. T-Bonds	$95^{21}/_{32}$	+1.0
£	1.4360	−2.8	Eurodollar	94.01	+.1
Gold	427.20	+2.6	Crude Oil	14.43	−4.2
			Japanese Bonds	103.36	+.3

QUANTUM FUND EQUITY $1,503,000,000
Net Asset Value Per Share $9,728
Change from 9/12/86   +1.2%
Change from 8/16/85   +122.2%

Portfolio Structure (in millions of dollars)

Investment Positions (1)	Long	Short	Net Change (2) from 9/12	Net Currency Exposure (6)	Long	Short	Net Change (2) from 9/12
Stocks				DM-related	990		+85
US Stocks	1,071	(53)	−49	Japanese Yen	295		−60
US Index				Pound Sterling		(10)	−13
Futures		(275)	−330	US Dollar	228		+7
Foreign				Other			
Stocks	623		−6	Currencies	238		−11
Bonds (3)							
US Gvt.							
Short							
Term (4)							
Long							
Term		(180)	−180				
Japanese							
(5)	1,986		−362				
Commodities							
Oil	94		−3				
Gold							

tion? The question is very similar to the one I asked at the beginning of the real-time experiment: what is going to be the outcome of the Imperial Circle? Indeed, the question could be phrased differently: is the "Golden Age of Capitalism" an enduring phenomenon or is it merely a temporary expedient that has run its course?

Many signs point to the latter alternative. I shall mention only a few: the steepening of the yield curve; the rise of gold; and the disarray in the Group of Five process. The stock market also shows signs of a major top, although it has not quite reached the state of euphoria that one would expect from "the bull market of a lifetime"; in other words, the bubble is not yet ripe for bursting. That is, in fact, the main reason why I have been so reluctant to recognize the topping action and preferred to think in terms of a technical correction. It is by no means certain that the bull market is over, but the break has been too severe to treat it as part of an ongoing bull market. It is better to declare the phase I have called the "Golden Age of Capitalism" as complete and to try to identify the next phase. Even if it turns out to be a new phase in the "bull market of a lifetime," it is bound to have so many different features as to justify giving it a different name. I am quite uncertain at present how the situation will unfold. By declaring it a new phase, even if it turns out to be a continuation of the old one, I avoid getting frozen into an inappropriate mold and force myself to maintain an open mind. It is far too early to come to any definite conclusions.

The previous phase was based on international cooperation that has made a controlled descent of the dollar and a coordinated reduction in interest rates possible.

The world economy remained sluggish so that monetary stimulation led to a big bull market in financial assets. The increasing disparity between the "real" and the "financial" economies of the world created strains that threaten to undermine international cooperation and require a new departure if a breakdown is to be avoided. Unfortunately, there are no signs of new policy initiatives, only squabbling among the allies. It is far too early to predict how the impasse will be resolved. I can see three major possibilities:

1. *Muddling through.* The J curve finally begins to work, providing some impetus to the U.S. economy while weakening our major trading partners. The world economy remains sluggish and monetary policy accommodating. Once it becomes clear that the disintegration of the international trading and financial system has been avoided, confidence returns and the tremendous

liquidity that has accumulated is once again invested in financial assets. If so, we may yet see "the bull market of a lifetime."

2. *A vicious circle.* A weak economy and a weak dollar reinforce each other to produce higher interest rates and higher budget deficits. Protectionism gains the upper hand and it provokes retaliation, including debt repudiation.

3. *New policy initiatives.* Under pressure from the financial markets (a falling dollar, falling bond and stock markets, and rising gold prices) the authorities get their act together. The dollar is stabilized at the same time as there is another round of interest rate reductions. The U.S. and the Soviet Union agree on a disarmament pact, allowing the military budget to be cut. International debt is finally recognized as a political problem and steps are taken to stimulate the economies of less developed countries.

Since the emergence of a vicious circle is bound to evoke a policy response, we may distinguish between two main alternatives: muddling through and a vicious circle followed by new policy initiatives. The actual course of events is likely to combine elements of both. Either way, financial markets are likely to remain under pressure in the near term.

After the OPEC meeting I made a bet that the quarrel between the United States and Germany will be patched up and we shall muddle through. I have started to hedge my bet recently; nevertheless, the outcome of the latest Group of Five meeting has proven me wrong. I intend to react to it vigorously.

I can understand how the impasse was reached. Baker needed a scapegoat and the Germans refused to be cast in the role. The elements of a deal were clearly visible: a U.S. commitment to stabilize the dollar in exchange for a German commitment to lower interest rates. I have the impression that it was Baker who balked. If so, it betrays the weakness of his position: he cannot agree to stabilize the dollar before the November elections because he has nothing else to offer to fend off protectionist pressures. There is plenty of time till the elections for the financial markets to elicit a more adequate policy response. I intend to do my share: I plan to increase my DM position by $500 million, my short position in U.S. government bonds from $180 to $500 million, and my stock index futures short position from $275 million to $750 million. I also want to go long $150 million in gold. The downside seems more open-ended than only a few weeks ago: by the time the policy disagreements are resolved a vicious circle may well be under way.

WEDNESDAY EVENING, OCTOBER 1, 1986

One tactical mistake begets another: everything I did on Monday, with the exception of the DM purchase, was wrong. I do not minimize the importance of the pre-summit meeting announced yesterday, but I must be careful not to embark on a vicious circle of my own. For the time

	Oct. 1, 1986				
	Closing 10/1/86	*% Change from 9/26*		*Closing 10/1/86*	*% Change from 9/26*
DM	2.0175	+1.7	S&P 500	233.60	+6
¥	153.85	+.5	U.S. T-Bonds	96 $^{22}/_{32}$	+1.1
£	1.4450	+.6	Eurodollar	94.03	0
Gold	425.20	−.5	Crude Oil	15.16	+5.1
			Japanese Bonds	103.02	−.3

QUANTUM FUND EQUITY $1,511,000,000
Net Asset Value Per Share $9,562
Change from 9/26/86   −1.7%
Change from 8/16/85   +118.4%

Portfolio Structure (in millions of dollars)

Investment Positions (1)	Long	Short	Net Change (2) from 9/26	Net Currency Exposure (6)	Long	Short	Net Change (2) from 9/26
Stocks				DM-related	1,415		+425
US Stocks	1,014	(83)	−87	Japanese Yen	282		−13
US Index				Pound Sterling	1		+11
Futures		(575)	−300	US Dollar		(187)	−415
Foreign				Other			
Stocks	635		+12	Currencies	240		+2
Bonds (3)							
US Gvt.							
Short							
Term (4)							
Long							
Term		(466)	−286				
Japanese							
(5)	1,987		+1				
Commodities							
Oil	99		+5				
Gold	150		+150				

being, I shall sit tight. Although I have lost money getting there, I believe my portfolio is reasonably well balanced. If so, I am prepared to sit out a rally in stocks and bonds, especially as I am going to China for a month.

WEDNESDAY, OCTOBER 22, 1986

I cut my trip to China short because I was worried about the Japanese portion of the portfolio. I am now on my way back to New York after spending a day in Tokyo.

The decline in the Japanese stock market has turned into a veritable rout in the last few days. The market as a whole has dropped by some 15%, but the stocks that I own, which are all real estate related, are off 25–40% from their recent highs. The bond market, where I have a large exposure, has also been weak.

Now that I have focused on it, I realize what is happening. The appreciation of the yen has gone too far: Japan is losing out to the newly industrialized countries of the Pacific Basin and exporting companies are hurting badly. An easy money policy is not enough to cope with the situation; indeed, it has become counterproductive by engendering a speculative boom that is bound to end in a bust. Recognizing this, the authorities have decided to relieve the upward pressure on the yen by actively encouraging capital outflows rather than by lowering interest rates any further. The policy succeeded, the yen has stabilized, and the market has collapsed.

I have been an active participant in one of the classic boom/bust sequences in history and I failed to get out in time. I am now badly caught. It is clear that I ought to get out of the market, but how and when? I don't know what to do because my knowledge of the Japanese market is extremely limited. I expect to pay a heavy price for my ignorance.

I find it somewhat embarrassing to get caught in the "bust of our lifetime" while writing about the "boom of our lifetime." Yet that is what has happened. I believe the collapse of the Japanese stock market will prove to be one of the landmarks of contemporary financial history. It resembles a classic crash more closely than anything we are likely to witness in our own market. The Japanese market has become grossly overvalued and complacency has become pervasive, as my own behavior testifies. Governor Satoshi Sumita of the Bank of Japan issued repeated warnings, but the market ignored it. I now hear that unit trusts were verbally guaranteeing 9% returns to investors—an unsound

Oct. 21, 1986

	Closing 10/21/86	% Change from 10/1		Closing 10/21/86	% Change from 10/1
DM	1.9845	+1.6	S&P 500	235.88	+1.0
¥	155.10	−.8	U.S. T-Bonds	$94\,^{22}/_{32}$	−2.1
£	1.4340	−.8	Eurodollar	93.92	−.1
Gold	425.20	0	Crude Oil	15.19	+.2
			Japanese Bonds	101.35	−1.6

QUANTUM FUND EQUITY　　　$1,488,000,000
Net Asset Value Per Share　　　$9,422
Change from 10/1/86　　　−1.5%
Change from 8/16/85　　　+115.2%

Portfolio Structure (in millions of dollars)

Investment Positions (1)	Long	Short	Net Change (2) from 10/1	Net Currency Exposure (6)	Long	Short	Net Change (2) from 10/1
Stocks				DM-related	1,316		−99
US Stocks	1,104	(108)	+65	Japanese Yen		(104)	−386
US Index				Pound Sterling	3		+2
Futures		(579)	−4	US Dollar	273		+460
Foreign				Other			
Stocks	572		−63	Currencies	235		−5
Bonds (3)							
US Gvt.							
Short							
Term (4)							
Long							
Term		(466)					
Japanese							
(5)	1,607		−380				
Commodities							
Oil	102		+3				
Gold	122		−28				

practice if ever there was one. I should have noticed these signs of speculative excess, but I failed to pay attention.

My only excuse is that I do not have a permanent presence in Japan: my previous foray was fifteen years ago. At that time I was a broker advising foreign investors; as a consequence I had the inside track, and I got out unscathed. Now I am a foreign investor, and my fate is typical of the occasional investor from abroad who is attracted by a boom: I bought in a rising market, and I shall have to sell in a falling one; having seen a large paper profit, I shall end up with a real loss.

The thesis that attracted me to Japan is no longer valid because it was based on excessive liquidity that created a land boom as well as a boom in the stock market. Railroad shares, which had been static since the last boom in 1973, were selling at a fraction of their asset value. Railroad companies have a way of accumulating assets without showing earnings: since the rate of return on commercial real estate is traditionally lower than the interest rate, they can shelter their earnings by borrowing money and investing it in additional real estate. Thus they enjoy physical growth as well as the appreciation of their land values. The fly in the ointment is that shareholders do not get any of the benefits: railroad companies are regulated, and if they want any rate increases they cannot increase their dividends. But changes are in the wind. The National Railroad is being converted to private ownership, and it needs to show better earnings in order to be salable to the public. Moreover, the pace of property development needs to be stepped up if domestic demand is to be stimulated. This means that railroad companies need external financing. As a consequence, both the companies and their underwriters have an interest in seeing their share prices rise, and most railroad companies have, in fact, been issuing bonds with warrants at rising prices. Foreign investors were the first to recognize this reflexive thesis, but to validate it domestic investors had to follow. That was also beginning to happen: at the beginning of the new fiscal year (October 1), the newly formed unit trusts (the ones that were guaranteeing a 9% return to investors) pushed real estate-related shares to an all-time high on record volume. As it turned out, that was the buying climax. The break in New York brought redemptions to Fidelity International Investment Trust, which was heavily invested in Japanese real estate-related stocks, and they were forced to sell in Japan. I was aware of that development at the time, and I intended to lighten up on the next rally; but the rally never came, and the decline turned into a rout. What I did not realize was the change in Japanese government policy in fostering capital exports. I should have taken my cue from the fact that the yen was stabilizing, but I was complacent. For that, there is no excuse. Now, the reflexive thesis has begun to work in reverse. The same factors that have punctured the stock market are likely to slow down the real estate boom. Although there is going to be a great increase in construction, the big increase in land prices is probably behind us. That is why I have to get out of my positions as best I can.

I must take great care not to compound my error by reacting emotionally. The hedges I put on prior to my departure did not protect me against the debacle in Japan; in fact they have cost me money. I can absorb my Japanese losses; but if I compound them with other losses, I could get badly hurt. Yet I cannot stand still, either. I must adjust to the changing circumstances. What are they?

First, the yen seems to have topped out, and it would not surprise me if it declined, say, 10%. Capital outflows far exceed the surplus on current account, and it is only because a large portion of the capital transactions have been hedged that the supply and demand for the yen have remained in balance for the last two months. As market participants gain confidence that the peak in the yen has passed, they may be more willing to hold dollars, bringing about a reversal of the trend. The government is unlikely to allow a decline in the yen to go too far, however, for fear of the political consequences.

I sold all my yen yesterday, and I intend to go short an amount equal to about half of my long position in DM. If the DM does not weaken in sympathy with the yen, I may even increase my long position in DM—half against dollars, half against yen. At the same time, I am cutting my long position in gold by half until I can see more clearly.

I have also sold some 20% of my Japanese bonds just to give me some flexibility, but I think it would be a mistake to liquidate my position at the current depressed prices. Yields have risen some 50–70 basis points. Contrary to previous occasions, the government is likely to resist a further backing up in interest rates, especially if the stock market continues to decline and the yen weakens.

By the same token, my short position in U.S. government bonds makes less sense than it did a few weeks ago: Japanese investors are likely to show up in force at the next auction. With the effect of the OPEC agreement fully felt by then, I intend to cover my short position on that occasion and perhaps even go long.

My U.S. stock portfolio seems reasonably well hedged at present, and I am happy to keep it that way. I am inclined to the short side, but I restrain myself lest I compound my mistakes. I have less hesitation in taking profits on Hong Kong real estate shares, which are currently at a peak largely as a result of Japanese buying.

I shall also be happy to sell my oil contracts by the second half of November, when they mature. Indeed, I am setting up for selling short at higher prices by going long in January and short in March at practically the same price. I expect the forward discount to widen as the price goes up.

I am now convinced that the "bull market of a lifetime" is behind us. There may be occasional flare-ups of speculative activity, more unsound than ever, but its main thrust is exhausted. The blind confidence, which is an essential ingredient in a mature bull market, cannot be reestablished in a hurry. The demise has been less spectacular than one could have expected from the "bull market of a lifetime," although there have been classic climaxes in Italy, France, and now Japan. The closest we came to a climax in the U.S. has been the momentary rush to redeem mutual funds in September. I feel pretty foolish for failing to recognize these signs. The fact is that the bull market was cut short by the monetary authorities before it reached its full extension. They may lower interest rates yet, but the effect will no longer be the same. The bull market was based on the flight from physical to monetary assets; further monetary stimulation is likely to engender a flight to liquidity, including gold.

At present, there is a temporary lull: OPEC has been patched up, but without a sound foundation; exchange rates have been stabilized, but without proper international cooperation; the U.S. economy is enjoying a temporary respite before the tax reform comes into effect; and the stock market is buoyed by deals that must be consummated before the end of the year for the same reason. What will next year bring?

SATURDAY, OCTOBER 25, 1986

I managed to sell $750 million worth of yen short before it broke. When the DM failed to resist the rise in the dollar, I reduced my DM position to $750 million. I am now fully hedged, long in DM and short in yen. I did not make any money on the maneuver, but I avoided giving back my profits.

Oct. 24, 1986					
	Closing 10/24/86	*% Change from 10/21*		*Closing 10/24/86*	*% Change from 10/21*
DM	2.0355	−2.6	S&P 500	238.26	+1.0
¥	161.7	−4.3	U.S. T-Bonds	95²⁹/₃₂	+1.3
£	1.413	−1.5	Eurodollar	93.99	+.1
Gold	407.5	−4.2	Crude Oil	15.02	−1.1
			Japanese Bonds	101.95	+.6

QUANTUM FUND EQUITY $1,455,000,000
Net Asset Value Per Share $9,214
Change from 10/21/86 -2.2%
Change from 8/16/85 +110.4%

Portfolio Structure (in millions of dollars)

Investment Positions (1)	Long	Short	Net Change (2) from 10/21	Net Currency Exposure (6)	Long	Short	Net Change (2) from 10/21
Stocks				DM-related	792		−524
US Stocks	1,069	(123)	−50	Japanese Yen		(735)	−631
US Index				Pound Sterling	2		−1
Futures		(675)	−96	US Dollar	1,396		+1,123
Foreign				Other			
Stocks	523		−49	Currencies	216		−19
Bonds (3)							
US Gvt.							
Short							
Term (4)							
Long							
Term		(465)	+1				
Japanese							
(5)	1,234		−373				
Commodities							
Oil	99		−3				
Gold	80		−42				

I also tried to unload half my Japanese stock positions on the first rally, but I failed: the Japanese broker reneged on his commitment and took only half the amount he committed for, equal to one-eighth of my total exposure. The worst of it is that he now knows my intention. This is going to be a bloody business.

I am beginning to feel uncomfortable with my short positions in U.S. government bonds and S&P futures. With the rally in the dollar, the case against higher interest rates is weakening, and, if bonds rally, the shorts in S&P futures may be run in. Everybody now expects the Japanese to buy the October government bond refunding; therefore, I must act before. There is a 7-year bond auction on Tuesday; I must move on that occasion. I can start to sell or reduce my long positions on the rally that I expect to follow a successful auction.

At present, the stock market is dominated by program trading and portfolio insurance schemes. These schemes are fundamentally unsound. They virtually assure a loss in exchange for peace of mind in a declining market. Only if the decline continued, or if the investor had the strength of character to take off the hedge in a weak market—which is unlikely, otherwise he would not have bought portfolio insurance in the first place—could he realize a profit. The very expression "portfolio insurance" is a false metaphor because it is based on an analogy with life insurance; but death is certain, while a crash is not.

A rally in the stock market would show up the flaw in portfolio insurance; afterward, the market would be in a better position to decline. I expect such a decline to follow the next reduction in short-term interest rates. In the meantime, the stock market could retest its recent high. Other things being equal, there ought to be a strong year-end rally because of all the tax-induced selling that will have preceded it. Of course, the November elections will also affect the market, but I do not know how.

SATURDAY, NOVEMBER 1, 1986

It was a hectic, difficult week. It started out with a collapse in oil prices due to the Saudi decision to engage in new "net-back" deals. I managed to liquidate most of my crude oil before the break, but the drop in oil prices made it more expensive to execute the rest of my plan. Nevertheless, by Tuesday afternoon I had covered half my stock index short and swung around from being $500 million short in government bonds to an $800 million long position. But the 7-year auc-

	Oct. 31, 1986				
	Closing *10/31/86*	*% Change* *from 10/24*		*Closing* *10/31/86*	*% Change* *from 10/24*
DM	2.0661	−1.5	S&P 500	243.98	+2.4
¥	163.25	−1.0	U.S. T-Bonds	98³/₃₂	+2.3
£	1.4065	−.5	Eurodollar	94.11	+.1
Gold	403.60	−1.0	Crude Oil	15.27	+1.7
			Japanese Bonds	102.96	+1.0

QUANTUM FUND EQUITY $1,469,000,000
Net Asset Value Per Share $9,296
Change from 10/21/86   +.9%
Change from 8/16/85   +112.3%

Portfolio Structure (in millions of dollars)

Investment Positions (1)	Long	Short	Net Change (2) from 10/24	Net Currency Exposure (6)	Long	Short	Net Change (2) from 10/24
Stocks				DM-related	1,280		+488
US Stocks	1,015	(99)	−30	Japanese Yen		(955)	−220
US Index				Pound Sterling	3		+1
Futures		(327)	+348	US Dollar	1,141		−255
Foreign				Other			
Stocks	460		−63	Currencies	201		−15
Bonds (3)							
US Gvt.							
Short							
Term (4)							
Long							
Term	1,073		+1,538				
Japanese							
(5)	1,232		−2				
Commodities							
Oil		(28)	−127				
Gold	79		−1				

tion did not go well—I must have been the biggest buyer—and by Tuesday night I was losing on all fronts. Then came two unexpected developments: the dismissal of Sheik Yamani as Saudi oil minister and the indication that the Japanese discount rate will be lowered. Suddenly, my position looked much brighter. I used the opportunity to reduce my holdings in Japanese real estate-related stocks and increased my holdings in U.S. government bonds to $1200 million. I also increased my cross position—long DM, short yen—to $1 billion. I have bought an additional $250 million worth of DM, giving me a modest net short position in the dollar.

My additional purchase of U.S. bonds turned out to be badly timed because oil rallied sharply, following a call by the new Saudi oil minister for an emergency meeting of the OPEC pricing committee. The situation is extremely confused, but the prevailing opinion is that the change represents a victory for Iran, and the Saudis will raise prices even if it means selling less oil. I take a different view, but I have not yet developed a high degree of conviction in it. In my opinion, the Saudis will publicly posture for fixing the oil price at $18, but they will not abandon their net-back deals and they will continue to play hardball in fighting for market share. Since it is impossible to maintain oil at $18 without reducing production all around, it is probable that negotiations will break down, and there will be another round in the price war. The Saudis have to be careful, however, not to anger Iran. I have started to short oil again, but only in small quantities because I cannot afford to take much risk. I am already exposed enough in bonds. If my bond play works out, I may become more courageous in oil—if it is not too late.

In the last two days of the week, a number of stronger economic figures were released, weakening my strategic position. The dollar rallied, but the yen/DM cross position has been working in my favor (see chart on p. 281), especially on Friday, after the joint Japanese-American statement was released. The statement confirms the thesis on which the cross position is based: whatever pressure develops against the dollar, it will be concentrated on European currencies—and possibly gold. If, however, the U.S. economy turns out to be stronger than I expected, the DM may decline even more than the yen because it has greater volatility. Thus, the position is not without risk; but I cannot see the dollar getting much stronger. My main risk is in bonds and in what has turned into a cross position: long bonds, short stock indexes. I am not unduly worried about the economic statistics because they merely confirm a temporary pickup prior to the tax changes; I am willing to take a view on oil; my main worry is the election next Tuesday, whose impact I cannot evaluate. The trouble is that my tolerance for losses has been reduced by the losses I have already sustained, both in my macro manipulations—the hedge I took on prior to my trip to China turned out to be quite costly—and in my investment portfolio, which continues to unravel. As a consequence, I feel nervous and somewhat overexposed.

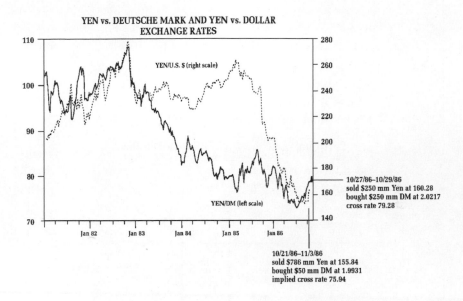

YEN vs. DEUTSCHE MARK AND YEN vs. DOLLAR EXCHANGE RATES

10/27/86–10/29/86
sold $250 mm Yen at 160.28
bought $250 mm DM at 2.0217
cross rate 79.28

10/21/86–11/3/86
sold $786 mm Yen at 155.84
bought $50 mm DM at 1.9931
implied cross rate 75.94

SATURDAY, NOVEMBER 8, 1986

The gamble on the government bond auction did not work out: an initial profit turned into a loss. I cut my position to limit the loss. The news on oil has been contradictory and I decided to withdraw to the sidelines; I also withdrew from gold at the same time. All I have now is a cross position—long bonds, short stock indexes—which I regard as a temporary expedient; a long position in Japanese bonds, which I may gradually liquidate or partially switch to German bonds; and my currency positions, which seem soundly based.

Most of my recent macro moves turned sour; only the decision to short the yen has saved the day. I can apply the profit on the yen either to offset the losses on the other moves or to protect my profits on the DM, but not both. Either way, my macro manipulations failed

	Closing 11/7/86	% Change from 10/31		Closing 11/7/86	% Change from 10/31
DM	2.0610	+.2	S&P 500	245.77	+.7
¥	163.00	+.2	U.S. T-Bonds	96 $^{10}/_{32}$	−1.8
£	1.4310	+1.7	Eurodollar	93.92	−.2
Gold	388.60	−3.7	Crude Oil	15.17	−.7
			Japanese Bonds	103.09	+.1

Nov. 7, 1986

QUANTUM FUND EQUITY $1,461,000,000
Net Asset Value Per Share $9,320
Change from 10/31/86 +.3%
Change from 8/16/85 +112.8%

Portfolio Structure (in millions of dollars)

Investment Positions (1)	Long	Short	Net Change (2) from 10/31	Net Currency Exposure (6)	Long	Short	Net Change (2) from 10/31
Stocks				DM-related	1,334		+54
US Stocks	1,022	(71)	+35	Japanese Yen		(956)	−1
US Index				Pound Sterling	7		+4
Futures		(544)	−217	US Dollar	1,076		−65
Foreign				Other			
Stocks	436		−24	Currencies	201		0
Bonds (3)							
US Gvt.							
Short							
Term (4)							
Long							
Term	750		−323				
Japanese							
(5)	983		−249				
Commodities							
Oil			+28				
Gold	41		−38				

to protect me against a deterioration in my investment positions and the asset value of the Fund has declined.

This is an opportune moment to end the real-time experiment because it is gradually deteriorating into a record of my day-to-day trading activity. It is not without interest—I follow a stochastic, trial-and-error method that seems to produce positive results on balance—but it is rather messy because of the prevalence of errors, and it takes us rather far afield from the original purpose of the experiment. I could justify taking the readers along the torturous course of my mega-manipulations for a while—if for no other reason than to give them a more balanced picture than Phase 1 alone would have done—but I must draw the line somewhere and return to the original question, namely, the resolution of the contradictions inherent in the Imperial Circle. Incidentally, I am beginning to worry that the process of recording my thoughts for public consumption may interfere with my ability to acknowledge and correct mistakes promptly because doing so makes the record even messier. I am thinking of the hedge I put on prior to my trip to China, which turned out to be so costly.

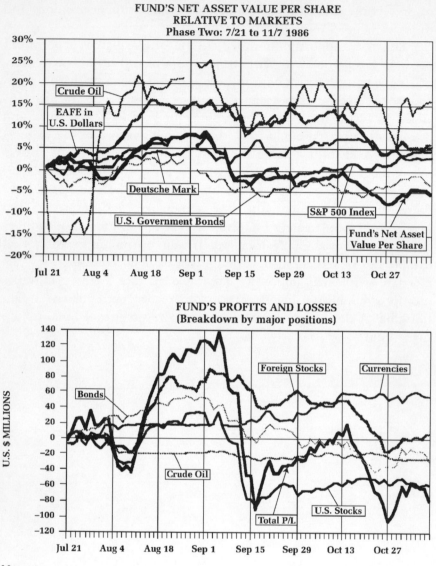

Notes:

(1) All prices are calculated as percent change over the first day shown.

(2) EAFE is Morgan Stanley's Capital International Index in U.S. dollars for European, Australian, and Far Eastern stock markets.

(3) The Oil and the Government Bond prices are the closing prices of the nearest futures contracts.

(4) Currency profits and losses include only forward and futures contracts. P&L on foreign stocks includes the currency gain or loss on the positions.

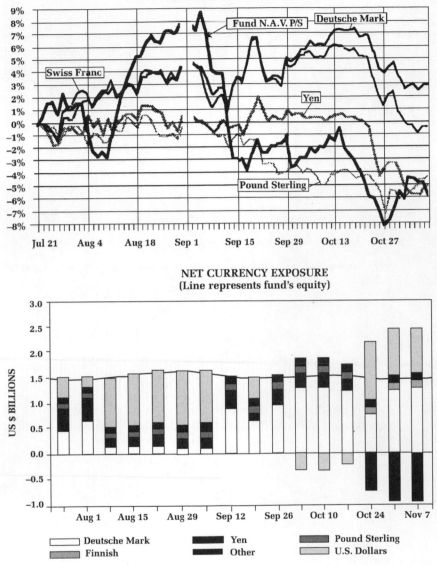

CURRENCY PRICES
Phase Two: 7/21 to 11/7 1986

NET CURRENCY EXPOSURE
(Line represents fund's equity)

Notes:

(1) Prices in U.S. dollars shown as percent change over the first day shown. New York closing prices are used.

(2) Net currency exposure includes stock, bonds, futures, forwards, cash, and margins, and equals the total equity of the fund. A short position in U.S. dollars indicates the amount by which the currency exposure exceeds the equity of the fund.

(3) Currency exposure shown as of end of week.

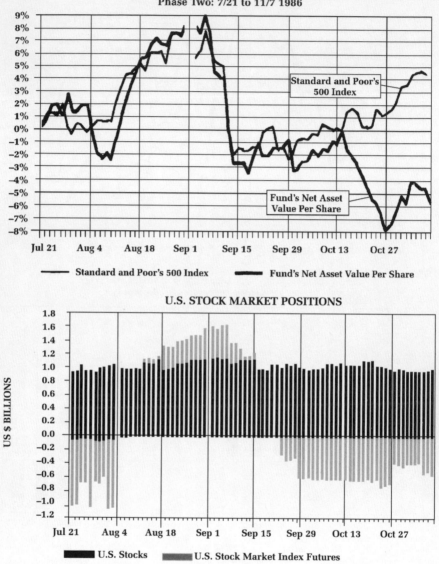

U.S. STOCK MARKET
Phase Two: 7/21 to 11/7 1986

Standard and Poor's 500 Index

Fund's Net Asset Value Per Share

— Standard and Poor's 500 Index   ▬ Fund's Net Asset Value Per Share

U.S. STOCK MARKET POSITIONS

US $ BILLIONS

■ U.S. Stocks   ▨ U.S. Stock Market Index Futures

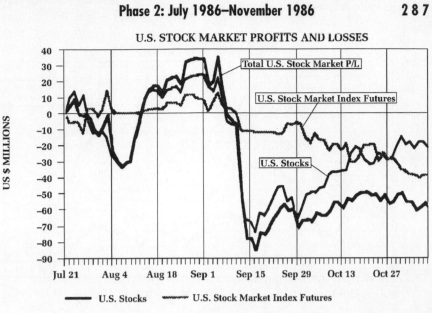

U.S. STOCK MARKET PROFITS AND LOSSES

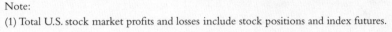

Note:

(1) Total U.S. stock market profits and losses include stock positions and index futures.

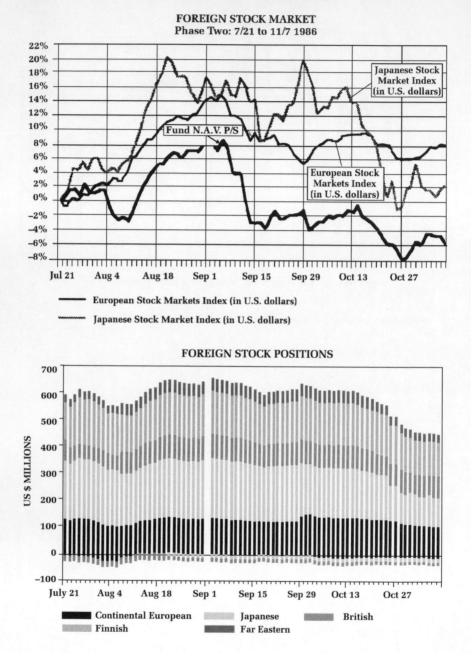

FOREIGN STOCK MARKET
Phase Two: 7/21 to 11/7 1986

Japanese Stock Market Index (in U.S. dollars)

Fund N.A.V. P/S

European Stock Markets Index (in U.S. dollars)

——— European Stock Markets Index (in U.S. dollars)
wwwww Japanese Stock Market Index (in U.S. dollars)

FOREIGN STOCK POSITIONS

US $ MILLIONS

■ Continental European   ▨ Japanese   ▨ British
▨ Finnish   ▨ Far Eastern

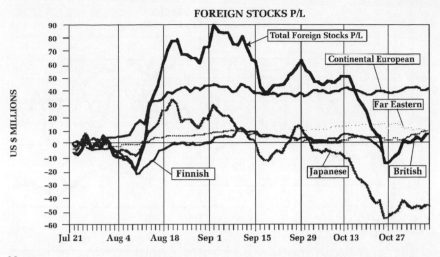

FOREIGN STOCKS P/L

Notes:

(1) Total foreign stock market profits and losses include foreign exchange gains or losses on foreign stock positions.

(2) Far Eastern positions include Hong Kong, Korea, Taiwan, Australia, and Thailand.

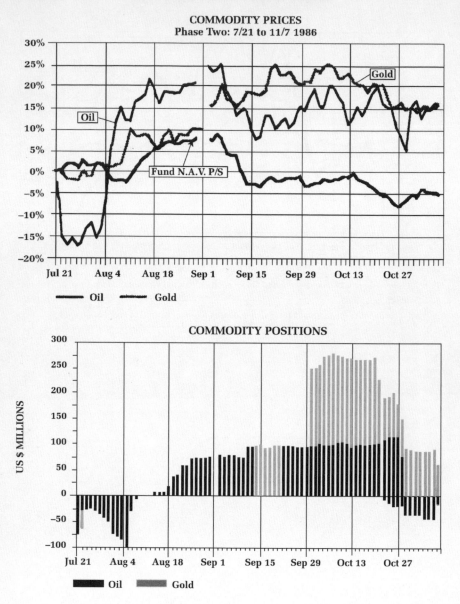

COMMODITY PROFITS AND LOSSES

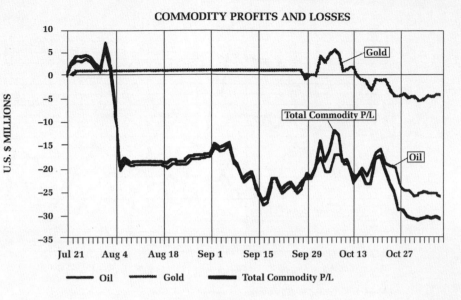

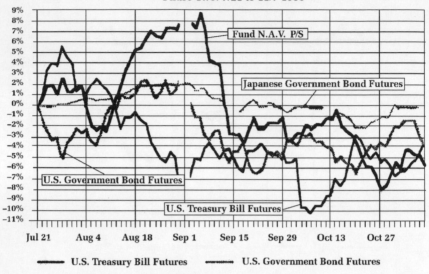

FIXED INCOME SECURITIES
Phase Two: 7/21 to 11/7 1986

U.S. Treasury Bill Futures   U.S. Government Bond Futures
Japanese Government Bond Futures

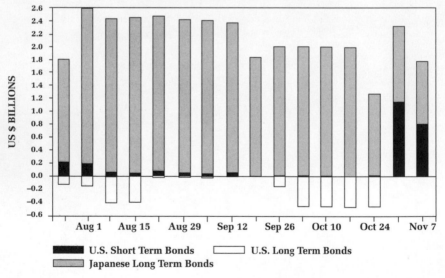

FIXED INCOME SECURITIES POSITION

U.S. Short Term Bonds   U.S. Long Term Bonds
Japanese Long Term Bonds

FIXED INCOME SECURITIES P&L

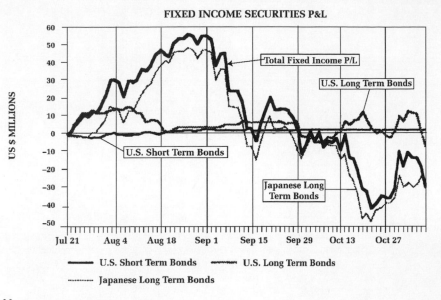

Legend:
- ━━━ U.S. Short Term Bonds
- ╍╍╍ U.S. Long Term Bonds
- ┄┄┄ Japanese Long Term Bonds

Notes:

(1) U.S. Short Term Bond positions and P&L include Treasury Bills, Treasury Bill and Eurodollar Futures, and Treasury Notes up to two years to maturity.

(2) All U.S. Government Bonds are reduced to a common denominator of 30-year Government Bonds. The basis of the conversion is the effect on price of a given change in yield. For instance, $100 million in face value of 4-year Treasury Notes are equivalent to $28.5 million in market value of 30-year Government Bonds.

(3) Japanese Government Bond Futures have considerably less volatility than U.S. Government Bonds. For instance, as of June 30, 1986, $100 million in face value of Japanese Government Bonds had the same volatility as roughly $66.2 million in 30-year U.S. Government Bonds. We have *not* adjusted for this difference.

(4) Positions shown as of end of week.

13

The Conclusion: November 1986

The "bull market of a lifetime" came to a premature end. I am not ruling out the possibility of another bull market, but that would be a distinct development.*

The very fact that the "bull market of a lifetime" was aborted provides a valuable insight into the overall situation. It is not the only sequence that has come to a premature end before it could have wreaked havoc. The Imperial Circle was another. Once we start looking for them, other examples abound. OPEC nearly came apart, but when the chasm opened the members pulled back from the brink. The same is true of international lending: I have analyzed collective lending as a system born of emergency which needs emergency conditions to survive and is so constructed as to generate the emergency conditions that are needed to keep it in existence. In the case of freely fluctuating exchange rates, I have argued that they are cumulatively unstable, but the Group of Five intervened before their destabilizing effect would have become intolerable, and we have turned to a system of "dirty float."

Looked at in this light, the U.S. budget deficit becomes another case in point. I had thought that 1985 would see the culmination of deficit financing and, with or without Gramm-Rudman, we would begin to

---

*P.S., January 1987: I spoke too soon. But if markets become euphoric, the "brink" model I shall outline in this chapter becomes all the more relevant.

see a gradual improvement. I must now revise this view. We did, in fact, reach a climax in 1985, but the turning point did not constitute a departure in the opposite direction. When the crisis receded, so did our resolution to deal with it. The budget deficit remains almost undiminished and it may easily swell to a crisis point again.

We may generalize from these instances and formulate the hypothesis that we live in a financial system that tends to go to the brink and then recoil. This hypothesis fits in well with the tendency of our economy to flirt with recession and then to rebound without gathering real strength. There is a logical connection between the two tendencies: it is the danger of a recession that prompts remedial action. Although we can expect the system to recoil from the brink every time it gets there, we cannot be sure; and the more confident we become, the greater is the danger that it will not. We could call this a system of self-defeating prophecies.

The system I am describing bears a certain similarity to the adjustment process in classical economic theory: after all, self-defeating prophecies are a kind of self-correcting mechanism. But there are some vital differences. First, the classical adjustment process tends toward equilibrium; in the system under consideration there is no such tendency. Second, the arrangement described here subordinates the real economy to the vagaries of the financial system. There is a flight from fixed assets to financial ones. The fortunes of particular industries rise and fall with exchange rates but, on balance, it is not unfair to say that the real economy is being sacrificed to keep the financial economy going. This fundamental instability creates tensions that may find political expression. The main dangers are protectionism at home and debt repudiation in the debtor countries. That is what makes the system so precarious.

It has not always been so. The first time we went to the brink was in 1982, although the situation had been getting progressively more unstable ever since the breakdown of fixed exchange rates in 1973—and that breakdown itself was a sign of instability. There seems to be a qualitative difference between conditions prior to 1982 and those afterward. Prior to 1982 the situation may have been deteriorating but the system was essentially viable; that is why it was allowed to disintegrate. Since 1982, the system has been basically unsound, and it has been kept together only by the threat of a breakdown. Could it be reconstituted on a sounder basis? I shall consider that question in Chapter 17. Here I must reconcile the system I am describing with the concept of a credit and regulatory cycle.

The fact that the normal, cyclical pattern has been broken was clear

to me from the outset; I emphasized that we were passing through uncharted territory. But I failed to understand the implications of this
fact; I tried to navigate through uncharted territory using the same old
cyclical chart. No wonder I kept going astray! First I was surprised by
the emergence of the Imperial Circle; then in the course of the experiment I was surprised by the premature demise of the Golden Age of
Capitalism. In Phase 2 of the experiment I was finally forced to realize
that the boom/bust pattern is inappropriate to the current situation. We
need a different model. The image that comes to mind is that of a nee-
dle stuck in a groove. But we need to be somewhat more analytical
about it.

The normal course of the credit cycle has been arrested by the intervention of the authorities. Thus we must look at their behavior for a
clue. When disaster threatens, they pull together; when the danger recedes, they pull apart. This is the mechanism that lies at the heart of the
"going-to-the-brink" phenomenon. The collective system of lending
provides the paradigm, but the other instances I have cited—the exchange rate system, the budget deficit, OPEC, even a 1929-style bull
market—also fit the pattern. The mechanism comes into play only
when a bust would have catastrophic consequences; that is why it has
been operating only since 1982. Sometimes it is effective before the climax is reached, as in the exchange rate system and the "bull market of a
lifetime"; sometimes only afterward, as in the international debt crisis
and in OPEC.

Why does the intervention of the authorities fail to produce a lasting reversal of the trend? Two factors are at play. First, past excesses are
not liquidated but merely contained; therefore they continue to fester.
This is particularly true of the accumulation of bad debt. Second, an
orderly correction or containment may not be sufficient to bring about
a decisive reversal in the prevailing bias. For instance, the banks continued on their expansionary path after 1982; the spirit of a bull market
could be easily rekindled, especially in the U.S., where the damage to
confidence has not been severe; and in the case of OPEC it remains to
be seen whether the experience of 1986 was sufficient to generate the
cohesion necessary to prevent a recurrence.

The impact of these two factors varies from case to case. As a
consequence, we do not get a clear-cut cyclical pattern but something much more indecisive and variegated: some trends are genuinely reversed; others go into temporary remission; yet others

manifest themselves in different forms. For instance, when bank regulation was tightened in 1984, many of the risks were transferred to
the financial markets.

How is it all going to end? In theory, we could keep going to
the brink indefinitely, but since nothing lasts forever, somehow we
are going to get out of the groove. It could happen in one of two
ways: the system could break down as the result of an accident, or
we could gradually work our way out of all the excesses and stop
going to the brink. As we bump along from crisis to crisis, many of
the excesses do get corrected. The banks are less exposed then they
were in 1982; many structural changes have occurred in the debtor
countries; both the budget and the trade deficits of the United
States seem to have culminated; and a 1929-style boom seems to
have come to a premature end. On the other hand, financial assets
continue to accumulate at a pace which outstrips the creation of
"real" wealth, and this disparity is one of the excesses that needs to
be corrected.

A positive resolution would require greater stability in exchange
rates, a continued decline in real interest rates, and an appreciation in
stock prices to a point where investment in "real" assets would offer
greater returns than would the purchase of securities. It is difficult to
see how such a point could be reached as long as the federal government continues to borrow at the present rate. A negative resolution
would involve increasing financial instability, protectionism, a worldwide recession, and a flight from financial to liquid assets. I cannot predict which outcome is more likely.

It can be seen that the model I arrived at has even less predictive
power than the boom/bust model. The boom/bust model did at least
indicate the direction and sequence of events; the "brink" model does
not even do that, because a climax is not necessarily followed by a
trend reversal. Nevertheless, the model is not without some explanatory power.

The question posed at the beginning of the experiment—what is
the eventual outcome—must remain unanswered. In that respect, Phase
2 of the experiment ends with a whimper rather than a bang. But there
is another, related, question that admits a more definite answer: which
brink are we going to next? A correct answer can help convert speculation from a random walk to a profitable exercise.

Clearly, the next brink is protectionism. With a Democratic Congress, some action is inevitable. Its severity will be greatly influenced by the pace of economic activity. If the experience of the last five years is any guide, protectionist pressures will be accommodated short of allowing the system to disintegrate. The administration has already indicated that it is willing to cooperate with Congress to that end. Nineteen eighty-seven may well see some measure of protectionism combined with some measure of debt relief.

The ultimate challenge to the system is a worldwide recession, and the first half of 1987 will be a severe test in that regard. Some of the economic activity in the final quarter of 1986 will have been borrowed from 1987 because of the Tax Reform Act of 1986. Undoubtedly, tax reform will help to eliminate distortions from the economy; but it is always when past excesses are corrected that their negative effect is most severely felt. The much-awaited retrenchment in consumer spending may finally be upon us. Moreover, the Japanese economy is weak, and Germany's is weakening. A worldwide recession coupled with protectionist legislation could sweep us over the brink.

What are the chances of a recession? I find the argument that a recession must be close at hand just because four years have elapsed since the last one quite unconvincing. In an expansionary phase, recessions are induced by the monetary authorities in their attempt to cool off an overheated economy. But we are not in an expansionary phase, and there is no overheating. A more convincing case can be made by arguing that we are in a phase of credit contraction in which the economy would naturally slip into a recession unless it is actively stimulated. It is difficult to see where the stimulation could come from. Still, the monetary authorities have at least one more round of interest rate reductions in their armory; the decline in the dollar may finally begin to make its effect felt on the trade balance; and the prospect of higher oil prices may encourage inventory accumulation. Instead of a recession, we may just have a few more years of substandard growth ahead of us.

My analysis is inconclusive, to say the least. What will happen in the financial markets in 1987? That will be the subject of an ongoing real-time experiment.

P.S., DECEMBER 29, 1986

Two major events have occurred since the conclusion of the experiment: the Boesky affair, and the OPEC agreement. Both have bullish implications. The Boesky affair constitutes a dramatic turning point in the speculative excesses of mergermania. In contrast to other turning points, it does not endanger the system; that is why it will be allowed to be played out in full. It will not bring corporate restructuring to a halt, but it will slow it down. The flow of funds into junk bonds will be reversed, greatly increasing the risk premiums they must carry. The effect will be to ease the demand for credit and to nudge the Federal Reserve toward easing the money supply. All these influences are positive for government bonds and, indirectly, for blue chips. It is noteworthy that the bond markets have shrugged off the news of an OPEC agreement. Higher oil prices are likely to encourage inventory accumulation, moderating downward pressures on the economy, especially in the first quarter of 1987.

I approach the year's end fairly fully invested in both bonds and stocks and do not intend to take my leave until after a discount-rate cut. The major cloud on the horizon is a renewed weakness of the dollar.

P.P.S., FEBRUARY 1987

Obviously, I spoke too soon when I said that the "bull market of our lifetime" came to a premature end. The stock market broke out of its doldrums immediately after the turn of the year and attained new high ground very soon thereafter. What I considered to be the end of the bull market turned out to be merely a temporary interruption that was due to selling pressures engendered by the abolition of the preferential tax treatment of long-term capital gains. As soon as the pressure lifted, the market took off.

The current advance qualifies as the third wave in the bull market that began in August 1982. It has many of the same features as the second wave that began in October 1985 but in some respects it is faster and wilder, as befits a more advanced stage. For instance, the first buying climax came sooner than last time and caused sharper price fluctuations (6% in the S&P futures, versus only 4.8% in 1986). The parallel with the bull market that led up to the crash of 1929 is widely recognized. The charts of the Dow Jones averages, when superimposed upon each other, show an uncanny similarity (see chart). Robert Prechter, a technician who bases his predictions on the Elliott wave theory, has become the prophet of our time whose predictions can move the market—indeed, he is largely responsible for the deviation from the pattern of 1928 that occurred on January 23, 1987.

Equally significant is the fact that the Japanese stock market has also recovered from the nasty break it suffered in October 1986 and reached new highs recently. How do these developments affect the validity and relevance of my conclusions?

The revival of the bull market fits in well with the "brink" model I developed at the end of the experiment. It is a distinguishing feature of the model that we may keep going to the same brink instead of experiencing a decisive trend reversal.

The ease with which the model can accommodate the revival of the bull market confirms my assertion that it has next to no predictive value. It merely offers a conceptual framework for understanding the course of events. The specific predictions must be

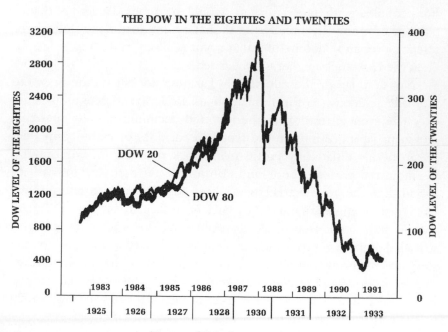

(Courtesy of Tudor Investment Corp.)

formulated by the user; the model provides only a general hypothesis about prevailing market expectations—namely, that they are likely to prove self-defeating.

The user's own prediction may turn out to be false; if so, it is up to him to correct it. When he is a participant in financial markets, he has a strong financial incentive to do so. In the case of financial advisers, academics, or politicians, it may be more advantageous to obfuscate one's mistakes than to admit them. The model can also be useful in that regard. Indeed, it could legitimately be asked whether I have tried to cover up my inability to predict the course of events by creating the "brink" model. If so, I shall pay a heavy price, because I intend to use the model in dealing with the renewed bull market. That is to say, I operate on the assumption that we are in a 1929-type bull market which will, however, abort long before it reaches the lofty heights of 1929.

Clearly, there is a long way to go before the internal dynamics—or, more accurately, dialectics—of the market render it ripe for a reversal. If anything, the correction in the second half of 1986, coupled with the further decline of the dollar, has extended the "natural" life span of the boom. If it is to be aborted again, the causes will have to be external. What these external constraints are has been amply discussed: a recession, coupled with protectionism, would be more dangerous than a buoyant economy. Eventually, the monetary authorities are unlikely to tolerate a runaway boom—but that point is a long way away, at least as far as the U.S. stock market is concerned.

Not so in Japan. The valuation of Japanese stocks has long ceased to bear any relevance to the fundamentals. Price/earnings multiples are excessive even in relation to the low and declining interest rates that prevail in Japan. Moreover, the reported earnings of many companies are artificially inflated by profits from stock transactions. The outlook for industrial profits is poor, and companies use their surplus cash to speculate in the stock market. Specialized funds have been set up to attract corporate investors, and they have been illegally promising a guaranteed minimum return. A governmental investigation of these so-called "tokkin funds" received a lot of publicity at the time of the stock market break of October 1986. Nevertheless, the market has recovered its poise and reached new highs early in 1987. How far can the boom go? Just as Italy was the market to watch for impending trouble in 1986, in 1987 it is Japan.

The Japanese stock market is fueled by liquidity and the liquidity is generated by the combination of a weak economy and a strong yen. When either Japanese or non-Japanese holders of dollars convert them into yen, some of those yen find their way into the stock market. The tendency is particularly strong when the yen are supplied by the central bank in an endeavor to keep the exchange rate from rising. When the central bank is not involved, there is at least a chance that the sellers of yen sell, or fail to buy, Japanese stocks in order to acquire assets denominated in dollars.

The Japanese government has engaged in a campaign to encourage investment abroad and, on the whole, it has been very successful: capital outflows consistently exceed the trade surplus. The yen continues to strengthen only because of an inflow of foreign capital and hedging by Japanese investors. Once market participants gain conviction that the trend is changing, they reduce their hedging, and the yen falls of its own accord. That is what happened last October, although the break in the stock market preceded the decline of the yen. It is likely to happen again. Since the end of the year, the upward pressure on the yen has built up again and the stock market boom gained a new lease on life. When the pressure abates, involuntary selling by the Bank of Japan will be replaced by voluntary selling by holders of yen. That is when the pool of liquidity will spring a leak. Given the inflated level of stock prices, a decline could easily turn into a rout.

There is a noteworthy similarity between the position of Japan today and that of the United States in the 1920s: it is emerging as the leading economic power and its stock market is less seasoned than that of the mature economies. But that is where the similarity ends. The Japanese authorities have a tradition of intervention and a firm grip on the participants in financial markets. Once before, in 1965, when the stock market collapsed, the government set up a corporation to buy, and hold, shares dumped on the market by distressed holders. Nineteen twenty-nine is not likely to repeat itself, even in Japan.

The initial impact of a decline in the Japanese stock market could well be positive for other markets because it is likely to be associated with a wholesale movement of funds from the Japanese to other stock markets. But if the decline turns into a rout, it is bound to send a shiver through the world.

Part Four

EVALUATION

14

The Scope for Financial Alchemy: An Evaluation of the Experiment*

The real-time experiment has turned out quite differently from what I had expected; moreover, the results of the second phase are quite different from those of the first: the evaluation I wrote in June 1986 had to be rewritten in light of what has happened since. Phase 1 shows my approach at work when it is successful, Phase 2 when it is not. This makes the task of evaluation more complex; but it will also render the judgment more complete.

In evaluating my approach we must distinguish between its ability to produce profits in financial markets and its ability to predict the future course of events. The fact that the distinction is necessary has far-reaching implications, which will be explored in the course of this chapter and the next one.

First, as to the financial results. Phase 1 coincided with the most prosperous period of my Fund. In the eleven months between the inception of the experiment and the end of the control period, Quantum Fund shares appreciated by 126%, as against 27% for the S&P index, 30% for Treasury bond futures, 23% for the DM, and 34% for the yen. Admittedly, these were prosperous times for most investors, even for those who were

____

*Written in June 1986; revised in December 1986.

on the wrong side of the currency trend; but few did as well as my Fund. Leverage is only part of the explanation, because leverage works in both directions: one has to be on the right side of the market to benefit from it.

Even if we make allowances for an element of coincidence, there can be no doubt that the process of formulating and testing hypotheses made a positive contribution to the results.

By contrast, Phase 2 shows a loss. Between July 21, 1986, and the end of the year Quantum Fund shares declined by 2% as against a 2% rise for the S&P index, a 2% fall for the Treasury bond futures, a 1% rise for the Japanese government bond futures, and a 5% rise for the Japanese stock index. The DM rose by 10%, the yen fell by 2%, gold rose by 14%, and oil rose by 40%. Putting both phases into the context of my entire performance, the results can be considered satisfactory.

The record shows that my trading was far from flawless even in Phase 1. I was too late in buying bonds and too early in selling them—although I had the courage to reestablish the position at a much higher price. I was also rather late in recognizing the "bull market of our lifetime" in stocks. My trading in currencies was the best: the insight that the level of risk had been reduced by the Plaza meeting of the Group of Five was highly rewarding.

Phase 2 is dominated by one major mistake: my reluctance to recognize that the "bull market of a lifetime" had run its course before it had truly earned its name. The consequences were particularly painful in Japan where I was participating in a classic boom/bust sequence and failed to get out in time. Once committed, the mistake was difficult to rectify; but at least the analytical framework made me aware of what I was up against. A method that produces outstanding results during good periods and helps to contain losses during bad ones must be declared a success.

Quantum Fund N.V. Class A Shares			
Year Ended	Net Asset Value Per Share	% Change from Preceding Year	Size of Fund
Dec. 31, 1984	$3,057.79		$488,998,187
Dec. 31, 1985	$6,760.59	+121.1%	$1,003,502,000
Dec. 31, 1986	$9,699.41	+43.5%	$1,567,109,000★
Mar. 31, 1987	$12,554.16	+29.4%	$2,075,679,000★
	Compounded annual appreciation:		
	1969–1986: +35.4%		
★Unaudited.	1984–1986: +78.1%		

My financial success stands in stark contrast with my ability to forecast events. In this context, we must distinguish between events in financial markets and events in the real world. Events in financial markets determine financial success; events in the real world are relevant only in evaluating the scientific merit of my approach.

Even in predicting financial markets my record is less than impressive: the best that can be said for it is that my theoretical framework enables me to understand the significance of events as they unfold—although the record is less than spotless. One would expect a successful method to yield firm predictions; but all my forecasts are extremely tentative and subject to constant revision in the light of market developments. Occasionally I develop some conviction and, when I do, the payoff can be substantial; but even then, there is an ever-present danger that the course of events fails to correspond to my expectations. The concept of the "bull market of a liftime" is a case in point: it was highly rewarding in Phase 1 but it became more of a hindrance than a help in Phase 2. My approach works not by making valid predictions but by allowing me to correct false ones.

With regard to events in the real world, my record is downright dismal. The outstanding feature of my predictions is that I keep on expecting developments that do not materialize. During the real-time experiment I often envisioned a recession that was just around the corner, but it never occurred; at the inception of the experiment I was contemplating a reversal of the Imperial Circle that was avoided only by the deus ex machina of the Plaza agreement of the Group of Five. Going further back, a collapse of the banking system has never been far from my thoughts since 1981. Similarly, I expected the collapse in oil prices to be followed by a tax on imported oil, of which there is no sign. To be fair, there were some developments that I anticipated correctly—the collapse in oil prices was one and the willingness of the Japanese to finance our budget deficit was another. Although I did not anticipate the Group of Five meeting at the Plaza Hotel, it fitted my framework perfectly and I responded to it correctly.

How can financial success and predictive failure be reconciled? That is the question I shall address in this chapter. But before I do so, I must remind the reader why it arises in the first place. If this were a scientific experiment, my financial success would serve as evidence of the validity of the hypotheses on which my decisions were based. But the experiment does not qualify as a scientific one. I need to raise only two considerations to make this point: one personal and the other pertaining to the subject matter.

My decision-making process was greatly influenced by personal factors such as my presence or absence from the office, and the real-time experiment itself was an important personal factor. The fact that the monetary results served as a possible criterion of the validity of my ideas made me try harder than I would have otherwise. This is borne out by the fact that my understanding was much hazier and my moves in the market more tentative during the control period than they were at the height of the experiment. Such haziness is quite common; it is the sharp focus that I managed to attain in the course of the experiment that is rather exceptional. I was greatly helped by the discipline of having to write down my thoughts. My arguments may not strike the reader as particularly well organized, but they are certainly more consistent than they would have been if I had not taken the trouble to formulate them in writing. I was also inspired by the fact that I was able to combine the two great abiding interests in my life: philosophical speculation and speculation in financial markets. Both seemed to benefit from the combination: together, they engaged me more than either one on its own.

The other consideration has to do with external events. Phase 1 happened to coincide with a moment in history when the authorities tried to assert their leadership: they cooperated first in pushing down the dollar and then in pushing down interest rates. The theoretical framework I was using was particularly well suited for dealing with these developments. After all, the interplay between markets and regulators is one of the main themes in the concept of a regulatory and credit cycle. My theoretical framework might have proven much less helpful at other moments in history.

For instance, I recall the time, in 1981–82, when the Federal Reserve sought to control the quantity of money and allowed market forces to set interest rates. The market for government bonds, and to a lesser extent for stocks and currencies, became like a casino, and my approach of formulating hypotheses and testing them against the market became worse than useless: by the time I recognized a market trend and formulated a hypothesis to explain it, the trend had already changed and I had to find a new hypothesis. The result was that I was always lagging behind the market and kept on getting whipsawed until I abandoned the hopeless struggle and delegated the task of gambling in government bond futures to someone more qualified. I found a computer-based speculator, Victor Niederhofer, who had developed a system using the assumption that the market is a casino. He operated successfully until the international debt crisis of 1982 changed the nature of the game. He had the rare fortitude to close the account before he had lost all the money he had made for me previously. I could argue that an approach which allows me to recognize when it does not work is a valid approach; still, it is somehow more convincing to demonstrate it at a juncture when it does work.

These two considerations go a long way toward explaining my financial success during the experiment. They also serve to disqualify it as a scientific experiment. First, the fact that an experiment is conducted is not supposed to influence the outcome; in my case it did. Second, scientific theories are supposed to be universally valid, while mine seems to operate only intermittently. But the divergence from scientific experiment goes much deeper. I have never claimed scientific status for my theoretical framework. On the contrary, I have argued that reflexive processes cannot be predicted by scientific method, and the real-time experiment was a deliberate attempt to explore an alternative method. To bring the point home, I have described the alternative method as alchemy. Scientific method seeks to understand things as they are, while alchemy seeks to bring about a desired state of affairs. To put it another way, the primary objective of science is the truth—that of alchemy, operational success.

In the sphere of natural phenomena, there is no distinction between the two objectives. Nature obeys laws that operate independently of whether they are understood or not; the only way man can bend nature to his will is by understanding and applying these laws. That is why alchemy has failed and natural science reigns supreme.

But social phenomena are different: they have thinking participants. Events do not obey laws that operate independently of what anybody thinks. On the contrary, the participants' thinking is an integral part of the subject matter. This creates an opening for alchemy that was absent in the sphere of natural science. Operational success can be achieved without attaining scientific knowledge. By the same token, scientific method is rendered just as ineffectual in dealing with social events as alchemy was in altering the character of natural substances. I shall revert to the predicament of the social sciences in the next chapter; here I want to explore the scope for alchemy.

The real-time experiment shows that my approach is more successful in dealing with financial markets than with the real world. The reason for it readily suggests itself: financial markets themselves function imperfectly as a mechanism for predicting events in the real world. There is always a divergence between prevailing expectations and the actual course of events. Financial success depends on the ability to anticipate prevailing expectations and not real-world developments. But, as we have seen my approach rarely produces firm predictions even about the future course of financial markets; it is only a framework for understanding the course of events as they unfold. If it has any validity it is because the theoretical framework corresponds to the way that financial markets operate. That means that the markets themselves can be viewed as formulating hypotheses about the future and then submitting them to the test of the actual course of events. The hypotheses that survive the test are reinforced; those that fail are discarded. The main difference between me and the markets is that markets seem to engage in a process of trial and error without the participants fully understanding what is going on, while I do it consciously. Presumably that is why I can do better than the market.

If this view is correct, financial markets bear a curious resemblance to scientific method: both involve the testing of hypotheses. But there is a fundamental difference: in science, testing serves to establish the truth; in financial markets, the criterion is operational success. In contradistinction with natural science, the two criteria do not coincide. How could they? Market prices always express a prevailing bias, whereas natural science works with an objective criterion. Scientific theories are judged by the facts; financial decisions are judged by the distorted views of the participants. Instead of scientific method, financial markets embody the method of alchemy.

This interpretation of financial markets as a mechanism for testing hypotheses by alchemy is both novel and challenging. The fact that it is not generally accepted adds to the challenge. How can markets be testing something when the participants don't know what they are doing? The answer is to be found in the results they achieve. Try to propound an unformulated hypothesis and you get a hit-or-miss result. By contrast, when you deliberately formulate your hypotheses, you can consistently outperform the market averages—provided your specific predictions are not too far off the mark. Treating the market as a mechanism for testing hypotheses seems to be an effective hypothesis. It produces results that are better than a random walk.

This conclusion validates the approach I have taken over a strictly scientific one. If we abide by the methods of natural science, we arrive at the random walk theory. The hypotheses that are being tested have to be disregarded because they do not constitute facts and what we are left with is a jumble of haphazard price fluctuations. On the other hand, if we look at the situation from the inside, from the vantage point of a participant, we discover a process of trial and error. It is not easy to make sense of the process: many people participate with only a vague idea of what is going on, and I must confess that the sensation of being on a random walk is not unfamiliar to me. My attempts at formulating conjectures about the future work only intermittently; oftentimes all I get is white noise. But when I succeed in formulating a worthwhile conjecture the results can be very rewarding, as Phase 1 of the experiment demonstrates; and even if my perceptions are flawed, as was often the case in Phase 2, I have a criterion that I can use to identify my mistakes: the behavior of the market.

The real-time experiment has shown how greatly my decision-making process is influenced by the market action. At first sight this seems to contradict my original contention that markets are always wrong. But the contradiction is more apparent than real. Markets provide the criterion by which investment decisions are judged. Moreover, they play a causal role in shaping the course of events. The information is more readily available than events in the real world; hence the market action offers the most convenient feedback mechanism by which one's expectations can be evaluated. One need not regard the market as always right in order to use it in that capacity. Indeed, if one believes that the market is always right there is little to be gained from having a feedback mechanism because the prospect of outperforming the market becomes a matter of pure chance.

As I shall argue in Chapter 16, the contention of classical economic theory that the market mechanism assures the optimum allocation of resources is false; its true merit is that it provides a criterion by which the participants can recognize their own misconceptions. But it is important to realize what kind of criterion the market provides: far from being always right, it always incorporates the prevailing bias. If participants labor under the misapprehension that the market is always right, the feedback they get is misleading. Indeed, the belief in efficient markets renders markets more unstable by short-circuiting the corrective process that would occur if particpants recognized that markets are always biased. The more the theory of efficient markets is believed, the less efficient the markets become.

How good are financial markets in predicting real-world developments? Reading the record, it is striking how many calamities that I anticipated did not in fact materialize. The financial markets must have come to reflect the same concerns; otherwise my false expectations could not have proven so rewarding. This raises an interesting possibility. Perhaps some of the developments I predicted were preempted by the very fact that they were anticipated by the market and the market provoked a reaction that prevented them from happening. This seems to hold true of the collapse of the banking system and of the collapse of the dollar, and also of the "bull market of our lifetime," which was to be followed by a crash 1929 style. The monetary authorities became so concerned about the excessive buoyancy of financial markets that in the end they refused to supply the excess liquidity that would create a speculative bubble. Their action was neither deliberate nor unanimous. In the U.S., Volcker was opposed to providing excess liquidity but he was defeated in the Open Market Committee and had to appeal to Germany to join in a round of interest rate reductions. When Secretary Baker pushed for another round, the Germans balked and the resulting row almost wrecked the Group of Five process. The Japanese devised their own medicine but by the time it took effect the speculative bubble was sufficiently developed to precipitate a more or less full-scale bust in the Japanese stock market. No wonder that I had difficulty in recognizing the premature demise of the bull market of a lifetime!★ It is possible that the United States will continue to create excess liquidity, but I consider it unlikely that it will cause a speculative bubble because confidence has been too badly shaken. It is more likely that investors would flee to liquidity and gold. When I finally recognized that

★Written before the revival of the bull market in January 1987.

markets can preempt the catastrophes they predict, I concluded that we live in an age of self-defeating prophecies.

The collapse of oil prices does not seem to fit the argument because it actually occurred; but that may be attributed to the fact that either I or the authorities have misjudged its dire consequences. I expected such severe repercussions on the banking system and on the economy as to make a levy on imported oil indispensable, while we seem to have gotten along fine without it. In the end, it was left to OPEC to pull itself together. The present arrangement is no more permanent than the Group of Five process; the drama has yet to be played out in both cases.

This line of argument opens up a fascinating vista. I may have discovered not just a reasonably effective way of operating in financial markets but an actual model of how the financial markets operate in the real world. Models currently in use are based on the misconception that markets can only foreshadow events, they cannot shape them. My approach recognizes that financial markets can also precipitate or abort future events. Following this line of argument, it is possible that we have indeed been teetering on the verge of both a deflationary spiral and a free fall of the dollar—not to mention all sorts of other financial calamities—and we have been saved from them only because of the danger signals emitted by the financial markets. In other words, financial markets constantly anticipate events, both on the positive and on the negative side, which fail to materialize exactly because they have been anticipated. No wonder that financial markets get so excited in anticipating events that seem quite harmless in retrospect! It is an old joke that the stock market has predicted seven of the last two recessions. We can now understand why that should be so. By the same token, financial crashes tend to occur only when they are unexpected.

This last point should not be overstated. There are many events that actually occur in spite of the fact that they were widely anticipated. The collapse in oil prices is a case in point; the outbreak of the Second World War was another. It has become fashionable to be a contrarian, but to bet against prevailing expectations is far from safe. It will be recalled that, in the boom/bust model, events tend to reinforce prevailing expectations most of the time and contradict them only at the inflection points; and inflection points are notoriously difficult to identify. Now that the contrarian viewpoint has become the prevailing bias, I have become a confirmed anti contrarian.

15

The Quandary of
the Social Sciences

We are now in a position to appreciate the predicament of the social sciences. Scientific method is based on the presumption that a successful experiment corroborates the validity of the hypothesis that it was designed to test. But in situations with thinking participants, experimental success does not assure the truth or validity of the statements that are being tested. The real-time experiment is a case in point: inconclusive and occasionally patently false predictions were crowned by financial success. Admittedly, the experiment was not a scientific one; I went to great lengths to emphasize its alchemical character. But the very fact that alchemy can succeed raises questions about scientific method; and the fact that scientific theories do not seem to be able to produce superior results compounds the predicament. I shall argue that social science is a false metaphor and we shall be better off if we recognize it as such.

Scientific method works whenever scientists have an objective criterion at their disposal by which the truth or validity of their statements can be evaluated. The scientists' understanding is never perfect; but the objective criterion allows misunderstandings to be corrected. Scientific method is an interpersonal process in which the contribution of each participant is subjected to the critical appraisal of all others. Only when all the participants are guided by the same criterion is the critical process capable of producing results that qualify as knowledge. That is why the availability of an objective criterion is indispensable to the success of scientific method.

The role of an objective criterion is filled by facts. Statements that correspond to the facts are true; those that do not are false. Unfortunately, the facts are not always as dependable as this simple statement makes them out to be. They can serve as an objective criterion only when they are totally independent of the statements that relate to them. That is the case in natural science where one fact follows another irrespective of what anybody thinks. But it is not the case in social science where events incorporate the participants' bias. It should be emphasized that the interference comes not only from scientists but also from participants. Indeed, if the participants' thinking did not play a causal role in shaping the course of events no observer could influence the course of events by making statements about it and the situation of the social scientist would be no different from that of the natural scientist. It is the participants' thinking that creates the problems.

The structure of events that have no thinking participants is simple: one fact follows another in an unending causal chain. The presence of thinking participants complicates the structure of events enormously: the participants' thinking affects the course of events and the course of events affects the participants' thinking. To make matters worse, participants influence and affect each other. If the participants' thinking bore some determinate relationship to the facts there would be no problem: the scientific observer could ignore the participants' thinking and focus on the facts. But the relationship cannot be accurately determined for the simple reason that the participants' thinking does not relate to facts; it relates to events in which they participate, and these events become facts only after the participants' thinking has made its impact on them. Thus the causal chain does not lead directly from fact to fact but from fact to perception and from perception to fact with all kinds of additional connections between participants that are not reflected fully in the facts.

How does this complex structure affect the ability of an observer to make valid statements about the course of events? His statements must also be more complex. In particular, they must allow for a fundamental difference between past and future: past events are a matter of record, while the future is inherently unpredictable. Explanation becomes an easier task than prediction—as the real-time experiment illustrates. Generalizations do not apply to the future with as much force as to the past, and the beautiful symmetry that characterizes the deductive-nomological (D-N) model of science is destroyed. This goes against the grain of scientific generalizations, which are supposed to be timelessly valid.

It is possible to establish universally valid generalizations—witness the ones I proposed about freely fluctuating exchange rates—but they cannot be used to predict the course of events. What is worse, the facts do not provide an adequate criterion by which the validity of generalization can be judged because there is more to the subject matter than facts. The fact that a prediction turns out to be true does not necessarily validate the theory on which it is based and, conversely, a valid theory does not necessarily generate predictions that can be checked against the facts.

Indeed, the sequence of social events cannot be properly understood if we confine our attention to facts. The participants' thinking is an integral part of the situation they participate in; to treat such a situation as if it were composed exclusively of facts distorts the subject matter. The D-N model of scientific method is based on a strict segregation of facts and statements. Thus we are forced to the conclusion that the D-N model is not applicable to the study of social events.

It would be a mistake to equate the D-N model with scientific method. Even the theory of science recognizes other models, notably statistical or probabilistic ones and laws relating to an ideal case as in economic theory. Moreover, the practice of science differs significantly from its theory and a study of these differences has given rise to further refinements in the theory of science since the D-N model was originally developed. Nevertheless, the D-N model embodies the ideal that scientific method strives for: universally valid generalizations that can be used for prediction and explanation with equal force and are amenable to testing. Natural science has so many accomplishments to its credit that it can dispense with theoretical models and pursue its investigations wherever they may lead; but social science, exactly because it has been less successful, is in greater need of the prestige that the D-N format can impart. To abandon the D-N model is to give up what is most valuable, persuasive, and attractive in science.

But that is only half the story. When the course of events is influenced by the participants' bias, future events are open to manipulation by observers in a way that is not possible in natural science. That is the point I was trying to make by speaking of alchemy. Since alchemy is unable to influence natural phenomena, the social sciences face a problem that has no parallel in the natural sciences. The critical process that is the foundation of science works smoothly only when the participants share the same objective. The avowed purpose of science is the pursuit of truth; but when the subject matter is open to manipulation, participants may be more interested in changing the course of events than in understanding it. The fact that they can enhance their influence by claiming scientific status for their views undermines the critical process even further.

How can scientific method protect itself against subversion? The first step is to recognize the danger. That requires the repudiation of the "doctrine of the unity of science." People participate in science with a variety of motivations. For present purposes we may distinguish between two main objectives: the pursuit of truth and the pursuit of what we may call "operational success." In natural science, the two objectives coincide: true statements work better than false ones. Not so in the social sciences: false ideas may be effective because of their influence on people's behavior and, conversely, the fact that a theory or prediction works does not provide conclusive evidence of its validity. Marxism provides an outstanding example of the first kind of divergence; and my own prediction of the "bull market of a lifetime" of the second.

The divergence between truth and operational or experimental success undermines scientific method in more ways than one. On the one hand, it renders scientific theories less effective; on the other, it allows nonscientific theories to achieve operational success. What is worse, an alchemical theory can profit from assuming a scientific guise.

We cannot remove the first two limitations because they are inherent in the subject matter; but we can protect against the third. All we have to do is to recognize the limitations of scientific method when it comes to dealing with social situations. This is what I propose to do by declaring social science a false metaphor. That means that the methods of natural science do not apply to the study of social events. It emphatically does not mean that we ought to abandon the pursuit of truth in the study of social events.

To try to argue about motivations would be totally counterproductive. Every contribution must be considered on its merit and not on the basis of its intentions, otherwise the critical process which is at the heart of the scientific method would turn to shambles. It is note-worthy that two schools of thought that insisted on judging contributions by their source rather than on their merit, namely, Marxism and psychoanalysis, were also the most successful in subverting scientific method.

The only way to protect against subversion is to establish a special convention for the study of social phenomena. Instead of demanding that contributions be cast in the D-N mold in order to qualify as scientific, theories of the D-N type would be treated as a form of social alchemy. The convention would not automatically disqualify every theory, prediction, or explanation that claims scientific status but it would put the burden of proof on them to justify their claim. It would prevent the abuse of scientific method for alchemical purposes and allow theories, like mine, that do not produce unconditional predictions to qualify as valid contributions. The convention is necessary because without it the arguments I am presenting here would have to be repeated in each and every case, and that would be impractical to say the least. Try to convince a Marxist that Marxism is not scientific!

I happen to be passionately interested in the pursuit of truth, but I am also fully cognizant of the need to attain operational success in order to get a hearing for my views. As I admitted earlier, that consideration was a major driving force behind the real-time experiment. My success in the stock market has had the liberating effect of allowing me to speak my mind. I am in the fortunate position of not needing operational success as a scientist, having been able to attain it as a participant.

But people in the academic professions are not so lucky: they compete directly with natural scientists for status and funds. Natural science has been able to produce universally valid generalizations and unconditional predictions. In the absence of a convention to the contrary, social scientists are under great pressure to come up with similar results. That is why they produce so many scientific-looking formulas. Declaring social science a false metaphor would liberate them from having to imitate natural science.

Apart from academia, there are many fields where participants can obtain operational success by claiming scientific status for their views. Financial forecasting is one; politics is another. The history of ideas is littered with examples. Marxism is the political creed that has used a scientific guise most deliberately, but laissez-faire policies also derive their intellectual force from a scientific theory—namely, the theory of perfect competition—and Freud was just as determined to claim scientific status as Marx.

I have no grounds for impugning the motivations of others. After all, I have just as overwhelming a desire to see my views accepted as everybody else, and I am marshaling whatever arguments I can to support my views. Moreover, in my previous incarnation as a securities analyst I often espoused views that I knew to be distorted for the sake of their operational effect, so that I am no holier than anyone else.

The question is not one of motivation but of operational effect. A consideration of the structure of social events shows that all predictions are contingent on the participants' decisions. Yet the pursuit of operational success often drives people to try to compete with natural science by making more unconditional predictions. This has the operational effect of endangering the pursuit of truth in the study of social phenomena. As long as the doctrine of the unity of science prevails, there is a direct conflict between the pursuit of truth and the pursuit of operational success. It can be resolved only by renouncing the doctrine.

I have managed to claim exemption from the rigorous requirements of the D-N model by renouncing the doctrine of the unity of science. I went even further: I asserted that the pursuit of truth prohibits unconditional predictions. Does that mean that the kinds of conjectures I produced are the best that can be hoped for? Certainly not. The real-time experiment is best regarded as an amateur effort that ought to be improved upon when the appropriate professional skills are developed.

Part Five

PRESCRIPTION

16

Free Markets Versus Regulation

It is almost redundant to criticize the concept of equilibrium any further. In the Introduction, I asserted that the concept is a hypothetical one whose relevance to the real world is open to question. In subsequent chapters I examined various financial markets as well as macroeconomic developments and showed that they exhibit no tendency towards equilibrium. Indeed, it makes more sense to claim that markets tend towards excesses, which sooner or later become unsustainable, so that they are eventually corrected.

Equilibrium is supposed to ensure the optimum allocation of resources. If markets do not tend towards equilibrium, the main agrument that has been used in favor of the market mechanism loses its validity: we have no grounds for believing that markets optimize anything.

This may sound like a startling conclusion, but it falls far short of that. The concept of an optimum is just as alien to a world in which participants function without the benefit of perfect knowledge as the concept of an equilibrium, and for the same reason: both concepts presuppose perfect knowledge. So it is not at all surprising if both of them are shown to have little relevance to the real world.

There are other arguments that can be advanced in favor of the market mechanism. Indeed, an interesting line of argument seems to emerge from the discussion in Chapter 14. I interpreted financial markets as a process that is somewhat akin to scientific method—that is to say, a process of trial and error in which the market price at the termination of the experiment serves as a criterion by which the experiment can be judged. The criterion does not meet the requirements of scientific method, because the market price is not independent of the participants' decisions in the way in which the events studied by natural scientists are independent of the statements that scientists make about them. Nevertheless, it is a useful criterion because it is just as real and just as amenable to scientific observation as any natural phenomenon. Moreover, it is of vital interest to market participants. Thus the market mechanism has the merit of providing an objective criterion albeit a biased one.

How great that merit is we can appreciate only when we consider what happens in its absence. For that purpose, we must look at centrally planned economies which, in revulsion against the deficiencies of market economies, have eschewed the use of the pricing mechanism. Output has to be measured in physical quantities, and the distortions are far worse than the excesses of the market.

Winston Churchill once said that democracy is the worst form of government except for all the others. The same can be said about the market mechanism: it is the worst system of allocating resources except for all the others. Indeed, there are significant similarities between the election mechanism and the market mechanism. It would be difficult to argue that elections optimize the political leadership of a country: the skills needed to attract votes bear little relevance to the qualities a candidate is going to need once he is in office. Nevertheless, the very fact that he has to run for election imposes a discipline which helps prevent some of the more egregious excesses.

The value of an objective criterion is perhaps best appreciated subjectively. We all live in a fantasy world. Having an affinity for abstract ideas, I am perhaps more apt to be carried away into a world of my own creation than many other people. The markets have always helped to preserve my sense of reality. It may seem paradoxical that my sense of reality should be rooted in the markets when markets often behave so strangely that they strike other onlookers as unreal; yet as a market participant, I am not merely aware of being connected to reality: I actually feel it in my guts. I react to events in the marketplace as an animal reacts to events in the jungle. For instance, I used to be able to anticipate an impending disaster because it manifested itself in the form of a backache. I was of course unable to tell what shape the disaster would take: by the time I could identify it, my backache would dissolve. There was a time when my involvement with the market was all embracing—much to the detriment of my relationships with human beings. Now that I have managed to distance myself, my market sense has suffered. Events often reach me as white noise: I cannot make sense of them. For instance, during the real-time experiment, market developments had sharp contours; during the control period, the outlines became more blurred.

It is interesting to observe how my market involvement relates to my ability to organize abstract ideas. One would think that being active in the market would interfere with writing, but the opposite seems to be the case: the discipline of having to make investment decisions prevents me from getting too far divorced from reality. During the three years that I was writing the *The Burden of Consciousness,* I lost my ability to make money in the stock market and eventually I got lost in my own abstractions. Again, during the three years when I was trying to make sense of the international debt problem I saw my ability to operate in the market diminish, and, what is worse, I sensed that my analysis of the debt problem was becoming increasingly removed from reality. By contrast, the real-time experiment brought both my investment activities and my ability to express myself to a high pitch.

I mention this because it may have more than subjective relevance. Had I been an academic, I could have persisted with my analysis of the debt problem, and if reality failed to conform to my expectations, I could have defended my analysis by blaming extraneous developments. Eventually, some of my expectations were fulfilled, albeit with a delay of several years. As a market-oriented man, I found such a delay intolerable, and I felt obliged to search for, and to recognize, the flaws in my argument. As an academic, I could have claimed to be vindicated. The point I am trying to make is that the market is a harder taskmaster than academic debate.

Yet it is easy to exaggerate the merits of having an objective criterion at our disposal. We have become so fixated on objective criteria that we are inclined to endow them with a value they do not intrinsically possess. Profit—the bottom line—*efficiency*—takes on the aspect of an end in itself, instead of being a means to an end. We tend to measure every activity by the amount of money it brings. Artists are valued according to the price their products sell for. What is worse, we often want to make a profit from activities that ought to be otherwise motivated. Politicians want to earn lecture fees and sell their memoirs; White House aides become lobbyists; generals in charge of procurement angle for lucrative jobs in industry, and so do lawyers working for regulatory agencies. The profit motive has become so all-embracing that we find it hard to accept when someone is motivated by considerations other than profit. An American executive finds it a nuisance when an Englishman is unwilling to relocate for the sake of a better job, a South African black who prefers to destroy civilization rather than put up with apartheid strikes us as positively barbaric—not to mention a phenomenon like Islamic fundamentalism which is totally beyond our ken. Values that motivate people cannot be readily translated into objective terms; and exactly because individual values are so confusing, we have elevated profit and material wealth—which can be readily measured in terms of money—into some kind of supreme value. Surely that is an exaggeration. The fact is that in a world of imperfect understanding, there is some kind of exaggeration or bias involved in every value. In our civilization, the value of profit is exaggerated and so is the value of objectivity.

Let us take a closer look at the kind of criterion market prices provide. The distinction we have drawn between scientific method and alchemy will come in useful. I have argued that in the study of social phenomena we need to distinguish between two kinds of validity: one associated with truth, the other with effectiveness. In natural science, the distinction is missing: theories are effective only if they are true; that is why alchemy does not work. Following this line of thought, we can argue that the market price provides a criterion of effectiveness but not a criterion of truth. Future market prices will determine how the various participants fare, but they will not determine whether their understanding is correct. Only if market prices tended towards an equilibrium would the two criteria merge: the market price would then be the "correct" price.

We can see now how important the concept of equilibrium is. It serves as a bridge between natural and social science and eliminates the disturbing dichotomy between truth and effectiveness that characterizes the study of social phenomena. Unfortunately, the bridge does not stand up, because imperfect understanding renders the concept of equilibrium inappropriate. Without an innate tendency towards equilibrium, the course of events cannot be determined by scientific method; but it can be shaped by the methods of alchemy.

The attempt to transpose the methods and criteria of natural science to the social sphere is unsustainable. It gives rise to inflated expectations that cannot be fulfilled. These expectations go far beyond the immediate issue of scientific knowledge and color our entire way of thinking. The belief that economic policy ought to aim at the optimum allocation of resources has dominated political thought—and political action—since the middle of the nineteenth century. Those on the left wanted the State to take charge of the allocation; those on the right wanted to leave it to the market mechanism. Under the influence of Marxism, the pursuit of the optimum led to the total abandonment of the market mechanism in large parts of the world. Even in market-oriented economies, the State was given a large role in correcting the imperfections of the market mechanism. Gradually, the harmful side effects of State intervention have become increasingly evident, and the prevailing bias has swung back in favor of free markets.

We are quite willing to recognize the fallacy in Marxism, but we are much less inclined to admit that the theory of perfect competition is imbued with a similar fallacy. Both are built on the assumption of perfect knowledge. In one case, the assumption produces market equilibrium; in the other, it finds expression in an unconditional prediction of the course of history. It is worth pointing out that both theories originated in the nineteenth century, when the limitations of knowledge were not yet recognized and science reigned supreme.

Once we recognize that the optimum is unattainable, we are in a better position to evaluate the merits and shortcomings of the market mechanism. I do not want to get involved in the problems connected with the distribution of wealth—not because I do not consider them important, but only because my analysis has little to contribute to the subject; I want to focus on one particular weakness of the market mechanism: its innate instability. Its cause has been identified: it derives from the two-way connection between thinking and reality that I have labeled reflexivity. It is not in operation in all markets at all times; but if and when it occurs, there is no limit to how far away both perceptions and events can move from anything that could be considered equilibrium.

Instability is not necessarily harmful; indeed, if it were described as dynamic adjustment, it would sound positively benign. But carried to extremes, it can give rise to sudden reversals that may take on catastrophic proportions. That is particularly the case where credit is involved, because the liquidation of collateral can lead to sudden compression of market prices. The prevention of excessive instability is therefore a necessary condition for the smooth functioning of the market mechanism. It is not a condition that the market mechanism can ensure on its own. On the contrary, I have presented evidence that unregulated financial markets tend to become progressively more unstable. The evidence is most clear-cut in the currency markets, but it is also quite persuasive with regard to the expansion and contraction of credit. Whether stock markets would prove inherently unstable if there were no credit involved remains an open question, because stock-market booms are always associated with credit expansion. Excessive instability can be prevented only by some sort of regulation.

How much instability is excessive is a matter of judgment. Standards vary with time. The degree of dislocation we are willing to tolerate today, as measured by unemployment figures, would have seemed inconceivable a few decades ago when the memories of the Great Depression were still fresh and the drawbacks of full-employment policies less evident. Similarly, the restrictions on corporate restructuring have been greatly relaxed between the conglomerate boom of the 1960s and the mergermania of the 1980s.

The trouble with regulation is that the regulators are also human, and apt to err. In order to avoid arbitrary behavior and abuse of power, rules and regulations need to be fixed in advance, and it is difficult to devise regulations that are flexible enough to meet all contingencies. Regulations tend to be rigid and to hinder innovation. The rigidities and distortions they introduce tend to be just as cumulative as the instability of an unregulated market. Income taxes provide a good example. The steeper the rates and the longer they stay in effect, the more widespread the tax avoidance and the more complex the tax code.

I do not want to keep the discussion at such a high level of generality much longer, because it can easily deteriorate into empty phrases. I shall try to make some policy suggestions in the next chapter; here I want to make only one general point. Both regulation and unrestrained competition can be harmful when carried to extremes, but the failure of one extreme is no justification for turning to the other. The two extremes should be treated not as alternatives, but as limits, within which the right balance needs to be struck. The task is complicated by our innate tendency to be biased in one direction or the other.

In *The Burden of Consciousness,* written some twenty-five years ago, I developed a rather elaborate scheme along these lines. I took the rate of change as my critical variable, and I argued that people, with their imperfect understanding, are bound to exaggerate it in one direction or the other. One extreme yields a traditional or a dogmatic mode of thinking according to which the existing arrangements have to be accepted as they are because it is inconceivable that they should be otherwise. The other extreme produces a critical mode of thinking in which everything is considered possible until disproved. Each mode of thinking is linked with a form of social organization which corresponds to it with the degree of imperfection that is appropriate to the imperfect understanding of the participants. In this way, the traditional mode of thinking is associated with tribal society, the dogmatic mode with totalitarian society, and the critical mode with Open Society. Needless to say, I was very much under the influence of Karl Popper. I opted for Open Society, but the choice was not without qualification. Each form of social organization was found wanting in something that could be found only in its opposite: totalitarian society lacked freedom; Open Society lacked stability. But given our innate bias, a stable equilibrium between the two is just as unlikely to be attained as a stable equilibrium in a free market. Sentiment is likely to swing in one direction or the other.

After nearly half a century of what now appears as excessive regulation, we have been moving towards excessive deregulation. The sooner we recognize that some kind of regulation is necessary in order to maintain stability, the better our chances of preserving the benefits of a nearly free market system.

17

Toward an
International Central Bank

We have concluded that financial markets are inherently unstable. What practical measures are needed to prevent them from breaking down? I find myself ill-qualified to provide an answer. My strength lies in identifying the flaws in any system and not in designing systems. I have long nurtured the fantasy of becoming an economic reformer a la Keynes but the closer I come to getting a hearing for my views, the more acutely aware I become of my own limitations. My particular expertise is derived from the insight that all systems are flawed; but my understanding of any particular system is always inferior to that of the experts. This holds true for security analysis as well as finance and economics. When I sat for an examination as supervisory security analyst, I failed in every subject; in analyzing the credit-cum-regulatory cycle, I felt the lack of a thorough grounding in the theory of money; and, as the reader saw, in the real-time experiment my greatest weakness was in economic forecasting. Both in my investment activities and in writing this book I could take the state of the art in any particular subject as given without actually possessing it; but when it comes to designing a new financial system, my lack of knowledge becomes a decided drawback.

Nevertheless, I feel I have a contribution to make, especially as the prevailing wisdom has so little to offer. Keynesianism (as distinct from Keynes) has been discredited by the inflation of the 1970s; monetarism is in the process of being shown to be irrelevant to a regime of variable exchange rates and large-scale international capital movements; and supply-side economics turns out to be not much more than a pun on the Keynesian emphasis of the demand side. There is a general malaise, but no clear ideas. In these circumstances even my vague and tentative ideas may prove useful.

First, I think we should distinguish between economic policy and systemic reform. Both are necessary, but neither is sufficient by itself. It is difficult to imagine how any system could function fully automatically. Experience shows that every system—be it the gold standard, Bretton Woods, or freely floating exchange rates—has broken down when it was not supported by the appropriate economic policies. It is equally difficult to see how economic policies could correct the prevailing imbalances without some sort of systemic reform. The various imbalances are interconnected and it is impossible to deal with one without affecting the others.

We are confronted with a disconcerting array of imbalances and instabilities. To mention but a few: unstable exchange rates, the international debt problem, the chronic budget and trade deficits of the United States, the chronic trade surplus of Japan, a chronic worldwide surplus of agricultural and mineral products, unstable commodity prices with particular emphasis on oil, unstable international capital movements, and unstable international financial markets. Some of these instabilities are caused by economic policies and can be altered only by pursuing different ones; others are inherent in the prevailing system and can be cured only by changing the system.

We can take as an example of the first kind of imbalance the desire of the Japanese to produce more than they consume and the apparent desire of the United States to consume more than it produces. If unchecked, these tendencies will lead, in due course, to the rise of Japan as the dominant economic power of the world and to the decline of the United States. The transition is bound to cause a great deal of commotion and dislocation, but its occurrence can be prevented only by changing economic and financial policies and not by changing the financial system. The system itself must be able to accommodate the transition, insofar as it occurs; otherwise it will break down to the detriment of all parties concerned.

An example of the second kind of imbalance is the prevailing system of exchange rates. As we have seen, freely floating exchange rates are cumulatively destabilizing. The fact has now been recognized by the authorities, and the Plaza agreement has committed them to managing the exchange rates. But there is no agreement on how to do it. Managing exchange rates is tantamount to coordinating economic policies. If coordination can be achieved on a voluntary basis, well and good. If not, a different system will have to be devised.

In this chapter I shall explore the possibilities for systemic reform; the appropriate economic policies will be discussed only tangentially.

In my opinion, there are three major problem areas that require systemic reform: exchange rates, commodity pricing with special emphasis on oil, and international debt. Each of these problem areas has a number of aspects that cannot be dealt with individually but only as part of the whole system. There is a fourth major problem area that is not even recognized as such: international capital markets. They reflect, accommodate, and help to generate the various other imbalances. Their rapid development is universally acclaimed as a welcome innovation and treated as yet another instance where markets spontaneously adjust to changing needs. I contend that, in retrospect, the rapid growth of international capital markets will be recognized as yet another excess, similar to the rapid growth of international bank lending in the 1970s. We all know that the international lending boom was based on faulty foundations; I believe it is only a matter of time before the flaws in international capital markets will be recognized.

At present, there is a strong predilection for treating problems on a case-by-case basis. It is now generally agreed, for instance, that exchange rates cannot be allowed to drift any further without interference; but it is also agreed that the interference has to be gradual and tentative. The debate revolves around the question of target zones: should they be tacit or explicit? The possibility of returning to fixed exchange rates is more or less ruled out. Similarly, there is a recognition that the international debt problem requires some new initiative; but the Baker Plan emphatically insists on a case-by-case approach. It is easy to see why. A concession granted to one country can easily spread to all others, so that any talk of systemic reform can precipitate a breakdown of the system. As far as oil prices are concerned, the matter is left to OPEC; the idea that consumer countries ought to cooperate to bring stability to the industry has not even been broached.

The step-by-step approach advocated by James Baker represents a significant advance over the hands-off approach taken by Donald Regan when he was at the Treasury. It constitutes a recognition that markets cannot be left to their own devices, that the authorities have to provide some direction if a breakdown is to be avoided. The initiative taken at the Plaza meeting of the Group of Five touched off a major rise in the world's stock and bond markets. But the momentum generated by the Plaza meeting has dissipated and we are once again drifting dangerously. If the momentum could be recaptured by ad hoc measures, well and good. But without effective international cooperation the dangers of protectionism, currency dislocations, and a breakdown in debt service loom larger than ever, and the need for systemic reform becomes correspondingly more pressing.

Once we turn to systemic reform, the approach has to be completely reversed. Instead of dealing with individual problems in isolation, we must tackle them all at the same time. Problems that appear intractable on their own may fall into place within a larger solution. The more comprehensive the scheme, the better its chance of success. Perhaps the three or four major problem areas I have mentioned could be treated separately, but it would be more effective to deal with them simultaneously. I realize that any radical change in prevailing arrangements goes against the grain, especially in matters of international cooperation where the common good has to be whittled down to accommodate national interests. But there are times when reforms are both possible and necessary. Usually, those are times of crisis.

In the following pages I shall discuss the major problem areas separately, but the solution I shall suggest will link them together. It involves the creation of an international central bank. Historically, central banking has evolved in response to crises. Each central bank has its own history, although developments in one financial center have also affected the others. The problems of the present time are primarily international; hence, the solution must also be international. We have the beginnings of international central banking institutions: the Bank for International Settlement was organized in 1930 in response to the German debt problem; the IMF and the World Bank were founded in 1944 at Bretton Woods. The next step ought to involve an enlargement of their functions or the establishment of a new institution.

EXCHANGE RATES

Exchange rate misalignments have become a major source of disruption for the world economy. They make it unsafe to make long-term investments, they endanger the value of investments already made, and they are at the root of protectionist sentiment in the United States. The market mechanism fails to bring currencies back into alignment. On the contrary, speculation tends to exaggerate currency moves. As we have seen, the system of freely floating currencies is cumulatively destabilizing.

The question is: what can be done about it? A number of arrangements are possible. Target zones, either tacit or explicit, constitute the least radical and therefore the most often mentioned alternative. We could also return to a system of fixed exchange rates, with or without relying on gold as the standard of value. Or, most daring of all, we could establish an international currency.

Whichever arrangement is chosen, a number of problems need to be resolved. First and foremost is the problem of international capital movements. The transfer of capital across national frontiers is highly desirable and ought to be encouraged; but speculative capital movements, as we have seen, are cumulatively destabilizing. We need a system that renders speculation unprofitable. Ideally, currency fluctuations ought to be kept within the confines of interest rate differentials; but that would entail a system of more or less fixed exchange rates.

Target zones are unlikely to discourage speculation. On the contrary, they may constitute an invitation to speculate against the authorities with limited risk. By endorsing a set of target zones, the authorities would expose themselves to speculative attack at a time and place chosen by the speculators. History shows that under these conditions the speculators usually win. It could be argued that an explicit target zone system constitutes the worst of all possible worlds because it would reward speculation within the system as well as encouraging speculative attacks against the system.

Unannounced target zones have a somewhat better chance of success. They would pit the authorities against speculators in an intricate cat and mouse game that the authorities have a chance of winning, provided they act in unison and mobilize larger resources than speculators.

Since they control the ultimate weapon—the printing press—their task is not impossible. A strong currency can always be prevented from appreciating futher provided the central bank is willing to supply it in unlimited quantities. The curious fact is that central banks have rarely had the nerve to do so.

If the authorities succeeded in stablizing exchange rates, hot money would eventually cool off and find its way into long-term investment—an essential prerequisite for a sounder world economy. But stabilizing the relative values of the major currencies is not enough: the value of all the currencies taken together must also be kept stable if we are to avoid inflationary and deflationary excesses on a worldwide scale. Gold has served as a stabilizer throughout history and it may play that role again in one form or another, although it has one great drawback at the present time: the bulk of fresh supplies is produced by two prison administrations—namely, South Africa and the Soviet Union. In any case, the problem is not only one of finding a suitable monetary base; given the reflexivity of credit, the credit structure that is erected on that base also needs to be regulated. What is needed is an institution that coordinates the growth of credit on a worldwide scale: an international central bank.

At this point in the argument, the other major problem areas, namely, international debt and commodity prices with special reference to oil, also need to be considered.

INTERNATIONAL DEBT

The burden of accumulated debt continues to weigh heavily on lenders and borrowers alike. It was hoped that they could grow their way out of the problem, but calculations failed to take into account the erosion of collateral values that occurs when debts are liquidated. In the case of balance-of-payments loans, the collateral consists of exports. Less developed countries export mainly commodities that face inelastic demand: as they try to increase their exports, commodity prices come under pressure.

Some of the major debtor countries managed to enter what I have called Phase 3 of the adjustment process but others seem permanently mired in a deficit position. Raising the production of traditional export commodities has become a dead end. Other avenues of growth need to be pursued. Exporting more sophisticated products is one possibility, but it is running into the road block of protectionism. That leaves domestic growth in less developed countries as the main route to recovery. Politically, it is highly desirable, because the United States may be more willing to absorb imports if exports showed some signs of picking up; moreover, public opinion in debtor countries is increasingly insistent on domestic growth.

The Baker Plan was designed to bring relief to heavily indebted countries by increasing the flow of new lending. The funds would come partly from international institutions, notably the World Bank and the Interamerican Development Bank, and partly from commercial banks. Commercial banks were asked to pledge $20 billion over three years. The loans would have cross-default claims, which would make them more secure than purely commercial loans. When the resources of the World Bank are exhausted, the administration would go to Congress to ask for a capital increase.

The plan is a step in the right direction, but it leaves two problems unresolved: one is the accumulation of additional debt by the borrowing countries at a time when they cannot meet their already existing obligations; the other is the accumulation of doubtful loans on the books of the commercial banks at a time when they already have too many such loans. The plan would mitigate the second problem because a large portion of new loans would come from government institutions, but it would not eliminate it altogether. On the other hand, it lays itself open to the accusation that it constitutes a bailout for the banks. This will make it difficult to get Congress to approve an increase in the World Bank's capital.

It is clear that the plan does not go far enough. It fails to deal with the legacy of past excesses. In the absence of government intervention the accumulated debt would have been liquidated in catastrophic fashion. If a policy of intervention is to succeed, it must reduce the accumulated debt in an orderly manner.

The experience of the last few years shows that, once the weight of accumulated debt passes a certain critical point, it cannot be reduced by a normal process of adjustment. In most Latin American countries, adjustment has been pushed to the limits of endurance and negative resource transfers have reached and already passed their maximum. Nevertheless, external debt has continued to accumulate and debt ratios have showed little, if any, improvement. Moreover, internal debt has been rising at an alarming rate.

In every advanced economy, special legal procedures have been established to deal with excessive indebtedness. Bankruptcy law serves to assure the orderly liquidation of bad debt without undue economic disruption. We are badly in need of some kind of bankruptcy procedure for international debt.

The principles of a bankruptcy reorganization are simple. The clock is stopped at a certain point in time. All existing assets and obligations are thrown into a pot, to be sorted out in lengthy litigation. In the meantime, the entity is allowed to function, if it is viable, free of the burdens of the past. The obligations of the ongoing entity take precedence over the obligations of its predecessor. It is this principle that allows the bankrupt entity to continue functioning.

International lending knows no equivalent procedure for settling bad debt. There have been many precedents where debts have not been paid in full. Usually, nonpayment has resulted in total default and the situation was normalized only several decades later, when the lenders were happy to settle for a few cents on the dollar. The most comprehensive attempts at debt reorganization without total default were the Dawes and Young plans for Germany in 1924 and 1929, respectively, and they did not have a happy outcome.

The example of domestic bankruptcy procedures is not directly applicable to the present situation because the amounts involved are so large that, if payments were suspended even temporarily, the lenders would also go bust; but the principle of drawing a line under the past is the correct one.

At present, all market participants are aware of an unresolved problem. Foreign lenders seek to keep their commitments to the minimum and domestic capital seeks shelter abroad. The economies of the heavily indebted countries continue to languish and political pressures intensify. These trends need to be reversed. We are dealing with a reflexive process. A reversal of trend requires a climactic event whose impact is sufficient to alter the prevailing bias. Only a comprehensive scheme of reorganization would constitute such an event.

I am not in a position to put forward a concrete plan of action. Such a plan would require a great deal of preparation and negotiation. All I can do here is to provide a rough sketch of what it may look like.

It will have to deal with at least five major topics: (1) the treatment of preexisting debt; (2) the provision of new credit; (3) the preservation of the banking system; (4) economic policies in the debtor countries; and (5) the repatriation of flight capital and the attraction of foreign investment. Senator Bradley proposed a plan in June 1986 that touches on all of these points.[1] Henry Kaufman outlined a plan very similar to my own on December 4, 1986.[2] These contributions are moving the discussion in the right direction.

The preexisting debt could be consolidated into long-term negotiable bonds with concessionary interest rates. The bonds would sell at a fraction of their par value and the banks holding the bonds would suffer substantial losses. To protect them, banks would be allowed to write down their bonds to the market value gradually over a period of years. During that time the bonds could be used at their gradually depreciating official value as collateral for borrowing at the discount window of the central bank. This would prevent a run on those banks whose financial positions had been impaired by the reorganization: they would be allowed to earn their way out of a hole.

To reorganize preexisting debt is not enough; a continuing flow of new credit must be secured to enable the heavily indebted countries to recover. Commercial banks cannot be counted on. They should not have provided credit for balance-of-payments purposes in the first place; they have learned their lesson and would be unwilling to lend even if they did not suffer any losses on their existing commitments. Balance-of-payments lending ought to be the province of an international lending institution that has the clout to insist that borrowing countries follow appropriate economic policies.

At present, the major internal problem in the heavily indebted countries is inflation. As long as the servicing of foreign debt generates a large budget deficit there is little hope of curbing it. But once the debt burden is reduced, domestic reforms would have a better chance of succeeding. With less inflation real interest rates would rise, flight capital would be encouraged to return, and perhaps even foreign capital could be attracted once again.

To provide an adequate flow of new credit, the World Bank (or a new institution designed for the purpose) would need a large amount of capital. At present, the political will to make the necessary capital available is missing: any enlargement of international financial institutions would be perceived as a bailout for the banks or for the debtor countries or for both. A comprehensive scheme that would require both creditors and debtors to contribute to the limits of their abilities ought to be able to overcome these objections. The new loans would not go to service existing debt; they would serve to stimulate the world economy at a time when the liquidation of bad debts is having a depressing effect and stimulation is badly needed.

OIL

There is a painless way in which the capital needed by the World Bank could be obtained. It involves a grand design that combines an oil stabilization scheme with a solution to the international debt problem. I first thought of it in 1982. I outlined it in an article that was rejected with scathing comments and never published. It was considered too far-fetched then and it will probably be considered the same today. The interesting point about the article is that the problem that prompted its writing has not gone away. The article is just as timely now as it was when it was written. The reader can judge for himself because I shall reproduce it more or less verbatim.

AN INTERNATIONAL BUFFER STOCK SCHEME FOR OIL*

This article will outline what could be achieved by international cooperation if the willingness to cooperate were present. There are many possibilities: I shall focus on the optimum that could be achieved. The point in doing so is to show that a workable solution is conceivable. This may help generate the will to put it into effect.

The optimum solution would require an agreement between the major oil-importing and oil-exporting countries. It would replace OPEC with an organization that would combine the essential features of a cartel—price fixing and production quotas—with those of an international buffer stock scheme.

It is not necessary or even desirable that all the consuming and producing countries should participate. Cooperation of the industrialized countries and the "moderate" members of OPEC is indispensable,

*Written in 1982.

but the scheme could work without including producers like Iran, Libya, or Algeria.

The scheme would work as follows. Production and consumption quotas would be established. The aggregate amount of the quotas would be in excess of the present level of consumption. The excess would go into a buffer stock. Since it is expensive to store oil, the buffer stock would exist mainly on paper: the oil would be kept in the ground.

Payment would be made not directly to the producing country but into a blocked account at a special facility of the IMF. The funds would be held in favor of the producing countries whose production quotas were not filled by actual sales. The oil would be paid for by those consuming countries that did not fill their consumption quotas with actual purchases. It would be held on the books of the buffer stock authority at the disposal of the country that paid for it. The buffer stock authority, in turn, would hold the oil in the ground of the producing country until needed. Obviously, the buffer stock authority would have to be satisfied that the oil in the ground is secure.

The consuming countries would impose a levy on imported oil. They would rebate a portion of the oil levy to those producing countries that participate in the scheme. Nonparticipating producers would not be entitled to a rebate to penalize them for not participating. The rebates would also be deposited into the blocked accounts at the special facility of the IMF. The blocked accounts would bear interest at a very low rate, say 1%.

Producers with large outstanding debts, such as Mexico, Venezuela, Nigeria, and Indonesia, could use their blocked accounts to repay their debt; countries with surpluses, such as Saudi Arabia and Kuwait, would build up credit balances.

Less developed countries would be exempted from having to participate in the buffer stock scheme. They would then have the advantage of being able to buy oil at a cheaper price than the industrialized countries. Their absence would not endanger the scheme.

For purposes of illustration, let us assume that the benchmark price were kept at $34; the levy would be quite large, say, $17, half of which, $8.50, would be rebated to producers. Quotas would be fixed quite high so that the buffer stock started accumulating at a daily rate of say 3 million barrels. If the industrialized countries were importing oil at a rate of only 15 million barrels a day, and 80% of the oil came from participating producers, they would realize $55.8 billion a year from the levy and pay out $28 billion for buffer stock purchases. The rest would contribute to a reduction of budget deficits putting the industrialized countries in a favorable position to provide the necessary equity capital to an enlarged World Bank. The IMF special facility would receive $65 billion a year, all for the credit of producing countries: $37.2 billion from the producers' share of the oil levy and $28 billion from the buffer stock. By comparison, the net increase of international lending was about $60 billion at its peak in 1980 and 1981.

What would happen to the market price of oil? Since the blocked account pays only 1% interest, there is an inducement to make physical sales rather than sales to the buffer stock. The price paid by the buffer stock would therefore serve as a ceiling: the free market price would settle somewhere below the benchmark price, less the unrebated portion of the levy, that is, $25.50. For consumers and producers in the industrialized countries, the price would of course include the levy. Should the price rise above the benchmark it would be an indication that demand is strong and it would be time to raise production quotas.

How to adjust quotas and prices presents a gamut of tough problems. Most attempts at market regulation flounder because a suitable adjustment mechanism is lacking. This is true even of the international monetary system: the Bretton Woods arrangement broke down because of the inflexibility of the price of gold. The more the scheme relies on price as the adjustment mechanism, the better its chances of survival. Recognizing this principle, the buffer stock should be used only to give the price mechanism time to do its work. That means that after the initial buildup of a buffer stock, whenever it is beginning to be drawn upon there would be an upward adjustment, first in production quotas and then in prices. When the buffer stock is beginning to build up again, there would be a reduction in production quotas down to the minimum established at the outset.

The allocation of production quotas is one of the thorniest problems. Initial quotas would be based on the irreducible financial needs of the countries involved; as the global amount of production is increased the allocation of the increased amounts would have to be guided more by considerations of unused production capacity, size of reserves, and rate of increase or decrease of reserves. The Saudi quota, for instance, would have to rise more than the Algerian or Venezuelan. Even if some formula could be developed, there would be a large element of discretionary judgment involved.

Eventually, as production capacity is more fully utilized, the unwillingness of individual producers to increase their quota could serve as the trigger mechanism for increasing prices. Again there would be an element of judgment involved.

The allocation of consumption quotas would be quite simple by comparison: estimates using actual consumption figures could serve as the basis.

To exercise discretionary powers, authority is required. How such an authority would be constituted and the voting rights divided presents the most difficult question of all. It can be settled only by hard bargaining; the outcome would reflect the bargaining power and bargaining skills of the parties involved.

Undoubtedly, there would be a major shift of power from the oil-producing to the industrialized countries. That is only appropriate when OPEC is being saved from collapse. It is my contention that the collapse of OPEC would have such calamitous consequences that it would have to be prevented one way or another. One of the major arguments in favor of embarking on the comprehensive scheme outlined here is that the industrialized countries might as well gain the maximum benefit from a development that they would have to acquiesce in anyhow. How much they can gain depends on the skill, courage, and cohesion they demonstrate. The scheme outlined here would be much more advantageous than patching up OPEC.

The ultimate merit of the scheme would depend on how the funds accumulating at the IMF special facility would be used. The amounts involved are very large: larger than the accumulation of international debt at its peak; they would remain very large even when the buffer stock stopped growing. The funds should be sufficient to finance a global reorganization plan for sovereign debt.

The blocked funds held by the IMF would be lent to the World Bank to provide credit to heavily indebted countries; they could also be used to buy up their outstanding debt at a discount. The cash income earned on these loans could, in turn, be used to unblock the blocked accounts at the IMF.

How would the various parties to the scheme fare? That would depend largely on the terms arrived at by negotiations. Nevertheless, the broad outlines are clear.

The industrialized countries would give up the benefits of a lower oil price in the near term in exchange for long-range price stability, the accumulation of a buffer stock, a solution for the international debt problem, and a significant contribution to government revenues. They would also have the benefit of protecting their domestic energy and oil service industries, if any.

Producing countries that participated would be assured of a market for their oil production at a volume substantially higher than at present. The price they receive would be less than at present, but higher than it would be if OPEC collapsed. They would have two powerful inducements to participate: the rebate on the oil levy and the ability to sell to the buffer stock. It is true that both would be paid into blocked accounts at the IMF, but oil-producing countries with debts would have access to the accounts for debt repayment purposes; those with surpluses would have their funds unblocked only after a long delay.

The less developed non–oil-producing countries would obtain substantial relief from being able to buy oil at a cheaper price than industrialized countries. Both producing and consuming countries would benefit from the global debt reorganization scheme.

This article does not deal with the problem of how such a comprehensive scheme could be brought into existence—how one could get from here to there. Probably it would require a worse crisis than is currently visible to bring the various parties together.

The plan outlined above would have to be revised in the light of changed circumstances. Both the benchmark price and the size of the levy would have to be substantially lower than the figures used above, reflecting the erosion in OPEC's monopoly profits that has occurred since the scheme was formulated.

I am reluctant to invest any effort in revising the plan because I recognize that it is totally unrealistic, given the prevailing bias. Any kind of buffer scheme would be instantly laughed out of court, and the dismissal would be justified by the past history of buffer stock schemes. But the argument can be turned around. Is the experience with the market mechanism any better? Look at the history of oil. The only periods of stability were those when there were excess supplies and a cartel-type arrangement was in operation. There were three such episodes: first, the monopoly established by Standard Oil; second, the production quota system operated by the Texas Railroad Commission; and third, OPEC. Each episode was preceded and followed by turmoil. If some sort of stabilization scheme is necessary, should the task be left to the producers? Ought not the consuming countries, whose vital interests are affected, take a hand in the arrangements? When the force of this argument is recognized, it will be time to take the plan out of the drawer.

AN INTERNATIONAL CURRENCY

Once the idea of a buffer stock scheme for oil is accepted, it is a relatively short step to the creation of a stable international currency. The unit of account would be based on oil. The price of oil would be kept stable by the buffer stock scheme although its value, in terms of other goods and services, may gradually appreciate if and when demand outstrips supply. In other words, national currencies would gradually depreciate in terms of the international currency.

The newly created international lending agency would use oil as its unit of account. Since its loans would be protected against inflation, they could carry a low rate of interest, say, 3%. The difference between interest earned (3%) and interest paid on blocked accounts (1%) could be used to unblock the accounts. As the blocked accounts diminish, the lending agency builds up its own capital.

The lending agency could be endowed with the powers that usually appertain to a central bank. It could regulate the worldwide money supply by issuing its own short-term and long-term obligations, and it could play a powerful role in regulating the volume of national currencies in terms of its own unit of account. It could exercise the various supervisory functions that are performed by central banks. Its unit of account would constitute an international currency.

Commercial loans could also be designated in the international currency. Eventually, the oil-based currency could replace the dollar and other national currencies in all types of international financial transactions. The transition would have to be carefully orchestrated and the institutional framework developed. This is not the place, and I am not the man, to design a comprehensive scheme. It is clear that an oil-based currency could eliminate speculative influences from international capital transfers.

Whether the establishment of such a currency would be acceptable to all parties concerned is the crucial question. The United States, in particular, has much to lose if the dollar ceased to be the main international currency. For one thing, the home country of the reserve currency is in an advantageous position to render financial services to the rest of the world. More important, the United States is at present the only country that can borrow unlimited amounts in its own currency. If the dollar were replaced by an international currency, the United

States could continue borrowing, but it would be obliged to repay its debt in full. At present, it is within the power of the U.S. government to influence the value of its own indebtedness and it is almost a foregone conclusion that the indebtedness will be worth less when it is repaid than it was at the time when it was incurred.

There are limits to the willingness of the rest of the world to finance the U.S. budget deficit and we may be currently approaching these limits. But the Japanese, for one, seem content to finance the United States even in the knowledge that they will never be repaid in full, because that is the way in which Japan can become "number one" in the world. Japan has already taken over the role of the United States as the major supplier of capital to the rest of the world and it is only a question of time before the yen takes over as the major reserve currency. The transition is likely to be accompanied by a lot of turmoil and dislocations, as was the transition from the pound sterling to the dollar in the interwar period.

The introduction of an international currency would avoid the turmoil. Moreover, it would help arrest the decay of the U.S. economy currently under way. We could no longer run up external debt on concessionary terms; therefore we would be forced to put our house in order. The question is whether our government has the foresight, and our people the will, to accept the discipline that an international currency would impose. Renouncing credit on easy terms makes sense only if we are determined to borrow less. That means that we must reduce both our budget and our trade deficits. It is at this point that the questions of systemic reform and economic policy become intertwined.

As far as trade is concerned, there are two alternative ways to go. One is to exclude imports through protectionist measures, and the other is to increase our exports. Protectionism is a recipe for disaster. It would precipitate the wholesale default of heavily indebted countries and lead to the unraveling of the international financial system. Even in the absence of financial calamity, the elimination of comparative advantages would cause a substantial lowering of living standards throughout the world. On the other hand, it is difficult to see how exports can be significantly increased without systemic reform. Debt reform would increase the purchasing power of debtor countries and monetary reform would provide the element of stability that is necessary for a successful adjustment process in the U.S.

It can be argued that excessive financial instability is doing great damage to the fabric of the American economy. Real assets cannot adjust to macroeconomic changes as fast as financial assets; hence there is a great inducement to transfer real assets into a financial form. This transfer is itself a major factor in weakening the "real" economy. When we examine how financial assets are employed we gain a true measure of the devastation that has occurred. The bulk of the assets is tied up in the Federal budget deficit, loans to heavily indebted countries, and leveraged buyouts. "Real" capital formation is actually declining. That would not be so disastrous if we could count on a steady flow of income from abroad. But our trade deficit is financed partly by debt service from less developed countries, which is precarious to say the least, and partly by capital inflows, which we shall have to service in turn. It is not an exaggeration to say that the "real" economy is being sacrificed to keep the "financial" economy afloat.

To reduce our dependence on capital inflows, the budget deficit needs to be tackled. The most alluring prospect, in my eyes, is a disarmament treaty with the Soviet Union on advantageous terms. The period of heavy defense spending under President Reagan could then be justified as a gigantic gamble that has paid off: the Imperial Circle would be replaced by a more stable configuration in which both our budget and our trade are closer to balance.

The Japanese can, of course, continue to produce more than they consume. There is nothing to stop them from becoming the premier economic power in the world as long as they are willing to save and to export capital. But the rise of Japan need not be accompanied by the fall of the United States; with the help of an international currency, two leading economic powers could coexist.

18

The Paradox
of Systemic Reform

I have provided the outlines not only of a viable international financial system but also of a viable economic policy for the United States. It is no more than a sketch or a vision but it could be elaborated to cover other aspects that I have not touched upon here.

Two fundamental problems present themselves; one is abstract, and the other personal. The abstract problem concerns all attempts at systemic reform. Given our inherently imperfect understanding, isn't there a paradox in systemic reform? How can we hope to design an internally consistent system? The personal problem concerns my aversion to bureaucracy; an international central bank would make bureaucracy inescapable.

I believe the paradox of systemic reform is spurious but it needs to be dealt with. Only if one could demand permanent and perfect solutions would it have any validity. But it follows from our imperfect understanding that permanent and perfect solutions are beyond our reach. Life is temporary; only death is permanent. It makes a great deal of difference how we live our lives; temporary solutions are much better than none at all.

There is a great temptation to insist on a permanent solution. To understand its source, we must consider the meaning of life and death. The fear of death is one of the most deeply felt human emotions. We find the idea of death totally unacceptable and we grasp at any straw to escape it. The striving for permanence and perfection is just one of the ways in which we seek to escape death. It happens to be a deception. Far from escaping the idea of death, we embrace it: permanence and perfection are death.

I have thought about the meaning of life and death long and hard and I have come up with a formulation that I have found personally satisfying. I shall sum it up here, although I realize that it may not be as meaningful to others as it is to me. The key is to distinguish between the fact of death and the idea of death. The fact of death is linked with the fact of life, whereas the idea of death stands in juxtaposition with the idea of consciousness. Consciousness and death are irreconcilable; but life and death are not. In other words, the fact of death need not be as terrifying as the idea.

The idea of death is overpowering: in terms of death, life and everything connected with it lose all significance. But the idea of death is only an idea and the correspondence between facts and ideas is less than perfect. It would be a mistake to equate the idea and the fact. As far as facts are concerned, the clear and present fact is that we are alive. Death as a fact looms in the distance, but, when we reach it, it will not be the same as the idea we have of it now. In other words, our fear of death is unlikely to be validated by the event.

In thinking about life and death, we have a choice: we can take life or death as our starting point. The two are not mutually exclusive: both need to be dealt with—as a fact and as a thought. But the point of view we adopt tends to favor one or the other. The bias we develop permeates all aspects of our thinking and existence. There are civilizations, like that of the Egyptians, that seem to be devoted to the cult of death; there are others, like that of the Greeks, where even the immortals seem to lead normal lives. In most instances the two points of view are at odds and the interplay between them makes history. The conflict between the spiritual and the temporal in Christianity is a case in point. The drama is now being reenacted in the Soviet Union where the demands of Communist ideology are difficult to reconcile with the demands of military strength and economic efficiency.

The clash of biases can manifest itself in many more subtle ways. Thus, we can take different attitudes with regard to economic regulation. One position is that regulation is useless because it introduces distortions that, left to themselves, eventually lead to a breakdown of the system. This point of view is powerfully reinforced by the argument that the market mechanism, left to itself, tends toward equilibrium. The opposite point of view is that perfection is not attainable either by the market or by regulation. Markets are too unstable, regulation too rigid. Markets need to be regulated but regulation cannot be left to itself either: it is in constant need of revision. The fact that no system is perfect is not a valid argument against trying to perfect the system. Take Bretton Woods: the fact that it eventually broke down does not alter the fact that it provided the basis for a quarter of a century of prosperity.

When it comes to a choice between the two attitudes, mine is clearly in favor of life and the temporary and imperfect structures we can create within it. Although I advocate a comprehensive reform of the financial system, I have no illusions that the new system will be any more flawless or permanent than the preceding ones. On the contrary: I regard the search for permanence and perfection as an illusion. The pitfall in a well-functioning system is that it lulls us into complacency. That is what happened to Bretton Woods, and that is what will happen to the next one if we design it too well.

This brings me to the personal problem I have with systemic reform. Systems are operated by bureaucrats, and I have an instinctive aversion to the bureaucratic mentality. In advocating a more regulated international financial system I seem to be wishing for something that I abhor.

The problem is real. The distinctive feature of every bureaucracy is its striving for self-perpetuation. Every system faces the danger that it becomes ossified in the hands of the bureaucracy that administers it. This holds true for Christianity as well as communism. The dead hand of bureaucracy is difficult to escape. Mao Tse-tung tried it by instigating the Cultural Revolution and the consequences were disastrous.

But the problem is not insurmountable. When bureaucrats are in charge of a market, market action serves to keep the bureaucrats on their toes. Experience shows that central banks are among the most flexible, innovative, and efficient institutions. The reason is that the market provides a criterion by which the results of their actions can be judged. They may come under the influence of false ideologies, just like anybody else, but when a policy does not work, they cannot help but notice it. For instance, the Federal Reserve adopted a monetarist stance in 1979, but abandoned it in August 1982. Similarly, the IMF operated with a rather rigid set of prescriptions in dealing with heavily indebted countries, but gradually it has been forced to abandon a formula that does not work. Central banks are often criticized for following the wrong policies; but the very fact that the failures can be demonstrated provides a potent discipline. Moreover, central banks have been surprisingly innovative in handling crises. The Bank of England invented the "lifeboat" in 1974, and the Federal Reserve applied it on a worldwide scale in the debt crisis of 1982. Volcker, in particular, proved to be a man who thrives on crises; but the fact that a man like Volcker could be at the helm of a central bank cannot be treated as an accident.★

In sum, the creation of an international central bank does not constitute a permanent solution. Indeed, the very idea that it constitutes a permanent solution carries with it the seeds of the next crisis.

★Compared with other bureaucracies, central banks constitute a lesser evil.

19

The Crash of '87

The stock market crash of 1987 is an event of historic significance. One must go back to the crashes of 1929, 1907 or 1893 to find a comparison. In many ways the most relevant is 1929, and it is also the most widely known; but in drawing the comparison we must be careful not to confuse the crash itself with its aftermath.

In the crash of 1929, the New York stock market fell by about 36%; this figure is almost identical with the loss that occurred in 1987. Subsequently, stocks recovered nearly half their losses, and then declined by another 80% in the long-drawn-out bear market between 1930 and 1932. It is that bear market, associated with the Great Depression, which preys on the public imagination. Exactly because it is so well remembered, we can be sure that history will not repeat itself. The immediate governmental reaction to the crash already bears out this contention. After 1929, the monetary authorities made a momentous mistake by not supplying enough liquidity; in the present case, they will make a different mistake. On the basis of their initial reaction, the danger is that they will destroy the stability of the dollar in their effort to avoid a recession, at least in an election year.

Technically, the crash of 1987 bears an uncanny resemblance to the crash of 1929. The shape and extent of the decline and even the day-to-day movements of stock prices track very closely. The major difference is that in 1929 the first selling climax was followed within a few days by a second one which carried the market to a lower low. In 1987, the second climax was avoided, and even if the market were to establish new lows in the future, the pattern would be different. The divergence bears witness to the determination of the authorities not to repeat the mistake of 1929. In the early stages of the crash President Reagan sounded remarkably like President Hoover, but by the time of his press conference on Thursday, October 22, he had been carefully coached to avoid the resemblance.

The crash of 1987 came just as unexpectedly as the crash of 1929. There had been a general awareness that the worldwide boom was unsound and unsustainable, but few people got their timing right. I was as badly caught as the next fellow. I was convinced that the crash would start in Japan; that turned out to be an expensive mistake.

In retrospect, it is easy to reconstruct the sequence of events that led to the crash. The boom had been fed by liquidity; it was a reduction in liquidity that established the preconditions for a crash. In this respect also 1987 resembles 1929: it will be recalled that the crash of 1929 was preceded by a rise in short-term money rates.

Exactly how the reduction in liquidity came about in 1987 is a thornier question, to which one cannot give a definitive answer without a great deal of research. One thing is clear: the agreement to defend the dollar played a crucial role. In the first few months following the Louvre Accord of February 1987, the dollar was defended by sterilized intervention; that is to say, domestic interest rates were not allowed to be affected. When the central banks found that they had to acquire more dollars than they had appetite for, they changed their tactics. After Nakasone's visit to Washington of April 29–May 2, 1987, they allowed interest-rate differentials to widen to levels at which the private sector was willing to hold dollars; in effect, they "privatized" the intervention.

What is not so clear yet is whether it was the sterilized or the unsterilized intervention that led to the reduction in liquidity. Sterilized intervention transferred large amounts of dollars to the coffers of the central banks, and the Federal Reserve may have failed to inject the equivalent amounts into the domestic money market. In that case, the effect would have made itself felt with a lag of several months. Alternatively, it may be that the monetary authorities in Japan and Germany got cold feet about the inflationary implications of unsterilized intervention and it was their attempt to rein in their domestic money supply that led to the worldwide rise in interest rates.

I favor the latter explanation, although I cannot rule out the possibility that the former was also a contributing factor. The Germans are well known to harbor a strong anti-inflationary bias. The Japanese are more pragmatic, and they did, in fact, allow their interest rates to fall after Nakasone's return to Tokyo. But when they found that an easy-money policy was merely reinforcing the already unhealthy speculation in financial assets, including land, they had second thoughts. They tried to slow down the growth of the Japanese domestic money supply and bank lending; but speculation was out of control by then. Even after the Bank of Japan started to rein in the money supply, the bond market continued to soar, and the yield on the bellwether Coupon #89 issue fell to only 2.6% in May before the bond market crashed in September, 1987.

The collapse of the Japanese bond market was the first in a sequence of events that will enter the annals of history as the Crash of 1987. There were large speculative long positions in September bond futures which could not be liquidated. Hedging led to a collapse of the December futures, and the yield on the Coupon #89 issue rose to more than 6% before the bottom was reached. I thought that the collapse would carry over into the stock market, which was even more overvalued than the bond market, but I was wrong. Speculative money actually moved from bonds to stocks in a vain attempt to recoup the losses. As a result, the Japanese stock market reached minor new highs in October.

The consequences for the rest of the world were more grievous. The government bond market in this country had become dependent on Japanese buying. When the Japanese turned sellers, even in relatively small quantities, our bond market suffered a sinking spell which went beyond any change justified by economic fundamentals. Undoubtedly our economy was somewhat stronger than had been expected, but the strength was in industrial production rather than in final demand. Commodity prices were rising, encouraging inventory accumulation and raising the specter of inflation. The fear of inflation was more a rationalization for the decline in bonds than its root cause; nevertheless, it served to reinforce the downtrend in the bond market.

The weakness in bonds widened the disparity between bond and stock prices that had been developing since the end of 1986. Such a disparity can persist indefinitely, as it did, for instance, in the 1960s, but as it widens it creates the preconditions for an eventual reversal. The actual timing of the reversal is determined by a confluence of other events. In this case, political considerations played a major role: President Reagan had lost his luster and the elections were approaching. The decisive factor was the renewed pressure on the dollar; and the internal instabilities of the stock market converted a decline into a rout.

The first crack came when a well-known and widely followed "guru," Robert Prechter, gave a bearish signal before the opening on October 6 and the market responded with a resounding fall of some 90 points. This was a sign of underlying weakness, but similar incidents had occurred in 1986 without catastrophic consequences. The situation deteriorated when the dollar also started to weaken. On Tuesday, October 13, Alan Greenspan, Chairman of the Federal Reserve, announced that the trade balance showed signs of a "profound structural improvement." The figures published on Wednesday, October 14, were all the more disappointing. The dollar came under severe selling pressure. The principle of unsterilized intervention would have required a rise in interest rates which would have been all the larger because of the rises that had occurred in Japan and Germany. The U.S. authorities were unwilling to undertake such a tightening, and by Thursday, as the stock market continued to decline, Treasury Secretary James Baker was reported to be pressing the Germans to lower their interest rates lest the dollar be allowed to fall. The stock market decline continued to accelerate amid reports that the House Ways and Means Committee was planning to limit the tax deductibility of junk bonds issued in leveraged buy-outs. Although the provision was abandoned by Friday, stocks that had been bid up in the expectation of a "corporate event" declined sufficiently to force the liquidation of positions held on margin by professional arbitrage traders.

Then came the sensational lead article in the Sunday edition of *The New York Times* in which Treasury officials were reported to be openly advocating a lower dollar and blaming the Germans in advance for the stock market fall which these remarks helped to precipitate. Some selling pressure on Monday, October 19, was inevitable because of the built-in instabilities; but the *New York Times* article had a dramatic effect, exacerbating the instabilities which had been allowed to accumulate. The result was the largest decline ever on a single day: the Dow Jones average lost 508 points, or 22% of its value.

Portfolio insurance, option writing and other trend-following devices allow, in principle, the individual participant to limit his risk at the cost of enhancing the instability of the system. In practice, the breakdown of the system did not allow the individual to escape unscathed. The market became disorganized, panic set in and the forced liquidation of collateral further compressed market values.

The collapse in New York had repercussions abroad, and the collapse of other markets affected New York in turn. London turned out to be more vulnerable than New York, and the normally staid Swiss market was even worse affected. Worst of all was Hong Kong, where a group of speculators in the futures market managed to arrange for a suspension of trading on the stock exchange for the rest of the week in the vain hope that they might be able to force a settlement of the futures contract at an artificial price. The ploy failed, the speculators were wiped out and the futures market had to be rescued by Government intervention. During the week that the Hong Kong market was suspended, selling from Hong Kong radiated to the other Australasian markets and to London. The selling pressure persisted for the better part of two weeks after Black Monday. While other stock markets continued to reach new lows, the New York market did not exceed the lows set in the initial selling climax.

The only stock market that escaped collapse was Japan's. There was a one-day panic following Black Monday, when prices fell the limit without many transactions taking place. (In Japan, daily price movements are limited by regulations.) Japanese stocks traded at large discounts in London the next morning; but by the time the Japanese market reopened the next day, the Ministry of Finance had made a few phone calls, the sell orders miraculously disappeared and large institutions were aggressive buyers. As a result, the market recouped a large part of the previous day's losses. Prices sagged further after the panic, and at the time of the gigantic Nippon Telephone & Telegraph issue, which involved raising about $37 billion from the public, it looked as if the market might unravel. But the authorities intervened again, this time permitting the four large brokers to trade for their own accounts—in effect, giving them a license to manipulate the market.

The two outstanding features of the Crash of 1987, then, are the absence of a second selling climax in New York and the relative stability of Tokyo. These two features deserve further exploration, because they can provide some insight into consequences of the crash.

The historic significance of the crash of 1929 derived from the fact that it precipitated the Great Depression. It occurred during a period when economic and financial power was moving from Europe to the United States. The shift in power caused a great deal of instability in exchange rates, and the end result was that the dollar supplanted sterling as the international reserve currency; but the crash of 1929 itself played no clearly defined role in the process.

By contrast, the historic significance of the Crash of 1987 lies in the fact that it marks the transfer of economic and financial power from the United States to Japan. Japan has been producing more than it consumes, and the United States has been consuming more than it produces for some time past. Japan has been accumulating assets abroad, while the United States has been amassing debts. The process received a great boost when President Reagan took office with a program of cutting taxes and increasing military expenditures (in this context, armaments are also a form of consumption), and it has been gaining momentum ever since. Both sides have been loath to acknowledge it: President Reagan wanted to make Americans feel good about being American and pursued the illusion of military superiority at the cost of rendering our leading position in the world economy illusory; while Japan wanted to keep growing in the shadow of the United States as long as possible.

The Crash of 1987 has revealed the strength of Japan and made the transfer of economic and financial power clearly visible. It was the collapse of the Japanese bond market that depressed our own bond market and set up our stock market for a crash. Yet Japan has been able to avert a collapse of its own stock market. To top it all, our authorities have been able to avert a second selling climax only by abandoning the dollar. Herein lies the significance of the two features of the crash I have singled out for special attention. Japan has, in effect, emerged as the banker to the world—taking deposits from the rest of the world, and making loans to and investing in the rest of the world. The dollar is no longer qualified to serve as the international reserve currency. Whether a new international currency system can be established without a Great Depression remains an open question.

Events are notoriously more difficult to predict than to explain. How can one anticipate decisions that have not yet been taken? Nevertheless, one can evaluate the implications of the decisions that have already been taken.

The Crash of 1987 confronted our Government with the question: which do we consider more important, averting a recession or preserving the value of the dollar? The response was unequivocal. By the middle of the second week after Black Monday, the dollar had been cut loose from its moorings, and by the end of that week Treasury Secretary James Baker made the news official. The dollar moved obediently lower, and a second selling climax in the stock market did not take place. The mistake of 1929 has been avoided, but only at the peril of committing a different kind of mistake. The decision to cut the dollar loose is painfully reminiscent of the competitive devaluations of the 1930s. Temporary relief may be bought at the cost of greater damage later.

Prospects are good that a severe recession in the United States can be avoided at least in the near future. Consumer spending was already declining prior to the crash, and the crash is bound to make consumers more cautious. But industrial production has been benefiting from the lower dollar, and industrial employment has been strong. The reduction in the budget deficit is too small and too illusory to have much of an effect. If American corporations slash their capital expenditures, foreign corporations expanding in the United States may take up the slack. It is unlikely, therefore, that the downturn in consumption would develop into much more than a flat first quarter or first half in 1988. Both Germany and Japan are likely to stimulate their own economies. The net result would be a continuation of the slow growth that has prevailed in the world economy since 1983. It may come as a surprise how little direct effect the stock market is going to have on the real economy.

The trouble with this scenario is that it leaves the imbalances that have precipitated the Crash of 1987 unresolved. Neither the budget deficit nor the trade deficit of the United States is likely to disappear. The aftermath of the crash may bring some temporary respite, but eventually the dollar is bound to come under pressure again—either because our economy is strong and the trade deficit persists, or because it is weak and lower interest rates are needed to stimulate it.

The United Kingdom found itself in a similar situation prior to the discovery of North Sea oil. The result was "stagflation" and a sequence of "stop-go" policies. The same is in store for us now. The major difference is that the United States is the largest economy in the world and its currency still serves as the international medium of exchange. As long as the dollar remains unstable, international financial markets will remain accident-prone. It should be recalled that while it was the Louvre Accord that created the preconditions for a crash, it was the actual fall in the dollar that precipitated it.

If the dollar continues to depreciate, owners of liquid assets will be driven to take refuge elsewhere. Once the movement gathers momentum, not even a rise in interest rates could arrest it, because the rate of depreciation in the dollar would outweigh the interest-rate differential in its favor. Eventually, the rise in interest rates would bring on a more severe recession than the one that the Administration sought to avoid.

It has happened before. In the last two years of the Carter Administration, speculative capital continued to move to Germany and Switzerland even when it had to pay a premium to be accepted there. The specter of a free-fall in the dollar is more real today than it has been at any time since President Carter was forced to sell bonds denominated in hard currencies in 1979.

Ever since the crash, stock markets worldwide have weakened whenever the dollar weakened, and vice versa. The message is clear: any further decline in the dollar would be counterproductive. The Administration seems to have received the message: all talk of a lower dollar has ceased, and now that a budget compromise of sorts has been accomplished, preparations are under way for reestablishing the Louvre Accord. Much depends on how successful the effort will be. Unfortunately, the Administration does not bring much to the table: the budget cut has been described as "a miserable pittance" by Senator Packwood. Moreover, the Crash of 1987 has demonstrated conclusively that the Administration is more concerned with avoiding a recession than with stabilizing the dollar. The burden of supporting the dollar will fall primarily to our trading partners.

The best way for the Japanese to protect their export markets is to transfer production to the dollar zone; the process had already started prior to the crash. Many Japanese companies, led by the car makers, are establishing manufacturing subsidiaries in the United States and Mexico. The process will be accelerated by the crash and the falling dollar, both of which make American assets cheaper to acquire and the American market less profitable to supply from abroad. The eventual solution of the trade deficit will be import substitution—by Japanese manufacturers. It echoes the solution to Europe's seemingly incurable "dollar gap" after the Second World War. That was the time when many American corporations became "multinational" and the United States consolidated its hegemony over the world economy. Similarly, the birth of Japanese multinational corporations will coincide with Japan's becoming the world's banker and economic leader.

Already, large-scale Japanese investments give Japan considerable political leverage in the United States. Almost every state in the Union has established trade-promotion offices in Japan. Their endeavors are not likely to make much headway if the Congressmen representing the state are too vocal in supporting protectionist measures. In spite of all the posturing, protectionism may no longer be a viable policy option. And in a few years' time, when the Japanese have built their factories, they may become the most ardent protectionists—to keep out competition from Korea and Taiwan.

There have been many instances in the course of history when economic and financial and, eventually, political and military leadership passed from one country to another. The latest instance was in the interwar period, when the United States supplanted Great Britain. Nevertheless, the prospect of Japan's emerging as the dominant financial power in the world is very disturbing, not only from the point of view of the United States but also from that of the entire Western civilization.

From the narrowly American standpoint, the damage is too obvious to deserve much elaboration. The loss of our preeminent position is bound to engender a crisis in our sense of national identity. Having just expended enormous sums in the pursuit of military superiority, albeit these sums were borrowed abroad, we are ill prepared to cope with the fact that we are losing our economic superiority. Our sense of national identity is less firmly grounded in tradition than in the case of Great Britain, so the crisis is bound to be all the more deeply felt. The consequences for our political behavior, both internally and internationally, are incalculable.

The implications for our civilization are equally profound but less obvious. The international trading system is an open system; its members are sovereign states which have to treat each other on the basis of equality. That would not change if Japan takes over leadership. On the contrary, the Japanese can be expected to step more gingerly than the Americans have on occasion.

The problem is more subtle. The United States and Great Britain are members of the same culture; that is not true of Japan. The Japanese have shown tremendous capacity to learn and to grow, but the society in which they live remains fundamentally different from ours. The Japanese think in terms of subordination and dominance. Contrast this with the notion that all men are created equal, and the difference between the two cultures is brought into focus.

Both the United States and Great Britain are open societies: internally, people enjoy a large degree of freedom; externally, the borders are open to the movement of goods, people, capital and ideas to various degrees. Japan is still, to a large extent, a closed society. The features of an open society, such as a democratic form of government, have been imposed by an occupying power after a lost war. But the value system which permeates Japanese society is a closed one: the interests of the individual are subordinated to the interests of the social whole.

This subordination is not achieved through coercion; Japan bears no resemblance whatsoever to a totalitarian state. It is merely a country with a very strong sense of national mission and social cohesion. The Japanese want to be part of a group that strives to be number one, whether it is their company or their nation; and they are willing to make considerable sacrifices in the service of that goal. They cannot be faulted for holding such values; indeed, it is more appropriate to criticize Americans for their unwillingness to suffer any personal inconvenience for the common good. Japan is a nation on the rise; we have become decadent.

The question is, whether the United States in particular and the rest of the world in general will allow itself to be dominated by an alien society with such a strong sense of national identity. The question is troubling not only for us but also for the Japanese. There is a strong school of thought that wants Japan to open up in order to become more acceptable to the rest of the world. But there is also a strong commitment to traditional values and an almost pathological fear, especially in the older generation, that Japan may lose its drive before it becomes number one. Japan is a society in transition, and it may well become much more open as it assumes the role of leadership. There are many internal tensions and contradictions which tend to undermine social cohesion and hierarchical values. Much depends on how fast the transition occurs. If the United States proved itself somewhat more viable than it has been of late, the value system of an open society would also become more attractive to the Japanese.

The closed character of Japanese society manifests itself in many areas. Formally a democracy, Japan has been ruled by one party since its present constitution was introduced; the succession of prime ministers is determined by negotiations behind closed doors. Although the domestic market is formally open, foreign companies find it impossible to penetrate it without a domestic ally. But nowhere is the difference between the openness of the Western system and the closed character of the Japanese more dramatically demonstrated than in the financial markets.

The Western world has gone overboard in allowing financial markets to function unhindered by any government regulation. That was a grievous mistake, as the Crash of 1987 has demonstrated. Financial markets are inherently unstable; stability can be maintained only if it is made an objective of public policy. Instability is cumulative. As I have tried to show elsewhere in this book, the longer markets are allowed to develop without regulation, the more unstable they become, until eventually they crash.

The Japanese attitude toward financial markets is totally different. The Japanese treat markets as a means to an end and manipulate them accordingly. The authorities and the institutional players are connected by a subtle system of mutual obligation.

Recent events have provided an insight into the way the system operates. The first time the market was set to collapse, after Black Monday, a telephone call from the Ministry of Finance was sufficient to rally the financial institutions. In the second instance, at the time of the public issue of Nippon Telephone & Telegraph shares, financial institutions proved less responsive, perhaps because the Ministry of Finance had used up its chits in the first phone call. It now had to rely on the brokers, whose survival was directly threatened. By giving them license to manipulate the market, the authorities avoided disaster.

Whether a collapse can be avoided indefinitely is one of the most fascinating questions about the current financial situation. It still awaits an answer. The authorities have allowed a speculative bubble to develop in Tokyo real estate and in the stock markets whose magnitude has few parallels in history. To illustrate, Nippon Telephone & Telegraph shares were sold to the public at 270 times earnings, while American Telephone & Telegraph was valued at 18 times. If this were a free market, it would have collapsed already. There has been no example in history when a bubble of this magnitude has been deflated in an orderly manner without bursting. The authorities have been unable to prevent a crash in the Japanese bond market, but they may be able to do so in the stock market. The continuing strength of the yen works to their advantage. If they succeed, it would represent a historic first, the dawn of a new era in which financial markets are manipulated for the benefit of the public good.

The effect of the crash was to move the Japanese stock market nearer to being a closed system. Foreigners owned less than 5% of Japanese stocks at the outset of the crisis, and they dumped much of their stock during and after it. The selling was absorbed, interestingly, not so much by Japanese institutions as by the Japanese public, which was encouraged by the brokers to go heavily into debt. Japanese brokers did, in fact, speak of buying stocks during the crisis as a patriotic duty whose accomplishment will set Japan apart from the rest of the world. Margin debt is at an all-time record. How to reduce the debt load without precipitating forced liquidation of margin accounts is the task now confronting the authorities.

Why did the Japanese authorities allow the speculative bubble to develop in the first place? That is another fascinating question about which one can only conjecture. There were external pressures—the United States was pushing for lower interest rates in Japan—but the Japanese would not have yielded if it had not suited them.

At first, the inflation of financial assets allowed the authorities to discharge their obligations toward the commercial banks at a time when the real economy was in deep trouble. Without the land and stock market boom, the commercial banks would have seen many of their loans to industrial companies turn sour, and their earnings would have suffered. Land and stock market speculation allowed them to expand their loan portfolios against seemingly good collateral and also allowed the industrial companies to make up for their earnings shortfall by earnings derived from "zaitech"—that is, financial manipulation. The land boom has also served another purpose: it helped to preserve a high domestic savings rate and a favorable trade balance in spite of the rise in the value of the yen. With the cost of housing rising faster than wages, Japanese wage earners had good reason to save an increasing portion of their income. With the domestic economy in recession, the savings were available for investing abroad. That was an ideal recipe for amassing wealth and power in the world, even if the foreign investments depreciated in value. I suspect that at least a fraction of the Japanese power elite would be quite pleased to see investors lose some money: it would prevent the Japanese from going soft before Japan has become great. How else can one explain the willingness of a democratic government to sell shares to its electorate at obviously inflated prices?

But rising land and stock prices soon started to have adverse consequences. The high savings rate brought additional pressure from abroad to stimulate the domestic economy, and the government finally had to give in. Moreover, the gap between those who owned land and those who did not widened to such an extent as to threaten social cohesion. As soon as the domestic economy began to recover, there was no need to allow banks to finance speculative transactions; on the contrary, it was appropriate to redirect their resources toward the real economy. The attempt to rein in bank lending and the money supply set off the chain of events I have reviewed earlier.

It is ironic that the Japanese should have a better understanding of the reflexive character of the financial markets than the Western world does, and it is regrettable that they should be using it to ensure the success of a closed system. If we don't like what is happening, we should take steps to develop a viable alternative.

The stock market boom has diverted our attention from the fundamental deterioration in the financial position of the United States. With the frenetic activity in financial markets and the lure of quick rewards, it was at least possible to pretend that the policies pursued by the Reagan Administration were working. The Crash of 1987 comes as a rude awakening. Many of the profits turned out to be illusory, and frenetic activity will soon be succeeded by the stillness of the morgue. Prospects are dismal. One way or another, we face a reduction in living standards. Much will depend on the route we choose.

The most likely path is the one I have outlined earlier. It is the path followed by Great Britain before us, and it is likely to produce similar results as far as the United States is concerned. The effect on the world economy may be much more negative because of the importance of the dollar.

There is also a temptation to pursue a protectionist policy, but for the reasons I have stated earlier, it is no longer a viable alternative. Nevertheless, it could do a lot of mischief.

Finally, there is the possiblity of reasserting the leadership we failed to exercise. This would involve not only putting our own house in order but also bringing a new international financial order into existence which is appropriate to the altered circumstances.

We cannot have a smoothly functioning international economy without a stable international currency. The monetary authorities began to recognize this fact with the Plaza Agreement of October 1985 and reconfirmed it with the Louvre Accord of February 1987. Unfortunately, the steps they took were inadequate, and the Louvre Accord fell apart in the Crash of 1987. Since the decision to stabilize the dollar can be held responsible, one way or another, for the crash, it is highly unlikely that the Louvre Accord can be patched up. Whatever agreement is reached, its credibility will have been diminished by the fact that when it came to the crunch, the previous agreement had been abandoned. And it is highly doubtful whether the Louvre Accord should be patched up—after all, it did cause the Crash of 1987.

Trying to protect the currency at an unsustainable level can plunge the country into protracted depression; that is what happened to Great Britain in 1926 when it returned to the gold standard at the prewar level.

It could be argued that the dollar is reasonably valued at DM1.65 and Y132 to the dollar. This is true in the sense that a further fall in its value would not bring any appreciable improvement in the trade balance in the near term. But this was already true when the dollar was 10% higher. The reason is that the adjustment process takes time, while a fall in the value of the currency has an immediate negative impact (the famous J-curve effect). Moreover, the more unstable the exchange rate, the more reluctant people are to make the investments necessary to adjust to it.

The argument only goes to prove that there is simply no realistic exchange rate at which the dollar can continue fulfilling its role as the international reserve currency: the dollar is unsound at any price. Holders of financial assets seek the best store of value, and the dollar no longer qualifies. A country with a large budget deficit and a large trade deficit cannot expect foreigners to accept an ever-increasing flow of its currency. Yet the international financial system cannot function without a stable currency as its foundation. This is the central lesson that emerges from the Crash of 1987.

We desperately need an international currency system that is not based on the dollar. Yet the yen is not yet ready to serve as the international reserve currency—partly because the Japanese financial markets are not sufficiently open, and partly because the rest of the world is not ready to accept Japanese hegemony. The ideal solution would be a genuine international currency, issued and controlled by a genuine international bank. International lending for balance-of-payments purposes would then be designated in the international currency, and the value of the currency would be tied to gold or to a basket of commodities, ensuring that debts would have to be repaid in full. Only when the dollar loses its privileged status will the United States cease to flood the world with dollars. The sooner we make the transition, the better the chances of arresting the economic decline of the United States.

Unfortunately, we are not yet ready to learn the central lesson of the crash. The prevailing wisdom still maintains that markets are self-correcting and exchange rates ought to be allowed to find their equilibrium levels. The Crash of '87 has, if anything, reinforced this line of thought. As a consequence, we can expect a period of continuing turmoil in financial markets, although the focus of attention may shift from the stock market to the currency market and the bond market and, eventually, to the market for precious metals.

The idea of an international currency and an international central bank has few supporters. Ironically, it is likely to get a more enthusiastic response in Japan than in the United States. There are many people in Japan who would like their country to develop into a more open society. The Japanese have still vivid memories of the Second World War when they tried to go it alone. They would much rather flourish within a worldwide trading and financial system than embark on the impossible task of creating their own. As newcomers, they would be willing to accept an arrangement that does not fully reflect their current strength.

Yet it is the United States that has the most to gain from a reform of the international currency system. It would allow us to consolidate our position in the world which we are otherwise in danger of losing. We are still in a position to strike a favorable deal, especially in view of our military might. Most important, we could preserve an open system in which Japan would be one of the leading members, becoming a more open society in the process. The alternative is a period similar to the 1930s: financial turmoil, beggar-thy-neighbor policies leading to worldwide depression and perhaps even war.

Epilogue

The unifying theme of this book is the concept of reflexivity: I have focused on its implications for the social sciences in general and financial markets in particular. I have left other areas largely unexplored. I should like to mention them briefly here, although my thoughts relating to them are not properly developed. They ought to form the subject of another book in the future, but I am afraid I may not have a chance to write it, especially if I remain involved in financial markets.

First, the question of values. Economic theory has trained us to take values as given, although the evidence suggests that they are shaped by a reflexive process. Most values can be reduced to economic terms nowadays—the most recent Nobel laureate in economics earned his prize by interpreting politics as an economic process in which the participants seek to maximize their own benefits—but that has not always been the case, and even today there are many parts of the world where profit-maximizing behavior takes second place to other motivations. Religion and tradition are less easily amenable to economic analysis than is politics in a materialistic culture. We have great difficulty in understanding a phenomenon like Islamic fundamentalism; at the other end of the scale, a movement that we profess to admire, Solidarity, is also alien to our way of thinking.

The predominance of economic values in Western and westernized societies is itself a function of our economic success. Values evolve in reflexive fashion: the fact that economic activity has borne positive results has enhanced the value we put on economic values. The same can be said about scientific method: the triumphs of natural science have raised the status of scientific method to unsustainable heights. Conversely, various forms of art have played a much bigger role in cultures not very far removed from our own just because it was easier to achieve positive results in art than in economic activity. Even today, poetry carries a weight in Eastern Europe, including the Soviet Union, that we find difficult to appreciate in the West. There is little doubt in my mind that our emphasis on material values, profit, and efficiency has been carried to an extreme.

Reflexive processes are bound to lead to excesses, but it is impossible to define what is excessive because in matters of values there is no such thing as normal. Perhaps the best way to approach the subject of values is to start from the position that they are rooted in fantasy rather than reality. As a consequence, every set of values has a flaw in it. We can then ask what are the elements of fantasy in a particular set of values and how the elements of fantasy and reality have interacted. Any other approach would introduce a bias in favor of our own flawed set of values.

Values are closely associated with the concept of self—a reflexive concept if ever there was one. What we think has a much greater bearing on what we are than on the world around us. What we are cannot possibly correspond to what we think we are, but there is a two-way interplay between the two concepts. As we make our way in the world our sense of self evolves. The relationship between what we think we are and what we are in reality is the key to happiness—in other words, it provides the subjective meaning of life.

I could readily provide a reflexive interpretation of my own development but I am reluctant to do so because it would be too revealing, not to say incriminating. It will come as no surprise to the reader when I admit that I have always harbored an exaggerated view of my self-importance—to put it bluntly, I fancied myself as some kind of god or an economic reformer like Keynes (each with his General Theory) or, even better, a scientist like Einstein (reflexivity sounds like relativity). My sense of reality was strong enough to make me realize that these expectations were excessive and I kept them hidden as a guilty secret. This was a source of considerable unhappiness through much of my adult life. As I made my way in the world, reality came close enough to my fantasy to allow me to admit my secret, at least to myself. Needless to say, I feel much happier as a result. I have been fortunate enough to be able to act out some of my fantasies—this book, in particular, fills me with a great sense of accomplishment. Reality falls far short of my expectations, as the reader can readily observe, but I no longer need to harbor a sense of guilt. Writing this book, and especially these lines, exposes me in a way I never dared to expose myself before, but I feel I can afford it: my success in business protects me. I am free to explore my abilities to their limits, exactly because I do not know where those limits are. Criticism will help me in this endeavor. The only thing that could hurt me is if my success encouraged me to return to my childhood fantasies of omnipotence—but that is not likely to happen as long as I remain engaged in the financial markets, because they constantly remind me of my limitations. Given my personality I have been extremely lucky in my career choice, but of course it was not really a choice but a reflexive process in the course of which both my career and my sense of self evolved in tandem. I could say a lot more on the subject, but as long as I have a career in business I have to plead the Fifth Amendment. There is a point beyond which self-revelation can be damaging and one of the flaws in my character, which I have not fully fathomed, is the urge to reveal myself. Perhaps I was exaggerating a minute ago when I said I am not afraid of exposing myself.

I also have some views on what could be called the meaning of life in the objective sense—if it were not a contradiction in terms to use the word "objective" in this context. I start from the position that every human endeavor is flawed: if we were to discard everything that is flawed there would be nothing left. We must therefore make the most of what we have; the alternative is to embrace death. The choice is a real one, because death can be embraced in a number of ways; the pursuit of perfection and eternity in all its manifestations is equivalent to choosing the idea of death over the idea of life. If we carry this line of argument to its logical conclusion, the meaning of life consists of the flaws in one's conceptions and what one does about them. Life can be seen as a fertile fallacy.

So far I have spoken mainly in terms of the individual. But the individual does not exist in isolation; his inherently imperfect understanding makes him all the more dependent on the society to which he belongs. The analysis that has led to the concept of reflexivity also throws some light on the relationship between the individual and society. It is a mistake to think that there are two separate entities involved:

the relationship is between a part and a whole. We have seen the cognitive difficulties that such a relationship gives rise to: neither the individual nor society can be defined without reference to the other. Given the structure of our language it is extremely difficult to recognize the contingent nature of the two entities, and as a matter of historical fact most discourses on the subject have taken either the whole or the part as their starting point. The choice of the starting point tends to infuse the rest of the discussion with a bias. The famous speech of Agrippa in which he compares society with an organism epitomizes one extreme, and Rousseau's social contract the other.

In order to avoid the bias inherent in these extremes new categories of speech need to be established. An appropriate language is beginning to emerge in the context of computer science and systems analysis, but it will take time to permeate general discourse.* Even if we learn to think in terms of reflexive and recursive relations, we are confronted with a substantive choice: should society take a predetermined shape or should its members be allowed to determine the form of society in which they live? The former kind of society has been described by Karl Popper as closed, the latter as open.

I have just come back from China where the issue is of vital significance. The country has passed through a horrendous period during which the collective terrorized the individual on a massive scale. It is now run by a group of people who had been on the receiving end of the terror. These people have ample reason to be passionately devoted to the cause of individual freedom; but they are up against a long tradition of feudalism, an all-pervasive bureaucracy, and the constraints of Marxist ideology.

I was surprised to find an avid interest in the concept of reflexivity. As I have noted in the book, reflexivity could also be described as a kind of dialectics, but I have eschewed using the word because of the heavy intellectual baggage it carries. It is exactly these connotations that make the concept so fascinating for the Chinese because it allows them to modify Marxist ideology without breaking with it. Hegel propounded a dialectic of ideas; Marx turned the idea on its head and espoused dialectic materialism; now there is a new dialectic that connects the partici-

---

*I have been much taken by Gregory Bateson, *Steps to an Ecology of Mind* (New York: Ballantine, 1975), and Douglas R. Hofstadter, *Gödel, Escher, Bach: An Eternal Golden Braid* (New York: Basic Books, 1979).

pants' thinking with the events in which they participate—that is, it operates between ideas and material conditions. If Hegel's concept was the thesis and Marxism the antithesis, reflexivity is the synthesis.

But there is a fundamental difference between Marxism and the new dialectic. Marx labored under the misapprehension that, in order to be scientific, a theory has to determine the future course of history. The new dialectic is emphatically not deterministic. Since the shape of society cannot be "scientifically" determined, it must be left to the participants to decide their own form of organization. Since no participant has a monopoly on truth, the best arrangement allows for a critical process in which conflicting views can be freely debated and eventually tested against reality. Democratic elections provide such a forum in politics, and the market mechanism provides one in economics. Neither markets nor elections constitute an objective criterion, only an expression of the prevailing bias; but that is the best available in an imperfect world. Thus, the concept of reflexivity leads directly to the concept of an open society—hence its "charm" in contemporary China. As far as I am concerned, it completes what Hofstadter would call a "recursive loop" between my concept of reflexivity, my interest in financial markets, and my devotion to the ideal of an open society.

Notes

INTRODUCTION

1. Roman Frydman and Edmund Phelps, *Individual Forecasting and Aggregate Outcomes: Rational Expectations Examined* (Cambridge: Cambridge University Press, 1983).

2. An amusing book by Norman Cantor describes how historians themselves often create history. *Inventing the Middle Ages: The Lives, Works, and Ideas of the Great Medievalists of the Twentieth Century* (New York: HarperCollins, 1993).

3. Karl R. Popper, *The Poverty of Historicism* (London: Routledge & Kegan Paul, 1957), p. 130.

4. Mancur Olson, *Power and Prosperity: Outgrowing Communist and Capitalist Dictatorships* (New York: Basic Books, 2000).

5. George Soros, *Open Society: Reforming Global Capitalism* (New York: PublicAffairs, 2000).

6. George Soros, "Bush's Inflated Sense of Supremacy," *Financial Times* (March 13, 2003).

7. My own interpretation of Gödel's theorem is different from Gödel's. He took a Platonic view of the universe of arithmetics: he regarded all the truths and proofs as preexisting, irrespective of what mathematicians thought. In my view, Gödel numbers were invented by Gödel, who enlarged the universe of arithmetics by inventing them.

8. To avoid any further terminological confusions, the human uncertainty principle should be regarded as just another, hopefully more catchy way of describing reflexivity as a universal human condition.

9. George Soros, "Don't Blame Brazil," *Financial Times* (August 13, 2002).

10. George Soros, *Opening the Soviet System* (London: Weidenfeld & Nicolson, 1990).

377

11. George Soros, "Bush's Inflated Sense of Supremacy," *Financial Times* (March 13, 2003).

12. Robert Solow, "The False Economies of George Soros," *New Republic* (February 8, 1999).

13. Joshua Chafin and Andrew Hill, "Enron & Wall Street," *Financial Times* (July 24, 2002).

14. Cf. Tivadar Soros, *Masquerade: Dancing around Death in Nazi-Occupied Hungary* (New York: Arcade Publishing, 2001), and *Soros on Soros: Staying Ahead of the Curve* (New York: John Wiley & Sons, 1995).

15. Michael T. Kaufman, *Soros: The Life and Times of a Messianic Billionaire* (New York: Alfred A. Knopf, 2002).

16. David Edmonds and John Eidinow, *Wittgenstein's Poker* (New York: Ecco/HarperCollins, 2001).

CHAPTER 2

1. Ragnar Nurske, *International Currency Experience: Lessons of the Interwar Period* (Geneva: League of Nations, Secretariat: Economic, Financial, and Transit Department, 1944).

2. Henry Kaufman, "Comments on Credit," May 3, 1985 (New York: Salomon Brothers Inc.).

CHAPTER 4

1. *The New York Times* (April 21, 1985).

2. Milton Friedman and Anna Schwartz, *A Monetary History of the United States, 1867–1960* (Princeton: Princeton University Press, 1963), and *Monetary Statistics of the United States* (New York: Columbia University Press, 1970).

CHAPTER 5

1. George Soros, "The International Debt Problem, Diagnosis and Prognosis," July 1983; "The International Debt Problem Revisited," March 1984 (New York: Morgan Stanley).

2. Anatole Kaletsky, *The Costs of Default* (New York: Twentieth Century Fund, 1985).

CHAPTER 6

1. Henry Kaufman, loc. cit., passim.

2. For example, Paul Volcker's testimony before the Senate Banking Committee, February 20, 1986.

Chapter 7

1. International Monetary Fund, *World Economic Outlook* (September 1, 1986).

2. Jonathan E. Gray, "Financial Corporation of America: Strategic Analysis ≠ Forecast," *Bernstein Research,* Dec. 28, 1983 (New York: Sanford C. Bernstein & Co.).

Chapter 17

1. The International Parliamentary Working Round Table on Exchange Rates and Coordination, Zurich, Switzerland; June 28, 29, and 30, 1986.

2. The U.S. Congressional Summit on Debt and Trade, New York, N.Y.; Dec. 3, 4, and 5, 1986.

Appendix

Prospect for
European Disintegration

I am very grateful to the Aspen Institute for giving me this opportunity to address an audience in Germany, and I have chosen a topic which ought to be of particular interest to people in Germany. My topic is the prospect of European disintegration.

It is a subject that engages me in three different ways. First, I am passionately devoted to the idea of Europe as an open society. Second, I have developed a theory of history which casts light on the process of European integration and disintegration. Third, I am a participant in the process.

Open society means a society based on the idea that nobody has a monopoly on truth; a society which is not dominated by the state or by any particular ideology, where minorities and minority opinions are respected. Using these criteria, the European Community is a highly desirable form of organization. Indeed, in some ways it is ideal, because it has a very interesting feature: all the participating states are in a minority. Respect for the minority is the basis of its construction. The unresolved question is: how much power should be delegated to the majority? How far should Europe be integrated?

The way Europe evolves will have a profound influence on what happens to the east of Europe, the region that was formerly under the sway of Communist ideology. Communism built a universal closed society, but Communism as an ideology is now well and truly dead. The line of least resistance leads to the break-up of the universal closed system into particular closed societies, based on the principle of national or ethnic identity. We can see the principle well advanced in the former Yugoslavia. The only possible escape from this fate is to make the transition from closed to open society. But that is not so easy. It requires time and effort to establish the rule of law, the institutions of civil society, and the critical way of thinking which are characteristic of an open society. Societies devastated by Communism cannot make the transition on their own. They need a Europe that is open and receptive and supportive of their effort. East Germany got too much help, the rest of Eastern Europe too little. I am deeply engaged in helping the rest of Eastern Europe. As you may know, I have set up a network of foundations devoted to this cause, and that is the bias that I bring to the subject of Europe.

My second involvement is that I have developed a theory of history which has guided me both in my activities in the financial markets and in setting up the foundation network. The key to my theory is the role that mistakes and misconceptions play in shaping the course of events. There is always a divergence between the participants' thinking and the actual state of affairs, but sometimes the divergence is relatively small and self-correcting—I call this "near-equilibrium"; and, at other times, the divergence is large, with no tendency to correct itself—I call this "far-from-equilibrium." The course of events has quite a different character in near-equilibrium and in far-from-equilibrium conditions. This point is not generally understood. My theory relates to far-from-equilibrium conditions. I have made a particular study of what I call the "boom/bust sequence," which can be observed from time to time in financial markets; and I think it is also applicable to the integration and disintegration of the European Community. Since the revolution of 1989 and the reunification of Germany, Europe has been in a condition of dynamic disequilibrium. Therefore it presents a very interesting case study for my theory of history.

And, finally, I am myself a participant in this process of dynamic disequilibrium because I am an international investor. I used to call myself a speculator and I used to joke that an investment is a speculation that has gone wrong but, in view of the campaign against speculators, I am no longer amused. International investors did play an important role in the breakdown of the Exchange Rate Mechanism, but it is impossible to have a common market without international capital movements. To blame speculators is like shooting the messenger.

I shall deal with my subject on the basis of my theory of history. The fact that I am also a participant does not interfere with my ability to apply the theory. On the contrary, it has allowed me to test it in practice. Nor does it matter that I bring a particular bias to the subject because it is part of my theory that participants in a historical process always act on the basis of a bias. And, of course, the same rule applies to the proponents of theories.

But I must confess that my particular bias—namely, that I want to see a united, prosperous and open Europe—does interfere with my activities as a participant in financial markets. I had no problem as long as I was an anonymous participant. Sterling would have left the ERM whether or not I speculated against it. But, after sterling left the ERM, I received a lot of publicity and I ceased to be an anonymous participant. I became a guru. I could actually influence the behavior of markets, and it would be dishonest of me to pretend otherwise. This has created opportunities and imposed responsibilities. Given my bias, I did not want to be responsible for the French franc being pushed out of the Exchange Rate Mechanism. I decided to abstain from speculating against the franc in order to be able to put forward a constructive solution; but nobody thanked me for it. Indeed, my public utterances seemed to annoy the monetary authorities even more than my activities in the financial markets, so I can't say I am doing well in my newfound role of guru. Nevertheless, given my bias, I must say what I am going to say, even if it is inconvenient for me as a participant.

The important point about my boom/bust theory is that there is nothing inevitable about it. The typical boom/bust sequence is initially self-reinforcing and, eventually, self-defeating, but it can be aborted or diverted at any point. It is in the light of this theory that I shall comment on the boom/bust process of European integration. I shall pay particular attention to the Exchange Rate Mechanism, which is playing such a crucial role in the process. It had worked perfectly well in near-equilibrium conditions, until the reunification of Germany. But the reunification has created conditions of dynamic disequilibrium. Since that time, the course of events has been shaped by mistakes and misunderstandings. The most tangible result is the disintegration of the Exchange Rate Mechanism which, in turn, is an important factor in the possible disintegration of the European Community.

Let me start at the point where near-equilibrium conditions were replaced by a condition of dynamic disequilibrium. This point can be fixed in time with great precision: it was the fall of the Berlin Wall. This opened the way to German reunification. Chancellor Kohl rose to the historic occasion. He decided that reunification must be complete, immediate and achieved in a European context. Actually, he had no choice in the matter, since the German constitution gave East Germans citizenship of Germany and Germany was a member of the European Community. But it makes all the difference whether you take charge of events or merely react to them. Chancellor Kohl exhibited real leadership. He went to President Mitterand and said to him, in effect, "I need your support and the support of Europe to achieve immediate and complete reunification." The French replied, in effect, "Let's create a stronger Europe in which the reunified Germany can be fully embedded." This gave a tremendous impulse towards integration. It set into motion the "boom" part of the boom/bust process. The British were opposed to the creation of a strong central authority; you will recall Margaret Thatcher's speech at Bruges. Tough negotiations ensued, but there was a sense of urgency, a self-imposed deadline. The result was the Treaty of Maastricht, the two main goals of which were to establish a common currency and a common foreign policy. It had a number of other provisions, but they were less important and, when the British objected, they were allowed to opt out of some of them. All in all, the Treaty was a giant step forward towards integration, a valiant attempt to create a Europe strong enough to cope with the revolutionary changes resulting from the collapse of the Soviet empire. It went, perhaps, further and faster than public opinion was prepared for; but that was a chance that the leaders took in order to cope with the revolutionary situation. Rightly so, in my opinion, because that is what leadership entails.

The trouble lay elsewhere. I shall not dwell on a side deal in which Germany got the agreement of the European Community to recognize Croatia and Slovenia as independent states. It was little discussed and little noticed at the time, but it had horrendous consequences. I want to focus on the internal disequilibrium in Germany which was generated by the reunification because it was that disequilibrium which has turned the boom into a bust.

The German government seriously underestimated the cost of reunification and was, in any case, unwilling to pay the full cost through higher taxation or a reduction of other government expenditures. This created tensions between the Bundesbank and the government on two levels: one was that the government acted against the express advice of the Bundesbank; the other was that a very loose fiscal policy—that is to say, a huge budget deficit—required a very tight monetary policy in order to reestablish monetary equilibrium. The injection of purchasing power through the exchange of East German currency at par created an inflationary boom, and the fiscal deficit added fuel to the fire. The Bundesbank was charged, by law, with the mission of maintaining the value of the Deutschmark and it acted with alacrity. It raised the repo rate to 9.70 percent. But that policy was very harmful to the other member countries of the European Monetary System. In other words, the monetary policy which was designed to reestablish equilibrium at home created a disequilibrium within the European Monetary System. It took some time for the disequilibrium to develop but, with the passage of time, the tight monetary policy imposed by the Bundesbank pushed all of Europe into the deepest recession it has experienced since the Second World War. The Bundesbank plays a dual role: it is the guardian of sound money at home and it is the anchor of the EMS. It acted as the transmission mechanism for turning the internal disequilibrium of the German economy into a force for the disintegration of the EMS.

There was also a third and deeper level of conflict between the Bundesbank and the German government. Chancellor Kohl, in order to obtain French support for German reunification, entered into the Treaty of Maastricht. That Treaty posed a profound threat to the institutional dominance, indeed, institutional survival, of the Bundesbank as the arbiter of European monetary policy. In the EMS, the German mark serves as the anchor. But, under the Maastricht Treaty, the role of the Bundesbank was to be replaced by a European central bank in which the Bundesbank would only have one vote out of twelve. Admittedly, the European Central Bank was based on the German model; but it makes all the difference in the world whether you serve as the model or whether you are actually in charge. The Bundesbank never openly acknowledged that it was opposed to this institutional change, and it remains unclear to what extent its actions were designed to prevent it. All I can tell you is that, as a market participant, I acted on the hypothesis that it was the Bundesbank's underlying motivation. I cannot prove to you that my hypothesis was correct; all I can say is that it worked.

For instance, I listened to Helmut Schlesinger warn that the markets are mistaken when they think that the ECU consists of a fixed basket of currencies. I asked him what he thought of the ECU as the future common currency of Europe. He said he would like it better if it were called the mark. I was guided accordingly. Shortly thereafter, the lira was forced out of the ERM.

I don't want to get into a blow-by-blow account of what happened because I want to establish a broad historical perspective. From that perspective, the salient features are that the Maastricht referendum was defeated in Denmark; it passed with a very narrow margin in France; and it barely squeaked through Parliament in Britain. The European Exchange Rate Mechanism has, for all intents and purposes, broken down and it has done so in several installments, of which the last one, namely, the broadening of the band in August, was the most far-reaching because it loosened the strongest tie within the European Community, the one which ties Germany and France together. What is in the long run even more important, Europe is in the midst of a deep recession from which there is no immediate prospect of recovery. Unemployment is a serious and still-growing problem which continues to be aggravated by monetary policies which are far too restrictive for this stage of the cycle. From these observations, I conclude that the trend towards the integration of Europe has passed its peak and has now been reversed.

The exact moment of reversal can be identified as the defeat in the Danish referendum. It could have brought forth a groundswell of support for the Maastricht Treaty; in that case, there would have been no reversal. Instead, it generated the breakdown of the Exchange Rate Mechanism. Europe is now in a process of disintegration. Since we are dealing with a boom/bust process, it is impossible to say how far it will go. But it may go much further than people are currently willing or able to envisage because a boom/bust process is self-reinforcing in both directions.

I can identify at least five elements which are mutually self-reinforcing. First and foremost is the recession; 11.7 percent unemployment in France, 14.1 percent in Belgium, and 22.25 percent in Spain, are simply not acceptable. They generate social and political unrest which is easily channeled in an anti-European direction. Second, there is the progressive disintegration of the Exchange Rate Mechanism. This is very dangerous because in the medium to long term the Common Market cannot survive without stability in exchange rates.

The ERM functioned perfectly well in near-equilibrium conditions for more than a decade. But the reunification of Germany has revealed a fundamental flaw in the mechanism, namely, that the Bundesbank plays a dual role: guardian of domestic monetary stability and anchor of the EMS. As long as the two roles are in harmony, there is no problem. But when there was a conflict, the Bundesbank gave precedence to domestic considerations to the detriment of its international obligations. This was clearly demonstrated, for instance, on Thursday, July 29th, when it refused to lower the discount rate in order to relieve the pressure on the French franc. It can be argued that the Bundesbank has no choice in the matter: it is obliged by law, the *Grundgesetz,* to give absolute priority to the preservation of the value of the German currency. In that case, there is an irreconcilable conflict between the ERM and the *Grundgesetz.*

This episode revealed another fundamental flaw in the ERM, namely, that there is an asymmetry between the obligations of the anchor currency and the currency which is under pressure. All the obligations fall on the weak currency. It will be recalled that, at the time of the Bretton Woods agreement, John Maynard Keynes emphasized the need for symmetry between the strong and the weak. He based his arguments on the experiences of the inter-war period. The current situation is increasingly reminiscent of that period and sometimes it seems as if Keynes had not lived.

This brings me to the third element, namely, mistaken economic and monetary policies. Here it is not so much the Bundesbank that is to blame but those who have opposed it, like the German government, or those who have been the victims of its policy, like the United Kingdom and France. The German government is, of course, responsible for creating the internal disequilibrium in the first place. The British committed an egregious error in joining the Exchange Rate Mechanism on October 8th, 1990 after the reunification of Germany. They did so on the basis of arguments which had been developed in 1985, but were strenuously resisted by Margaret Thatcher. When her position weakened, she finally gave in, but by that time, the arguments which had been valid in 1985 were no longer applicable. So the British made two mistakes—one in 1985 and one in 1990.

They were particularly hard hit by the high interest rate regime imposed on them by the Bundesbank because they were already in a recession when they went into the ERM. Being pushed out of the ERM brought them much-needed relief. They ought to have welcomed it, but they were too dazed to react. They did the right thing eventually and lowered interest rates, but they failed to seize the initiative. This has made it harder to build up confidence and it will make it much harder to reassert control over wages when the economy does pick up.

One would have thought the French would learn from the British experience. But they are proving even more inflexible. One could sympathize with their efforts to defend the *franc fort* policy because they fought so long and so hard to establish it, and they were on the verge of reaping the benefits in the form of improved competitiveness vis-a-vis Germany when the reward was snatched from their hands by recurrent attacks on the franc. But, once the *franc fort* policy proved untenable, they ought to have adjusted their approach to the new situation. Instead, they are sticking voluntarily with a regime which proved so disastrous when it was imposed on them by the ERM. I think I understand their motivation: they are concerned with rebuilding their reserves and repaying the debt that the Banque de France incurred with the Bundesbank in defending the parity. But they got their priorities wrong. France is in a serious recession and it needs to lower interest rates. That is what brought on the August crisis. To try and keep the French franc close to the Deutschmark by keeping interest rates high is self-defeating. The only way to have a strong franc is to have a strong economy.

The Bundesbank itself has been remarkably consistent in the pursuit of its objectives, especially if we include institutional self-preservation among those objectives, and amazingly successful. It found itself in an impossible situation after the reunification of Germany: a sudden increase in the stock of money, an enormous budget deficit, and a threat to its institutional survival. Yet it came out victorious. Whether it was worth the cost—a Europe-wide recession and the breakdown of the ERM—is another question.

A few months ago I was convinced that the Bundesbank was following the wrong monetary policy, even for domestic purposes, because Germany was in a recession and monetary policy ought to be counter-cyclical. The Bundesbank stuck to its medium-term monetary targets, but I thought that M3—which had worked well as a target in near-equilibrium conditions—had been rendered irrelevant in today's far-from-equilibrium conditions; and I thought that the Bundesbank had overstayed its course in following a tight monetary policy.

But that was before the widening of the bands in the ERM. Since then, the Deutschmark has rallied, the German long bonds have strengthened and, on top of it all, the German economy is showing some signs of strength. I must now admit that I may have been wrong and the Bundesbank may have been successful in its pursuit of its domestic policy goals. But, if anything, that strengthens my argument that there is a conflict of interest between the domestic responsibilities of the Bundesbank and its role as the anchor of the EMS. The events of the last two months have clearly demonstrated that the needs of Germany and the rest of Europe are very different. Germany needs low interest rates on long bonds because it borrows at the long end, whereas the rest of Europe needs lower interest rates at the short end because the liquidity of the banking system needs to be rebuilt and lower short-term rates are needed to stimulate economic activity. Germany got what it needs, but the rest of Europe did not.

The fact that I may have been wrong on the Deutschmark brings me to the fourth factor. It is not only the authorities who make mistakes, but also market participants. Markets are often wrong. Specifically, they were wrong when they assumed that the path to a common currency would follow a straight line. International investors, particularly managers of international bond funds, went for the highest yields, ignoring exchange rate risks. Helmut Schlesinger was right in warning that the ECU does not consist of a fixed basket of currencies. There had been large capital movements into weak-currency countries like Italy, Spain and Portugal. The movement was initially self-reinforcing but eventually self-defeating. It created excessive rigidity in exchange rates in the first place, and excessive instability in the second. The errors of the market compounded the errors of the authorities in creating dynamic disequilibrium.

Finally, there is a fifth factor that reinforces the trend toward disintegration. It may be called the emotional amplifier. When things are going wrong, especially when mistakes are being made, there is an impulse to blame someone else. Who would have thought that respected officials like Jacques Delors and the Finance Minister of Belgium and the newly appointed head of the Banque de France really believed in an Anglo-Saxon conspiracy to destroy the Franco-German alliance? These attitudes then color subsequent discussions as in the case of the GATT negotiations.

There is also a sixth element which needs to be considered; namely, the instability of Eastern Europe and particularly of the former Yugoslavia.

I believe that this factor is working in the opposite direction. The threat of instability and the influx of refugees are good reasons to band together and build a "Fortress Europe." At the same time, the lack of unity in the European Community has the effect of reinforcing the political instability and economic decline in Eastern Europe. The outcome is going to be a European Community which is a far cry from the open society to which the people whom I support in Eastern Europe aspire.

All this is truly disturbing and depressing. I realize that I sound more like a prophet of gloom and doom than a guru. But let me remind you that there is nothing determinate about the boom/bust sequence; that the direction of the process can be reversed practically at any time. Indeed, a reversal of direction is an essential part of a boom/bust sequence. What I am trying to say is that events are now going in the wrong direction and they will continue to go in that direction until we recognize that there is something fundamentally wrong and we take resolute action to correct it.

There can be no doubt that there is something fundamentally wrong with the European Monetary System as it is currently constituted. First, the domestic obligations of the Bundesbank have proven to be irreconcilable with its role as the anchor currency; indeed, one could argue that the Bundesbank has exploited its role as the anchor currency in order to solve its domestic problems. Second, there is an asymmetry between the obligations of the strong and the weak currencies. And most importantly, there is asymmetry between the risks and rewards of international investors, that is to say, speculators. These structural faults were there from the beginning, but they only became apparent in the course of the last year. Once they became known, it is impossible to return to the conditions which prevailed previously. The best way to eliminate the faults of the ERM is to have no exchange rate mechanism at all. But freely floating exchange rates would destroy the Common Market. Hence the necessity for a common currency. That means implementing the Maastricht Treaty. At the time the treaty was negotiated, the path leading to the common currency was envisaged as a gradual, near-equilibrium path. But the gradual path has run into unexpected obstacles. To continue on a gradual path will now lead in the opposite direction because there has been a trend reversal and we are now in a process of disintegration. Therefore we must find a different path. If we can't get there gradually, it is better to get there all at once than not to get there at all.

At the emergency meeting on August 1st, an official from Portugal reportedly proposed that the introduction of a common currency should be speeded up. A German participant reportedly reacted by saying, "Surely, you must be joking!" If my line of argument is correct, it is time to take the suggestion seriously. This may sound a little too facile, and it is. My argument will be taken seriously only if I can show a path that would lead to a common currency. Since we are in dynamic disequilibrium, the path has to be a disequilibrium one. At present, the first priority of the French monetary authorities is to rebuild their reserves. In order to do so, they are trying to keep the French franc strong. That is wrong. The first priority ought to be to stimulate the French economy, and the maturity of the French debt to the Bundesbank ought to be extended for, say, two years so that France could lower interest rates now. When I say lower interest rates, I mean three percent. The rate reduction ought to be coordinated with the other members of the EMS, excluding Germany and Holland. The Deutschmark would undoubtedly appreciate. The overvaluation of the Deutschmark would have a negative effect on the German economy, hastening the decline in German interest rates. As the German economy weakened and the rest of Europe picked up, the trend in exchange rates would be reversed and they may eventually settle down not very far from where they were before the bands were widened. The main difference would be in economic activity. The rest of Europe would recover, first at the expense of Germany; but eventually Germany would also join the recovery. When that happened, the dynamic disequilibrium would have been corrected, and the march towards a common currency could be resumed in near-equilibrium conditions. The whole process would not take more than two years. After that, you could move to a common currency directly, without reinstituting the narrow bands. But you cannot get there in a straight line. Right now, you are caught in a vicious circle; you need to turn it around and make it a virtuous circle. This has already happened, up to a point, in Italy. It could be done in the rest of Europe.

I have not dealt with issues of foreign policy, the future of NATO and the fate of Eastern Europe, but I have covered too much ground already. In any case, those issues are intricately interlinked with monetary policy. European monetary policy is wrong and it can be corrected.